Poems in Context

Poems in Context

LEE A. JACOBUS   WILLIAM T. MOYNIHAN

University of Connecticut

 HARCOURT BRACE JOVANOVICH, INC.

New York   Chicago   San Francisco   Atlanta

© 1974 by Harcourt Brace Jovanovich, Inc.

All rights reserved. No part of this publication may be reproduced or transmitted in any form or by any means, electronic or mechanical, including photocopy, recording, or any information storage and retrieval system, without permission in writing from the publisher.

ISBN: 0-15-570652-7

Library of Congress Catalog Card Number: 73-21081

Printed in the United States of America

COPYRIGHTS AND ACKNOWLEDGMENTS

LÉONIE ADAMS. For "Country Summer." Reprinted by permission of the author from *Poems: A Selection*, Funk and Wagnalls' New York.

ATHENEUM PUBLISHERS, INC. For "The Pietà, Rhenish, 14th C., The Cloisters" from *To See, To Take* by Mona Van Duyn. Copyright © 1970 by Mona Van Duyn. Reprinted by permission of Atheneum Publishers.

PAUL BREMAN LTD. For "Award" by Ray Durem from *The Writing on the Wall: 108 American Poems of Protest*, edited by Walter Lowenfels.

BROADSIDE PRESS. For "A Poem Looking for a Reader" from *Don't Cry, Scream*. Copyright © 1969 by Don L. Lee; for "The Idea of Ancestry" from *Poems from Prison*. Copyright © 1968 by Etheridge Knight. Reprinted by permission of Broadside Press, Detroit, Michigan.

CITY LIGHTS. For "Supermarket in California" from *Howl and Other Poems*. Copyright © 1956, 1959 by Allen Ginsberg. Reprinted by permission of City Lights Books.

CLARENDON PRESS. For "The Limits of Submission" by Faarah Nuur from *Somali Poetry* by D. W. Andrzejewski and I. M. Lewis, © 1964 Oxford University Press, reprinted by permission of the Clarendon Press, Oxford.

ROSICA COLIN, LTD. For "Evening" by Richard Aldington.

COLLINS-KNOWLTON-WING, INC. For "The Persian Version" by Robert Graves from *Collected Poems*. Reprinted by permission of Collins-Knowlton-Wing, Inc. Copyright © 1958, 1961 by Robert Graves.

Pages 495-501 constitute a continuation of the copyright page.

Preface

For more than a generation, the study of poetry has concentrated almost exclusively on elements of language. Textbook emphasis on imagery, diction, paradox, irony, and verbal structures has caused us to lose sight of other useful ways of approaching poetry. Poetry that does not lend itself to this technique of criticism has been omitted from the college classroom. However, it should be self-evident that any partial or narrow approach to poetry will finally be just that—partial or narrow. Thus, this book places the verbal approach in a context of other approaches. It makes a wider range of poetry available to students by employing a wider range of critical perspectives.

We have employed a technique analogous to an ecological approach in biology or a Gestalt approach in psychology. When the ecologist studies a species, he not only studies it as an organism but also considers its place in a context of relationships with other similar species and their environment. The Gestalt therapist is concerned not only with the individual human organism but with the physical and social environment in which that organism lives. Fritz Perls, a Gestalt therapist, uses the expression "organism" to describe his attitude toward the psyche, saying "you cannot . . . separate the organism and the environment." This is precisely the perspective we have adopted for our study of poetry. We examine the poem as a whole—the poem and its environment.

A poem's environment is more than its language: it consists of other poems written on the same theme over a period of time; it includes the author's life, his theory of poetry, the period in which he writes, and his other works. It also includes style, genre, tradition, aesthetics, and culture. This book shows how a poem can be studied in terms of such broad perspectives.

Our organization depends upon the distinction between the internal contexts of language, which include matters of style, and the external contexts, which consider the poem's environment. For instance, our opening three sections concentrate on the internal context of the poem's language as it relates to prose, to light verse, and to dramatic speech. In parts two and three, the external contexts of theme and form are emphasized, as—to an extent—they are in the final part, which deals with poetry influenced by visual arts, music, and dance. Our discussions of diction and meter treat internal contexts, and they do so by introducing comparative materials from a wide range of poems whose diction or meter is of particular interest.

The historical circumstances, represented by poems of the metaphysical, romantic, and imagistic periods, affect both the external and internal contexts of poems. The historical periods can be seen as implying an internal contextual problem in that our attention is drawn to style. But since the individual poem's style is most clearly defined in its historical relation to other poems of a limited period, the style itself also contains external influences. The problems of biography are clearly those of the external sort, as are those that rise from considerations of culture and of nationality. Our ultimate purpose is to slight none of these contexts, but to help clarify the way each affects the understanding and pleasure we get from reading poetry.

We feel that *Poems in Context* offers a genuine alternative to the approaches that seem to have taken over the classroom in the last two decades. It is not an approach based on a flashy anticritical polemic. We feel we are offering a simple, pertinent aesthetic of poetry that will be useful to a wide variety of people. It is based on nothing more than the facts of poetic life as most critics and readers know them. Our approach is neither an antihistorical nor an antiphilosophical view; it is fundamentally an aesthetic view that takes into account more than one mode of a poem's existence.

This approach has already proved a boon and a relief to our students. We hope it will prove so to you as well.

Lee A. Jacobus   William T. Moynihan

Contents
Topical

Preface	v
Introduction	1

LANGUAGE CONTEXTS, 15

Prose and Poems	15
Verse and Poems	35
Dramatic Speech and Poems	50

THEMATIC CONTEXTS, 69

Poems of Love	72
Poems on Spring	91
Elegies	97

FORMAL CONTEXTS, 119

The Ballad	119
The Sonnet	145
The Ode	161

STYLISTIC CONTEXTS, 213

Diction — 213

Rhythm and Meter — 236

HISTORICAL CONTEXTS, 275

Metaphysical Poetry: Early Seventeenth Century — 276

Romantic Poetry: Early Nineteenth Century — 297

Imagistic Poetry: Early Twentieth Century — 314

BIOGRAPHICAL CONTEXTS, 337

Walt Whitman (1819–1892) — 339

William Butler Yeats (1865–1939) — 363

Emily Dickinson (1830–1886) — 374

CULTURAL CONTEXTS, 393

Protest Poetry — 393

   Poems of War Protest — 395

   Poems of Black American Protest — 406

The Poetry of Other Cultures — 423

   African Poems — 426

   Chinese Poems — 448

AESTHETIC CONTEXTS, 465

Visual Arts, Music, and Dance — 465

Contents

Author and Title

Preface	v
Introduction	1
Robert Frost *Design*	6
Robert Frost *In White*	8
Walt Whitman *A Noiseless Patient Spider*	10
Robert Francis *The Orb Weaver*	10

LANGUAGE CONTEXTS, 15

Prose and Poems	15
Stephen Crane *To the Maiden...*	17
T. S. Eliot *Hysteria*	19
Robert Frost *"Out, Out—"*	21
William Butler Yeats *Diary Entry*	23
William Butler Yeats *Words*	24
William Wordsworth *With Ships the Sea*	24
William Wordsworth From *A Letter to Lady Beaumont*	25
Thomas Hobbes From *Leviathan (I, iii)*	26
John Wilmot, Earl of Rochester *Love and Life: A Song*	26
Raphael Holinshed From *Chronicles of England, Scotland and Ireland (1577)*	27
William Shakespeare From *King Lear (Act I, sc. i)*	27
Plutarch From *The Lives of Noble Grecians and Romans*	29
William Shakespeare From *Antony and Cleopatra (Act II, sc. ii)*	30
Ralph Waldo Emerson From *Commodity*	31
Ralph Waldo Emerson *The Rhodora*	31
John Milton From *The Christian Doctrine*	32
John Milton From *Paradise Lost (Book VIII)*	32

ix

x   Contents

| Thomas Traherne   From *Centuries of Meditations* | 33 |
| Thomas Traherne   *Wonder* | 34 |

Verse and Poems 35
John Dryden   *Mac Flecknoe*   38
Arthur Hugh Clough   *The Latest Decalogue*   39
Robert Graves   *The Persian Version*   40
Hilaire Belloc   *Epitaph on the Politician*   41
Anonymous   *It Isn't the Cough*   42
William Blake   *If You Trap the Moment*   42
Andrew Marvell   *To His Coy Mistress*   42
Matthew Prior   *To the Honorable Charles Montague, Esq.*   44
Lewis Carroll   *The Crocodile*   45
James Stephens   *A Glass of Beer*   45
W. H. Auden   *Foxtrot from a Play*   46
Anonymous   *The Dying Airman*   47
Anonymous   *Relativity*   47
Anonymous   *A Happy Time*   48
Anonymous   *Mind and Matter*   48
John Heywood   *Of Loving a Dog*   48
John Heywood   *Of Late and Never*   48
F. R. Higgins   *Grace Before Beer*   49
Ogden Nash   *The Turtle*   49
Langston Hughes   *Gone Boy*   49
e. e. cummings   *Buffalo Bill's*   50

Dramatic Speech and Poems   50
Walter Savage Landor   *I Strove with None*   51
Anonymous   *Western Wind*   54
Walt Whitman   *To the States*   55
Thomas Hardy   *The Walk*   56
D. H. Lawrence   *A Youth Mowing*   57
Lord Herbert of Cherbury   *To a Lady
    Who Did Sing Excellently*   59
John Milton   *To Leonora Baroni, Singing at Rome*   60
William Wordsworth   *The Solitary Reaper*   60
Percy Bysshe Shelley   *To Constantia, Singing*   61
Thomas Hardy   *The Curtains Now Are Drawn: Song*   63
Wallace Stevens   *The Idea of Order at Key West*   63
D. H. Lawrence   *Piano*   65
Ezra Pound   *Envoi*   65
X. J. Kennedy   *In a Prominent Bar in Secaucus One Day*   66

THEMATIC CONTEXTS, 69

Poems of Love | 72
From Song of Solomon *The Voice of the Turtle* | 72
Sappho *Letter to Anaktoria* | 73
Catullus *Kisses* | 74
Ovid *The Universal Lover* | 75
John Donne *The Baite* | 77
Emily Dickinson *"Why Do I Love" You, Sir?* | 78
Rainer Maria Rilke *Love Song* | 79
D. H. Lawrence *Love on the Farm* | 79
Laurie Lee *First Love* | 81
Vassar Miller *Love's Eschatology* | 82
Donald Justice *Love's Map* | 82
Adrienne Rich *Two Songs* | 83
Keith Waldrop *To Rosmarie in Bad Kissingen* | 84
Robert Bagg *Madonna of the Cello* | 85
Michael Dennis Browne *News from the House* | 88
Brian Patten *Party Piece* | 90

Poems on Spring | 91
John Lyly *To Welcome in the Spring* | 91
Thomas Nashe *Spring, the Sweet Spring* | 91
John Webster *All the Flowers of the Spring* | 92
William Blake *To Spring* | 92
Gerard Manley Hopkins *Spring* | 93
William Carlos Williams *Spring Strains* | 93
D. H. Lawrence *Spring Morning* | 94
e. e. cummings *O sweet spontaneous* | 95
Dylan Thomas *Hold Hard, These Ancient Minutes in the Cuckoo's Month* | 96

Elegies | 97
John Milton *Lycidas* | 97
Walt Whitman *When Lilacs Last in the Dooryard Bloom'd* | 103
William Butler Yeats *In Memory of Major Robert Gregory* | 111
John Crowe Ransom *Bells for John Whiteside's Daughter* | 114
W. H. Auden *In Memory of W. B. Yeats* | 115
Raymond R. Patterson *At That Moment* | 117

FORMAL CONTEXTS, 119

The Ballad		**119**
Anonymous	*Sir Patrick Spens*	123
Anonymous	*Bonny Barbara Allan*	124
Anonymous	*The Bailiff's Daughter of Islington*	125
Anonymous	*Johnie Armstrong*	127
Anonymous	*Get Up and Bar the Door*	128
Anonymous	*Frankie and Albert*	130
Anonymous	*Poor Omie*	131
Anonymous	*Jesse James*	132
Anonymous	*The Jam on Gerry's Rock*	133
Anonymous	*John Henry*	134
A. E. Housman	*The True Lover*	138
Ezra Pound	*Ballad of the Goodly Fere*	139
Langston Hughes	*Ballad of the Landlord*	141
W. H. Auden	*O What Is That Sound*	142
Gwendolyn Brooks	*The Ballad of Rudolph Reed*	143
X. J. Kennedy	*Down in Dallas*	144
The Sonnet		**145**
John Keats	*On First Looking into Chapman's Homer*	146
William Shakespeare	*Sonnet 18*	147
William Shakespeare	*Sonnet 30*	148
William Shakespeare	*Sonnet 73*	148
William Shakespeare	*Sonnet 97*	149
William Shakespeare	*Sonnet 116*	149
William Shakespeare	*Sonnet 129*	150
William Shakespeare	*Sonnet 147*	150
John Donne	*Holy Sonnet 5*	151
John Donne	*Holy Sonnet 7*	151
John Donne	*Holy Sonnet 10*	152
John Donne	*Holy Sonnet 14*	152
John Milton	*How Soon Hath Time*	153
John Milton	*On Shakespeare*	153
John Milton	*When I Consider How My Light Is Spent*	154
William Wordsworth	*It Is a Beauteous Evening*	154
William Wordsworth	*London, 1802*	155
William Wordsworth	*Composed upon Westminster Bridge, September 3, 1802*	155
William Wordsworth	*The World Is Too Much with Us*	156
William Wordsworth	*Mutability*	156
William Wordsworth	*After-Thought*	157

Jones Very *The Dead*	157
Christina Rossetti *In an Artist's Studio*	158
Gerard Manley Hopkins *God's Grandeur*	158
William Butler Yeats *Leda and the Swan*	159
Edwin Arlington Robinson *New England*	159
Trumbull Stickney *Mt. Lykaion*	160
Edna St. Vincent Millay *Love Is Not All: It Is Not Meat Nor Drink*	160
e. e. cummings *sonnet*	161

The Ode   161

Ben Jonson *To the Immortal Memory and Friendship of That Noble Pair, Sir Lucius Cary and Sir Henry Morrison*	164
John Dryden *A Song for St. Cecilia's Day, 1687*	168
Thomas Gray *Ode on a Distant Prospect of Eton College*	170 ✓
William Collins *Ode to Evening*	172 ✓
William Wordsworth *Ode: Intimations of Immortality from Recollections of Early Childhood*	174
William Wordsworth *Ode to Duty*	179
Samuel Taylor Coleridge *Dejection: An Ode*	181 ✓
Percy Bysshe Shelley *Ode to the West Wind*	185
John Keats *To Autumn*	187 ✓
John Keats *Ode to a Nightingale*	188
John Keats *Ode on Melancholy*	191
William Butler Yeats *Among School Children*	192
Léonie Adams *Country Summer*	194
Allen Tate *Ode to the Confederate Dead*	195
Dylan Thomas *Poem in October*	198
Robert Lowell *For the Union Dead*	200
Sylvia Plath *Point Shirley*	202

STYLISTIC CONTEXTS, 213

Diction	**213**
Gerard Manley Hopkins *The Windhover: To Christ Our Lord*	214
e. e. cummings *in Just—*	215
Lewis Carroll *Jabberwocky*	215
Ezra Pound From *Canto I*	218
John Milton From *Paradise Regained*	219
William Blake *The Mockers*	220

xiv   Contents

Robert Lowell *Memories of West Street and Lepke*	221
Theodore Roethke *Root Cellar*	223
Li Po (Rihaku) *A Song of Ch'ang-Kan*	224
Ezra Pound *The River-Merchant's Wife: A Letter*	225
Dylan Thomas *A Refusal to Mourn the Death,*	
by Fire, of a Child in London	228
William Butler Yeats *A Prayer for My Daughter*	228
Anne Sexton *The Fortress*	231
Walt Whitman *A Noiseless Patient Spider*	232
Robert Lowell *Mr. Edwards and the Spider*	233
Ted Hughes *The Hawk in the Rain*	234
Dylan Thomas *Over Sir John's Hill*	235
Rhythm and Meter	**236**
William Blake *The Tyger*	244
John Skelton *Mannerly Margery Milk and Ale*	247
Thomas Nashe *A Litany in Time of Plague*	248
Ben Jonson *Still to Be Neat, Still to Be Drest*	249
Robert Herrick *Delight in Disorder*	249
William Blake *And Did Those Feet in Ancient Time*	250
Alfred, Lord Tennyson *Ulysses*	250
Robert Browning *Love Among the Ruins*	252
Algernon Charles Swinburne *The Garden of Proserpine*	255
Robert Frost *Fire and Ice*	257
T. S. Eliot *The Love Song of J. Alfred Prufrock*	258
e. e. cummings *anyone lived in a pretty how town*	262
Langston Hughes *Harlem Sweeties*	263
Elizabeth Bishop *Invitation to Miss Marianne Moore*	264
Dylan Thomas *Fern Hill*	266
Allen Ginsberg *A Supermarket in California*	268
Anne Sexton *Ringing the Bells*	269
Jonathan Williams *Fastball*	269
Sylvia Plath *Ariel*	270
Imamu Amiri Baraka (LeRoi Jones) *In Memory of Radio*	271

HISTORICAL CONTEXTS, 275

Metaphysical Poetry: Early Seventeenth Century	**276**
John Donne *The Flea*	277
John Donne *Song*	278
John Donne *A Valediction Forbidding Mourning*	279
John Donne *Elegie: Going to Bed*	280

Lord Herbert of Cherbury	*A Fly That Flew into My Mistress Her Eye*	282
Lord Herbert of Cherbury	*Sonnet of Black Beauty*	282
George Herbert	*Easter-Wings*	283
George Herbert	*The Collar*	284
Edmund Waller	*Of the Last Verses in the Book*	285
Richard Crashaw	*Sainte Mary Magdalene or The Weeper*	286
Richard Crashaw	*On Our Crucified Lord Naked, and Bloody*	292
Henry Vaughan	*The World*	293
Henry Vaughan	*The Lampe*	294
Henry Vaughan	*The Dedication*	295

Romantic Poetry: Early Nineteenth Century — 297

Thomas Gray	*Elegy Written in a Country Church Yard*	298
William Blake	*The Garden of Love*	302
William Blake	*Mad Song*	302
William Blake	*London*	303
William Wordsworth	*To My Sister*	304
William Wordsworth	*To Toussaint L'Ouverture*	305
Samuel Taylor Coleridge	*Kubla Khan*	306
Samuel Taylor Coleridge	*Sonnet*	307
George Gordon, Lord Byron	*Stanzas for Music: There Be None of Beauty's Daughters*	308
George Gordon, Lord Byron	*Stanzas for Music: There's Not a Joy the World Can Give Like That It Takes Away*	308
Percy Bysshe Shelley	*Sonnet: England in 1819*	309
Percy Bysshe Shelley	*Ozymandias*	310
John Keats	*To——*	310
John Keats	*La Belle Dame Sans Merci*	312
John Keats	*On Seeing the Elgin Marbles*	313

Imagistic Poetry: Early Twentieth Century — 314

Amy Lowell	*The Pond*	315
H. D.	*Oread*	316
Archibald MacLeish	*Ars Poetica*	317
John Peale Bishop	*Speaking of Poetry*	321
Joseph Langland	*Hunters in the Snow: Brueghel*	324
William Carlos Williams	*III The Hunters in the Snow*	325
John Berryman	*Winter Landscape*	326
William Carlos Williams	*II Landscape with the Fall of Icarus*	327
W. H. Auden	*Musée des Beaux Arts*	328
Amy Lowell	*Venus Transiens*	329

Wallace Stevens *Disillusionment of Ten O'Clock*	329
Wallace Stevens *Study of Two Pears*	330
William Carlos Williams *The Red Wheelbarrow*	331
William Carlos Williams *Nantucket*	331
William Carlos Williams *Daisy*	332
William Carlos Williams *Dawn*	333
Ezra Pound *In a Station of the Metro*	333
Ezra Pound *Doria*	333
Ezra Pound *Imerro*	334
H. D. *Heat*	334
Richard Aldington *Evening*	334
Denise Levertov *October*	335

BIOGRAPHICAL CONTEXTS, 337

Walt Whitman (1819–1892)	**339**
From *Song of Myself*	341
A Woman Waits for Me	360
Full of Life Now	362
William Butler Yeats (1865–1939)	**363**
The Pity of Love	365
The Lover Tells of the Rose in His Heart	366
He Tells of the Perfect Beauty	366
He Hears the Cry of the Sedge	366
When You Are Old	367
The Folly of Being Comforted	367
Never Give All the Heart	367
O Do Not Love Too Long	368
Against Unworthy Praise	368
Fallen Majesty	369
Friends	369
The People	370
A Thought from Propertius	371
A Deep-Sworn Vow	371
Presences	372
Quarrel in Old Age	372
A Bronze Head	373
Emily Dickinson (1830–1886)	**374**
For Each Ecstatic Instant	376
He Was Weak	376
I'm "Wife"	376

Wild Nights	377
I Reason, Earth Is Short	377
After Great Pain, a Formal Feeling Comes	378
Of Course—I Prayed	378
The First Day's Night Had Come	378
Much Madness Is Divinest Sense	379
I Reckon—When I Count at All	379
It Would Have Starved a Gnat	380
They Shut Me Up in Prose	380
Ourselves Were Wed One Summer—Dear	381
I Dwell in Possibility	381
Again—His Voice Is at the Door	382
One Need Not Be a Chamber	383
It Dropped So Low	383
Because the Bee May Blameless Hum	383
How Happy I Was If I Could Forget	384
If I Can Stop One Heart from Breaking	384
Struck, Was I, Not Yet by Lightning	384
I Felt a Cleaving in My Mind	385
When They Come Back	385
To Whom the Mornings Stand for Nights	386
A Great Hope Fell	386
Like Rain It Sounded Till It Curved	387
I Thought That Nature Was Enough	387
A Little Madness in the Spring	387
My Maker—Let Me Be	388
The Fact That Earth Is Heaven	388
It Was a Quiet Seeming Day	388
One Joy of So Much Anguish	389
"Heavenly Father"	389
The Bible Is an Antique Volume	389
Of God We Ask One Favor	390
Is It Too Late to Touch You, Dear?	390
If All the Griefs I Am to Have	390
Rearrange a "Wife's" Affection!	391
Lad of Athens	391

CULTURAL CONTEXTS, 393

Protest Poetry	393
Poems of War Protest	395
From II Samuel David's Lament	395
Li Po The Nefarious War	396

A. E. Housman *Epitaph on an Army of Mercenaries* 396
William Butler Yeats *An Irish Airman Foresees His Death* 397
Siegfried Sassoon *Counter-Attack* 397
Edna St. Vincent Millay *Conscientious Objector* 398
Wilfred Owen *Arms and the Boy* 399
Wilfred Owen *Spring Offensive* 400
Wilfred Owen *Exposure* 401
Wilfred Owen *Dulce et Decorum Est* 402
e. e. cummings *i sing of Olaf glad and big* 403
Kenneth Patchen *The Known Soldier* 404
John William Corrington *A Trip to Omaha (Normandy 6.VI.44)* 405

Poems of Black American Protest 406
Claude McKay *If We Must Die* 406
Claude McKay *The Negro's Tragedy* 407
Claude McKay *The Lynching* 407
Langston Hughes *Let America Be America Again* 408
Countee Cullen *A Brown Girl Dead* 410
Countee Cullen *Scottsboro, Too, Is Worth Its Song* 410
Richard Wright *Between the World and Me* 411
Owen Dodson *Jonathan's Song* 413
Ray Durem From *Award* 414
Etheridge Knight *The Idea of Ancestry* 415
Imamu Amiri Baraka (LeRoi Jones) *Vice* 416
Imamu Amiri Baraka (LeRoi Jones) *The New Sheriff* 418
Ishmael Reed *off d pig* 419
Don L. Lee *A Poem Looking for a Reader* 420
Anonymous From *Back of the Bus* 422

The Poetry of Other Cultures 423
Bashō *The Old Pond* 425

African Poems 426
Tshakatumba *Prayer Without Echo* 426
Sembène Ousmane *Nostalgia* 427
Boevi Zankli *The Dream of African Unity* 429
John M. Ruganda *The Image of God* 430
Ezekiel Mphahlele *Death* 431
Taban Lo Liyong *Uncle Tom's Black Humour* 434
Faarah Nuur *The Limits of Submission* 439
Léopold Sédar Senghor *Prayer to the Masks* 440
Birago Diop *Breath* 441

David Diop *Africa*	443
Bernard B. Dadié *The Lines of Our Hands*	444
Gabriel Okara *Piano and Drums*	445
Kwesi Brew *Ancestral Faces*	446
John Pepper Clark *Night Rain*	447
Chinese Poems	**448**
Anonymous *A Confucian Ode: Blessings*	448
Anonymous *A Confucian Ode: The Legend of Shang*	449
Anonymous *A Confucian Ode: Minister of War*	450
Tu Fu *Déjeuner Sur L'Herbe*	451
Tu Fu *The Excursion*	452
Tu Fu *The Emperor*	452
Tu Fu *The Autumn Wastes*	453
Tu Fu *At the Corner of the World*	454
Han Yu From *The South Mountains*	455
Li Ho *The Northern Cold*	457
Li Ho *An Arrowhead from the Ancient Battlefield of Ch'ang-P'ing*	458
Li Ho *The Grave of Little Su*	459
Lui Chi *A Poet Thinks*	459
Mao Tse-Tung *The Snow*	460
Mao Tse-Tung *The Long March*	461
Mao Tse-Tung *After Swimming Across the Yangtze River*	461
Feng Chi *Sonnet XVI*	462

AESTHETIC CONTEXTS, 465

Visual Arts, Music, and Dance	**465**
John Milton *At a Solemn Music*	467
Alexander Pope *Ode on St. Cecilia's Day*	468
William Carlos Williams *Picture of a Nude in a Machine Shop*	472
William Carlos Williams *Ol' Bunk's Band*	473
Siegfried Sassoon *Sheldonian Soliloquy*	474
Siegfried Sassoon *Concert-Interpretation*	475
Marianne Moore *Arthur Mitchell*	476
Edna St. Vincent Millay *On Hearing a Symphony of Beethoven*	477
Kenneth Fearing *Art Review*	477
Stephen Spender *Art Student*	478

Contents

John Berryman *Beethoven Triumphant*	479
Mona Van Duyn *The Pietà, Rhenish, 14th C., The Cloisters*	485
J. D. O'Hara *Aristotle Contemplating the Bust of Homer: After Rembrandt*	487
Andrey Voznesensky *Maya*	487
Bob Kaufman *Mingus*	489
Bob Kaufman *Walking Parker Home*	490
Sandra Hochman *The Museum*	491
Marge Piercy *The Peaceable Kingdom*	491

Index 502

Introduction

Writers of poetry textbooks are in somewhat the same position as the three blind men before the elephant. One version of that story has it that the three were placed before an elephant and asked to describe what was there. One grabbed the trunk and said he had a snake, the second felt a side and said it was a wall, while the third wrapped his arms around a leg and said he had a tree. Poems, like the elephant, can present similar difficulties to those who try to describe them. Thus, before a great poem we sometimes seem like those blind men, grasping now one part, now another, and never seeing the whole.

While there is no easy solution to the awesome and mysterious task of describing poems, we should, at least, avoid the same mistake the blind men made. We must not take hold of one part and say, "This is it, I have found the answer." Instead, we should move around the object we would describe. We should begin by trying to grasp a sense of the whole. Like scientists and detectives, we can make repeated hypotheses, examining each hypothesis by appealing to the evidence—in this case, the poem and the circumstances in which it exists. We must guess and test. We might begin by touching a side and saying, "This seems to be a wall." But we must not stop there. We must touch other parts, and eventually we must ask what kind of wall it is that breathes, stands on four trees, and has a huge snake at one end. If we use such simple logic, we can soon put together the parts of even the most complicated poem and come up with an informative description of any poem we study.

Unfortunately for writers, one page must follow another. And although writers might wish to present all their chapters in the form of a circle, allowing the reader to pick and choose among the chapters as his need and interest require, books cannot be printed that way. All we, as writers, can do is stress at the outset that the reader must move around the poem, read it, examine it from the inside and the outside, begin at the end and end at the beginning. Like a detective, he must infer, he must gather testimony and witnesses, he must make guesses and evaluate them in light of every possible kind of information, he must find the "motive" behind the poem, he must understand the structure of the poem by reconstructing it as a poetic act. In addition, he may find it necessary to examine the poem in light of the poet's other works, the poet's life, or in terms of other poems of similar kinds and on similar themes.

There is, however, no sure place to begin to formulate such a description of a poem. Critics and readers invariably make false starts, ask the wrong questions, are baffled by some simplicity or ambiguity, and make wrong guesses. But eventually trial and error pay off. Despite the fact that this book advocates an intelligent tentativeness as the best attitude with which to begin reading poetry, it is organized in consecutive chapters. These chapters are based on the conception of a poem existing in an almost infinite number of contexts. Behind this notion of context is a loose distinction—that between internal and external. Some chapters are organized around a poem's internal contexts, some are concerned with external contexts.

We have selected a half dozen different kinds of external contexts as being the most rewarding and interesting. These are the Thematic (Love, Spring, Elegy), Formal (Ballad, Sonnet, Ode), Historical (Metaphysical, Romantic, Imagistic), Biographical (Walt Whitman, William Butler Yeats, Emily Dickinson), Cultural (Social Protest, Chinese, African), and Aesthetic (Visual Arts, Music, Dance). The internal contexts we deal with are those that may be seen from a perspective of Language (Prose, Light Verse, Dramatic Speech), and those that seem best viewed from the perspective of Style (Diction, Meter and Rhythm).

We begin our consideration of external contexts by examining some of the ways poems on similar subjects may be related to one another. We recognize that the logical extension of thematic analysis of this kind is archetypal criticism—the gathering and evaluation, for example, of all the images, character types, and plot situations that are generally connected with romance or with tragedy. Such an ambitious goal is beyond the purposes of this book. Our aim is much more limited: to show what similarities and what differences may be involved when different authors treat the same general subject. Specifically, we are concerned with the choices the poet makes; for example, what it means when he decides to treat the pain of love rather than the joy of love, and what it means for a contemporary poet to write a love poem with several centuries of love poems to look back on (no matter how vaguely).

Out of the numerous technical forms in English we have selected three as best suited to illustrate the influence of poetic conventions: the ballad, the sonnet, and the ode. These three forms have been used by English poets for four centuries. Of the three, the oldest—the ballad—is currently the form most popular among contemporary poets. This may be due to the fact that the ballad allows room for extraordinary variation and individuality. This is less true of the ode and even less true of the sonnet. The possibilities for meaningful variation in the fourteen-line sonnet were so nearly exhausted by the last century that only rare geniuses and foolhardy neophytes were left to experiment with the form. And although perfect sonnets have been written in the twentieth century, this perfection has been achieved in the face of the overwhelming accomplishments of previous poets in this same mode. The few poets who have successfully confronted the achievements of the past and added to these accomplishments have, however, provided the student of poetry with singular examples of how poetic forms channel poetic talent, and allow the critic to make precise appraisals of poetic originality. As for the ode, it would seem to be more significant as an historical development than as a viable form in which poets today seek the same aesthetic ends as poets of earlier centuries. The formal requirements of the Pindaric and Horatian odes appear to have been found too restrictive by poets since the eighteenth century, and since that time the name "ode" has been applied more broadly, covering such different poems as John Keats's "Ode on a Grecian Urn," Percy Bysshe Shelley's "Ode to the West Wind," Dylan Thomas's "Fern Hill," and Allen Tate's "Ode to the Confederate Dead." Despite the collapse of the strict ode forms, the evolution of radically different kinds of odes provides a valuable background for the study of what we might loosely call medium-length lyric poems.

Any text attempting to deal with the environment of English poetry might well deal with eleven or more historical periods—for example, the medieval, Renaissance, metaphysical, Restoration, Age of Reason, romantic, Victorian, yellow nineties, imagistic, modern, and even the contemporary. In treating poetic forms, however, we have had to make a choice among these periods. The three we felt most useful were the metaphysical, the romantic, and the imagistic. While our need to select was determined by space, our selections were based on the belief that these three eras were the most influential in the development of poetry in English and that because of this they could best provide models for students to explore historical considerations. Certainly, the student who is interested, or the instructor who is an expert in another period, should not hesitate to substitute or add to this brief review of historical contexts.

But schools and periods are not the only contexts in which we can see poems. Every poem is written from experience, whether real or imagined, and most poems are better understood if we have some insight into the biographical circumstances surrounding its writing. For this book we have chosen three poets—Walt Whitman, William Butler Yeats, and Emily Dickinson—whose works are autobiographical in order to illustrate the context most clearly. Some of their poems are significant only because they shed light on how the poets felt and thought. Thus the poems we have chosen may be supplemented by those that may be found in any standard anthology. But no matter which of their poems you read, you will understand them more fully if you see their poetry in relation to their lives. This is not to suggest that all poems are illustrations of a poet's life; it is only to assert that some poets use their experiences more directly than do others. When they do this we can get a great deal more from their work by seeing it in the context of their lives. Just as the words poets use are defined outside the poems—in dictionaries—the events or moods or moments of experience the poems embody are sometimes defined outside the poems—in the poet's lives.

Most books about poetry do not include poems from other languages, or poems not in the "great tradition" of English poetry. This is not true of this book. We include non-English poems in translation, and we include poems whose main interest is thematic —not formal, or even aesthetic. If one is concerned only with the internal contexts of language, it is not profitable to consider non-English poems, or didactic and controversial poetry. Yet an enormously important body of poetry exists outside our culture, and outside the academic traditions of English poetry. It is not reasonable to ignore such poetry, because some of the most pertinent and controversial poetry is in the polemic context, and particularly because some of the best creative work of our time is in the translation of non-English poetry. Since we are interested in the effects of a culture on poetry, we can easily include poetry as diverse from our own as that of China and Africa, poems of black protest, and poems protesting war. These latter—seen in the context they were written —represent some of the oldest kinds of poetry and carry out some of the most time-honored purposes of poetry that we have record of.

Chinese poems may be difficult to discuss if we isolate one or two instances and try to present them in the same way we do a poem of T. S. Eliot. But if we do not demand tight internal relationships and consider only the poems in their cultural context, we can gain a new awareness and appreciation of both our own and foreign cultural contexts. If nothing else, this poetry can give us a highly valuable insight into a poetry that is clearly different from the one our traditional critics have been examining. We may understand why some modern poets have been so obviously influenced by Oriental poetry. We can also see how much the African poet has in common with poets around the world who share the same basic concerns about life.

Much African poetry can be discussed in the context of black American protest poetry, since a large portion of it is also protest poetry. Traditional analysis often will not help us understand this highly vigorous work. However, if we concentrate on its purposes, its own specific rhetoric, and its relation to poems in the same mode, we can learn a good deal. Our interests in this book are primarily critical and aesthetic when we treat African poetry, but we believe poems with such political intentions have an aesthetic premise that differs from the premises of the traditional poems that critics usually deal with.

In the section on aesthetic contexts, we look at several poems that refer to other arts. Here the poet establishes a contextual relationship between his poem and a given work of art or artistic medium. Without an awareness of the work or the medium, our responses to the poem are somewhat limited. At the same time, poems that refer to artifacts have much in common, which is perceptible even when we do not have access to the artifacts in question. Here the external context is crucial, although we can still examine the internal contextual relationships of words, images, and other poetic elements with some possibility of enjoyment.

When we speak of internal contexts we mean the relationship of a given word, speech, character, sound, meter, idea, image, or trope to another in a given poem. If Shakespeare, for example, begins a sonnet by talking about an experience in terms of legal language, we will want to know how he works out the associations in order to make good on his initial reference. In such cases we are concerned with the structure the poet builds in the poem.

While our handling of internal contexts necessarily touches on the same considerations as more traditional texts, even here our approach is not conventional. We take a much more concrete and pragmatic attitude toward language. We start from the observable fact that poetry is a verbal expression related to prose, to verse, and to dramatic speech. The advantage of such an attitude is that it

6 Introduction

begins with what *is* rather than with a theory of what *should be*. It simply accepts the fact that a poem has things in common with prose, verse, and dramatic speech, and in the process of clarifying that commonness it creates a working definition of poetry and provides some basic questions for analyzing and judging poems. The Diction and Meter and Rhythm chapters are the most traditional in the book. They deal with two of the most common ways of examining the style of poems—by considering a poet's word choices and by considering the metrical or rhythmical organization of the poem.

Three types of questions are asked in this text. They are posed at various points in the book, depending on the context and kind of poem being analyzed. One type of question is textural—new critical in a sense. It concentrates on words and lines. It deals with speaker, drama, ideas, and tone in the dramatic situation. Quite literally, it seeks to find out what is happening in the poem. Such questions aim at a paraphrase, a gloss, or a "translation" of a poem. A second kind of question is formal. It does not so much seek to learn what a word, scene, or action means, as why the poet used that word, scene, or action as he did. It aims at eliciting information about a poem's design, about the *ordering* of the language and ideas, and about the *emphasis* given to respective parts. The third type of question— and the type generally used in chapters dealing with external contexts—seeks to draw comparisons among poems. It not only looks at broad themes and types of poetic expression, it evaluates one poem's presentation in terms of another poem's presentation.

It is possible to sum up almost all of the contexts we have outlined by reference to a single poem by Robert Frost. The most economical way to do this is by simply listing some of the kinds of information derived from each context, or by asking the questions required to elicit such information. For internal contexts, all the necessary information will be found in the poem itself; for the external contexts, it will be necessary to provide facts and circumstances—especially for the biographical context—so that the student who knows little of Frost will have a clear idea of exactly what is being described.

The poem that will serve as our model is Frost's "Design."

    I found a dimpled spider, fat and white,
    On a white heal-all holding up a moth
    Like a piece of rigid satin cloth—
    Assorted characters of death and blight,
    Mixed ready to begin the morning right   5

> Like the ingredients of a witches' broth—
> A snow-drop spider, a flower like froth,
> And dead wings carried like a paper kite.
>
> What had that flower to do with being white,
> That wayside blue and innocent heal-all?   10
> What brought the kindred spider to that height,
> Then steered the white moth thither in the night?
> What but design of darkness to appall?—
> If design govern in a thing so small?

The Context of Dramatic Speech—The Preliminary Questions
In analyzing a poem, as any verbal communication, the first thing to do is clarify the context in which the words are spoken. The following questions may prove useful: Do the words on the page express an idea, create a dramatic scene, or describe a picture? (If the words appear to do more than one of these things, try to determine how the idea, drama, and picture are related, and which seems to be most important to the whole poem. If the poem appears to be an "idea" poem, clarify the idea, show how the various parts of the poem help to present the speaker's thought, and determine if there is any logical or chronological relationship between the parts of the poem. If the poem creates a drama, clarify the relationship between the speaker and the scene.) Is there an implied audience? Is there a dramatic unfolding—a basic situation, a rising action, a climax, a resolution—in the poem? Can the plot be summarized? What are the circumstances of the action? If the chief end of the poem seems to be to describe a picture, or to give the feeling of a scene, explain how the words do this. What are the chief features of the picture so described, or the mood so depicted? Is the significance of the picture all on the surface, or does it have some implied or hidden meaning?

The Context of Diction
When we examine the words of a poem, we are concerned with three things: those words that call attention to themselves, the effective ordering of all the words in the poem, and the overall tone that the language of the poem helps to underline. If we translate these concerns into questions, we might ask the following: What words call attention to themselves? (In the first line of "Design" the words "dimpled" and "white" are such attention-demanding words.) How are the words ordered for effectiveness? (Consider the structure of the first sentence, the significance of the three

questions that conclude the poem, and the rhyme words.) What is the tone of the poem? Is there a mixture of lightness and seriousness? Why, for example, is there a comic touch in the line "Mixed ready to begin the morning right"?)

The essential information we seek when we examine poetic diction will always answer two questions: Why did the poet use the words he did? Were his choices successful? The best way to answer such questions is to substitute different words for those the poet actually used. Are your substitutes as effective as the words the poet chose? A convenient way to ask such a question for this particular poem is to consider some of the actual words Frost discarded as he worked "Design" toward its final form. Here is an earlier version of the poem:

IN WHITE

A dented spider like a snow drop white
On a white heal-all, holding up a moth
Like a white piece of lifeless satin cloth—
Saw ever curious eye so strange a sight?—
Portent in little, assorted death and blight   5
Like the ingredients of a witches' broth?—
The beady spider, the flower like a froth,
And the moth carried like a paper kite.

What had that flower to do with being white,
The blue prunella every child's delight.   10
What brought the kindred spider to that height?
(Make me no thesis of the Miller's plight.)
What but design of darkness and of night?
Design, design! Do I use the word aright?

Compare the words of the two poems line by line. List those words that seem most effective and least effective, and be ready to explain why there is this variation in effectiveness.

The Context of Meter and Rhythm

We are looking for one thing when we examine the poem's meter or rhythm: How does the poet want us to read his poem? One way we determine this is to find the pattern of accents, or stresses, the poet has used, and then note where he varies the pattern. Once we have determined the metrical norm and the main variations, we can ask what the emotional and intellectual results of these variations are. The metrical pattern of "Design" is iambic pentameter (pages 237–38). There are several meaningful variations from the iambic norm, but perhaps the most meaningful is contained in the last line, where the regular iambic meter is varied by an abbreviated first foot that causes the opening word "If" to receive a heavy stress. What does it mean when the meter requires that we stress the opening word in the final line: "*If* design govern in a thing so small"?

The Context of Prose: The Context of Verse
We study the relationships between poetry and prose and poetry and verse in order to make judgments about the effectiveness of particular poems. Here, for example, Lawrance Thompson, Frost's biographer, discusses a book (William James's *Pragmatism*) that may have been in the back of Frost's mind when he wrote "Design."

> It pleased Frost to find that James, in *Pragmatism*, very wittily mocked the old-fashioned claim, for example, that God had designed every minute physical detail in nature for a special end. James says that some of these details, "if designed, would argue an evil rather than a good designer." Then to illustrate how much depends on the point of view he singles out a grub and a woodpecker: "To the grub under the bark the exquisite fitness of the woodpecker's organism to extract him would certainly argue a diabolic designer." (Lawrance Thompson, *Robert Frost: The Early Years* [New York, 1966], p. 386.)

This comment contains much of the idea of "Design," plus one clever example not found in Frost's poem. So we might say it contains "the idea" of "Design" and something else. But we could not say it is the poem. Why? Why is a prose paraphrase not comparable to the actual poem? When we can answer that question, we will be able to make the most necessary and rudimentary kind of judgment about what constitutes effective poetry. And in order to make such a basic judgment, it is necessary that we observe an idea in the context of prose and verse.

The Context of Theme
A much more concrete way of answering some of the questions we have already posed is to read Frost's poem in light of other poems that have spiders as their subjects. Here are two poems that may help us to see Frost's poem in a fresh light:

A NOISELESS PATIENT SPIDER

Walt Whitman (1819–1892)

A noiseless patient spider,
I mark'd where on a little promontory it stood isolated,
Mark'd how to explore the vacant vast surrounding,
It launch'd forth filament, filament, filament, out of itself,
Ever unreeling them, ever tirelessly speeding them.   5

And you O my soul where you stand,
Surrounded, detached, in measureless oceans of space,
Ceaselessly musing, venturing, throwing, seeking the spheres to
     connect them,
Till the bridge you will need be form'd, till the ductile anchor hold,
Till the gossamer thread you fling catch somewhere, O my soul.   10

THE ORB WEAVER

Robert Francis (b. 1901)

Here is the spinner, the orb weaver,
Devised of jet, embossed with sulphur,
Hanging among the fruits of summer,

Hour after hour serenely sullen,
Ripening as September ripens,   5
Plumping like a grape or melon.

And in its winding-sheet the grasshopper.

The art, the craftsmanship, the cunning,
The patience, the self-control, the waiting,
The sudden dart and the needled poison.   10

I have no quarrel with the spider
But with the mind or mood that made her
To thrive in nature and in man's nature.

When we read "Design" in the context of these other two poems, we are able to grasp more immediately the essential conception, the "motive" behind "Design." Furthermore, we can see how each poet emphasizes different qualities of the spider, each establishes a different tone, and each arrives at a still different conclusion. The context of theme enables us to perceive similarity and dissimilarity immediately and clearly. It enables us to see a poem in the context of like poems and thus helps us to achieve a fuller understanding of poetic form and thought.

Formal and Historical Contexts
   Ordinarily a poem's form and its place in literary history are separate concerns. But this is not true of Frost's poem. The form of "Design" is the best way to see its historical context. "Design" is a sonnet, and as such it immediately gives the reader a sense of controlled expression ordinarily associated with that form. But being a twentieth-century sonnet, it has characteristics that clearly suggest its modernity. The proper place to explore the formal characteristics of "Design" is in the section on the sonnet (pages 145–61), but two brief points may be made here. Frost uses a traditional rhyme scheme in his octave (*abba abba*), but he uses a rhyme scheme that only a twentieth-century poet would be likely to employ in the sestet (*ab aa bb*). This is like few other English sonnets in its rhyme scheme—just three rhyme sounds in fourteen lines is unusual for a sonnet. Second, there is the ironical—perhaps even flippant—attitude toward *design*, toward the order of the universe. This single thematic quality alone is enough to mark it as a twentieth-century poem.

Cultural Context
   The further we explore ways in which the poem questions the nature and order of the universe, the further we identify Frost's poem as a representative of the twentieth-century *Zeitgeist*. If we are aware of Jonathan Edwards's admiration for the spider's industry, or recall Whitman's analogy of the spider's activity to the activities of man's soul, we can immediately see a difference between attitudes toward nature in the eighteenth and nineteenth centuries compared with the twentieth-century attitudes of Frost and Robert Francis. Another cultural aspect of this poem may be seen if we simply think about the use of "white" in the poem. It is difficult, maybe impossible, to be exact about the use of "white" but it certainly is not the way a poet writing in China or Africa would be likely to use the word.

Biographical Context
   Our understanding of the biographical context covers a wide range of matters related to the author's life and work. We have

already dipped into biographical considerations in pointing out that Frost may have had William James's *Pragmatism* in the back of his mind when he wrote "Design." The earlier version of the poem, "In White," is also biographical. Everything in the poet's body of work and life that casts light on his poem is covered by the phrase "biographical context." We would, if we wanted to be thorough, look into Frost's other poems to discover his customary ideas on design and order in the universe. Further, we would want to know that he sent this poem to a clergyman, the Reverend Ward, after having argued with him about the extent of God's providence. We would also do well to read relevant passages in the poet's letters and biography to determine just what Frost's views on God were around the time he wrote this poem. Frost, for example, disagreed with Reverend Ward about the *extent* of God's presence in the universe; he did not deny the existence of God. Thompson provides us with a convenient summary of the kind of information we look for when we try to see a poem in the "biographical context." Thompson discusses Frost's reading of the philosophers William James and Henri Bergson. He discusses Frost's rejection of the Reverend Ward's conviction that "God's plan" governs everything in the universe—no matter how insignificant. Finally, drawing on his knowledge of Frost's thinking over many years, and his knowledge of Frost's poetry, Thompson makes an evaluation of just what Frost meant by the puzzling last lines of the sonnet. Here is Thompson's concluding comment on the poem's biographical context:

> William Hayes Ward, reading the first draft of this poem in the letter of thanks, might have thought he found in it a confirmation of his fear that Robert Frost had come powerfully under the influence of "atheistical" writers like Bergson and had thus become an atheist himself; but he would have been incorrect. If his more perceptive sister placed the first draft of this poem side by side with "My Giving," she may have seen correspondences between the two artistic procedures of carrying a sentimental notion to an absurd extreme. She knew Frost well enough to be certain that the coincidences did not for a moment convince him that this "design" suggested proof that the Designer must be evil. Frost, habitually the prey to dark moods which temporarily upset his religious affirmations, was perfectly capable of understanding—and even of sympathizing with—the possibility that his little study in white could be interpreted as being akin to Melville's very bitter chapter, "The Whiteness of the Whale," in *Moby Dick*. But Melville enjoyed the agony of luxuriating in blasphemous negations, and Frost never

did. Instead, he so desperately needed the consolation of positive religious belief that he was never long without it. Although he could briefly and intermittently entertain the notion that the Designer might be evil, he preferred to manipulate the notion in a detached way to tease and mock those whose religious beliefs seemed to him to be sentimental. Even in teasing, however, he still very firmly agreed with James and Bergson (as opposed to William Hayes Ward) that all the important purposes of the Designer are benevolent.

The Limits of Context

We have included only a small number of the contexts that might be explored for a more complete understanding of poems. We do not seek to be exhaustive, only suggestive. Although we placed "Design" in most of our contexts, we did so only as an illustration. Ordinarily a single poem is sufficiently analyzed if viewed in one or two of the contexts outlined in this text. We consider a poem in various contexts in order to perceive different facets of its meaning. Yet it is sometimes simply a matter of taste that determines which context any given poem in this book has been placed in. Many of these poems could be moved from chapter to chapter. This is not a defect of this book; it is a fact of poetic life. We wish to encourage the exploration of all appropriate contexts. If we have used a poem to demonstrate a metrical point, the student should not hesitate to view the same poem in a thematic or an historical perspective. Any context that provides a "way in" to a poem, or clarifies a poem, is useful.

Language Contexts

Prose and Poems

Almost every critic feels he knows what poetry is, yet no single definition seems to please everyone. Wordsworth said that much confusion had "been introduced into criticism" because the terms "prose" and "poetry" were commonly contrasted. He felt that the correct opposition was between "poetry and matter of fact, or science," but that "the only strict antithesis to Prose is Metre." Although Wordsworth's distinctions point in the right direction, they too are a bit confusing. For the term "poetry" is not defined simply by distinguishing it from verse or "matter-of-fact" prose. A practical understanding of poetry requires that we consider it in relation to two types of prose, to verse, and to the conventions that define the idea of the poem itself.

Verse, in the sense of metrical language, is the single most common characteristic of poetry, and, as Wordsworth remarked, is one of the ways we distinguish poetry from prose. Verse is regularly accented and unaccented language; prose is not. But there is some poetry that is not metrical. To describe this kind of poetry, it is necessary for us to draw further distinctions between poetry and prose. In order to do this we should recognize two types of prose: one "Matter of Fact, or Scientific," the other concerned with literary expression. The former deals with verifiable facts, the latter with the imagination. In describing literary prose there is sometimes a tendency to employ a phrase such as "poetic prose," or "vivid prose." The term "fiction" itself is another way of distinguishing

15

imaginative prose from ordinary prose. And herein lies a prime source of difficulty in defining poetry: imaginative prose is often poetic and may be poetry. Poetic passages from the Bible, or from the novels of James Joyce, Virginia Woolf, or Ernest Hemingway, certainly are poetry. However, these passages are not poems. Another way of putting this is to say that any imaginative expression may be poetic, but only a poet writes a poem. Let us look at some examples of these distinctions.

George Orwell rewrote a passage from the Bible (Ecclesiastes 9:11) in order to illustrate the difference between matter-of-fact prose and poetry:

> Objective consideration of contemporary phenomena compels the conclusion that success or failure in competitive activities exhibits no tendency to be commensurate with innate capacity, but that a considerable element of the unpredictable must invariably be taken into account. ("Politics of the English Language," from *Shooting an Elephant and Other Essays* [New York, 1950].)

Here is the poetic translation of the year 1611:

> I returned, and saw under the sun, that the race is not to the swift, nor yet the battle to the strong, neither yet bread to the wise, nor yet riches to men of understanding, nor yet favor to men of skill; but time and chance happeneth to them all.

Whatever our preference, the first version is undeniably prosaic. We call the second poetic because it is dramatic, rhythmic, and concrete. The sense of drama is conveyed by a speaker saying something of importance to him. The rhythmic quality results from the grammatical balancing of antitheses and parallelisms. But perhaps the most striking difference is one Orwell himself pointed out: the first contains only abstract phrases and vague language, while the second contains "six vivid images, and only one phrase ('time and chance') that could be called vague." This vivid, concrete way of using words and the effect of these words on readers led Wallace Stevens to assert that "poetry is the subject of the poem." It is not the conception itself but the way the conception is expressed, and the effect of the language on the reader that lies at the center of poetry.

The distinctions between a free-verse poem and poetic prose are difficult to describe. Essentially, we have to compare poetry in a poem and poetry in a piece of prose. Such an effort should help us to concentrate on different uses of language.

It is no disparagement of the following passage not to call it a poem:

> None of them knew the color of the sky. Their eyes glanced level, and were fastened upon the waves that swept toward them. These waves were of the hue of slate, save for the tops, which were of foaming white, and all of the men knew the colors of the sea. The horizon narrowed and widened, and dipped and rose, and at all times its edge was jagged with waves that seemed thrust up in points like rocks. Many a man ought to have a bathtub larger than the boat which here rode upon the sea. These waves were most wrongfully and barbarously abrupt and tall, and each frothy top was a problem in small-boat navigation.

It may be that word-painting like this is more obviously poetic than some works we call poems. The lines are the opening sentences of Stephen Crane's short story "The Open Boat." Crane himself acknowledged, in an indirect way, that the experience could be handled in a more formal kind of poetry when he wrote the following poem:

TO THE MAIDEN...

Stephen Crane (1871–1900)

> To the maiden
> The sea was blue meadow,
> Alive with little froth-people
> Singing.
>
> To the sailor, wrecked, 5
> The sea was dead grey walls
> Superlative in vacancy,
> Upon which nevertheless at fateful time
> Was written
> The grim hatred of nature. 10

The naïve person who says the latter *is* poetry because the words are lined up on the left-hand margin but not on the right, while the former version is *not* poetry because the words are lined up on both margins, may receive patronizing smiles from the sophisticated, but he happens to be saying something that is not too far off the mark. Both are poetry, but only one should be called a poem. This is because a poem is a convention and a poet tells us he is writing a poem by observing these conventions. (Some poets alter our conception of what a poem should be either by forging new conventions or reminding us of old ones that have not previously been employed in the language: Walt Whitman is one such poet.) Indenting each line is one convention a person observes when he wishes to tell his readers he is writing a poem. In this way poets in our culture have testified that they do not like their line endings to be at the mercy of the typographer. When we say poets shape language differently from prose writers, we are referring to the most obvious thing about the poem. Ordinarily the prose writer indents his paragraph as an aid to the reader, the poet indents every line with the intention of giving every line the importance of the opening line of a paragraph. The rapid eye movement from the righthand end of a line of type to the left-hand end of the line below is, in the reading of prose, a complete waste, a time when no information is reaching the brain; in the reading of verse it may be a time of reflection:

> Superlative in vacancy

—these words are isolated for leisurely inspection and reflection before we go on to the next line. What in prose might be rather clumsy writing

> Was written

—a case of awkward or unnecessary use of the passive voice—is actually, in Crane's context, disturbing, even ominous.

To such ideas as drama, rhythm, concreteness, and typography should be added the idea of compression. Poets seek to achieve their effects within a severely limited space. This does not mean that a poem will always be shorter than a comparable piece of prose. It means that a poet seeks to say what must be said in the most economical manner possible. Novels, plays, and even short stories (like "The Open Boat") require more "elbow room." William Butler Yeats confessed that he enjoyed reading *War and Peace*, but he regretted not having some actual words to remember after the experience of reading had passed. It is these memorable words, this visual language, that the lyric poet commonly supplies; and he tends to keep the poem short so that the reader can keep the whole thing in his mind at once. As a result, it is probably true that the ten lines of "To the Maiden . . ." contain as much concentrated feeling about the sea as the eight thousand words of "The Open Boat" contain more diffusely. This is perhaps what Thomas Hardy meant when he said he "could get the whole of a novel into three pages of verse."

Although we distinguish verse and prose most confidently on the grounds that verse has rhyme and meter and is printed with each line indented, such distinctions have less validity today than in the recent past. Modern poets disagree about the most apparent conventions of poems—rhyme, meter, and typography. This has led some to use the phrase "prose poem" to describe such poetry as the following:

HYSTERIA

T. S. Eliot (1888–1965)

As she laughed I was aware of becoming involved in her laughter and being part of it, until her teeth were only accidental stars with a talent for squad-drill. I was drawn in by short gasps, inhaled at each momentary recovery, lost finally in the dark caverns of her throat, bruised by the ripple of unseen muscles. An elderly waiter with trembling hands was hurriedly spreading a pink and white checked cloth over the rusty green iron table, saying: "If the lady and gentleman wish to take their tea in the garden . . ." I decided that if the shaking of her breasts could be stopped, some of the fragments of the afternoon might be collected, and I concentrated my attention with careful subtlety to this end.

We have said that poetic language is concrete, vivid, and economical, and that it creates a sense of drama and excitement. We have also said that a poem observes conventions of sound, rhyme, meter, or rhythm, and usually signals that it is a poem by its appearance on the page. We call "Hysteria" a prose poem, but Eliot could also have arranged the rhythmic units of "Hysteria" in separate lines. In that event, we would simply assume that he had written a free-verse poem—that is, a poem without regular meter. It might be interesting to rearrange "Hysteria" in this manner, and to speculate as to why Eliot chose to present the poem to his readers in the form of a prose paragraph.

But, the most important single consideration to keep in mind is the object of the writer. Coleridge, in his *Biographia Literaria,* said that demonstrable truth was the object of science, recorded experience that of history, and pleasure the object of imaginative writing. This pleasure is attained, according to Coleridge, by "studied selection and artificial arrangement" of language, and by a poem's "exciting continuous and equal attention in its parts." These are rather large considerations, but they can serve us well whether we trace them in detail (page 213), or whether we simply ask the basic questions about the poet's objectives and his arrangement of language in order to achieve these objectives.

Below are a number of poems paired with examples of other kinds of poetry and prose. Although we ask several questions about the first pair—the newspaper clipping and the Frost poem—we offer only two questions about those that come after in order to guide you: (1) What is the writer's objective? (2) How is that objective achieved by his selection and arrangement of language in the poem?

Do not be content merely to define the poet's objective as pleasure—that is meaningless. Reflect on precisely what the writer appears to be doing and on how he makes his material interesting to the reader.

Lawrance Thompson, Robert Frost's biographer, has identified the following newspaper story as a journalistic account of an episode on which Frost based his poem "Out, Out—."

The Littleton Courier 31 March 1901

"Sad Tragedy at Bethlehem
"Raymond Fitzgerald, a Victim
"Of fatal Accident

Raymond Tracy Fitzgerald, one of the twin sons of Michael G. and Margaret Fitzgerald of Bethlehem, died at his home Thursday afternoon, March 24, as a result of an accident by which one of his hands was badly hurt in a sawing machine. The young man was assisting in sawing up some wood in his own dooryard with a sawing machine and accidently hit the loose pulley, causing the saw to descend upon his hand, cutting and lacerating it badly. Raymond was taken into the house and a physician was immediately summoned, but he died very suddenly from the effects of the shock, which produced heart failure. . . ." (Quoted in Lawrance Thompson, *Robert Frost: The Early Years* [New York, 1966], p. 567.)

"OUT, OUT—"

Robert Frost (1874–1963)

The buzz saw snarled and rattled in the yard
And made dust and dropped stove-length sticks of wood,
Sweet-scented stuff when the breeze drew across it.
And from there those that lifted eyes could count
Five mountain ranges one behind the other   5
Under the sunset far into Vermont.
And the saw snarled and rattled, snarled and rattled,
As it ran light, or had to bear a load.
And nothing happened: day was all but done.
Call it a day, I wish they might have said   10
To please the boy by giving him the half hour
That a boy counts so much when saved from work.
His sister stood beside them in her apron
To tell them "Supper." At the word, the saw,
As if to prove saws knew what supper meant,   15
Leaped out at the boy's hand, or seemed to leap—
He must have given the hand. However it was,
Neither refused the meeting. But the hand!
The boy's first outcry was a rueful laugh,
As he swung toward them holding up the hand   20
Half in appeal, but half as if to keep
The life from spilling. Then the boy saw all—
Since he was old enough to know, big boy
Doing a man's work, though a child at heart—
He saw all spoiled. "Don't let him cut my hand off—   25
The doctor, when he comes. Don't let him, sister!"
So. But the hand was gone already.
The doctor put him in the dark of ether.
He lay and puffed his lips out with his breath.
And then—the watcher at his pulse took fright.   30

No one believed. They listened at his heart.
Little—less—nothing!—and that ended it.
No more to build on there. And they, since they
Were not the one dead, turned to their affairs.

QUESTIONS

1. Describe the purpose behind the newspaper account; describe Frost's objective. In what ways do Frost and the newspaper have the same purpose? How do their purposes differ?
2. Consider other possible ways Frost could have recounted this experience. What might conceivably have been gained, what lost, if Frost had written a meditation on death, that is, if he had gone into the boy's life more deeply and had dealt with how the boy's death affected him and others around him? What effect might Frost have achieved if he had used a tight rhyme scheme? Consider carefully the following observations and questions before deciding finally on Frost's objective and how he carried it out:

   Title   "Out, Out—" are words from a famous soliloquy in Shakespeare's *Macbeth*. How are they appropriate?

   Line 1   There is a general regularity of accents in each line of the poem. Ordinarily, how many accents fall in each line? Where do exceptions occur? What is the effect of the exceptions? Note the repetition, here and later on, of the phrase "snarled and rattled." Comment.

   Lines 2–6   Between the two occurrences of "snarled and rattled" are five lines of picturesque description and quiet tone. What do these lines add to the poem?

   Line 8   Comment on the exactness of this line.

   Lines 10–12   The speaker's identity becomes slightly more evident in these lines.

   Line 13   What does the sister's presence add to the poem? Imagine that she was never mentioned. What would be missing?

Lines 14–17   Why does Frost emphasize the word "supper"?
Line 19   What precise aspects of the accident are implied by "The boy's first outcry was a rueful laugh"?
Lines 19–26   Why does Frost concentrate on the boy's concern with loss of his hand—as though this loss were going to be the major part of the narrative?
Lines 24–25   Comment on the character of the speaker as revealed in these lines.
Line 27   Why is "so" set apart?
Line 28   "The doctor put him in the dark of ether." This is another instance of remarkable economy. Throughout the poem, a great deal is said in the briefest possible manner. From this point in particular, each line is a summary of the essence of many small details. Can you explain what each line summarizes?
Lines 32–34   Comment on the tone of the concluding lines. Is there any implication of blame in the concluding sentence? Does the speaker feel those present should not have returned to their affairs?

SELECTIONS FOR FURTHER STUDY

Diary entry describing a poem, followed by the poem

Diary Entry

William Butler Yeats (1865–1939)

To-day the thought came to me that P.I.A.L. (Maud Gonne) never really understands my plans, or nature or ideas. Then came the thought—what matter? How much of the best I have done and still do is but the attempt to explain myself to her? If she understood I should lack a reason for writing, and one can never have too many reasons for doing what is so laborious. (Quoted in J. M. Hone, *W. B. Yeats 1865–1939* [London, New York, 1942, 1962], p. 228.)

WORDS

William Butler Yeats

I had this thought a while ago,
"My darling cannot understand
What I have done, or what would do
In this blind bitter land."

And I grew weary of the sun   5
Until my thoughts cleared up again,
Remembering that the best I have done
Was done to make it plain;

That every year I have cried, "At length
My darling understands it all,   10
Because I have come into my strength,
And words obey my call";

That had she done so who can say
What would have shaken from the sieve?
I might have thrown poor words away   15
And been content to live.

A sonnet by Wordsworth and his explication of the sonnet

WITH SHIPS THE SEA

William Wordsworth (1770–1850)

With Ships the sea was sprinkled far and nigh,
Like stars in heaven, and joyously it showed;
Some lying fast at anchor in the road,
Some veering up and down, one knew not why.
A goodly Vessel did I then espy   5
Come like a giant from a haven broad;
And lustily along the bay she strode,
Her tackling rich, and of apparel high.
This Ship was nought to me, nor I to her,
Yet I pursued her with a Lover's look;   10
This Ship to all the rest did I prefer:
When will She turn, and whither? She will brook

No tarrying; where She comes the winds must stir:
On went She, and due north her journey took.

from A Letter to Lady Beaumont

I am represented in the Sonnet as casting my eyes over the sea, sprinkled with a multitude of Ships, like the heavens with stars, my mind may be supposed to float up and down among them in a kind of dreamy indifference with respect either to this or that one, only in a pleasurable state of feeling with respect to the whole prospect. "Joyously it showed," this continued till that feeling may be supposed to have passed away, and a kind of comparative listlessness or apathy to have succeeded, as at this line, "Some veering up and down, one knew not why." All at once, while I am in this state, comes forth an object, an individual, and my mind, sleepy and unfixed, is awakened and fastened in a moment. "Hesperus, that led The starry host," is a poetical object, because the glory of his own Nature gives him the pre-eminence the moment he appears; he calls forth the poetic faculty, receiving its exertions as a tribute; but this Ship in the Sonnet may, in a manner still more appropriate, be said to come upon a mission of the poetic Spirit, because in its own appearance and attributes it is barely sufficiently distinguished to rouse the creative faculty of the human mind; to exertions at all times welcome, but doubly so when they come upon us when in a state of remissness. The mind being once fixed and roused, all the rest comes from itself; it is merely a lordly Ship, nothing more:

> This Ship was nought to me, nor I to her,
> Yet I pursued her with a Lover's look.

My mind wantons with grateful joy in the exercise of its own powers, and, loving its own creation,

> This Ship to all the rest did I prefer,

making her a sovereign or a regent, and thus giving body and life to all the rest; mingling up this idea with fondness and praise—

> where She comes the winds must stir;

and concluding the whole with

> On went She, and due north her journey took.

Thus taking up again the Reader with whom I began, letting him know how long I must have watched this favorite Vessel, and inviting him to rest his mind as mine is resting. (Ernest de Selincourt, ed., *The Letters of William and Dorothy Wordsworth: The Middle Years* [Oxford, 1937] I, 128–29.)

A philosopher and a poet on time

from Leviathan (I, iii)

Thomas Hobbes (1588–1679)

"The *present* only has a being in nature; things *past* have a being in the memory only, but things *to come* have no being at all; the *future* being but a fiction of the mind, applying the sequels of actions past, to the actions that are present; which with most certainty is done by him that has most experience, but not with certainty enough. And though it be called prudence, when the event answereth our expectation; yet in its own nature, it is but presumption."

LOVE AND LIFE
A SONG

John Wilmot, Earl of Rochester (1647–1680)

> All my past Life is mine no more,
>   The flying Hours are gone:
> Like transitory Dreams giv'n o'er,
> Whose Images are kept in store,
>   By Memory alone.   5
>
> The Time that is to come is not;
>   How can it then be mine?
> The present Moment's all my Lot;
> And that, as fast as it is got,
>   *Phillis*, is only thine.   10
>
> Then talk not of Inconstancy,
>   False Hearts, and broken Vows;
> If I, by Miracle, can be
> This live-long Minute true to thee,
>   'Tis all that Heav'n allows.   15

Holinshed's Leir and Shakespeare's Lear

from Chronicles of England, Scotland and Ireland (1577)

Raphael Holinshed (?–1580?)

When this Leir therefore was come to great years, and began to wax unwieldy through age, he thought to understand the affections of his daughters toward him, and prefer her whom he best loved to the succession over the kingdom. Whereupon he first asked Gonorilla, the eldest, how well she loved him: who calling her gods to record, protested that she loved him more than her own life, which by right and reason should be most dear unto her. With which answer the father being well pleased, turned to the second, and demanded of her how well she loved him: who answered (confirming her sayings with great oaths) that she loved him more than tongue could express, and far above all other creatures of the world.

Then called he his youngest daughter Cordellia before him, and asked of her what account she made of him, unto whom she made this answer as followeth: "Knowing the great love and fatherly zeal that you have always born toward me (for the which I may not answer you otherwise than I think, and as my conscience leadeth me) I protest unto you that I have loved you ever, and will continually (while I live) love you as my natural father. And if you would more understand of the love that I bear you, ascertain yourself that so much as you have, so much you are worth, and so much I love you, and no more."

from King Lear (Act I, sc. i)

William Shakespeare (1564–1616)

LEAR
　Tell me, my daughters
　Since now we will divest us both of rule,
　Interest of territory, cares of state,　　　　　　　　　　50
　Which of you shall we say doth love us most
　That we our largest bounty may extend
　Where nature doth with merit challenge. Goneril,
　Our eldest-born, speak first.

GONERIL
    Sir, I love you more than word can wield the matter,   55
    Dearer than eyesight, space, and liberty;
    Beyond what can be valued, rich or rare;
    No less than life, with grace, health, beauty, honor;
    As much as child e'er loved or father found;
    A love that makes breath poor, and speech unable;   60
    Beyond all manner of so much I love you.
CORDELIA (*Aside*)
    What shall Cordelia speak? Love, and be silent.
LEAR
    Of all these bounds, even from this line to this,
    With shadowy forests and with champains riched,
    With plenteous rivers and wide-skirted meads,   65
    We make thee lady. To thine and Albany's issues
    Be this perpetual. What says our second daughter,
    Our dearest Regan, wife to Cornwall? Speak.
REGAN
    I am made of that self metal as my sister,
    And prize me at her worth. In my true heart   70
    I find she names my very deed of love;
    Only she comes too short, that I profess
    Myself an enemy to all other joys
    Which the most precious square of sense professes,
    And find I am alone felicitate   75
    In your dear highness' love.
CORDELIA (*Aside*)   Then poor Cordelia!
    And yet not so, since I am sure my love's
    More ponderous than my tongue.
LEAR
    To thee and thine hereditary ever
    Remain this ample third of our fair kingdom,   80
    No less in space, validity and pleasure
    Than that conferred on Goneril. Now, our joy,
    Although the last and least; to whose young love
    The vines of France and milk of Burgundy
    Strive to be interest; what can you say to draw   85
    A third more opulent than your sisters? Speak.
CORDELIA   Nothing, my lord.
LEAR   Nothing?
CORDELIA   Nothing.
LEAR
    Nothing will come of nothing. Speak again.   90

CORDELIA
   Unhappy that I am, I cannot heave
   My heart into my mouth. I love your majesty
   According to my bond, no more nor less.
LEAR
   How, how, Cordelia? Mend your speech a little,
   Lest it may mar your fortunes.
CORDELIA   Good my lord,   95
   You have begot me, bred me, loved me. I
   Return those duties back as are right fit,
   Obey you, love you, and most honor you.
   Why have my sisters husbands, if they say
   They love you all? Haply, when I shall wed,   100
   That lord whose hand must take my plight shall carry
   Half my love with him, half my care and duty.
   Sure I shall never marry like my sisters,
   To love my father all.

Plutarch's "Anthony and Cleopatra" and Shakespeare's Antony and Cleopatra

from **The Lives of Noble Grecians and Romans**

(Sir Thomas North's translation)

Plutarch (46?–120?)

So she furnished herself with a world of gifts, store of gold and silver and of riches and other sumptuous ornaments, as is credible enough she might bring from so great a house and from so wealthy and rich a realm as Egypt was. But yet she carried nothing with her wherein she trusted more than in herself, and in the charms and enchantment of her passing beauty and grace. Therefore when was sent unto by divers letters, both from Antonius himself and also from his friends, she made so light of it and mocked Antonius so much that she disdained to set forward otherwise but to take her barge in the river of Cydnus, the poop whereof was of gold, the sails of purple, and the oars of silver, which kept stroke in rowing after the sound of the music of flutes, hautboys, cithers, viols, and such other instruments as they played upon in the barge. And now for the person of herself: She was laid under a pavilion of cloth-of-gold of tissue, appareled and attired like the goddess Venus commonly drawn in picture; and hard by her, on either hand of her, pretty fair boys, appareled as painters do set forth god Cupid, with little fans in their hands with the which they fanned wind upon her. Her ladies and gentlewomen also, the fairest of them, were appareled like the nymphs Nereides (which are the mermaids of the waters) and like the Graces, some steering the helm, others tending the tackle and ropes of the barge, out of the which there came a wonderful passing sweet savor of perfumes that perfumed the wharf's side, pestered with innumerable multitudes of people. Some of them followed the barge all along the river's side, others also ran out of the city to see her coming in, so that in the end there ran such multitudes of people one after another to see her that Antonius was left post-alone in the market place in his imperial seat to give audience. And there went a rumor in the people's mouths that the goddess Venus was come to play with the god Bacchus for the general good of all Asia.

from Antony and Cleopatra (Act II, sc. ii)

William Shakespeare

The barge she sat in, like a burnished throne,
Burned on the water: the poop was beaten gold,
Purple the sails, and so perfumèd that   195
The winds were lovesick with them; the oars were silver,
Which to the tune of flutes kept stroke and made
The water which they beat to follow faster,
As amorous of their strokes. For her own person,
It beggared all description: she did lie   200
In her pavilion, cloth-of-gold of tissue,
O'erpicturing that Venus where we see
The fancy outwork nature; on each side her
Stood pretty dimpled boys, like smiling Cupids,
With divers-colored fans, whose wind did seem   205
To glow the delicate cheeks which they did cool,
And what they undid did.

An essay and a poem

from **Commodity**

Ralph Waldo Emerson (1803–1882)

The misery of man appears like childish petulance, when we explore the steady and prodigal provision that has been made for his support and delight on this green ball which floats him through the heavens. What angels invented these splendid ornaments, these rich conveniences, this ocean of air above, this ocean of water beneath, this firmament of earth between? this zodiac of lights, this tent of dropping clouds, this striped coat of climates, this fourfold year? Beasts, fire, water, stones, and corn serve him. . . .

Nature, in its ministry to man, is not only the material, but is also the process and the result. All the parts incessantly work into each other's hands for the profit of man. The wind sows the seed; the sun evaporates the sea; the wind blows the vapor to the field; the ice, on the other side of the planet, condenses rain on this; the rain feeds the plant; the plant feeds the animal; and thus the endless circulations of the divine charity nourish man.

THE RHODORA

Ralph Waldo Emerson

ON BEING ASKED, WHENCE IS THE FLOWER?

In May, when sea-winds pierced our solitudes,
I found the fresh Rhodora in the woods,
Spreading its leafless blooms in a damp nook,
To please the desert and the sluggish brook.
The purple petals, fallen in the pool, 5
Made the black water with their beauty gay;
Here might the red-bird come his plumes to cool,
And court the flower that cheapens his array.
Rhodora! if the sages ask thee why
This charm is wasted on the earth and sky, 10
Tell them, dear, that if eyes were made for seeing,
Then Beauty is its own excuse for being:
Why thou wert there, O rival of the rose!
I never thought to ask, I never knew:

> But, in my simple ignorance, suppose 15
> The self-same Power that brought me there brought you.

A view of God—Prose and Poetry

from The Christian Doctrine

John Milton (1608–1674)

When we speak of knowing God, it must be understood with reference to the imperfect comprehension of man; for to know God as he really is far transcends the powers of man's thoughts, much more of his perception.... Our safest way is to form in our minds such a conception of God, as shall correspond with his own delineation and representation of himself in the sacred writings. For granting that both in the literal and figurative descriptions of God, he is exhibited not as he really is, but in such a manner as may be within the scope of our comprehensions, yet we ought to entertain such a conception of him, as he, in condescending to accommodate himself to our capacities, has shown that he desires we should conceive.

from PARADISE LOST (Book VIII)

John Milton

> Solicit not thy thoughts with matters hid,
> Leave them to God above, him serve and fear;
> Of other Creatures, as him pleases best,
> Wherever plac't, let him dispose: joy thou
> In what he gives to thee, this Paradise 5
> And thy fair Eve: Heav'n is for thee too high
> To know what passes there; be lowly wise:
> Think only what concerns thee and thy being;
> Dream not of other Worlds, what Creatures there
> Live, in what state, condition or degree, 10
> Contented that thus far hath been reveal'd
> Not of Earth only but of highest Heav'n.

Infancy: A prose meditation and a poem

from **Centuries of Meditations**

Thomas Traherne (1636–1674)

Will you see the infancy of this sublime and celestial greatness? Those pure and virgin apprehensions I had from the womb and that divine light wherewith I was born are the best unto this day wherein I can see the universe. By the gift of God they attended me into the world, and by His special favor I remember them till now. Verily they seem the greatest gifts His wisdom could bestow, for without them all other gifts had been dead and vain. They are unattainable by book, and therefore I will teach them by experience. Pray for them earnestly; for they will make you angelical and wholly celestial. Certainly Adam in Paradise had not more sweet and curious apprehensions of the world than I when I was a child.

All appeared new and strange at first, inexpressibly rare and delightful and beautiful. I was a little stranger, which at my entrance into the world was saluted and surrounded with innumerable joys. My knowledge was divine. I knew by intuition those things which, since my apostasy, I collected again by the highest reason. My very ignorance was advantageous. I seemed as one brought into the estate of innocence. All things were spotless and pure and glorious; yea, and infinitely mine, and joyful and precious. I knew not that there were any sins, or complaints, or laws. I dreamed not of poverties, contentions, or vices. All tears and quarrels were hidden from mine eyes. Everything was at rest, free and immortal. I knew nothing of sickness or death or rents or exaction, either for tribute or bread. In the absence of these I was entertained like an angel with the works of God in their splendor and glory. I saw all in the peace of Eden; heaven and earth did sing my Creator's praises, and could not make more melody to Adam than to me. All time was eternity, and a perpetual Sabbath. Is it not strange that an infant should be heir of the whole world and see those mysteries which the books of the learned never unfold?

The corn was orient and immortal wheat, which never should be reaped nor was ever sown. I thought it had stood from everlasting to everlasting. The dust and stones of the street were as precious as gold; the gates were at first the end of the world. The green trees, when I saw them first through one of the gates, transported and ravished me: their sweetness and unusual beauty made my heart to leap and almost mad with ecstasy, they were such strange and wonderful things. . . .

WONDER

Thomas Traherne

How like an angel came I down!
How bright are all things here!
When first among His works I did appear,
O how their glory me did crown!
The world resembled His eternity,   5
    In which my soul did walk;
    And everything that I did see
        Did with me talk.

The skies in their magnificence,
    The lively, lovely air,   10
Oh how divine, how soft, how sweet, how fair!
    The stars did entertain my sense;
And all the works of God so bright and pure,
    So rich and great did seem
    As if they ever must endure   15
        In my esteem.

A native health and innocence
    Within my bones did grow;
And while my God did all His glories show,
    I felt a vigor in my sense   20
That was all spirit: I within did flow
    With seas of life like wine;
    I nothing in the world did know
        But 'twas divine.

Harsh, ragged objects were concealed: 25
    Oppressions, tears, and cries,
Sins, griefs, complaints, dissensions, weeping eyes
    Were hid, and only things revealed
Which heavenly spirits and the angels prize:
    The state of innocence   30
    And bliss, not trades and poverties,
        Did fill my sense.

>   The streets were paved with golden stones;
>   The boys and girls were mine:
>   Oh how did all their lovely faces shine!
>   The sons of men were holy ones;
>   In joy and beauty they appeared to me;
>   And everything which here I found,
>   While like an angel I did see,
>   Adorned the ground.
>
>   Rich diamond and pearl and gold
>   In every place was seen;
>   Rare splendors, yellow, blue, red, white, and green,
>   Mine eyes did everywhere behold.
>   Great wonders clothed with glory did appear;
>   Amazement was my bliss;
>   That and my wealth was everywhere;
>   No joy to this!

Verse and Poems

We detected some characteristics of poetic language by comparing poetry and prose: vividness, drama, economy, and typography. Through a comparison of poetry and verse, we will find additional aspects, such as wit, humor, paradox, irony, understatement, and hyperbole.

There are several common uses of the term "verse": in one, the word is a synonym for poetry; another signifies a single line of a poem. Generally the word means poetry that possesses rhythmic or metric regularity. But it is another use of the term in which we are chiefly interested here—that is, to denote poetry that seems to lack seriousness of feeling or idea. This use is usually signaled by phrases such as "light verse" and "mere verse." The phrase "light verse" implies that the poem is clever, witty, or humorous, but the phrase "mere verse" involves some complicated value judgments. "Mere verse" is often used to refer to poems that are purely didactic, unintentionally humorous, or metrical, but lacking not only the qualities of vivid writing, but also the merits of light verse. Let us consider some examples. One quality that may be expected in verse but is usually found unpleasant in poetry is overt didacticism. One of the most famous uses of such didacticism may be found in the *New England Primer*:

> In Adam's Fall
> We sinned all.
>
> Peter deny'd
> His Lord and cry'd.
>
> Zaccheus he
> Did climb the tree
> Our Lord to see.

This didactic impulse is everywhere in verse, whether in TV commercials or in most common formulas for relaying information:

> Snow in Chattertown
> Means skiing in Gore,
> No snow in Chattertown
> Drive 50 miles more.

Samuel Taylor Coleridge (1772–1834) conveys an amazing amount of information about metric feet in these verses:

> Trochee trips from long to short;
> From long to long in solemn sort
> Slow Spondee stalks; strong foot! yet ill able
> Ever to come up with Dactyl trisyllable;
> Iambics march from short to long;
> With a leap and a bound the swift Anapests throng;
> One syllable long, with one short at each side;
> Amphibrachys hastes with a stately stride;
> First and last being long, middle short, Amphimacer
> Strikes his thundering hoofs like a proud high-bred racer.

These lines, however, indicate most clearly how verse becomes indistinguishable from poetry—by intellectual aptness. Although clever charades, anagrams, acrostics, and logograms possess some of the verbal and intellectual excitement that we associate with poetry, these verbal games cannot make poetry by themselves. Here is a very ingenious and once-popular logogram by Lord Macaulay:

> Cut off my head, how singular I act:
> Cut off my tail, and plural I appear;
> Cut off my head and tail—most curious fact!
> Although my middle's left, there's nothing there!
> What is my head, cut off: A sounding sea!
> What is my tail, cut off? A howling river!
> Amid the mingling depths I fearless play,
> Parent of softest sounds, though mute forever.

The answer to this puzzle (as provided by J. H. Vincent, editor of *The Home Book*) is:

> Cod; and every line reveals a fresh play upon the word. Cut off its head, and it is od, (odd), singular; its tail, and it is plural, Co., (the abbreviation for company;) cut off its head and tail and it is 0 (nothing;) the head cut off, is a sounding sea, (C); its tail, a flowing river—D (Dee). [Dee: The name of a river in England.] Amid their depths (the sea and the Dee) the Cod may play, parent of softest sounds (the air bladder of the cod, a favorite delicacy to many), yet mute forever.

Thus, while sheer intellectual gamesmanship may not produce poetry, it can produce extremely entertaining verse—a difficult feat to perform.

However, among those kinds of cleverness that do result in poetry, the most common are vaguely categorized as wit, paradox, and irony. John Dryden defined wit as "a Propriety of Thoughts and Words; or in other Terms, Thoughts and Words elegantly adapted to the Subject." Wit conveys a verbal excitement and precision that makes us immediately feel "this could not possibly have been more cleverly expressed." It provides the perfect balance of explicitness and implicitness and of thought and humor. The statement of the poem and the sound of the words have a certainty, like a key turning in a lock, to paraphrase Yeats. The opening of Dryden's own "Mac Flecknoe" is a classical illustration of the most engaging kind of wit (we will see more of this when we discuss the metaphysical poems—page 276).

MAC FLECKNOE

John Dryden (1631–1700)

All human things are subject to decay,
And, when fate summons, monarchs must obey.
This Flecknoe found, who, like Augustus, young
Was called to empire, and had governed long:
In prose and verse was owned, without dispute,   5
Through all the realms of nonsense, absolute.
The aged Prince, now flourishing in peace,
And blessed with issue of a large increase,
Worn out with business, did at length debate
To settle the succession of the state;   10
And, pond'ring which of all his sons was fit
To reign, and wage immortal war with wit,
Cried, "Tis resolved! For nature pleads that he
Should only rule who most resembles me.
Sh—— alone my perfect image bears,   15
Mature in dullness from his tender years.
Sh—— alone, of all my sons, is he
Who stands confirmed in full stupidity.
The rest to some faint meaning make pretense,
But Sh—— never deviates into sense.   20

Paradox and irony are closely related to one another and to a third, more common, use of language: sarcasm. Sarcasm is plain insult, such as saying of a football player who has just bungled a play: "He tripped over his own feet." An ironic statement says one thing and means the opposite: "That was one of the great plays of all time." A paradoxical statement might be appropriate if, for example, the player had missed a pass and by oddest chance scored a touchdown: "He let the defender catch the ball so he could steal it and score." Or, in such a case, the statement might take the form of hyperbole: "Even a man with four left feet and a handful of thumbs can look good against this team." Another possibility in this situation would be understatement: "That's all right for the first quarter; we're saving the really unusual plays for the second half."

Mac Flecknoe. This is used as a representative of the poor poet. **3–4. This ... long:** Augustus became emperor of the Roman Empire at thirty-two. **15. Sh——:** Thomas Shadwell, a contemporary with whom Dryden was often in strong disagreement.

Below are poems whose appreciation depends on our perception of their irony and verbal cleverness:

THE LATEST DECALOGUE

Arthur Hugh Clough (1819–1861)

Thou shalt have one God only; who
Would be at the expense of two?
No graven images may be
Worshipped, except the currency.
Swear not at all; for, for thy curse   5
Thine enemy is none the worse.
At church on Sunday to attend
Will serve to keep the world thy friend.
Honor thy parents; that is, all
From whom advancement may befall.   10
Thou shalt not kill; but need'st not strive
Officiously to keep alive.
Do not adultery commit;
Advantage rarely comes of it.
Thou shalt not steal; an empty feat,   15
When it's so lucrative to cheat.
Bear not false witness; let the lie
Have time on its own wings to fly.
Thou shalt not covet, but tradition
Approves all forms of competition.   20

QUESTIONS

1. A quick glance at the Ten Commandments will increase understanding of this poem. The essential form is the restatement of a traditional commandment in approximately one line, then the modern reason for obeying. Which juxtaposition do you find most clever; which seems close to doggerel?
2. Clough obviously does not mean what he actually says, but it may be difficult to know what he does feel about the Ten Commandments. What do you think can be safely inferred about his attitude toward the Commandments?

THE PERSIAN VERSION

Robert Graves (b. 1895)

Truth-loving Persians do not dwell upon
The trivial skirmish fought near Marathon.
As for the Greek theatrical tradition
Which represents that summer's expedition
Not as a mere reconnaissance in force   5
By three brigades of foot and one of horse
(Their left flank covered by some obsolete
Light craft detached from the main Persian fleet)
But as a grandiose, ill-starred attempt
To conquer Greece—they treat it with contempt;   10
And only incidentally refute
Major Greek claims, by stressing what repute
The Persian Monarch and the Persian nation
Won by this salutary demonstration:
Despite a strong Defence and adverse weather   15
All arms combined magnificently together.

QUESTIONS

1. Who is the speaker of the poem? (The author is an Englishman, but no biographical information would be relevant to understanding this poem.)
2. Examine the language of the poem. What phrases are similar to those used in official government announcements dealing with military activities?
3. Compare the Clough and Graves poems in terms of understatement and exaggeration.

Poetry is distinguished from verse not only by the kinds of verbal cleverness we have been discussing, but also by an emotional quality imparted by the poet, but not the versifier. Consider this famous piece of verse:

>Thirty days hath September,
>April, June and November;
>All the rest have thirty-one,
>Save February and it alone
>Has twenty-eight
>Till Leap Year gives it twenty-nine.

Recasting this as an unsuccessful poem, we are able to see another important distinction between poetry and verse—an emotional impulse that would be dangerously distracting on such a practical occasion:

> Alas then! Only thirty days in all pied April?
> Surely too few for her to vaunt her uncertain glories?
> Rather a short September benefiting schoolboys,
> And thereupon to lengthen June (queen of the year)
> For longer dreaming on ere winter come.

Although this is not poetry (it reads instead like a poor parody of Shakespeare), the poetic impulse is nonetheless operating, whereas it is not in "Thirty days hath September." The poetic impulse is seen in the cry from the heart "Alas then," in the unusual adjective "pied" (stolen from Shakespeare), in the spirited verb "vaunt," in the accurate observation (also stolen) represented by "uncertain glories" as applied to the weather of April, in the rather lighthearted wit of the third line, and so forth. These are all examples of poetic word choice, or diction (pages 213–36). However, for our purposes it is important to note that "Thirty days hath September" is acually a more efficient device to help us remember than "Alas then! Only thirty," whose energetic diction tends to distract one from the practical business at hand—whether to write May 1 or April 31. We may thus conclude that poetry is a Fine Art, verse a Practical Art.

POEMS FOR FURTHER STUDY

In some of the poems that follow the poetic impulse is clearly evident; in others it seems absent. An appropriate general question for all of these poems is whether each should be called poetry or verse. It is appropriate to ask such a question *not* because there is a clear-cut answer but simply because such a question forces us to think seriously about the nature of poetry.

EPITAPH ON THE POLITICIAN

Hilaire Belloc (1870–1953)

Here richly, with ridiculous display
The politician's corpse was laid away.

While all of his acquaintance sneered and slanged
I wept: for I had longed to see him hanged.

IT ISN'T THE COUGH

Anonymous

It isn't the cough
That carries you off;
It's the coffin
They carry you off in.

IF YOU TRAP THE MOMENT

William Blake (1757–1827)

If you trap the moment before it's ripe,
The tears of repentance you'll certainly wipe;
But if once you let the ripe moment go,
You can never wipe off the tear of woe.

TO HIS COY MISTRESS

Andrew Marvell (1621–1678)

Had we but world enough, and time,
This coyness, lady, were no crime.
We would sit down and think which way
To walk, and pass our long love's day;
Thou by the Indian Ganges' side   5
Shouldst rubies find; I by the tide
Of Humber would complain. I would
Love you ten years before the Flood;
And you should, if you please, refuse
Till the conversion of the Jews.   10
My vegetable love should grow
Vaster than empires, and more slow.

An hundred years should go to praise
Thine eyes, and on thy forehead gaze;
Two hundred to adore each breast,   15
But thirty thousand to the rest;
An age at least to every part,
And the last age should show your heart.
For, lady, you deserve this state,
Nor would I love at lower rate.   20
    But at my back I always hear
Time's winged chariot hurrying near;
And yonder all before us lie
Deserts of vast eternity.
Thy beauty shall no more be found,   25
Nor in thy marble vault shall sound
My echoing song; then worms shall try
That long preserved virginity,
And your quaint honor turn to dust,
And into ashes all my lust.   30
The grave's a fine and private place,
But none, I think, do there embrace.
    Now therefore, while the youthful hue
Sits on thy skin like morning dew,
And while thy willing soul transpires   35
At every pore with instant fires,
Now let us sport us while we may;
And now, like amorous birds of prey,
Rather at once our time devour,
Than languish in his slow-chapped power.   40
Let us roll all our strength, and all
Our sweetness, up into one ball;
And tear our pleasures with rough strife
Through the iron gates of life.
Thus, though we cannot make our sun   45
Stand still, yet we will make him run.

QUESTIONS

1. This poem has three parts. Compare the tone of the first and third parts with the second. Why is the understatement in lines 31–32 particularly effective?

2. List the hyperboles and the rhyme words and comment on their effectiveness.
3. This poem has a commonplace subject—the proposal of a man that a woman go to bed with him. Yet it is one of the best known poems in English poetry. Why?
4. Compare the sun imagery of lines 21–22 with that of lines 45–46.

TO THE HONORABLE CHARLES MONTAGUE, ESQ.

Matthew Prior (1664–1721)

Howe'er, 'tis well, that while mankind
   Through Fate's perverse meander errs,
He can imagined pleasure find,
   To combat against real cares.

Fancies and notions he pursues,   5
   Which ne'er had being but in thought:
Each, like the Grecian artist, woos
   The image he himself has wrought.

Against experience he believes;
   He argues against demonstration;   10
Pleased, when his reason he deceives;
   And sets his judgment by his passion.

The hoary fool, who many days
   Has struggled with continued sorrow,
Renews his hope, and blindly lays   15
   The desperate bet upon tomorrow.

Tomorrow comes; 'tis noon, 'tis night;
   This day like all the former flies:
Yet on he runs, to seek delight
   Tomorrow, till tonight he dies.   20

Our hopes, like towering falcons, aim
   At objects in an airy height:
The little pleasure of the game
   Is from afar to view the flight.

    Our anxious pains we, all the day,   25
        In search of what we like, employ:
    Scorning at night the worthless prey,
        We find the labor gave the joy.

    At distance through an artful glass
        To the mind's eye things well appear: 30
    They lose their forms, and make a mass
        Confused and black, if brought too near.

    If we see right, we see our woes:
        Then what avails it to have eyes?
    From ignorance our comfort flows.   35
        The only wretched are the wise.

    We wearied should lie down in death:
        This cheat of life would take no more;
    If you thought fame but empty breath;
        I, Phillis but a perjured whore.   40

THE CROCODILE

Lewis Carroll (1832–1898)

    How doth the little crocodile
        Improve his shining tail,
    And pour the waters of the Nile
        On every shining scale!

    How cheerfully he seems to grin,   5
        How neatly spreads his claws,
    And welcomes little fishes in
        With gently smiling jaws!

A GLASS OF BEER

James Stephens (1882–1950)

The lanky hank of a she in the inn over there
Nearly killed me for asking the loan of a glass of beer:
May the devil grip the whey-faced slut by the hair,
And beat bad manners out of her skin for a year.

That parboiled imp, with the hardest jaw you will see 5
On virtue's path, and a voice that would rasp the dead,
Came roaring and raging the minute she looked at me,
And threw me out of the house on the back of my head!

If I asked her master he'd give me a cask a day;
But she with the beer at hand, not a gill would arrange! 10
May she marry a ghost and bear him a kitten and may
The High King of Glory permit her to get the mange.

FOXTROT FROM A PLAY

W. H. Auden (1907–1973)

Man
 The soldier loves his rifle
  The scholar loves his books
 The farmer loves his horses
  The film star loves her looks
 There's love the whole world over 5
  Wherever you may be
 Some lose their rest for gay Mae West
  But you're my cup of tea

Woman
 Some talk of Alexander
  And some of Fred Astaire 10
 Some like their heroes hairy
  Some like them debonair
 Some prefer a curate
  And some an A.D.C.
 Some like a tough to treat 'em rough 15
  But you're my cup of tea

Man
 Some are mad on Airedales
  And some on Pekinese
 On tabby cats or parrots
  Or guinea-pigs or geese 20
 There are patients in asylums
  Who think that they're a tree
 I had an aunt who loved a plant
  But you're my cup of tea

Woman
 Some have sagging waistlines 25
  And some a bulbous nose

                And some a floating kidney
                    And some have hammer toes
                Some have tennis elbow
                    And some have housemaid's knee   30
                And some I know have got B.O.
                    But you're my cup of tea

Together   The blackbird loves the earthworm
                    The adder loves the sun
                The polar bear an iceberg   35
                    The elephant a bun
                The trout enjoys the river
                    The whale enjoys the sea
                And dogs love most an old lamp-post
                    But you're my cup of tea   40

THE DYING AIRMAN

Anonymous

A handsome young airman lay dying,
And as on the aerodrome he lay,
To the mechanics who round him came sighing,
These last dying words he did say:

"Take the cylinders out of my kidneys,   5
The connecting-rod out of my brain,
Take the cam-shaft from out of my backbone,
And assemble the engine again."

RELATIVITY

Anonymous

    There was a young lady named Bright,
    Who travelled much faster than light,
        She started one day
        In the relative way
    And returned on the previous night.

A HAPPY TIME

Anonymous

There was a young fellow named Hall,
Who fell in the spring in the fall;
   'Twould have been a sad thing
   If he'd died in the spring,
But he didn't—he died in the fall.

MIND AND MATTER

Anonymous

There was a faith-healer of Deal,
Who said, "Although pain isn't real,
   If I sit on a pin
   And it punctures my skin,
I dislike what I fancy I feel."

OF LOVING A DOG

John Heywood (1497–1580)

Love me, love my dog: by love to agree
I love thy dog as well as I love thee.

OF LATE AND NEVER

John Heywood

Better late than never: yea, mate,
But as good never as too late.

GRACE BEFORE BEER

F. R. Higgins (1896–1941)

For what this house affords us,
Come, praise the brewer most—
Who caught into a bottle
The barley's gentle ghost—
Until our parching throttles   5
In silence we employ—
Like geese that drink a mouthful,
Then stretch their necks with joy!

THE TURTLE

Ogden Nash (1902–1971)

The turtle lives 'twixt plated decks
Which practically conceal its sex.
It think it clever of the turtle
In such a fix to be so fertile.

GONE BOY

Langston Hughes (1902–1967)

Playboy of the dawn,
Solid gone!
Out all night
Until 12–1–2 a.m.

Next day   5
When he should be gone
To work—
Dog-gone!
He ain't gone.

BUFFALO BILL'S

e. e. cummings (1894–1963)

<pre>
Buffalo Bill's
defunct
        who used to
        ride a watersmooth-silver
                                    stallion   5
and break onetwothreefourfive pigeonsjustlikethat
                                                 Jesus
he was a handsome man
                      and what i want to know is
how do you like your blueeyed boy   10
Mister Death
</pre>

Dramatic Speech and Poems

Poetry, broadly defined, is a type of communication, one of the many ways man tries to speak with other men. It is distinguished from other kinds of communication in the way the poet, whether speaking or writing, composes his address. At times the poet uses language comparable to vivid prose, other times the language is comparable to verse—clever and witty, with metrical qualities such as rhyme and meter. In general, however, the poet strives to make his language memorable or dramatic. We described one aspect of this effort as the "poetic impulse." We might call another specific and significant manifestation of this effort the "dramatic impulse."

The use of the word "dramatic" to refer to certain effects of poetry may be confusing. Ordinarily we associate drama with plays, the stage, and acting. Some poems are, of course, dramatic in much the same sense—they are brief plays, two or more people speak, and, given actors to take the parts, they could be performed. Yet when we speak of a poem possessing dramatic qualities, we can mean many things not readily associated with stage dramas. Essentially we mean that the poet *shows* us something rather than *tells* us something. His words build up a scene, or constitute a monologue or soliloquy. Further, we mean that the words of a poem are interesting, they seem important, or they make demands on our curiosity about the human dimensions of their subject. Above all, "dramatic" in its most basic sense means that the poet is conveying a sense of life.

This sense of life is derived from direct experience, but the experience may be either imaginary or actual. The words on the page may be those of the poet himself speaking, or they may be those of a person created by the poet to speak them. We generally assume that the poet is not speaking autobiographically unless we have biographical information linking the poem to the poet's life.

The poet must achieve his dramatic effects with words only, as in the following poem:

I STROVE WITH NONE

Walter Savage Landor (1775–1864)

I strove with none, for none was worth my strife,
Nature I loved, and next to Nature, Art;
I warmed both hands before the fire of life;
It sinks, and I am ready to depart.

Landor uses nothing but words—but notice how he organizes them and how easily he creates a tone and a sense of personality so succinctly. In the first line, without sounding like a man with a superiority complex, he conveys a sense of proud, haughty, aristocratic disdain for the common desire to get ahead. Although such men may be contentious and stormy, he is aloof and calm, and his words—simple, direct, balanced—connote this. The second line, like the first, is balanced, pivoting, so to speak, on the commas following the fourth syllable. If the man of the first line seems a little too cool, detached, and Olympian to be human, that impression begins to be modified in the second line and is completely erased in the third and fourth lines. The second line suggests something like: "Yes, dear reader, I liked May and October and landscapes even as you do, and gave no exaggerated importance to the representations of those things, but still had to admit that in a world of Business, Commerce, Industry, and the like, Art is second only to Nature." The last two lines imply pleasure in life and at the same time a stoic willingness to leave it. This willingness is suggested further by the punctuation of the fourth line. The tempo of the line slows with the comma following the phrase, "It sinks," but then resumes its normal pace with the longer concluding phrase, "and I am ready to depart." The tenses also add to the willingness to accept the inevitable expressed in the concluding phrase. The past tenses of the first three lines give way to the present tenses of the last line.

We might, then, say that the qualities most frequently found in the language of dramatic expression are economy, implicitness, and some complexity of emotion—in sum, a balance or accord between the words and the sense of life which they convey. But we cannot really talk about these qualities abstractly; they are not absolutes that immediately signify dramatic achievements in poetry. All can be lacking and yet a poem may still have some indefinable tone that makes it dramatic. In romantic poetry, for example, even when dramatic, instead of economy we may find the repetitiousness and lengthy descriptions necessary to sustain the emotional mood of the poem. Although economy, implicitness, and the like are usually found in successful poems, the point is not whether such qualities are present but whether the qualities present actually work together to produce poetry.

We can, for example, compose four lines of rhymed iambic pentameter, faintly resembling Landor's "I Strove with None," which possess some of the qualities we have called dramatic. But we will not have composed a successful poem:

I WOKE AT NINE

> I woke at nine, for nine caused me no strife,
> I love my Ford, though not as much as of old;
> I warmed my hands before the stove of life,
> The stove is out, and I am getting cold.

The conception of the poem, or the experience from which it springs, is that of a man who rises late, is losing his interest in his car, has to sit by his stove, and gets cold when the stove goes out. The language is flat, the regularity of its meter is commonplace, and the lack of metrical variation is depressing. Further, the personality it conveys is stereotyped, and the poem is economical, only because it says nothing. And, while it uses vivid language (its "stove of life" is actually more concrete than Landor's "fire of life"), it achieves only an unintentional comic effect.

Perhaps the best way to demonstrate what is lacking in "I Woke at Nine" is to compare it with "I Strove with None." Here are some questions that might serve to guide such a comparison:
(1) Do you think that a direct experience motivated each poem? If so, describe as clearly as possible the experience pertinent to each. Compare these experiences.
(2) One of Landor's editors entitled his poem "On His Seventy-Fifth Birthday." What quality would such a title add to the poem? What title could you supply to the second poem? If the first poem suggests the words of a seventy-five-year-old man, characterize the person suggested by the words of the second.
(3) Do the words of "I Woke at Nine" convey the same sense of "memorable speech" as those of "I Strove with None"? Can you indicate specific places in either poem where a dramatic quality is lacking?

Robert Frost summarized the view that every line of poetry is like a line in a drama when he wrote:

> Everything written is as good as it is dramatic.... A dramatic necessity goes deep into the nature of the sentence. Sentences are not different enough to hold the attention unless they are dramatic. ... All that can save them is the speaking tone of the voice somehow entangled in the words and fastened to the page for the ear of the imagination. That is all that can save poetry from sing-song. ... [A poem is] heard or sung by a person in a scene—in character, in a setting, where and when is the question. (Lawrance Thompson, *Robert Frost: The Early Years* [New York, 1966], pp. 418–434).

These, then, are some of the elements of poetic utterance: memorable language (memorable because it is intellectually or emotionally exciting), special attention to figurative and rhythmical language, and a dramatic quality that may be said to spring from experience, revealing a quality of mind or a personality. In subsequent chapters we will deal extensively with memorable language when we discuss meter, rhythm and diction in more detail. Now, however, let us turn to some basic questions touching on the intellectual and emotional drama inherent in short lyrical poems.

We will ask four kinds of questions: questions dealing with the poem's *speaker, tone, action* (expressed through drama or ideas), and *emphasis*. Examples of questions touching on the speaker are the most obvious: Who is speaking? What are the circumstances of his address or reflection? What attitude does he reveal toward the reader and toward his subject? Is any relationship implied between the speaker and another person in the poem? Questions dealing with tone are essentially concerned with the manner of the utterance. Initially these questions touch on the emotional context of the poem: Is the poem whispered or shouted, expressed cynically or passionately? Questions dealing with tone also would include those about the poem's diction, imagery, form, meter, and rhythm. Questions aimed at a poem's action seek to determine what goes on in the poem. Such questions include those dealing with the poem's grammar and eventually probe into any event or idea in the poem. After determining *what* occurs in a poem, we must ask *why* the events or ideas occur in the order that they do. This leads us to emphasis. Here, we are concerned with matters of order, intensity, and proportion. We want to know why things are treated in a particular order or why their repetition, length, or prominence determine their stress—in brief, why does one scene or idea receive five lines and another only one line?

We may ask many other questions about poems, but these are the essential kinds we ask about the context of a poem's language. And although we have listed these questions in sequence, we do so only for convenience. These questions may be asked in any order—as a particular poem demands. To be aware of such questions and to employ them in reading poems should enable us to perceive a poem's intellectual and emotional qualities. Let us see if this is true of the following brief poems:

WESTERN WIND

Anonymous (15th century)

Western wind, when wilt thou blow
The small rain down can rain?
Christ, if my love were in my arms
And I in my bed again!

QUESTIONS

speaker Who is the speaker? Is he addressing anyone? What are the circumstances of his address?

tone (manner) What is the effect of the word "Christ" occurring where it does? What is achieved by a question followed by an exclamation? Is there any significance between the desire for rain and the speaker's desire for his beloved?

action Literally, what is the speaker asking for? What is the "Western Wind"? The "small rain"? There was a love song popular among Vietnamese troops in 1972 that contained the line, "maybe when it rains we can get together again." Does this cast any light on "Western Wind"?

emphasis State as specifically as possible the emotion expressed by the speaker. How does the poem make clear that this emotion is being expressed rather than another, similar emotion?

TO THE STATES

Walt Whitman (1819–1892)

To the States or any one of them, or any city of the States,
    Resist much, obey little,
Once unquestioning obedience, once fully enslaved,
Once fully enslaved, no nation, state, city of this earth,
    Ever afterwards resumes its liberty.

QUESTIONS

speaker Describe the speaker (preferably without reference to Whitman's life), the conceivable circumstances of his address, and his possible audience. What kind of speaker would "address" the states? Compare the speaker's attitude toward his audience in "Western Wind" with that in Whitman's poem.

action Paraphrase the poet's exhortation. What does he mean by "resist"? by "obey"?

tone (manner) These lines are sweeping, grandiose, and assertive. How does the poet manage to impart these qualities? One of the chief technical features of this poem is its use of parallelisms. Cite instances of this device.
emphasis This poem may be divided into three parts: the salutation, the message, and the reasons for the message. Indicate these parts. What is the effect of the italics? Do you find the poem moving, persuasive, timely? Explain. Do you think that the poet wants to convince you of the truth of his argument, or does he want to portray a man making a political assertion?

THE WALK

Thomas Hardy (1840–1928)

You did not walk with me
Of late to the hill-top tree
  By the gated ways,
  As in earlier days;
  You were weak and lame,   5
  So you never came,
And I went alone, and I did not mind,
Not thinking of you as left behind.

I walked up there to-day
Just in the former way;   10
  Surveyed around
  The familiar ground
  By myself again:
  What difference, then?
Only that underlying sense   15
Of the look of a room on returning thence.

QUESTIONS

1. When Hardy said that he "could get the whole of a novel into three pages of verse," he meant that the most intense

emotional moments of an entire novel might be conveyed in a few lines of poetry. This is a poem about an intense emotional experience. Before trying to describe that experience, supply some of the background that the poem only hints: Who is the speaker? Who is "you"? What is their relationship?
2. Carefully clarify the time references: line 2, "Of late"; line 4, "earlier days"; and line 9, "to-day."
3. Line 14 reflects the sense of something different that is the principal emphasis of the poem. The last two lines are somewhat obscure, but they clearly imply that something has drastically changed since the couple used to climb the hill together, and the speaker has been climbing the hill alone ever since. His walk is now dominated by the sense of change. What change has occurred? (Lines 5 and 6 give some indication of what may have changed.)
4. What elements of balance between thought and feeling does the poem reveal? What elements of economy, implicitness, and complexity?

A YOUTH MOWING

D. H. Lawrence (1885–1930)

There are four men mowing down by the Isar;
I can hear the swish of the scyth-strokes, four
Sharp breaths taken; yea, and I
Am sorry for what's in store.

The first man out of the four that's mowing   5
Is mine, I claim him once and for all;
Though it's sorry I am, on his young feet, knowing
None of the trouble he's led to stall.

And he sees me bringing the dinner, he lifts
His head as proud as a deer that looks   10
Shoulder-deep out of the corn; and wipes
His scythe-blade bright, unhooks

The scythe-stone and over the stubble to me.
Lad, thou has gotten a child in me,
Laddie, a man thou'lt ha'e to be,   15
Yea, though I'm sorry for thee.

QUESTIONS

1. Robert Frost said of a poem, "All that can save the sentences is the speaking tone of the voice." Describe the speaking tone of the voice in Lawrence's poem. Who is speaking? What are the circumstances? How many times does the speaker use the word "sorry"? Are the repetitions artfully varied? Explain. (Note: This poem is a good instance of why we should not say the author of a poem is speaking in every poem. Clearly D. H. Lawrence is not speaking in this poem. He has adopted a *persona*, that of a young woman, and the entire poem is spoken from her point of view.)
2. What is the effect of the sensuous details of the poem—especially the sounds of the scythe-strokes and the breathing of the men? Find others. Also, what is the effect of the strange diction—words like "yea," and "ha'e"?
3. Observe the sentence structure. The first and second stanzas are each one sentence. The third stanza and the first line of the fourth stanza, however, are one long sentence, and the sentence is quite complex, almost disjointed. Why do you think this was done?
4. Can you explain the ordering of the events? Examine each new bit of information as it is provided. Why is the information provided when it is?

Although we have discussed the dramatic context of poems by referring almost exclusively to short lyric poems, these are not the only kinds of poems that exist in a dramatic setting. These poems are relatively brief, there is only one speaker, and the dramatic qualities of scene and circumstances are often more implied than expressed. But if we were to take a dramatic lyric like Lawrence's "A Youth Mowing" and extend it by revealing more of the girl's personality, we would have what is called a dramatic monologue. Or, if as soon as the last line was spoken—"Yea, though I'm sorry for thee."—the poem went on with the boy responding, we would have the beginning of a genuinely dramatic poem. And if Lawrence's poem were developed by adding elements of description and details to the story, we would call it a narrative, or—depending on its dramatic qualities—a dramatic narrative. In each of these instances, however, we should keep in mind the distinction between the intellectual and emotional emphases in the poem. For if a monologue is principally concerned with ideas, we should perhaps call it a meditative or a philosophical poem. And if a dramatic poem with speakers is principally concerned with ideas, we may have something resembling a debate or a symposium more than a drama. Below are poems that illustrate some of this dramatic range.

These poems are all more or less concerned with women singing. The women in three of the poems have been identified. According to Milton's chief biographer, W. R. Parker, Milton heard Leonora Baroni sing in the autumn of 1638. Shelley's singer is usually identified as Claire Clairmont, later Byron's mistress, and the second wife of the philosopher William Godwin. Hardy's singer is generally thought to be his wife, who died sixteen years before he did. The singers in the Pound and Stevens poems represent the muse, creativity, or the imagination. Because they all share a general subject, these poems can be compared with one another. Perhaps the easiest way to make this comparison is to consider each poem individually in terms of speaker, tone, action, and emphasis, and then compare one poem with another.

TO A LADY WHO DID SING EXCELLENTLY

Lord Herbert of Cherbury (1583–1648)

When our rude and unfashion'd words, that long
   A being in their elements enjoy'd,
     Senseless and void,
Come at last to be formed by thy tongue,
   And from thy breath receive that life and place,   5
     And perfect grace,
That now thy power diffus'd through all their parts
   Are able to remove
All the obstructions of the hardest hearts,
   And teach the most unwilling how to love;   10

When they again, exalted by thy voice,
   Tun'd by thy soul, dismiss'd into the air,
     To us repair,
A living, moving, and harmonious noise,
   Able to give the love they do create   15
     A second state,

And charm not only all his griefs away,
   And his defects restore,
But make him perfect, who, the Poets say,
   Made all was ever yet made heretofore;   20

When again all these rare perfections meet,
   Composed in the circle of thy face,
      As in their place,
So to make up of all one perfect sweet,
   Who is not then so ravish'd with delight   25
      Ev'n of thy sight,
That he can be assur'd his sense is true,
   Or that he die, or live,
Or that he do enjoy himself, or you,
   Or only the delights, which you did give?   30

TO LEONORA BARONI, SINGING AT ROME

John Milton (1608–1674)

Another Italian beauty of your name,
Leonora d'Este, so inflamed the poet
Torquato Tasso that her brother Alphonso
Had to put him away for seven years.
Poor Tasso! Better had he been mad for thee,   5
For thee this moment, lovelier Leonora.
Thy singing as thou pluckst the golden wires
Of the harp thy mother trusted to thy keeping
Traces the Muses' torrents to their font.
And though old Tasso's eyes had rolled more wildly   10
Than the eyes of Pentheus drunk against his will
Thy voice could also bring him back to his senses,
Breathe peace and balm over his morbid madness,
Restore the poet who sang Zion restored.

THE SOLITARY REAPER

William Wordsworth (1770–1850)

Behold her, single in the field,
Yon solitary Highland Lass!
Reaping and singing by herself;
Stop here, or gently pass!

Alone she cuts and binds the grain, 5
And sings a melancholy strain;
O listen! for the Vale profound
Is overflowing with the sound.

No Nightingale did ever chant
More welcome notes to weary bands 10
Of travelers in some shady haunt,
Among Arabian sands;
A voice so thrilling ne'er was heard
In springtime from the Cuckoo bird,
Breaking the silence of the seas 15
Among the farthest Hebrides.

Will no one tell me what she sings?—
Perhaps the plaintive numbers flow
For old, unhappy, far-off things,
And battles long ago; 20
Or is it some more humble lay,
Familiar matter of today?
Some natural sorrow, loss or pain,
That has been, and may be again?

Whate'er the theme, the Maiden sang 25
As if her song could have no ending;
I saw her singing at her work,
And o'er the sickle bending—
I listened, motionless and still;
And, as I mounted up the hill, 30
The music in my heart I bore,
Long after it was heard no more.

TO CONSTANTIA, SINGING

Percy Bysshe Shelley (1792–1822)

I

Thus to be lost and thus to sink and die,
  Perchance were death indeed!—Constantia; turn,
In thy dark eyes a power like light doth lie,
  Even though the sounds which were thy voice, which burn
Between thy lips, are laid to sleep; 5
    Within thy breath, and on thy hair, like odor, it is yet,

And from thy touch like fire doth leap.
Even while I write, my burning cheeks are wet,
Alas, that the torn heart can bleed, but not forget!

II

A breathless awe, like the swift change 10
   Unseen, but felt in youthful slumbers,
Wild, sweet, but uncommunicably strange,
   Thou breathest now in fast ascending numbers.
The cope of heaven seems rent and cloven
   By the enchantment of thy strain, 15
And on my shoulders wings are woven,
   To follow its sublime career
Beyond the mighty moons that wane
   Upon the verge of Nature's utmost sphere,
Till the world's shadowy walls are past and disappear. 20

III

Her voice is hovering o'er my soul—it lingers
   O'ershadowing it with soft and lulling wings,
The blood and life within those snowy fingers
   Teach witchcraft to the instrumental strings.
My brain is wild, my breath comes quick— 25
   The blood is listening in my frame,
And thronging shadows, fast and thick,
   Fall on my overflowing eyes;
My heart is quivering like a flame;
   As morning dew, that in the sunbeam dies, 30
I am dissolved in these consuming ecstasies.

IV

I have no life, Constantia, now, but thee,
   Whilst, like the world-surrounding air, thy song
Flows on, and fills all things with melody.—
   Now is thy voice a tempest swift and strong, 35
On which, like one in trance upborne,
   Secure o'er rocks and waves I sweep,
Rejoicing like a cloud of morn.
   Now 'tis the breath of summer night,
Which when the starry waters sleep, 40
   Round western isles, with incense-blossoms bright,
Lingering, suspends my soul in its voluptuous flight.

THE CURTAINS NOW ARE DRAWN
SONG

Thomas Hardy (1840–1928)

I

The curtains now are drawn,
And the spindrift strikes the glass,
Blown up the jaggèd pass
By the surly salt sou'-west,
And the sneering glare is gone 5
Beyond the yonder crest,
    While she sings to me:
"O the dream that thou art my Love, be it thine,
And the dream that I am thy Love, be it mine,
And death may come, but loving is divine." 10

II

I stand here in the rain,
With its smite upon her stone,
And the grasses that have grown
Over women, children, men,
And their texts that "Life is vain"; 15
But I hear the notes as when
    Once she sang to me:
"O the dream that thou art my love, be it thine,
And the dream that I am thy Love, be it mine,
And death may come, but loving is divine." 20

POEMS FOR FURTHER STUDY

THE IDEA OF ORDER AT KEY WEST

Wallace Stevens (1879–1955)

She sang beyond the genius of the sea.
The water never formed to mind or voice,
Like a body wholly body, fluttering

Its empty sleeves; and yet its mimic motion
Made constant cry, caused constantly a cry, 5
That was not ours although we understood,
Inhuman, of the veritable ocean.

The sea was not a mask. No more was she.
The song and water were not medleyed sound
Even if what she sang was what she heard, 10
Since what she sang was uttered word by word.
It may be that in all her phrases stirred
The grinding water and the gasping wind;
But it was she and not the sea we heard.

For she was the maker of the song she sang. 15
The ever-hooded, tragic-gestured sea
Was merely a place by which she walked to sing.
Whose spirit is this? we said, because we knew
It was the spirit that we sought and knew
That we should ask this often as she sang. 20

If it was only the dark voice of the sea
That rose, or even colored by many waves;
If it was only the outer voice of sky
And cloud, of the sunken coral water-walled,
However clear, it would have been deep air, 25
The heaving speech of air, a summer sound
Repeated in a summer without end
And sound alone. But it was more than that,
More even than her voice, and ours, among
The meaningless plungings of water and the wind, 30
Theatrical distances, bronze shadows heaped
On high horizons, mountainous atmospheres
Of sky and sea.

                It was her voice that made
The sky acutest at its vanishing.
She measured to the hour its solitude. 35
She was the single artificer of the world
In which she sang. And when she sang, the sea,
Whatever self it had, became the self
That was her song, for she was the maker. Then we,
As we beheld her striding there alone. 40
Knew that there never was a world for her
Except the one she sang and singing, made.

Ramon Fernandez, tell me, if you know,
Why, when the singing ended and we turned
Toward the town, tell why the glassy lights   45
The lights in the fishing boats at anchor there,
As the night descended, tilting in the air,
Mastered the night and portioned out the sea,
Fixing emblazoned zones and fiery poles,
Arranging, deepening, enchanting night.   50

Oh! Blessed rage for order, pale Ramon,
The maker's rage to order words of the sea,
Words of the fragrant portals, dimly-starred,
And of ourselves and of our origins,
In ghostlier demarcations, keener sounds.   55

PIANO

D. H. Lawrence (1885–1930)

Softly, in the dusk, a woman is singing to me;
Taking me back down the vista of years, till I see
A child sitting under the piano, in the boom of the tingling strings
And pressing the small, poised feet of a mother who smiles as
    she sings.

In spite of myself, the insidious mastery of song   5
Betrays me back, till the heart of me weeps to belong
To the old Sunday evenings at home, with winter outside
And hymns in the cozy parlor, the tinkling piano our guide.

So now it is vain for the singer to burst into clamor
With the great black piano appassionato. The glamour   10
Of childish days is upon me, my manhood is cast
Down in the flood of remembrance, I weep like a child for the past.

ENVOI

Ezra Pound (1885–1972)

Go, dumb-born book,
Tell her that sang me once that song of Lawes;

Hadst thou but song
As thou hast subjects known,
Then were there cause in thee that should condone   5
Even my faults that heavy upon me lie
And build her glories their longevity.   slowing down

Tell her that sheds
Such treasure in the air,
Recking naught else but that her graces give   10
Life to the moment,
I would bid them live
As roses might, in magic amber laid,
Red overwrought with orange and all made
One substance and one colour   15
Braving time.

Tell her that goes
With song upon her lips
But sings not out the song, nor knows
The maker of it, some other mouth,   20
May be as fair as hers,
Might, in new ages, gain her worshippers,
When our two dusts with Waller's shall be laid,
Siftings on siftings in oblivion,
Till change hath broken down   25
All things save Beauty alone.

IN A PROMINENT BAR IN SECAUCUS ONE DAY

X. J. Kennedy (b. 1929)

In a prominent bar in Secaucus one day
Rose a lady in skunk with a topheavy sway,
Raised a knobby red finger—all turned from their beer—
While with eyes bright as snowcrust she sang high and clear:

"Now who of you'd think from an eyeload of me   5
That I once was a lady as proud as could be?
Oh I'd never sit down by a tumbledown drunk
If it wasn't, my dears, for the high cost of junk.

"All the gents used to swear that the white of my calf
Beat the down of the swan by a length and a half.   10
In the kerchief of linen I caught to my nose
Ah, there never fell snot, but a little gold rose.

"I had seven gold teeth and a toothpick of gold,
My Virginia cheroot was a leaf of it rolled
And I'd light it each time with a thousand in cash—   15
Why the bums used to fight if I flicked them an ash.

"Once the toast of the Biltmore, the belle of the Taft,
I would drink bottle beer at the Drake, never draught,
And dine at the Astor on Salisbury steak
With a clean tablecloth for each bite I did take.   20

"In a car like the Roxy I'd roll to the track,
A steel-guitar trio, a bar in the back,
And the wheels made no noise, they turned over so fast
Still it took you ten minutes to see me go past.

"When horses bowed down to me that I might choose,   25
I bet on them all, for I hated to lose.
Now I'm saddled each night for my butter and eggs
And the broken threads race down the backs of my legs.

"Let you hold in mind, girls, that your beauty must pass
Like a lovely white clover that rusts with its grass.   30
Keep your bottoms off barstools and marry you young
Or be left—an old barrel with many a bung.

"For when time takes you out for a spin in his car
You'll be hard-pressed to stop him from going too far
And be left by the roadside, for all your good deeds.   35
Two toadstools for tits and a face full of weeds."

All the house raised a cheer, but the man at the bar
Made a phonecall and up pulled a red patrol car
And she blew us a kiss as they copped her away
From that prominent bar in Secaucus, N.J.   40

Thematic Contexts

Poets have always written on such themes as love, spring, war, death, and gods. Indeed, we expect poets to treat themes that are universal in nature—shared by all men at all times. Yet, it may not occur to most of us that anyone who writes on such a universal theme assumes a relationship to all writers who have written on that theme. This is not to say that all poets who write about love have read Catullus, or even should have read Catullus. It simply means that what Catullus wrote is significant to anyone who tries either to write love poetry or to comprehend a poetic treatment of the theme of love.

Some poets may not agree with this idea. Critics themselves may feel that the concept does not affect them. But the point remains: All poems on love will set a precedent for all other poems on love. Or as Robert Frost put it: Every poem is written in light of every other poem ever written.

Even if a poet is not conscious of what a predecessor has done, he may be influenced nonetheless. If, for example, he has not read the "Song of Solomon" in the Bible, it does not mean that he is unaffected by what Solomon has written. So long as he is aware of any love poetry, he is influenced by the "Song of Solomon," for that poem and its form permeate the whole tradition of Western love poetry. In the poetry of Sappho or Catullus, the influence need not be immediate or conscious. It may be indirect and unconscious. But no matter which, it will be effective.

We all desire something new, something novel, in our poetry or in our art. We do not want anyone to rewrite the "Song of Solomon." We do not respond to a poet for having said the same things in the same ways as older poets. However, it is not just a desire for novelty that impels us to look for new modes of expression, but a desire for more knowledge, more insight, and more awareness concerning the most profound regions of human experience. We can be sure that love poems will be written until the end of time—or until poetry suffers an eclipse, whichever comes first. But, as long as people live and love, poets will have a subject to write about. This subject will be shared with ancient Egyptian poets as well as with poets of the present. Every poet who writes about love will find himself unconsciously competing with the past. The competition will be marked by an interest in what has not yet been done or what has not yet been expressed. The theme of love is forever old and forever new. And when we read a new love poem in an historical (or even a nonhistorical) context, we become aware once again that love is both the same and different for everyone. The point of Elizabeth Barrett Browning's "How do I love thee? Let me count the ways," is that the ways are not countable or measurable like other facets of human experience. The complete definition of love cannot be realized. It is the total of all that has been felt, written, said, and done in (and sometimes out of) its name. The context that appears here, as brief and as suggestive of larger dimensions as it is, should make that clear. Love is being examined, felt, responded to, defined, and enlarged on by poets from Solomon to Brian Patten. It is not a small thing to compare the ways these poets write about ecstatic moments in human experience, particularly since we are experts of a sort on the subject of love. Perhaps our capacities to express ourselves about love are not equal to theirs, but can it be said that we are not capable of feeling love or responding to it as deeply as they?

All this is true of the poems on spring and the elegies. To say something new or fresh about such subjects is extremely difficult. This difficulty becomes particularly apparent as we become more familiar with the ways poets have treated these subjects in the past. To perceive clearly this difficult and complex task the poet faces is one of the main reasons for studying poems in thematic contexts, and once we have grasped the problem faced by the poet we will be ready to study the extent of his achievement. However, first we must become aware of what the poet might have written—how he might otherwise have treated his subject. Then we are able to perceive the skill with which he accomplished his task.

Essentially, a group of related poems assists us in understanding the dimensions and varieties of the subject. It is almost meaningless to say a poem is "about love," or spring, or death.

There are hundreds of poems on these themes. Thus it is necessary to know the poet's real subject. Does he deal with love's joy, its loss, its tragedy, its fickleness? The thematic approach enables us to determine the writer's conception exactly and to see more clearly how he goes about expressing this conception.

It is possible to summarize the value of using a thematic context by pointing out three advantages of such an approach. First, our understanding of a particular poem is increased because we are able to see the poet's subject—his conception—more precisely. Second, the poet's technical virtuosity is made clearer when one poem is seen in relation to another poem on a similar subject. Further, we are better able to evaluate the relative effectiveness of each poem. And third, studying poems in a thematic context increases the reader's sense of historical relationships. This is so because a poet is an inveterate reader and borrower. It is true of great poets who have emotional "news" for us, just as it is of lesser poets who simply rework familiar areas of emotional interest. Poets of the second rank say what has always been said and accepted. They are often popular for a brief time, but, since they are creating nothing substantially original, their work does not last. Once such a poet has been viewed in a contextual relation with poets who have tried the same things and succeeded better, the relative success of their work becomes apparent.

It is probably fair to say that no critical view of any substance can be maintained without reconstructing a thematic context that takes into account the older, classically successful poems on the subject. We need to know what has already been written in order to know if what is now being written has lasting, imperishable value. We do not value cheap imitations in most human endeavors; yet, because most readers of poetry do not have a clear knowledge of the history of poetry—of what has already been said brilliantly—imitations are often the only successful poems of an age. Such a statement may need qualification; still, it does imply that poems on love, sorrow, or death for which popular success is the main criterion will have an audience virtually ignorant of other poetry. Clearly the task of such popularity-oriented poets is much simpler than that of the poet who writes with Shakespeare and Catullus fresh in the minds of his readers.

Great poets write not for those who are unaware, but for those who are aware of the achievements of the past. Reading Keith Waldrop's love poem is a peculiar experience partly because Waldrop is aware of Sappho and Rainer Maria Rilke, as well as hundreds of other poets whose poems do not appear here. He is not anxious to repeat or negate their work. He relies on our knowing that he has done something they did not do. To be appreciated, he must have an audience that has, at very least, a semblance of knowledge about older poetry. That his readership is small can be blamed largely on the difficulty of acquiring the background information needed to thoroughly understand him.

One reason many modern poems appear difficult to us is that their meaning depends on knowledge we may not have. Not only do some poems allude to poems of the past—something we are not directly worried about here—but they build on both poems and poetic attitudes of the past. Consider Michael Dennis Browne's poetic attitude toward love in contrast with that of Catullus, or John Donne's in relation to D. H. Lawrence's. By making such comparisons we become aware of earlier influences, and we find things explicit that are otherwise implicit in the later poems. However, these things will only be revealed to us and gain meaning if we are prepared to observe them.

The selections that follow are designed to help you make new observations and develop new insights. In addition to helping you gain a perspective on poems in this section, the contextual approach will make it possible for you to see more clearly the achievement of poems you have yet to read, or of poems not yet written. This is one of the most important functions of establishing thematic contexts of this kind: poems about love or the seasons can never end. Indeed, they ought never to be thought of as having an end.

Poems of Love

THE VOICE OF THE TURTLE

from SONG OF SOLOMON

The voice of my beloved!
Behold, he cometh
leaping upon the mountains,
skipping upon the hills.
My beloved is like a roe or a young hart: 5

behold, he standeth behind our wall,
he looketh forth at the windows,
showing himself through the lattice.
My beloved spake, and said unto me,
Rise up, my love, my fair one, and come away.   10
For, lo, the winter is past,
the rain is over *and* gone;
the flowers appear on the earth;
the time of the singing *of birds* is come,
and the voice of the turtle is heard in our land;   15
the fig tree putteth forth her green figs,
and the vines *with* the tender grape give a *good* smell.
Arise, my love, my fair one, and come away.
O my dove, *that art* in the clefts of the rock,
in the secret *places* of the stairs,   20
let me see thy countenance,
let me hear thy voice;
for sweet *is* thy voice,
and thy countenance *is* comely.
Take us the foxes, the little foxes, that spoil the vines: 25
for our vines *have* tender grapes.

My beloved *is* mine, and I *am* his:
he feedeth among the lilies.
Until the day break,
and the shadows flee away,   30
turn, my beloved,
and be thou like a roe or a young hart
upon the mountains of Bether.

LETTER TO ANAKTORIA

Sappho (7th Century B.C.)

For some the fairest thing on the dark earth is Thermopylae
and the Spartan phalanx lowering lances to die—
Salamis and the half-moon of Athenian triremes
sprinting to pin down the Persian fleet;
nothing is as fair as my beloved.   5

I can easily make you understand this:
dwell on the gentleness of his footstep,
the shimmer of his shining face fairer than ten thousand

barbarous scythe-wheeled Persian chariots,
or the myriad hanging gardens in Persepolis.

Helen forgot her husband and dear children
to cherish Paris,
the loveliest of mortals,
the murderer of Troy—
she bestowed her heart far off.

How easily a woman is led astray!
She remembers nothing of what is nearest at hand:
her loom, her household, her helots . . .
Anaktoria, did you cherish my love,
when the Bridegroom was with you?

A woman seldom finds what is best—
no, never in this world,
Anaktoria! Pray
for his magnificence I once pined to share . . .
to have lived is better than to live!

Translated by Robert Lowell

KISSES

Catullus (87?–55? B.C.)

Come and let us live, my dear,
Let us love and never fear
What the sourest fathers say:
Brightest Sol that dies to-day
Lives again as blithe to-morrow;
But if we dark sons of sorrow
Set, O then, how long a night
Shuts the eyes of our short light!
Then let amorous kisses dwell
On our lips, begin and tell
A thousand, and a hundred score,
An hundred and a thousand more,
Till another thousand smother
That, and that wipe off another.
Thus at last when we have numbred

Many a thousand, many a hundred,
We'll confound the reckoning quite,
And lose ourselves in wild delight:
While our joys so multiply
As shall mock the envious eye.   20

                Translated by Richard Crashaw

THE UNIVERSAL LOVER

Ovid (43 B.C.–17? A.D.)

This I admit: I'm very far from perfect.
I can't defend myself
with obvious lies—
if pleading guilty helps me, I'll confess—
say I've gone mad—then here's my list of crimes.   5
(I hate myself:
although I long to be what I am not—
if anyone got rid of all his sins,
he'd throw the greater part
of his weight away. I'm much too weak   10
to practice self-control: in storms mid-sea,
I'm like a boat that's rocked between the waves.

No single type of beauty is enough
to hold me fixed forever in her arms,
rather a hundred!
          If the girl's modest   15
and, like a virgin, keeps her eyes downcast,
I turn to flames, her innocence my ruin.
Yet, if she makes advances,
I love a girl who's not a bashful kitten—
she gives me hopes at once   20
of half a dozen pretty tricks in bed!
Or if she stand aloof,
as cold and rigid as a Sabine matron,
then I suspect she waits on invitation,
eager to strip   25
and drop her strange disguise.
(Ladies, if you love study,

join me tonight
in adult education.
Or, if you're unrefined, 30
I'm sure to praise refreshed simplicities!)

And if some beauty
calls Callimachus' songs "provincial rubbish"
compared to mine,
and proves it while she's naked in my arms— 35
I love the girl, and like myself the better.
Or, if she plays the critic,
says I'm no poet, scolds my little verses,
I love to lure
such critics between the sheets, 40
and as I mount them, hear them moan and cry.

One girl
has feet as light as air—I love her footfall—
another walks as though her feet were lead,
yet she's the kind that turns 45
to melting softness
the moment that she feels the touch of love.
Because one beauty
sings a pretty song
and charms me with her sweet facility, 50
I'd love to try those lips at deep-drawn kisses.
And what of her
              whose fingers stroke the harp
to wheedle music from the querulous string?
Who would not love such gifted, clever hands?
And still another 55
enraptures me with curves and turns in dancing—
herself is music when she takes the floor:
look at the quivering
of her hips and shoulders!
Since I'm susceptible to female rhythms, 60
I stand erect with all my blood on fire—
cold Hippolytus,
if he were in my skin, would be Priapus!

(And O blonde beauty,
tall as the daughters of our ancient heroes, 65
you fill the bed with love from head to foot—
yet I believe

a short girl, cute and naked, does as well—
for both destroy me—
I take them as they are, or great or small.)   70

If a girl's dowdy,
I dream of how she looks in décolleté,
and if she's smart,
she knows the art of showing off her beauty.
A girl with fair white skin and golden hair   75
turns to another
Venus in my arms—
she's my destruction—if her skin is dark,
I love a sun-tanned look—she's warm and easy,
yet if she's white as snow   80
with raven hair,
I'll not forget that Leda's hair was black—
or if it's auburn,
think of Aurora with her flaming curls!

My love would fit all heroines of history—   85
yet girls of ten or twelve
always attract me,
so does a matron who is ripe and eager:
one has experience—
and yet the others   90
charm me with promises of fresh delight.

Look, ladies, I am ready:
wherever girls are praised in this great city,
I'm there to hold them in my waiting arms!

Translated by Horace Gregory

THE BAITE

John Donne (1572?–1631)

Come live with mee, and bee my love,
And wee will some new pleasures prove
Of golden sands, and christall brookes,
With silken lines, and silver hookes.

There will the river whispering runne   5
Warm'd by thy eyes, more then the Sunne.
And there the'inamor'd fish will stay,
Begging themselves they may betray.

When thou wilt swimme in that live bath,
Each fish, which every channell hath,   10
Will amorously to thee swimme,
Gladder to catch thee, then thou him.

If thou, to be so seene, beest loath,
By Sunne, or Moone, thou darknest both,
And if my selfe have leave to see,   15
I need not their light, having thee.

Let others freeze with angling reeds,
And cut their legges, with shells and weeds,
Or treacherously poore fish beset,
With strangling snare, or windowie net: 20

Let coarse bold hands, from slimy nest
The bedded fish in banks out-wrest,
Or curious traitors, sleavesilke flies
Bewitch poore fishes wandring eyes.

For thee, thou needst no such deceit,   25
For thou thy selfe art thine owne bait;
That fish, that is not catch'd thereby,
Alas, is wiser farre then I.

"WHY DO I LOVE" YOU, SIR?

Emily Dickinson (1830–1886)

"Why do I love" You, Sir?
Because—
The Wind does not require the Grass
To answer—Wherefore when He pass
She cannot keep Her place.   5

Because He knows—and
Do not You—
And We know not—
Enough for Us
The Wisdom it be so—   10

The Lightning—never asked an Eye
Wherefore it shut—when He was by—
Because He knows it cannot speak—
And reasons not contained—
—Of Talk— 15
There be—preferred by Daintier Folk—

The Sunrise—Sir—compelleth Me—
Because He's Sunrise—and I see—
Therefore—Then—
I love Thee— 20

LOVE SONG

Rainer Maria Rilke (1875–1926)

How should I hold my spirit back, how weight
it lest it graze your own? How should I raise
it high above your head to other things?
Oh gladly I would simply relegate
my soul to something lost that darkly clings 5
to a strange silent place, a place that stays
quite still when your own inmost depths vibrate.
But all that grazes us, yourself and me,
is like a bow to us and joins two strings
together, so that one voice only sings. 10
To what stringed instrument have we been bound?
And in what player's hands do we resound?
Sweet melody.

Translated by Michael Hamburger

LOVE ON THE FARM

D. H. Lawrence (1885–1930)

What large, dark hands are those at the window
Grasping in the golden light
Which weaves its way through the evening wind
    At my heart's delight?

Ah, only the leaves! But in the west
I see a redness suddenly come
Into the evening's anxious breast—
 'Tis the wound of love goes home!

The woodbine creeps abroad
Calling low to her lover:
 The sun-lit flirt who all the day
 Has poised above her lips in play
 And stolen kisses, shallow and gay
 Of pollen, now has gone away—
  She woos the moth with her sweet, low word;
And when above her his moth-wings hover
Then her bright breast she will uncover
And yield her honey-drop to her lover.

Into the yellow, evening glow
Saunters a man from the farm below;
Leans, and looks in at the low-built shed
Where the swallow has hung her marriage bed.
 The bird lies warm against the wall.
 She glances quick her startled eyes
 Towards him, then she turns away
 Her small head, making warm display
 Of red upon the throat. Her terrors sway
 Her out of the nest's warm, busy ball,
 Whose plaintive cry is heard as she flies
 In one blue stoop from out the sties
 Into the twilight's empty hall.

Oh, water-hen, beside the rushes
Hide your quaintly scarlet blushes,
Still your quick tail, lie still as dead,
Till the distance folds over his ominous tread!

The rabbit presses back her ears,
Turns back her liquid, anguished eyes
And crouches low; then with wild spring
Spurts from the terror of *his* oncoming;
To be choked back, the wire ring
Her frantic effort throttling:
 Piteous brown ball of quivering fears!
Ah, soon in his large, hard hands she dies,
And swings all loose from the swing of his walk!
Yet calm and kindly are his eyes

And ready to open in brown surprise
Should I not answer to his talk
Or should he my tears surmise.

I hear his hand on the latch, and rise from my chair
Watching the door open; he flashes bare 50
His strong teeth in a smile, and flashes his eyes
In a smile like triumph upon me; then careless-wise
He flings the rabbit soft on the table board
And comes towards me: ah! the uplifted sword
Of his hand against my bosom! and oh, the broad 55
Blade of his glance that asks me to applaud
His coming! With his hand he turns my face to him
And caresses me with his fingers that still smell grim
Of the rabbit's fur! God, I am caught in a snare!
I know not what fine wire is round my throat; 60
I only know I let him finger there
My pulse of life, and let him nose like a stoat
Who sniffs with joy before he drinks the blood.

And down his mouth comes to my mouth! and down
His bright dark eyes come over me, like a hood 65
Upon my mind! his lips meet mine, and a flood
Of sweet fire sweeps across me, so I drown
Against him, die, and find death good.

FIRST LOVE

Laurie Lee (b. 1914)

That was her beginning, an apparition
of rose in the unbreathed airs of his love,
her heart revealed by the wash of summer
sprung from her childhood's shallow stream.

Then it was that she put up her hair, 5
inscribed her eyes with a look of grief,
while her limbs grew as curious as coral branches,
her breast full of secrets.

But the boy, confused in his day's desire,
was searching for herons, his fingers bathed 10
in the green of walnuts, or watching at night
the Great Bear spin from the maypole star.

It was then that he paused in the death of a game,
felt the hook of her hair on his swimming throat,
saw her mouth at large in the dark river   15
flushed like a salmon.

But he covered his face and hid his joy
in a wild-goose web of false directions,
and hunted the woods for eggs and glow-worms,
for rabbits tasteless as moss.   20

And she walked in fields where the crocuses
branded her feet, and mares' tails sprang
from the prancing lake, and the salty grasses
surged round her stranded body.

LOVE'S ESCHATOLOGY

Vassar Miller (b. 1924)

I touch you all over
as if every part were a petal
when now you are away.

Never has your body
before so budded to my senses   5
as to my empty fingers.

Love, may we in Heaven
view all for the first time forever
through the lens of the last.

LOVE'S MAP

Donald Justice (b. 1925)

Your face more than others' faces
Maps the half-remembered places
I have come to while I slept—
Continents a dream had kept
Secret from all waking folk   5
Till to your face I awoke,
And remembered then the shore,
And the dark interior.

TWO SONGS

Adrienne Rich (b. 1929)

1

Sex, as they harshly call it,
I fell into this morning
at ten o'clock, a drizzling hour
of traffic and wet newspapers.
I thought of him who yesterday　　　　　　　5
clearly didn't
turn me to a hot field
ready for plowing,
and longing for that young man
piercéd me to the roots　　　　　　　　　10
bathing every vein, etc.
All day he appears to me
touchingly desirable,
a prize one could wreck one's peace for.
I'd call it love if love　　　　　　　　　15
didn't take so many years
but lust too is a jewel
a sweet flower and what
pure happiness to know
all our high-toned questions　　　　　　　20
breed in a lively animal.

2

That "old last act"!
And yet sometimes
all seems post coitum triste
and I a mere bystander.　　　　　　　　　25
Somebody else is going off,
getting shot to the moon.
Or, a moon-race!
Split seconds after
my opposite number lands　　　　　　　　30
I make it—
we lie fainting together
at a crater-edge

24. **Post coitum triste:** sadness after sexual intercourse.

heavy as mercury in our moonsuits
till he speaks— 35
in a different language
yet one I've picked up
through cultural exchanges . . .
we murmur the first moonwords:
Spasibo. Thanks. O.K. 40

TO ROSMARIE IN BAD KISSINGEN

Keith Waldrop (b. 1932)

I just squashed a fat
fly who was buzzing me, but he's
more disgusting dead.

If we go by numbers, my old
zoology prof used to say, this 5
is the age of insects,
more specifically, of beetles.

This is also the age of information.

I hope the church bells
of Bad Kissingen aren't 10
keeping you awake—though it's
nice, hearing tones decay. You
won't let the bells chase you to church.

Somebody, just the other day, claimed
that you and I haven't 15
any roots (he thinks that's bad). It's
true enough that we've fallen between
two generations—one drunk, the other
stoned. The one has
inhibitions to get rid of (you know 20
what that means—liquor and
analysis); the other, a great
blank space to fill.

The wars of the young I
think will be wars of religion. 25

But all this letter is really
meant to say is that you should
leave those kraut Quasimodos at their
glockenspiels and
hurry back here, because whatever we 30
don't see together has for me always
a dead spot somewhere,

even though I know that one
place is much the same as another,

and all the air we could 35
breathe anywhere in the world
has already, numberless times, been the
breath of a fern and
a marigold
and an oak. 40

MADONNA OF THE CELLO

Robert Bagg (b. 1935)

"My child will be born soon,"
    Through a halo of her own pain.
In the warm grasp of her open thighs
    Her cello rests on the biding child.
Wakeful quintets of her senses watch 5
    With the restraint of angels
Over this baby that her body holds.
    She cannot touch, but heralds.

Her tiptoeing fingerings are perilously
    Leisurely, 10
    Docile sounds
Follow the beckons of her firm right hand.
    In strokes as surely drawn,
    Chestfilling as her breaths,
She draws out the reticent sad girl in the strings. 15

For women with child come by in holiness,
A donkey shall unravel winding hills
    To Bethlehem,
But this girl with her maidenhood
Scattered to the five winds of sense   20
    Has no comfort beyond
The wonderful body which surrounds her heart.

Her eyes may be seen as champions
    Intrigued with the war of white
And red roses in her complexion.   25
    Her lips bless her throat's peaceful
        Swanpale
Skin disappearing under her clothes.

    She has let her hair grow
        Anticipating curls,   30
    But the strands still fall
        Faithful to her neck.

From their far reaches after sadness
    Her eyes look home to merry sidelong wrists,
        Blue wrist veins risen,   35
            Sinking into her fingers.

A few bars from the end
She gives in to jubilant vibrations
In the part of her that's now child.
    The bow lifting from the strings   40
Becomes the moment after they both came,
    Each falling from ecstasy
        Into the other's arms.
"Some legend has gone on without us,"
    Her lover said.   45
"Believe your tears, before they evaporate
    Like notes of music from your cheeks
And your heart goes back to marking time."
        And they had sat, side
        By side on the stone stairs   50
    Of her white colonial home.
Sliding tears drew out of her eyes
    The things she saw:
Her mother staring into the whorls
    Of the washing machine,   55

    Her father's eyes receding,
Her own body growing beyond her control.

Along her highstrung Puritan lineaments
    All her promises gambol again.
She nestles to the cello's gnarled flourish.   60
        Those doomed
    Untouchable happenings,
        Once wild,
    Soon bewildered,
Overflow her cello's rosewood curves,   65
    Confined to a melody
        Which aches inside her,
        Sleeps with her,
           Swells.
    It is growing into a man.   70

    He remembered
Her throbbing metabolism,
    When his hand reached for her shoulder,
        Lifted her breast to his passing forearm,
Almost buried her sentences in dreamy breathing,   75
        Carried merry water to her eyes,
            Sweat to her stomach,
        Moved her from her clothes
            Like a soul from its body:
        It now feeds her child   80
Bread eaten with a spirited appetite,
    Sirloin, spinach and grapefruit, her
        Particular vice,
Where the child's capillaries touch her capillaries.
    Fingers once curled restless into her lover's   85
        Walk on the sonata's nerves
            Singing itself to sleep.

    Silence, after music, awakens the child.
        Her lover opens his palm
            Over her turbulent belly, where the child   90
            Troubles it with his footprints, turning
                Against the flesh.
                "He was conceived when my body
                    Opened to you.
                When my body opens to the world   95
                He shall be born."

NEWS FROM THE HOUSE

Michael Dennis Browne (b. 1940)

Love, I have warmed the car,
the snow between us lies

shaking at the sound of my wheels
pawing the ground, my radio

snorting through its shimmering
nostrils.
            I
have command of the seats,
the trunk has been blessed

by Eskimos, and the hood
(or British Bonnet) anointed
with a stern steam.
            There
is no time like the present,
send for me.

            Love, over
what dark miles do I come, shall I,
dark

as the wind round the house
I lie in,

the great bed, the long
night draining me,
            Love,
in what season may it, tell me
the green date mice may

swear by, and the vast
branches spread dizzy those
distances my eyes too well
see through this winter. What
I have done that you

weep, what you have
worked that I
pace continually

this most sad house, meals
of its emptiness in every 35
corner, that the wind
          sounds,

the house refusing to be musical,

in the sheerest dark. Tell me
the previous times, hear my 40

greed for you. Under it all
and the cold ground
          we
sleeping you said, and ending,
the April waking, that trap 45
sprung.
      Love, in my
solitude my hands
garrisoned, hear them

nightly beside me muttering 50
of freedoms they were

warm in. How
on these nights the house
refusing to be musical
          I 55

lie stone, seed-
cold, kernel of this

husked house, the white
miles between us

coiled soft as roads inside 60
me, my walls the blood
of rabbits, the bathroom
          a lodge for hunters,
the bath

of fur and stained.
          Love, 65

in what season, tell
me, I may unwrap this house
from me, these walls

remove, from my pockets
these stairs, drink 70
such dark no more
    nor wear ever
this most sad hat of shadows. Tell
me, make me instructions, 75
send them like news
from a dairy.
        I will feed
no more on this print and milk,
wait, crouch, mad in the sad house 80
refusing to be musical,
though I sing it each night the notes
my longest body is learning.

PARTY PIECE

Brian Patten (b. 1942)

   He said:
"Let's stay here
Now this place has emptied
& make gentle pornography with one another,
While the partygoers go out 5
& the dawn creeps in,
Like a stranger.

Let us not hesitate
Over what we know
Or over how cold this place has become, 10
But let's unclip our minds
And let tumble free
The mad, mangled crocodiles of love."

So, they did,
Right there among the woodbines and guinness stains, 15
And later he caught a bus and she a train
And all there was between them then
was rain.

Poems on Spring

TO WELCOME IN THE SPRING

John Lyly (1554?–1606)

What Bird so sings, yet so dos wayle?
O'tis the rauish'd Nightingale.
Iug, Iug, Iug, Iug, tereu, shee cryes,
And still her woes at Midnight rise.
Braue prick song! who is't now we heare?   5
None but the Larke so shrill and cleare;
How at heauen's gats she slaps her wings,
The Morne not waking till shee sings.
Heark, heark, with what a pretty throat
Poore Robin red-breast tunes his note;   10
Heark how the jolly Cuckoes sing
Cuckoe, to welcome in the spring,
Cuckoe, to welcome in the spring.

SPRING, THE SWEET SPRING

Thomas Nashe (1567–1601)

Spring, the sweet spring, is the year's pleasant king;
Then blooms each thing, then maids dance in a ring,
Cold doth not sting, the pretty birds do sing:
   Cuckoo, jug-jug, pu-we, to-witta-woo!

The palm and may make country houses gay,   5
Lambs frisk and play, the shepherds pipe all day,
And we hear aye birds tune this merry lay:
   Cuckoo, jug-jug, pu-we, to-witta-woo!

The fields breathe sweet, the daisies kiss our feet,
Young lovers meet, old wives a-sunning sit,   10
In every street these tunes our ears do greet:
   Cuckoo, jug-jug, pu-we, to-witta-woo!
      Spring, the sweet spring!

ALL THE FLOWERS OF THE SPRING

John Webster (1580–1625)

All the flowers of the spring
Meet to perfume our burying;
These have but their growing prime,
And man doth flourish but his time:
Survey our progress from our birth;   5
We are set, we grow, we turn to earth.
Courts adieu, and all delights,
All bewitching appetites.
Sweetest breath and clearest eye,
Like perfumes, go out and die;   10
And consequently this is done
As shadows wait upon the sun.
Vain the ambition of kings
Who seek by trophies and dead things
To leave a living name behind.   15
And weave but nets to catch the wind.

TO SPRING

William Blake (1757–1827)

O thou with dewy locks who lookest down
Through the clear windows of the morning, turn
Thine angel eyes upon our western isle,
Which in full choir hails thy approach, O Spring!

The Hills tell each other, and the listening   5
Valleys hear; all our longing eyes are turned
Up to thy bright pavillions: issue forth,
And let thy holy feet visit our clime,

Come o'er the eastern hills, and let our winds
Kiss thy perfumed garments; let us taste   10
Thy morn and evening breath; scatter thy pearls
Upon our love-sick land that mourns for thee.

O deck her forth with thy fair fingers; pour
Thy soft kisses on her bosom; and put
Thy golden crown upon her languished head,   15
Whose modest tresses were bound up for thee.

SPRING

Gerard Manley Hopkins (1844–1889)

Nothing is so beautiful as spring—
   When weeds, in wheels, shoot long and lovely and lush;
   Thrush's eggs look little low heavens, and thrush
Through the echoing timber does so rinse and wring
The ear, it strikes like lightning to hear him sing;   5
   The glassy peartree leaves and blooms, they brush
   The descending blue; that blue is all in a rush
With richness; the racing lambs too have fair their fling.

What is all this juice and all this joy?
   A strain of the earth's sweet being in the beginning   10
In Eden garden.—Have, get, before it cloy,
   Before it cloud, Christ, lord, and sour with sinning,
Innocent mind and Mayday in girl and boy,
   Most, O maid's child, thy choice and worthy the winning.

SPRING STRAINS

William Carlos Williams (1883–1963)

In a tissue-thin monotone of blue-grey buds
crowded erect with desire against the sky
      tense blue-grey twigs
slenderly anchoring them down, drawing
them in—   5
      two blue-grey birds chasing
a third struggle in circles, angles,
swift convergings to a point that bursts
instantly!
      Vibrant bowing limbs   10
pull downward, sucking in the sky
that bulges from behind, plastering itself
against them in packed rifts, rock blue
and dirty orange!
      But—   15
(Hold hard, rigid jointed trees!)
the blinding and red-edged sun-blur—
creeping energy, concentrated
counterforce—welds sky, buds, trees,

rivets them in one puckering hold! 20
Sticks through! Pulls the whole
counter-pulling mass upward, to the right
locks even the opaque, not yet defined
ground in a terrific drag that is
loosening the very tap-roots! 25
On a tissue-thin monotone of blue-grey buds
two blue-grey birds, chasing a third,
at full cry! Now they are
flung outward and up—disappearing suddenly!

SPRING MORNING

D. H. Lawrence (1885–1930)

Ah, through the open door
Is there an almond tree
Aflame with blossom!
   —Let us fight no more.

Among the pink and blue 5
Of the sky and the almond flowers
A sparrow flutters.
   —We have come through.

It is really spring!—See,
When he thinks himself alone 10
How he bullies the flowers.
   —You and me

How happy we'll be!—See him,
He clouts the tufts of flowers
In his impudence. 15
   —But, did you dream

It would be so bitter? Never mind
It is finished, the spring is here.
And we're going to be summer-happy
   And summer-kind. 20

We have died, we have slain and been slain
We are not our old selves any more.
I feel new and eager
   To start again.

It is gorgeous to live and forget. 25
And to feel quite new.
See the bird in the flowers?—he's making
   A rare to-do!

He thinks the whole blue sky
Is much less than the bit of blue egg 30
He's got in his nest—we'll be happy
   You and I, I and you.

With nothing to fight any more—
In each other, at least.
See, how gorgeous the world is 35
   Outside the door!

O sweet spontaneous

e. e. cummings (1894–1962)

O sweet spontaneous
earth how often have
the
doting

   fingers of 5
prurient philosophers pinched
and
poked

thee
  has the naughty thumb 10
of science prodded
thy

  beauty   ,how
often have the religions taken
thee upon their scraggy knees 15
squeezing and

buffeting thee that thou mightest conceive
gods
  (but
true 20

to the incomparable
couch of death thy
rhythmic
lover

    thou answerest   25

them only with

    spring)

HOLD HARD, THESE ANCIENT MINUTES IN THE CUCKOO'S MONTH

Dylan Thomas (1914–1953)

Hold hard, these ancient minutes in the cuckoo's month,
Under the land, fourth folly on Glamorgan's hill,
As the green blooms ride upward, to the drive of time;
Time, in a folly's rider, like a county man
Over the vault of ridings with his hound at heel,   5
Drives forth my men, my children, from the hanging south.

Country, your sport is summer, and December's pools
By crane and water-tower by the seedy trees
Lie this fifth month unskated, and the birds have flown;
Hold hard, my country children in the world of tales,   10
The greenwood dying as the deer fall in their tracks,
This first and steepled season, to the summer's game.

And now the horns of England, in the sound of shape,
Summon your snowy horsemen, and the four-stringed hill,
Over the sea-gut loudening, sets a rock alive;   15
Hurdles and guns and railings, as the boulders heave,
Crack like a spring in a vice, bone breaking April,
Spill the lank folly's hunter and the hard-held hope.

Down fall four padding weathers on the scarlet lands,
Stalking my children's faces with a tail of blood,   20
Time, in a rider rising, from the harnessed valley;
Hold hard, my county darlings, for a hawk descends,
Golden Glamorgan straightens, to the falling birds.
Your sport is summer as the spring runs angrily.

Was there a time when dancers with their fiddles 25
In children's circuses could stay their troubles?
There was a time they could cry over books,
But time has set its maggot on their track.
Under the arc of the sky they are unsafe.
What's never known is safest in this life. 30
Under the skysigns they who have no arms
Have cleanest hands, and, as the heartless ghost
Alone's unhurt, so the blind man sees best.

Elegies

LYCIDAS

John Milton (1608–1674)

In this Monody the Author bewails a learned Friend, unfortunately drown'd in his passage from Chester on the Irish Seas, 1637. And by occasion foretells the ruine of our corrupted Clergie then in their height.

Yet once more, O ye Laurels, and once more
Ye Myrtles brown, with Ivy never sear,
I com to pluck your Berries harsh and crude,
And with forc'd fingers rude,
Shatter your leaves before the mellowing year. 5
Bitter constraint, and sad occasion dear,
Compells me to disturb your season due:
For *Lycidas* is dead, dead ere his prime,
Young *Lycidas*, and hath not left his peer:

Lycidas. Lycidas is the name Milton gave Edward King, a schoolmate at Cambridge who died in his twenty-fifth year (Milton was twenty-nine). The poem was written for a tribute published by the university and appeared with a number of other pieces on the same theme. The opening lines imply that Milton did not feel he was ready to write a poem on so heavy a theme as the loss of a worthy man, and his references to the laurel, myrtle, and ivy are symbolic, since these evergreen ("never sere") plants had long been symbols of the poetic imagination and were woven into a crown for poets. King and Milton were both well known in the Cambridge community as budding poets.

Who would not sing for *Lycidas?* he knew 10
Himself to sing, and build the lofty rhyme.
He must not flote upon his watry bear
Unwept, and welter to the parching wind,
Without the meed of som melodious tear.
    Begin then, Sisters of the sacred well, 15
That from beneath the seat of *Jove* doth spring,
Begin, and somewhat loudly sweep the string.
Hence with denial vain, and coy excuse,
So may some gentle Muse
With lucky words favour my destin'd Urn, 20
And as he passes turn,
And bid fair peace be to my sable shrowd.
For we were nurst upon the self-same hill,
Fed the same flock; by fountain, shade, and rill.
    Together both, ere the high Lawns appear'd 25
Under the opening eye-lids of the morn,
We drove a field, and both together heard
What time the Gray-fly winds her sultry horn,
Batt'ning our flocks with the fresh dews of night,
Oft till the Star that rose, at Ev'ning, bright, 30
Toward Heav'ns descent had slop'd his westering wheel.
Mean while the Rural ditties were not mute,
Temper'd to th' Oaten Flute,
Rough *Satyrs* danc'd, and *Fauns* with clov'n heel,
From the glad sound would not be absent long, 35
And old *Damætas* lov'd to hear our song.
    But O the heavy change, now thou art gon,
Now thou art gon, and never must return!
Thee Shepherd, thee the Woods, and desert Caves,
With wilde Thyme and the gadding Vine o'regrown, 40

15. **Sisters of the sacred well:** the muses, who inspire poets; they inhabit Helicon, the mountain that held an altar to Jove. The introductory passage—the prologue—ends with line 14, and lines 15–84 represent an invocation of the muses. A procession of mourners begins at line 85, and the consolation—a typical ingredient of poems on the subject of death, since everyone in grief needs to be consoled—begins at line 132. The last lines—186–93—are an epilogue; they also represent a puzzling change in voice from the first person in the prologue to the third person. The last eight lines are also tightly rhymed (actually an Italian form, *ottava rima*), whereas the opening of the poem suggests an almost random rhyme scheme.   36. **old Damaetas:** possibly a teacher with whom Milton and King had studied at Cambridge. The references to shepherds feeding the same flock are a pastoral fiction representing their time at Cambridge together performing similar academic functions.

And all their echoes mourn.
The Willows, and the Hazle Copses green,
Shall now no more be seen,
Fanning their joyous Leaves to thy soft layes.
As killing as the Canker to the Rose, 45
Or Taint-worm to the weanling Herds that graze,
Or Frost to Flowers, that their gay wardrop wear,
When first the White Thorn blows;
Such, *Lycidas,* thy loss to Shepherds ear.
    Where were ye Nymphs when the remorseless deep 50
Clos'd o're the head of your lov'd *Lycidas*?
For neither were ye playing on the steep,
Where your old *Bards,* the famous *Druids,* ly,
Nor on the shaggy top of *Mona* high,
Nor yet where *Deva* spreads her wisard stream: 55
Ay me, I fondly dream!
Had ye bin there—for what could that have don?
What could the Muse her self that *Orpheus* bore,
The Muse her self for her inchanting son
Whom Universal nature did lament, 60
When by the rout that made the hideous roar,
His goary visage down the stream was sent,
Down the swift *Hebrus* to the *Lesbian* shore.
    Alas! What boots it with uncessant care
To tend the homely slighted Shepherds trade, 65
And strictly meditate the thankless Muse,
Were it not better don as others use,
To sport with *Amaryllis* in the shade,
Or with the tangles of *Neæra's* hair?
Fame is the spur that the clear spirit doth raise 70
(That last infirmity of Noble mind)
To scorn delights, and live laborious dayes;
But the fair Guerdon when we hope to find,
And think to burst out into sudden blaze,
Comes the blind *Fury* with th' abhorred shears, 75

54. Mona: Isle of Anglesey. **55. Deva:** river Dee, associated with the Elizabethan wizard, John Dee. **58. the Muse her self that Orpheus bore:** Calliope, the special muse of music. Orpheus was a legendary poet and priest—a good parallel for Edward King, who was a poet and also a minister in the Church of England. **63. Hebrus:** Orpheus's severed head was carried down the Hebrus River to the shore of the island of Lesbos. The Thracian women had torn him apart. **68, 69. Amaryllis, Neaera:** characters of Theocritus (Greek pastoral poet) and Virgil (Latin pastoral poet), classical poets well known in Milton's time, and also writers of pastoral elegies.

And slits the thin spun life. But not the praise,
Phœbus repli'd, and touch'd my trembling ears;
Fame is no plant that grows on mortal soil,
Nor in the glistering foil
Set off to th' world, nor in broad rumour lies,   80
But lives and spreds aloft by those pure eyes,
And perfet witnes of all-judging *Jove;*
As he pronounces lastly on each deed,
Of so much fame in Heav'n expect thy meed.
   O Fountain *Arethuse,* and thou honour'd floud,   85
Smooth-sliding *Mincius,* crown'd with vocal reeds,
That strain I heard was of a higher mood:
But now my Oat proceeds,
And listens to the Herald of the Sea
That came in *Neptune's* plea,   90
He ask'd the Waves, and ask'd the Fellon Winds,
What hard mishap hath doom'd this gentle swain?
And question'd every gust of rugged wings
That blows from off each beaked Promontory;
They knew not of his story,   95
And sage *Hippotades* their answer brings,
That not a blast was from his dungeon stray'd,
The Air was calm, and on the level brine,
Sleek *Panope* with all her sisters play'd.
It was that fatal and perfidious Bark   100
Built in th' eclipse, and rigg'd with curses dark,
That sunk so low that sacred head of thine.
   Next *Camus,* reverend Sire, went footing slow,
His Mantle hairy, and his Bonnet sedge,
Inwrought with figures dim, and on the edge   105
Like to that sanguine flower inscrib'd with woe.
Ah; Who hath reft (quoth he) my dearest pledge?
Last came, and last did go,
The Pilot of the *Galilean* lake,

77. Phoebus: Phoebus Apollo, leader of the Muses and father of inspiration. **85. Fountain Arethuse:** a Sicilian spring associated with Theocritus. **86. Mincius:** the birthplace of Virgil. **88. Oat:** shepherd's pipe, here a symbol of the song (poem) being sung. **91. Fellon Winds:** wild winds associated with Neptune and the sea. **96. Hippotades:** Neptune, god of the sea. **99. Panope:** a sea nymph. **103. Camus:** the river Cam, symbolic of Cambridge University. **109. The Pilot of the Galilean lake:** may be St. Peter, the first pope, who was given two keys in Matthew 16:19. Milton delivers a ruthless attack in these next lines on the corrupt clergy in order to emphasize society's loss in King's death; King had a reputation for being high-minded and opposed to corruption.

Two massy Keyes he bore of metals twain, 110
(The Golden opes, the Iron shuts amain)
He shook his Miter'd locks, and stern bespake,
How well could I have spar'd for thee, young swain,
Anow of such as for their bellies sake,
Creep and intrude, and climb into the fold? 115
Of other care they little reck'ning make,
Then how to scramble at the shearers feast,
And shove away the worthy bidden guest;
Blind mouthes! that scarce themselves know how to hold
A Sheep-hook, or have learn'd ought els the least 120
That to the faithful Herdmans art belongs!
What recks it them? What need they? They are sped;
And when they list, their lean and flashy songs
Grate on their scrannel Pipes of wretched straw,
The hungry sheep look up, and are not fed, 125
But swoln with wind, and the rank mist they draw,
Rot inwardly, and foul contagion spread:
Besides what the grim Woolf with privy paw
Daily devours apace, and nothing sed,
But that two-handed engine at the door, 130
Stands ready to smite once, and smite no more.
 Return *Alpheus*, the dread voice is past,
That shrunk thy streams; Return *Sicilian* Muse,
And call the Vales, and bid them hither cast
Their Bells, and Flourets of a thousand hues. 135
Ye valleys low where the milde whispers use,
Of shades and wanton winds, and gushing brooks,
On whose fresh lap the swart Star sparely looks,
Throw hither all your quaint enameld eyes,
That on the green terf suck the honied showres, 140
And purple all the ground with vernal flowres.
Bring the rathe Primrose that forsaken dies.
The tufted Crow-toe, and pale Gessamine,
The white Pink, and the Pansie freakt with jeat,
The glowing Violet. 145
The Musk-rose, and the well attir'd Woodbine,

120. **els**: else.   124. **scrannel**: thin. This is the first appearance in print of this word.   128. **the grim Woolf with privy paw**: a reference to the Roman church, which English churchmen felt was hopelessly corrupt.   132. **Alpheus**: a sacred river.   133. **Sicilian Muse**: Theocritus. The line calls for a return to the conventions of the Greek and Latin pastoral.   134. **Vales**: valleys.   142. **rathe**: early.   144. **jeat**: black.

With Cowslips wan that hang the pensive head,
And every flower that sad embroidery wears:
Bid *Amarantus* all his beauty shed,
And Daffadillies fill their cups with tears,   150
To strew the Laureat Herse where *Lycid* lies.
For so to interpose a little ease,
Let our frail thoughts dally with false surmise.
Ay me! Whilst thee the shores, and sounding Seas
Wash far away, where ere thy bones are hurl'd,   155
Whether beyond the stormy *Hebrides*
Where thou perhaps under the whelming tide
Visit'st the bottom of the monstrous world;
Or whether thou to our moist vows deny'd,
Sleep'st by the fable of *Bellerus* old,   160
Where the great vision of the guarded Mount
Looks toward *Namancos* and *Bayona's* hold;
Look homeward Angel now, and melt with ruth.
And, O ye *Dolphins*, waft the haples youth.
    Weep no more, woful Shepherds weep no more,   165
For *Lycidas* your sorrow is not dead,
Sunk though he be beneath the watry floar,
So sinks the day-star in the Ocean bed,
And yet anon repairs his drooping head,
And tricks his beams, and with new spangled Ore,   170
Flames in the forehead of the morning sky:
So *Lycidas* sunk low, but mounted high,
Through the dear might of him that walk'd the waves
Where other groves, and other streams along,
With *Nectar* pure his oozy Lock's he laves,   175
And hears the unexpressive nuptial Song,
In the blest Kingdoms meek of joy and love.
There entertain him all the Saints above,
In solemn troops, and sweet Societies
That sing, and singing in their glory move,   180
And wipe the tears for ever from his eyes.

149. Amarantus: Amarinth, a flower growing in Paradise.   **163. Look homeward Angel:** refers to the angel Michael, patron saint of mariners, who guards the Cornish coast facing south. The references to Bellerus (line 160), Namancos (line 162), and Bayona (line 162) emphasize the threat that Catholic forces represented to England and underscore the necessity for Michael's protection. **ruth:** compassion.   **170. new spangled Ore:** glints of light as the sun rises. **173. him that walk'd the waves:** Christ.   **176. unexpressive nuptial Song:** Revelation; thus it cannot be heard.

Now *Lycidas* the Shepherds weep no more;
Henceforth thou art the Genius of the shore,
In thy large recompense, and shalt be good
To all that wander in that perilous flood. 185
    Thus sang the uncouth Swain to th' Okes and rills,
While the still morn went out with Sandals gray,
He touch'd the tender stops of various Quills,
With eager thought warbling his *Dorick* lay:
And now the Sun had stretch'd out all the hills, 190
And now was dropt into the Western Bay;
At last he rose, and twitch'd his Mantle blew:
To morrow to fresh Woods, and Pastures new.

WHEN LILACS LAST IN THE DOORYARD BLOOM'D

Walt Whitman (1819–1892)

I

When lilacs last in the dooryard bloom'd,
And the great star early droop'd in the western sky in the night,
I mourn'd, and yet shall mourn with ever-returning spring.

Ever-returning spring, trinity sure to me you bring,
Lilac blooming perennial and drooping star in the west, 5
And thought of him I love.

II

O powerful western fallen star!
O shades of night—O moody, tearful night!
O great star disappear'd—O the black murk that hides the star!
O cruel hands that hold me powerless—O helpless soul of me! 10
O harsh surrounding cloud that will not free my soul.

---

186. uncouth Swain: the unknown youth who spoke the lines of the poem.
189. Dorick lay: rural song.
    When Lilacs Last in the Dooryard Bloom'd. This is an elegy on the death of Abraham Lincoln, whom Whitman greatly admired. The lilac, the hermit thrush, and the evening star are symbols of eternal return. They also represent symbolic aspects of Lincoln's meaning for Whitman. The lilac may be a symbol of love between men; the hermit thrush a symbol of the permanence of song or utterance; the evening star a symbol of vision and hope.

III

In the dooryard fronting an old farm-house near the white-wash'd
    palings,
Stands the lilac-bush tall-growing with heart-shaped leaves of rich
    green,
With many a pointed blossom rising delicate, with the perfume
    strong I love,
With every leaf a miracle—and from this bush in the dooryard,   15
With delicate-colour'd blossoms and heart-shaped leaves of rich
    green,
A sprig with its flower I break.

IV

In the swamp in secluded recesses,
A shy and hidden bird is warbling a song.
Solitary the thrush,   20
The hermit withdrawn to himself, avoiding the settlements,
Sings by himself a song.

Song of the bleeding throat,
Death's outlet song of life (for well, dear brother, I know,
If thou wast not granted to sing thou would'st surely die).   25

V

Over the breast of the spring, the land, amid cities,
Amid lanes and through old woods, where lately the violets peep'd
    from the ground, spotting the grey débris,
Amid the grass in the fields each side of the lanes, passing the
    endless grass,
Passing the yellow-spear'd wheat, every grain from its shroud in
    the dark-brown fields uprisen,
Passing the apple-tree blows of white and pink in the orchards,   30
Carrying a corpse to where it shall rest in the grave,
Night and day journeys a coffin.

VI

Coffin that passes through lanes and streets,
Through day and night with the great cloud darkening the land,

33. **Coffin ... streets:** Lincoln's funeral train brought his coffin from Washington, D.C., to Springfield, Illinois. Thousands mourned him on the way.

With the pomp of the inloop'd flags with the cities draped in
    black, 35
With the show of the States themselves as of crepe-veiled women
    standing,
With processions long and winding and the flambeaus of the night,
With the countless torches lit, with the silent sea of faces and the
    unbared heads,
With the waiting depot, the arriving coffin, and the somber faces,
With dirges through the night, with the thousand voices rising
    strong and solemn, 40
With all the mournful voices of the dirges poured around the coffin,
The dim-lit churches and the shuddering organs—where amid these
    you journey,
With the tolling tolling bells' perpetual clang,
Here, coffin that slowly passes,
I give you my sprig of lilac. 45

VII

(Nor for you, for one alone,
Blossoms and branches green to coffins all I bring,
For fresh as the morning, thus would I chant a song for you O sane
    and sacred death.

All over bouquets of roses,
O death, I cover you over with roses and early lilies, 50
But mostly and now the lilac that blooms the first,
Copious I break, I break the sprigs from the bushes,
With loaded arms I come, pouring for you,
For you and the coffins all of you O death.)

VIII

O western orb sailing the heaven, 55
Now I know what you must have meant as a month since I walked,
As I walked in silence the transparent shadowy night,
As I saw you had something to tell as you bent to me night after
    night,
As you drooped from the sky low down as if to my side (while the
    other stars all looked on),
As we wandered together the solemn night (for something I know
    not what kept me from sleep), 60

As the night advanced, and I saw on the rim of the west how full
    you were of woe,
As I stood on the rising ground in the breeze in the cool transparent
    night,
As I watched where you passed and was lost in the netherward
    black of the night,
As my soul in its trouble dissatisfied sank, as where you, sad orb,
Concluded, dropped in the night, and was gone.   65

IX

Sing on there in the swamp,
O singer bashful and tender, I hear your notes, I hear your call,
I hear, I come presently, I understand you,
But a moment I linger, for the lustrous star has detained me,
The star, my departing comrade, holds and detains me.   70

X

O how shall I warble myself for the dead one there I loved?
And how shall I deck my song for the large sweet soul that has
    gone?
And what shall my perfume be for the grave of him I love?

Sea-winds blown from east and west,
Blown from the Eastern sea and blown from the Western sea, till
    there on the prairies meeting,   75
These and with these and the breath of my chant,
I'll perfume the grave of him I love.

XI

O what shall I hang on the chamber walls?
And what shall the pictures be that I hang on the walls,
To adorn the burial-house of him I love?   80

Pictures of growing spring and farms and homes,
With the Fourth-month eve at sundown, and the gray smoke lucid
    and bright,
With floods of the yellow gold of the gorgeous, indolent, sinking
    sun, burning, expanding the air,
With the fresh sweet herbage under foot, and the pale green leaves
    of the trees prolific,
In the distance the flowing glaze, the breast of the river, with a wind-
    dapple here and there,   85

With ranging hills on the banks, with many a line against the sky, and shadows,
And the city at hand with dwellings so dense, and stacks of chimneys,
And all the scenes of life and the workshops, and the workmen homeward returning.

XII

Lo, body and soul—this land,
My own Manhattan with spires, and the sparkling and hurrying tides, and the ships, 90
The varied and ample land, the South and the North in the light, Ohio's shores and flashing Missouri,
And ever the far-spreading prairies covered with grass and corn.

Lo, the most excellent sun so calm and haughty,
The violet and purple morn with just-felt breezes,
The gentle soft-born measureless light, 95
The miracle spreading, bathing all, the fulfilled noon,
The coming eve delicious, the welcome night and the stars,
Over my cities shining all, enveloping man and land.

XIII

Sing on, sing on you gray-brown bird,
Sing from the swamps, the recesses, pour your chant from the bushes, 100
Limitless out of the dusk, out of the cedars and pines.

Sing on dearest brother, warble your reedy song,
Loud human song, with voice of uttermost woe.

O liquid and free and tender!
O wild and loose to my soul—O wondrous singer! 105
You only I hear—yet the star holds me (but will soon depart),
Yet the lilac with mastering odor holds me.

XIV

Now while I sat in the day and looked forth,
In the close of the day with its light and the fields of spring, and the farmers preparing their crops,
In the large unconscious scenery of my land with its lakes and forests, 110

In the heavenly aerial beauty (after the perturbed winds and the
    storms),
Under the arching heavens of the afternoon swift passing, and the
    voices of children and women,
The many-moving sea-tides, and I saw the ships how they sailed,
And the summer approaching with richness, and the fields all busy
    with labor,
And the infinite separate houses, how they all went on, each with
    its meals and minutia of daily usages, 115
And the streets how their throbbings throbb'd, and the cities pent
    —lo, then and there,
Falling upon them all and among them all, enveloping me with
    the rest,
Appear'd the cloud, appear'd the long black trail,
And I knew death, its thought, and the sacred knowledge of death.

Then with the knowledge of death as walking one side of me, 120
And the thought of death close-walking the other side of me,
And I in the middle as with companions, and as holding the hands
    of companions,
I fled forth to the hiding receiving night that talks not,
Down to the shores of the water, the path by the swamp in the
    dimness,
To the solemn shadowy cedars and ghostly pines so still. 125

And the singer so shy to the rest receiv'd me,
The gray-brown bird I know receiv'd us comrades three,
And he sang the carol of death, and a verse for him I love.

From deep secluded recesses,
From the fragrant cedars and the ghostly pines so still, 130
Came the carol of the bird.

And the charm of the carol rapt me,
As I held as if by their hands my comrades in the night,
And the voice of my spirit tallied the song of the bird.

Come lovely and soothing death, 135
Undulate round the world, serenely arriving, arriving,
In the day, in the night, to all, to each,
Sooner or later delicate death.

Prais'd be the fathomless universe,
For life and joy, and for objects and knowledge curious, 140
And for love, sweet love—but praise! praise! praise!
For the sure-enwinding arms of cool-enfolding death.

Dark mother always gliding near with soft feet,
Have none chanted for thee a chant of fullest welcome?
Then I chant it for thee, I glorify thee above all, 145
I bring thee a song that when thou must indeed come, come
    unfalteringly.

Approach strong deliveress,
When it is so, when thou hast taken them, I joyously sing the dead,
Lost in the loving floating ocean of thee,
Laved in the flood of thy bliss, O death. 150
From me to thee glad serenades,
Dances for thee I propose saluting thee, adornments and feastings
    for thee,
And the sights of the open landscape and the high-spread sky are
    fitting,
And life and the fields, and the huge and thoughtful night.

The night in silence under many a star, 155
The ocean shore and the husky whispering wave whose voice I
    know,
And the soul turning to thee, O vast and well-veil'd death,
And the body gratefully nestling close to thee.

Over the tree-tops I float thee a song,
Over the rising and sinking waves, over the myriad fields and the
    prairies wide, 160
Over the dense-pack'd cities all and the teeming wharves and ways,
I float this carol with joy, with joy to thee, O death.

XV

To the tally of my soul,
Loud and strong kept up the gray-brown bird,
With pure deliberate notes spreading, filling the night. 165

Loud in the pines and cedars dim,
Clear in the freshness moist and the swamp-perfume,
And I with my comrades there in the night.

While my sight that was bound in my eyes unclosed,
As to long panoramas of visions. 170

And I saw askant the armies,
I saw as in noiseless dreams hundreds of battle-flags,
Borne through the smoke of the battles and pierc'd with missiles
    I saw them,

And carried hither and yon through the smoke, and torn and bloody,
And at last but a few shreds left on the staffs (and all in silence), 175
And the staffs all splinter'd and broken.

I saw battle-corpses, myriads of them,
And the white skeletons of young men, I saw them,
I saw the débris and débris of all the slain soldiers of the war,
But I saw they were not as was thought, 180
They themselves were fully at rest, they suffered not,
The living remained and suffered, the mother suffered,
And the wife and the child and the musing comrade suffered,
And the armies that remained suffered.

XVI

Passing the visions, passing the night, 185
Passing, unloosing the hold of my comrades' hands,
Passing the song of the hermit bird and the tallying song of my soul,
Victorious song, death's outlet song, yet varying, ever-altering song,
As low and wailing, yet clear the notes, rising and falling, flooding the night,
Sadly sinking and fainting, as warning and warning, and yet again bursting with joy, 190
Covering the earth and filling the spread of the heaven,
As that powerful psalm in the night I heard from recesses,
Passing, I leave thee lilac with heart-shaped leaves,
I leave thee there in the dooryard, blooming, returning with spring.

I cease from my song for thee, 195
From my gaze on thee in the west, fronting the west, communing with thee,
O comrade lustrous with silver face in the night.

Yet each to keep and all, retrievements out of the night,
The song, the wondrous chant of the gray-brown bird,
And the tallying chant, the echo aroused in my soul, 200
With the lustrous and drooping star with the countenance full of woe,
With the holders holding my hand nearing the call of the bird,
Comrades mine and I in the midst, and their memory ever to keep, for the dead I loved so well,
For the sweetest, wisest soul of all my days and lands—and this for his dear sake,
Lilac and star and bird twined with the chant of my soul, 205
There in the fragrant pines and the cedars dusk and dim.

IN MEMORY OF MAJOR ROBERT GREGORY
William Butler Yeats (1865–1939)

I

Now that we're almost settled in our house
I'll name the friends that cannot sup with us
Beside a fire of turf in th' ancient tower,
And having talked to some late hour
Climb up the narrow winding stairs to bed: 5
Discoverers of forgotten truth
Or mere companions of my youth,
All, all are in my thoughts to-night being dead.

II

Always we'd have the new friend meet the old
And we are hurt if either friend seem cold, 10
And there is salt to lengthen out the smart
In the affections of our heart,
And quarrels are blown up upon that head;
But not a friend that I would bring
This night can set us quarrelling, 15
For all that come into my mind are dead.

III

Lionel Johnson comes the first to mind,
That loved his learning better than mankind,
Though courteous to the worst; much falling he
Brooded upon sanctity 20
Till all his Greek and Latin learning seemed
A long blast upon the horn that brought
A little nearer to his thought
A measureless consummation that he dreamed.

In Memory of Major Robert Gregory. Robert Gregory was the son of Yeats's long-time friend, Lady Augusta Gregory, with whom Yeats helped found the Irish Literary Theater. The house Yeats refers to was Thoor Ballylee in Galway, an ancient square Norman tower the Yeats's moved into in 1919. Major Gregory was killed flying an engagement over Italy in 1917.   **17. Lionel Johnson:** a member of the Rhymer's Club and an early influence on Yeats.

IV

And that enquiring man John Synge comes next, 25
That dying chose the living world for text
And never could have rested in the tomb
But that, long travelling, he had come
Towards nightfall upon certain set apart
In a most desolate stony place, 30
Towards nightfall upon a race
Passionate and simple like his heart.

V

And then I think of old George Pollexfen,
In muscular youth well known to Mayo men
For horsemanship at meets or at racecourses, 35
That could have shown how pure-bred horses
And solid men, for all their passion, live
But as the outrageous stars incline
By opposition, square and trine;
Having grown sluggish and contemplative. 40

VI

They were my close companions many a year,
A portion of my mind and life, as it were,
And now their breathless faces seem to look
Out of some old picture-book;
I am accustomed to their lack of breath, 45
But not that my dear friend's dear son,
Our Sidney and our perfect man,
Could share in that discourtesy of death.

VII

For all things the delighted eye now sees
Were loved by him: the old storm-broken trees 50
That cast their shadows upon road and bridge;
The tower set on the stream's edge;
The ford where drinking cattle make a stir

25. **John Synge** (pronounced "sing"): the first genius of the Irish Literary Theater. He died in 1909 after having written such classics as *Riders to the Sea* and *The Playboy of the Western World*.   33. **George Pollexfen:** Yeats's uncle and a strong influence on him in his youth. They sometimes practiced cabalism and telekinesis together—both longstanding interests of Yeats. 47. **Sidney:** Sir Philip Sidney was, like Gregory, a military man who died in battle. He is often cited as a paragon of the renaissance English ideal. The similarity is emphasized in line 70, "Soldier, scholar, horseman," used as a refrain.

Nightly, and startled by that sound
The water-hen must change her ground;
He might have been your heartiest welcomer.

VIII

When with the Galway foxhounds he would ride
From Castle Taylor to the Roxborough side
Or Esserkelly plain, few kept his pace;
At Mooneen he had leaped a place
So perilous that half the astonished meet
Had shut their eyes; and where was it
He rode a race without a bit?
And yet his mind outran the horses' feet.

IX

We dreamed that a great painter had been born
To cold Clare rock and Galway rock and thorn,
To that stern colour and that delicate line
That are our secret discipline
Wherein the gazing heart doubles her might.
Soldier, scholar, horseman, he,
And yet he had the intensity
To have published all to be a world's delight.

X

What other could so well have counselled us
In all lovely intricacies of a house
As he that practised or that understood
All work in metal or in wood,
In moulded plaster or in carven stone?
Soldier, scholar, horseman, he,
And all he did done perfectly
As though he had but that one trade alone.

XI

Some burn damp faggots, others may consume
The entire combustible world in one small room
As though dried straw, and if we turn about
The bare chimney is gone black out
Because the work had finished in that flare.
Soldier, scholar, horseman, he,

As 'twere all life's epitome.
What made us dream that he could comb grey hair?

XII

I had thought, seeing how bitter is that wind
That shakes the shutter, to have brought to mind 90
All those that manhood tried, or childhood loved
Or boyish intellect approved,
With some appropriate commentary on each;
Until imagination brought
A fitter welcome; but a thought 95
Of that late death took all my heart for speech.

BELLS FOR JOHN WHITESIDE'S DAUGHTER

John Crowe Ransom (b. 1888)

There was such speed in her little body,
And such lightness in her footfall,
It is no wonder that her brown study
Astonishes us all.

Her wars were bruited in our high window. 5
We looked among orchard trees and beyond,
Where she took arms against her shadow,
Or harried unto the pond

The lazy geese, like a snow cloud
Dripping their snow on the green grass, 10
Tricking and stopping, sleepy and proud,
Who cried in goose, Alas,

For the tireless heart within the little
Lady with rod that made them rise
From their noon apple dreams, and scuttle 15
Goose-fashion under the skies!

But now go the bells, and we are ready;
In one house we are sternly stopped
To say we are vexed at her brown study,
Lying so primly propped. 20

IN MEMORY OF W. B. YEATS

W. H. Auden (1907–1973)

d. Jan. 1939

I

He disappeared in the dead of winter:
The brooks were frozen, the airports almost deserted,
And snow disfigured the public statues;
The mercury sank in the mouth of the dying day.
What instruments we have agree
The day of his death was a dark cold day.

Far from his illness
The wolves ran on through the evergreen forests,
The peasant river was untempted by the fashionable quays;
By mourning tongues
The death of the poet was kept from his poems.

But for him it was his last afternoon as himself,
An afternoon of nurses and rumours;
The provinces of his body revolted,
The squares of his mind were empty,
Silence invaded the suburbs,
The current of his feeling failed; he became his admirers.

Now he is scattered among a hundred cities
And wholly given over to unfamiliar affections,
To find his happiness in another kind of wood
And be punished under a foreign code of conscience.
The words of a dead man
Are modified in the guts of the living.

But in the importance and noise of to-morrow
When the brokers are roaring like beasts on the floor of the Bourse,
And the poor have the sufferings to which they are fairly
    accustomed,
And each in the cell of himself is almost convinced of his freedom,
A few thousand will think of this day
As one thinks of a day when one did something slightly unusual.
What instruments we have agree
The day of his death was a dark cold day.

II

You were silly like us; your gift survived it all:
The parish of rich women, physical decay,
Yourself. Mad Ireland hurt you into poetry.
Now Ireland has her madness and her weather still, 35
For poetry makes nothing happen: it survives
In the valley of its making where executives
Would never want to tamper; flows on south
From ranches of isolation and the busy griefs,
Raw towns that we believe and die in; it survives, 40
A way of happening, a mouth.

III

Earth, receive an honoured guest:
William Yeats is laid to rest.
Let the Irish vessel lie
Emptied of its poetry. 45

In the nightmare of the dark
All the dogs of Europe bark,
And the living nations wait,
Each sequestered in its hate;

Intellectual disgrace 50
Stares from every human face,
And the seas of pity lie
Locked and frozen in each eye.

Follow, poet, follow right
To the bottom of the night, 55
With your unconstraining voice
Still persuade us to rejoice;

With the farming of a verse
Make a vineyard of the curse,
Sing of human unsuccess 60
In a rapture of distress;

In the deserts of the heart
Let the healing fountain start,
In the prison of his days
Teach the free man how to praise. 65

AT THAT MOMENT

Raymond R. Patterson (b. 1929)

FOR MALCOLM X

When they shot Malcolm Little down
On the stage of the Audubon Ballroom,
When his life ran out through bullet holes
(Like the people running out when the murder began)
His blood soaked the floor   5
One drop found a crack through the stark
Pounding thunder—slipped under the stage and began
Its journey: burrowed through concrete into the cellar,
Dropped down darkness, exploding like quicksilver
Pellets of light, panicking rats, paralyzing cockroaches—   10
Tunneled through rubble and wrecks of foundations,
The rocks that buttress the bowels of the city, flowed
Into pipes and powerlines, the mains and cables of the city:
A thousand fiery seeds.
At that moment,   15
Those who drank water where he entered . . .
Those who cooked food where he passed . . .
Those who burned light while he listened . . .
Those who were talking as he went, knew he was water
Running out of faucets, gas running out of jets, power   20
Running out of sockets, meaning running along taut wires—
To the hungers of their living. It is said
Whole slums of clotted Harlem plumbing groaned
And sundered free that day, and disconnected gas and light
Went on and on and on. . . .   25
They rushed his riddled body on a stretcher
To the hospital. But the police were too late.
It had already happened.

QUESTIONS

1. What additional poems do you feel should be included in the preceding contexts? Choose additional poems for each group and suggest reasons for including them.

2. Have you, in looking for more poems, found any that seem inferior (or superior) when compared with the poems presented here? Explain your answer.
3. How does reading poems in a thematic context give you a basis for criticism? How does it help you in making comparisons?
4. The poems that appear here are historically presented: the oldest appear first. Does this arrangement contribute in any way to a better understanding of the theme? Is it irrelevant here? Do you think it irrelevant in general?
5. Are there constants in these selections? Do you find the same core of interest or concern repeating itself? Do you find this in other poems on the same subject?
6. Try this experiment: Choose another theme, select some poems that seem appropriate, and put them together. What is the result of your effort? Do you find that your understanding or appreciation of them has increased? Do you find it makes a difference to those who read your collection? If not, why?

Formal Contexts

The Ballad

There are three kinds of ballad we ought to distinguish. One is the "ballad proper"—the ballad of the folklorist, the primitive ballad, the folksong. Another, which arises from this great mass of words and music, is the folksong that, printed as a poem, has come to assume an independent identity as a poem. Finally, there are poems—sometimes called literary ballads—that arose in modern, sophisticated, and literary circumstances; these are ballads only in the sense that the poet consciously drew on the traditions and characteristics of the ballad proper in order to create his poem. In this book we cannot be as concerned as we would like with the primitive ballads since they require music and must be performed. We have, however, presented a selection of folk ballads that have become part of literature as well as more recent literary ballads written under the influence of earlier folksongs.

The origin of a folk ballad, whether in tenth-century England or twentieth-century Appalachia, is musical and tribal. Ballads are songs of a folk—of a particular group of people—and, as such, they are meant to be sung, not published. The author is not interested in copyright but simply in performance. While these ballads are created by unusual individuals, they are also products of a group—dependent on a strong sense of community. Tristram P. Coffin remarks:

> A ballad survives among folk because it embodies a basic human reaction to a dramatic situation. This reaction is re-interpreted by

each person who renders a ballad. As an emotional core it dominates the artistic act, and melody setting, character, and plot are used only as a means to get it across. This core is more important to the singers and listeners than the details of the action. . . . Ballads resemble gossip. They are transmitted like gossip, and their variation comes about in much the same way gossip variation occurs. (MacEdward Leach, ed., *Critics and the Ballad* [Carbondale, Ill., 1961], p. 247.)

Robert Graves goes further in stressing the sense of communal participation. He recounts how the shared experiences of danger, hardship, isolation, and deprivation in the trenches in the First World War gave rise to genuine folk ballads. He continues:

When the word ballad was adopted by English singers, though the association with dancing did not survive, there remained latent in it the sense of rhythmic group action. . . . wherever this sense of group action remains in a ballad, let that ballad be distinguished as ballad proper. . . . (Robert Graves, *The English Ballad* [London, 1927], p. 8.)

The group actions Graves has in mind are such things as work songs, sea chanties, and marching songs.

It should be apparent why the ballad of oral traditions, the folksong, assumes a separate identity when published. It is divorced from its music, it is read instead of heard (or spoken instead of recited), and it takes on a meter instead of its original melody. Finally, it exists as literature rather than folksong, and, as literature, it affects poets and leads to new forms of poetic expression.

Historically, the process of removing the ballad from its origins began in the late eighteenth century when ballads began to be collected and published as examples of primitive literary efforts. Those editions of folk ballads were instrumental in the renewed interest of poets in the form and heralded the publication of such literary ballads as Samuel Taylor Coleridge's *Rime of the Ancient Mariner*. The impulse to adapt devices of ballad artistry to literary ends has continued unabated since the nineteenth-century Romantics; Robert Burns, Walter Scott, and Willam Wordsworth have been followed by John Masefield, William Butler Yeats, and Dylan Thomas. Additionally, a considerable body of impressive poetry related to, but distinct from, the folk ballad has been written, and is still being written.

The difficulty of defining primitive folksongs—not to mention their literary accretions—has been a frustrating problem. An early editor of ballads was reduced to the following definition: "What is a ballad?—A ballad is the 'Milldams of Binmorie' and 'Sir Patrick Spens' and 'The Douglas Tragedy' and 'Lord Randal' and 'Child Maurice,' and things of that sort." All of which means that anyone who has sung or heard "Jesse James," "Barbara Allen," or "John Henry" knows what a ballad is.

We will, however, list some general characteristics of the ballad. These characteristics are present in primitive ballads and more or less imitated by writers of more sophisticated literary ballads:

(1) All poetry has an oral tradition, and all lyric poetry is meant to be spoken. But ballads are meant to be sung. The ballad proper—not the literary ballad—cannot be separated from music and instruments.

(2) The song of the ballad is a narrative. It always tells a story marked by brevity. (The ballad is to narrative poetry what the short story is to the novel.) The ballad begins its story at or near the final act. Previous events are generally ignored or implied. This leads to a general sense of mystery, sometimes to simple confusion.

(3) The emphasis in the ballad narrative is on action. Character is not developed, circumstances are not explained in detail, causality and verisimilitude are not emphasized. The events of the story are meant to be self-explanatory; if there are gaps, the ballad singer does not worry.

(4) The tone of a ballad narrative is dramatic. The drama is foreshortened and intensified by its terseness and brevity. The tone is also impersonal and objective. There is little attempt by the author to interpret or to influence. And, since he is not telling his own story but a story for his community, he lets his narrative speak for itself.

(5) Many metrical effects are possible for the ballad writer, but essentially the meter of the ballad is dipodic. In a typical ballad line there are four feet, but the feet should be considered pairs because one foot has a slightly stronger stress than the other—thus imparting a lilting effect common in ballads. Here is an example:

$$\text{Her breath} \overset{/}{\text{grew strong}} \overset{/}{\text{her hair}} \overset{/}{\text{grew long,}}$$
$$\overset{/}{\text{And}} \overset{/}{\text{twisted}} \overset{/}{\text{thrice about}} \overset{/}{\text{the tree}}$$

The second and fourth stresses receive slightly greater emphasis.
(6) Ballads are written in varying combinations of the four-stress lines. Perhaps the most frequent is the four-stress quatrain:

> O was it wolf into the wood,
> Or was it fish intill the sea,
> Or was it man, or wily woman,
> My love, that misshapit thee?

But the most distinctive ballad form is the quatrain that has a four-stress line followed by a three-stress line:

> There lived a wife at Usher's Well
> And a stealthy wife was she;
> She had three stout and stalwart sons
> And sent them o'er the sea.

There is some evidence that such ballads were actually sung in couplets with seven stresses in each line. We see traces of this composition in some Anglo-American ballads. A native Maine ballad, for example, "The Jam on Gerry's Rock," begins:

> Come all of you brave shanty boys, wherever you may be,
> I pray you pay attention and listen unto me,
> Concerning six brave Canadian boys, so manfully and brave,
> Breaking a jam on Gerry's Rock they met a watery grave.

(7) Typically, a ballad—whether ancient or modern—deals with a single moment of tragedy or near-tragedy. There are notable exceptions to this such as "Get Up and Bar the Door," which has a humorous subject.
(8) The oral nature of the ballad requires a direct and straightforward language. As a result, similar situations or even similar phrases continually appear in different ballads. These phrases, along with repetitions and refrains, are used both because they help the singer remember the ballad, and because they have an emotional impact.

The more poems we know, the greater our ability to appreciate, analyze, and evaluate them. This is especially true when we know many poems of the same kind. Thus, the ability to cope with the following selections should steadily increase as we progress from ballads of earlier periods to those of the present age. And, knowing the characteristics and techniques of ballads in general will enhance the enjoyment and understanding of any ballad.

SIR PATRICK SPENS

Anonymous

The king sits in Dumferling town,
   Drinking the blude-reid wine:
"O whar will I get guid sailor,
   To sail this ship of mine?"

Up and spak an eldern knicht, 5
   Sat at the king's richt knee:
"Sir Patrick Spens is the best sailor
   That sails upon the sea."

The king has written a braid letter
   And signed it wi' his hand, 10
And sent it to Sir Patrick Spens,
   Was walking on the sand.

The first line that Sir Patrick read,
   A loud lauch lauched he;
The next line that Sir Patrick read, 15
   The tear blinded his ee.

"O wha is this has done this deed,
   This ill deed done to me,
To send me out this time o' the year,
   To sail upon the sea? 20

"Mak haste, mak haste, my mirry men all,
   Our guid ship sails the morn."
"O say na sae, my master dear,
   For I fear a deadly storm.

"Late, late yestre'en I saw the new moon 25
   Wi' the auld moon in hir arm,
And I fear, I fear, my dear master,
   That we will come to harm."

O our Scots nobles were richt laith
   To weet their cork-heeled shoon,
But lang or a' the play were played
   Their hats they swam aboon.

O lang, lang may their ladies sit,
   Wi' their fans into their hand,
Or ere they see Sir Patrick Spens
   Come sailing to the land.

O lang, lang may the ladies stand
   Wi' their gold kems in their hair,
Waiting for their ain dear lords,
   For they'll see them na mair.

Half o'er, half o'er to Aberdour
   It's fifty fadom deep,
And there lies guid Sir Patrick Spens
   Wi' the Scots lords at his feet.

BONNY BARBARA ALLAN

Anonymous

It was in and about the Martinmas time,
   When the green leaves were a falling,
That Sir John Graeme, in the West Country,
   Fell in love with Barbara Allan.

He sent his man down through the town,
   To the place where she was dwelling:
"O haste and come to my master dear,
   Gin ye be Barbara Allan."

O hooly, hooly rose she up,
   To the place where he was lying,
And when she drew the curtain by:
   "Young man, I think you're dying."

"O it's I'm sick, and very, very sick,
   And 'tis a' for Barbara Allan."
"O the better for me ye's never be,
   Though your heart's blood were a spilling.

"O dinna ye mind, young man," said she,
  "When ye was in the tavern a drinking,
That ye made the healths gae round and round,
  And slighted Barbara Allan?" 20

He turned his face unto the wall,
  And death was with him dealing:
"Adieu, adieu, my dear friends all,
  And be kind to Barbara Allan."

And slowly, slowly raise she up, 25
  And slowly, slowly left him,
And sighing said, she could not stay,
  Since death of life had reft him.

She had not gane a mile but twa,
  When she heard the dead-bell ringing, 30
And every jow that the dead-bell geid,
  It cried, "Woe to Barbara Allan!"

"O mother, mother, make my bed!
  O make it saft and narrow!
Since my love died for me to-day, 35
  I'll die for him to-morrow."

THE BAILIFF'S DAUGHTER OF ISLINGTON

Anonymous

There was a youth, and a well beloved youth,
  And he was a esquire's son,
He loved the bailiff's daughter dear,
  That lived in Islington.

She was coy, and she would not believe 5
  That he did love her so,
No, nor at any time she would
  Any countenance to him show.

But when his friends did understand
  His fond and foolish mind, 10
They sent him up to fair London,
  An apprentice for to bind.

And when he had been seven long years,
   And his love he had not seen:
"Many a tear have I shed for her sake   15
   When she little thought of me."

All the maids of Islington
   Went forth to sport and play;
All but the bailiff's daughter dear;
   She secretly stole away.   20

She put off her gown of gray,
   And put on her puggish attire;
She's up to fair London gone,
   Her true love to require.

As she went along the road,   25
   The weather being hot and dry,
There was she aware of her true love,
   At length came riding by.

She stepped to him, as red as any rose,
   And took him by the bridle-ring: 30
"I pray you, kind sir, give me one penny,
   To ease my weary limb."

"I prithee, sweetheart, canst thou tell me
   Where that thou wast born?"
"At Islington, kind sir," said she,   35
   "Where I have had many a scorn."

"I prithee, sweetheart, canst thou tell me
   Whether thou dost know
The bailiff's daughter of Islington?"
   "She's dead, sir, long ago."   40

"Then will I sell my goodly steed,
   My saddle and my bow;
I will into some far country,
   Where no man doth me know."

"O stay, O stay, thou goodly youth!   45
   She's alive, she is not dead;
Here she standeth by thy side,
   And is ready to be thy bride."

"O farewell grief, and welcome joy,
   Ten thousand times and more!   50
For now I have seen my own true love,
   That I thought I should have seen no more."

JOHNIE ARMSTRONG

Anonymous

There dwelt a man in fair Westmoreland,
    Johnie Armstrong men did him call,
He had neither lands nor rents coming in,
    Yet he kept eight score men in his hall.

He had horse and harness for them all,   5
    Goodly steeds were all milk-white;
O the golden bands an about their necks,
    And their weapons, they were all alike.

News then was brought unto the king
    That there was sic a one as he,   10
That livéd lyke a bold outlaw,
    And robbéd all the north country.

The king he writ an a letter then,
    A letter which was large and long;
He signéd it with his owne hand,   15
    And he promised to do him no wrong.

When this letter came Johnie untill,
    His heart it was as blythe as birds on the tree:
"Never was I sent for before any king,
    My father, my grandfather, nor none but me.   20

"And if we go the king before,
    I would we went most orderly;
Every man of you shall have his scarlet cloak,
    Laced with silver laces three.

"Every one of you shall have his velvet coat,   25
    Laced with silver lace so white;
O the golden bands an about your necks,
    Black hats, white feathers, all alike."

By the morrow morning at ten of the clock,
    Towards Edinburgh gone was he,   30
And with him all his eight score men;
    Good Lord, it was a goodly sight for to see!

When Johnie came before the king,
    He fell down on his knee;
"O pardon, my sovereign liege," he said,   35
    "O pardon my eight score men and me!"

"Thou shalt have no pardon, thou traitor strong,
  For thy eight score men nor thee;
For tomorrow morning by ten of the clock,
  Both thou and them shall hang on the gallow-tree." 40

But Johnie looked over his left shoulder,
  Good Lord, what a grevious look looked he!
Saying, "Asking grace of a graceless face—
  Why there is none for you nor me."

But Johnie had a bright sword by his side, 45
  And it was made of the metal so free,
That had not the king stepped his foot aside,
  He had smitten his head from his fair body.

Saying, "Fight on, my merry men all,
  And see that none of you be ta'en; 50
For rather than men shall say we were hanged,
  Let them report how we were slain."

Then, God wot, fair Edinburgh rose,
  And so beset poor Johnie round,
That fourscore and ten of Johnie's best men 55
  Lay gasping all upon the ground.

Then like a mad man Johnie laid about,
  And like a mad man then fought he,
Until a false Scot came Johnie behind,
  And run him through the fair body. 60

Saying, "Fight on, my merry men all,
  And see that none of you be ta'en;
For I will stand by and bleed but awhile,
  And then will I come and fight again."

News then was brought to young Johnie Armstrong, 65
  As he stood by his nurse's knee,
Who vowed if e'er he lived for to be a man,
  O' the treacherous Scots revenged he'd be.

GET UP AND BAR THE DOOR

Anonymous

It fell about the Martinmas time,
  And a gay time it was then,

When our goodwife got puddings to make,
    And she's boiled them in the pan.

The wind sae cauld blew south and north,   5
    And blew into the floor;
Quoth our goodman to our goodwife,
    "Gae out and bar the door."

"My hand is in my hussyfskap.
    Goodman, as ye may see;   10
An it should nae be barred this hundred year,
    It s' no be barred for me."

They made a paction 'tween them twa,
    They made it firm and sure,
That the first word whae'er should speak,   15
    Should rise and bar the door.

Then by there came two gentlemen,
    At twelve o'clock at night,
And they could neither see house nor hall,
    Nor coal nor candle-light.   20

"Now whether is this a rich man's house,
    Or whether is it a poor?"
But ne'er a word wad ane o' them speak,
    For barring of the door.

And first they ate the white puddings,   25
    And then they ate the black;
Though muckle thought the goodwife to hersel,
    Yet ne'er a word she spak.

Then said the one unto the other,
    "Here, man, tak ye my knife;   30
Do ye tak aff the auld man's beard,
    And I'll kiss the goodwife."

"But there's nae water in the house,
    And what shall we do then?"
"What ails ye at the pudding-bree,   35
    That boils into the pan?"

O up then started our goodman,
    An angry man was he:
"Will ye kiss my wife before my een,
    And scad me wi' pudding-bree?"   40

Then up and started our goodwife,
Gied three skips on the floor:
"Goodman, you've spoken the foremost word,
Get up and bar the door."

FRANKIE AND ALBERT

Anonymous

Frankie and Albert were sweethearts, everybody knows,
Frankie spent a hundred dollars just to get her man some clothes;
   He was her man, but he done her wrong.

Frankie went down to the corner, took along a can,
Says to the lovin' bartender, "Has you seen my lovin' man?   5
   He is my man, but he's doin' me wrong."

"Well, I ain't gonna tell you no story, ain't gonna tell you no lie,
Albert went by 'bout an hour ago, with a girl called Alice Fry;
   He was your man, but he's doin' you wrong."

Frankie's gone from the corner, Frankie ain't gone for fun,   10
Underneath her apron she's got Albert's gatlin' gun;
   He was her man, but he done her wrong.

Albert sees Frankie comin', out the back door he did scoot,
Frankie pulled out the pistol, went roota-de-toot-toot-toot.
   He was her man, but she shot him down.   15

Frankie shot him once, Frankie shot him twice,
Third time she shot him the bullet took his life;
   He was her man, but he done her wrong.

When Frankie shot Albert, he fell down on his knees,
Looked up at her and said, "Oh, Frankie, please,   20
   Don't shoot me no mo', don't shoot me no mo'.

"Oh, turn me over, doctor; turn me over slow,
Turn me over on my right side, 'cause the bullet am hurtin' me so.
   I was her man, but I done her wrong."

Now its rubber-tired carriages, decorated hack,   25
Eleven men went to the graveyard, and only ten come back;
   He was her man, but he's dead and gone.

Frankie was a-standin' on the corner, watchin' de hearse go by,
Throwed her arms into the air, "Oh, let me lie
   By the side of my man, what done me wrong."   30

Frankie went to the graveyard, bowed down on her knees,
"Speak one word to me, Albert, an' give my heart some ease.
   You was my man, but I done you wrong."

Sheriff arrested Frankie, took her to the county jail,
Locked her up in a dungeon cell, and throwed the keys away.   35
   She shot her man, said he done her wrong.

Judge tried lil' Frankie, under an electric fan;
Judge says, "Yo' free woman now, go kill yourself anothah man.
   He was yo' man, now he's dead an' gone."

POOR OMIE

Anonymous

"You promised to meet me at Adam's spring;
Some money you would bring me, or some other fine thing."

"No money, no money, to flatter the case,
We'll go and get married, it will be no disgrace.

"Come jump up behind me and away we will ride   5
To yonder fair city; I will make you my bride."

She jumped up behind him and away they did go
To the banks of deep waters where they never overflow.

"O Omie, O Omie, I will tell you my mind;
My mind is to drown you and leave you behind."   10

"O pity! O pity! Pray spare me my life,
And I will deny you and not be your wife."

"No pity, no pity, no pity have I;
In yonder deep water your body shall lie."

He kicked her and stomped her, he threw her in the deep;   15
He jumped on his pony and rode at full speed.

The screams of poor Omie followed after him so nigh,
Saying: "I am a poor rebel not fitten to die."

She was missing one evening, next morning was found
In the bottom of Siloty below the mill dam.   20

Up stepped old Miss Mother, these words she did say:
"James Luther has killed Omie and he has run away.

"He has gone to Elk River, so I understand,
They have got him in prison for killing a man."

They have got him in Ireland, bound to the ground;   25
And he wrote his confession and sent it around.

"Go hang me or kill me, for I am the man
That drowned little Omie below the mill dam."

JESSE JAMES

Anonymous

It was on a Wednesday night, the moon was shining bright,
    They robbed the Glendale train.
And the people they did say, for many miles away,
    'Twas the outlaws Frank and Jesse James.

Refrain—Jesse had a wife to mourn all her life,   5
    The children they are brave.
'Twas a dirty little coward shot Mister Howard,
    And laid Jesse James in his grave.

It was Robert Ford, the dirty little coward,
    I wonder how he does feel,   10
For he ate of Jesse's bread and slept in Jesse's bed,
    Then he laid Jesse James in his grave.

It was his brother Frank that robbed the Gallatin bank,
    And carried the money from the town.
It was in this very place that they had a little race,   15
    For they shot Captain Sheets to the ground.

They went to the crossing not very far from there,
    And there they did the same;
And the agent on his knees he delivered up the keys
    To the outlaws Frank and Jesse James.   20

It was on a Saturday night, Jesse was at home
    Talking to his family brave,
When the thief and the coward, little Robert Ford,
    Laid Jesse James in his grave.

How people held their breath when they heard of Jesse's death,   25
    And wondered how he ever came to die.
'Twas one of the gang, dirty Robert Ford,
    That shot Jesse James on the sly.

Jesse went to his rest with his hand on his breast.
    The devil will be upon his knee.   30
He was born one day in the county of Clay,
    And came from a solitary race.

THE JAM ON GERRY'S ROCK

Anonymous

Come all of you brave shanty boys, wherever you may be,
I pray you pay attention and listen unto me,
Concerning six brave Canadian boys, so manfully and brave,
Breaking a jam on Gerry's Rock they met a watery grave.

It being on a Sunday morning, the truth you shall hear,   5
Our logs were piled up mountain high, we could not keep them clear;
The foreman says: "Turn out, my boys, without no dread or fear,
We'll break the jam on Gerry's Rock and for Logantown we'll
    steer."

And some of them were willing, whilst others did stand back,
For to work upon a Sunday they did not think 'twas right,   10
Whilst six of those brave shanty boys did volunteer to go
To break the jam on Gerry's Rock, with their foreman young
    Munroe

They had not been on the jam long when the boss to them did say:
"I would have you be on your guard, for the jam will soon give
    way."
And scarcely had he spoke those words, when the jam did break
    and go,   15
Carrying off those six brave shanty boys and the foreman young
    Munroe.

When the rest of those brave shanty boys sad tidings came to hear,
For to search for their dead bodies to the river they did steer,
And amongst those reckless bodies to their sad grief and woe,
All cut and mangled on the beach was the head of young Munroe.   20

They raised it from the watery grave, combed down his raven hair;
There was one fair form among them whose groans did rent the air,
[There was one fair form among them], a girl from Sidney town,
Whose groans and cries did rent the skies for her lover who was
    drowned.

They buried him quite decently, being on the first of May;   25
It's come all of you brave shanty boys and for your comrade pray.
They engraved it on a tree close by his grave doth grow,
His age—his name—the drowning of that hero young Munroe.

Miss Carro was a handsome girl, likewise [the] Rogueman's
    friend,
Her mother was a widow, lived by the River Glenn,   30
And the wages of her own true love the boss to her did pay,
And a little subscription she secured from the shanty boys next day.

Miss Carro did not long survive to her sad grief and woe,
In a space of six months after Death called on her to go,
And her request was granted to be buried with young Munroe.   35

Now it's come all of you brave shanty boys, who'd like to
    come and see
A little mound by the river side, where grew a hemlock tree.
The shanty boys they cut their woods—two lovers they lie low;
There lies Miss Carro in her grave and her foreman young Munroe.

JOHN HENRY

Anonymous

Lissen to my story;
'Tis a story true;
'Bout a mighty man,—John Henry was his name,
An' John Henry was a steel-driver too—
Lawd,—Lawd,—   5
John Henry was a steel-driver too.

John Henry had a hammah;
Weighed nigh fo'ty poun';
Eb'ry time John made a strike
He seen his steel go 'bout two inches down,
Lawd,—Lawd,—
He seen his steel go 'bout two inches down.

John Henry's woman, Lucy,—
Dress she wore was blue;
Eyes like stars an' teeth lak-a marble stone,
An' John Henry named his hammah "Lucy" too,—
Lawd,—Lawd,—
John Henry named his hammah "Lucy" too.

Lucy came to see him;
Bucket in huh han';
All th' time John Henry ate his snack,
O Lucy she'd drive steel lak-a man,—
Lawd,—Lawd,—
O Lucy she'd drive steel lak-a man.

John Henry's cap'n Tommy,—
V'ginny gave him birth;
Loved John Henry like his only son,
And Cap' Tommy was the whitest man on earth,—
Lawd,—Lawd,—
Cap' Tommy was th' whitest man on earth.

One day Cap' Tommy told him
How he'd bet a man;
Bet John Henry'd beat a steam-drill down,
Jes' cause he was th' best in th' lan',—
Lawd,—Lawd,—
'Cause he was th' best in th' lan'.

John Henry tol' Cap' Tommy;
Lightnin' in his eye;
"Cap'n, bet yo' las' red cent on me,
Fo' I'll beat it to th' bottom or I'll die,—
Lawd,—Lawd,—
I'll beat it to the bottom or I'll die.

"Co'n pone's in my stomach;
Hammah's in my han';
Haint no steam-drill on dis railroad job

Can beat 'Lucy' an' her steel-drivin' man,
Lawd,—Lawd,—
Can beat 'Lucy' an' her steel-drivin' man.

"Bells ring on de engines;
Runnin' down th' line;   50
Dinnah's done when Lucy pulls th' co'd;
But no hammah in this mountain rings like mine,—
Lawd,—Lawd,—
No hammah in this mountain rings like mine."

Sun shined hot an' burnin'   55
Wer'n't no breeze at-tall;
Sweat ran down like watah down a hill
That day John Henry let his hammah fall,—
Lawd,—Lawd,—
That day John Henry let his hammah fall.   60

John Henry kissed his hammah;
White Man turned on steam;
Li'l Bill held John Henry's trusty steel,—
'Twas th' biggest race th' worl' had ever seen,—
Lawd,—Lawd,—   65
Th' biggest race th' worl' had ever seen.

White Man tol' John Henry,—
"Niggah, dam yo' soul,
You might beat dis steam an' drill o' mine
When th' rocks in this mountain turn to gol',—   70
Lawd,—Lawd,—
When th' rocks in this mountain turn to gol'."

John Henry tol' th' white man;
Tol' him kind-a sad:
"Cap'n George, I want-a be yo' fr'en;   75
If I beat yo' to th' bottom, don't git mad,—
Lawd,—Lawd,—
If I beat yo' to th' bottom don't git mad."

Cap' Tommy sees John Henry's
Steel a-hitin' in;   80
Cap'n slaps John Henry on th' back,
Says, "I'll give yo' fifty dollars if yo' win,
Lawd,—Lawd,—
I'll give yo' fifty dollars if yo' win."

White Man saw John Henry's   85
Steel a-goin' down;
White Man says,—"That man's a mighty man,
But he'll weaken when th' hardes' rock is foun',—
Lawd,—Lawd,—
He'll weaken when th' hardes' rock is foun'."   90

John Henry, O John Henry,—
John Henry's hammah too;
When a woman's 'pendin' on a man
Haint no tellin' what a mighty man can do,—
Lawd,—Lawd,—   95
No tellin' what a mighty man can do.

John Henry, O John Henry!
Blood am runnin' red!
Falls right down with his hammah to th' groun',
Says, "I've beat him to th' bottom but I'm dead,—   100
Lawd,—Lawd,—
I've beat him to the bottom but I'm dead."

John Henry kissed his hammah;
Kissed it with a groan;
Sighed a sigh an' closed his weary eyes,   105
Now po' Lucy has no man to call huh own,—
Lawd,—Lawd,—
Po' Lucy has no man to call huh own.

Cap' Tommy came a-runnin'
To John Henry's side;   110
Says, "Lawd, Lawd,—O Lawdy, Lawdy, Lawd,—
He's beat it to th' bottom but he's died,—
Lawd,—Lawd,—
He's beat it to th' bottom but he's died."

Lucy ran to see him;   115
Dress she wore was blue;
Started down th' track an' she nevvah did turn back,
Sayin', "John Henry, I'll be true—true to you,—
Lawd,—Lawd,—
John Henry, I'll be true—true to you."   120

John Henry, O John Henry!
Sing it if yo' can,—
High an' low an' ev'ry where yo' go,—

He died with his hammah in his han',—
Lawd,—Lawd,— 125
He died with his hammah in his han'.

Buddie, where'd yo' come from
To this railroad job?
If yo' wantta be a good steel-drivin' man,
Put yo' trus' in yo' hammah an' yo' God,— 130
Lawd,—Lawd,—
Put yo' trus' in yo' hammah an' yo' God.

THE TRUE LOVER

A. E. Housman (1859–1936)

The lad came to the door at night,
  When lovers crown their vows,
And whistled soft and out of sight
  In shadow of the boughs.

"I shall not vex you with my face 5
  Henceforth, my love, for aye;
So take me in your arms a space
  Before the east is grey.

"When I from hence away am past
  I shall not find a bride, 10
And you shall be the first and last
  I ever lay beside."

She heard and went and knew not why;
  Her heart to his she laid;
Light was the air beneath the sky 15
  But dark under the shade.

"Oh do you breathe, lad, that your breast
  Seems not to rise and fall,
And here upon my bosom prest
  There beats no heart at all?" 20

"Oh loud, my girl, it once would knock,
  You should have felt it then;

But since for you I stopped the clock
    It never goes again."

"Oh, lad, what is it, lad, that drips   25
    Wet from your neck on mine?
What is it falling on my lips,
    My lad, that tastes of brine?"

"Oh like enough 'tis blood, my dear,
    For when the knife has slit   30
The throat across from ear to ear
    'Twill bleed because of it."

Under the stars the air was light
    But dark below the boughs,
The still air of the speechless night,   35
    When lovers crown their vows.

BALLAD OF THE GOODLY FERE

Ezra Pound (1885–1972)

Simon Zelotes speaketh it somewhile after the Crucifixion.

Ha' we lost the goodliest fere o' all
For the priests and the gallows tree?
Aye lover he was of brawny men,
O' ships and the open sea.

When they came wi' a host to take Our Man   5
His smile was good to see,
"First let these go!" quo' our Goodly Fere,
"Or I'll see ye damned," says he.

Aye he sent us out through the crossed high spears
And the scorn of his laugh rang free,   10
"Why took ye not me when I walked about
Alone in the town?" says he.

Oh we drank his "Hale" in the good red wine
When we last made company,
No capon priest was the Goodly Fere   15
But a man o' men was he.

I ha' seen him drive a hundred men
Wi' a bundle o' cords swung free,
That they took the high and holy house
For their pawn and treasury.   20

They'll no' get him a' in a book I think
Though they write it cunningly;
No mouse of the scrolls was the Goodly Fere
But aye loved the open sea.

If they think they ha' snared our Goodly Fere   25
They are fools to the last degree.
"I'll go to the feast," quo' our Goodly Fere,
"Though I go to the gallows tree."

"Ye ha' seen me heal the lame and blind,
And wake the dead," says he,   30
"Ye shall see one thing to master all:
'Tis how a brave man dies on the tree."

A son of God was the Goodly Fere
That bade us his brothers be.
I ha' seen him cow a thousand men.   35
I have seen him upon the tree.

He cried no cry when they drave the nails
And the blood gushed hot and free,
The hounds of the crimson sky gave tongue
But never a cry cried he.   40

I ha' seen him cow a thousand men
On the hills o' Galilee,
They whined as he walked out calm between,
Wi' his eyes like the grey o' the sea,

Like the sea that brooks no voyaging   45
With the winds unleashed and free,
Like the sea that he cowed at Genseret
Wi' twey words spoke' suddenly.

A master of men was the Goodly Fere,
A mate of the wind and sea,   50
If they think they ha' slain our Goodly Fere
They are fools eternally.

I ha' seen him eat o' the honey-comb
Sin' they nailed him to the tree.

BALLAD OF THE LANDLORD

Langston Hughes (1902–1967)

Landlord, landlord,
My roof has sprung a leak.
Don't you 'member I told you about it
Way last week?

Landlord, landlord,   5
These steps is broken down.
When you come up yourself
It's a wonder you don't fall down.

Ten Bucks you say I owe you?
Ten Bucks you say is due?   10
Well, that's Ten Bucks more'n I'll pay you
Till you fix this house up new.

What? You gonna get eviction orders?
You gonna cut off my heat?
You gonna take my furniture and   15
Throw it in the street?

Um-huh! You talking high and mighty.
Talk on—till you get through.
You ain't gonna be able to say a word
If I land my fist on you.   20

Police! Police!
Come and get this man!
He's trying to ruin the government
And overturn the land!

Copper's whistle!   25
Patrol bell!
Arrest.

Precinct Station.
Iron cell.
Headlines in press: 30

MAN THREATENS LANDLORD

TENANT HELD NO BAIL

JUDGE GIVES NEGRO 90 DAYS IN COUNTY JAIL

O WHAT IS THAT SOUND

W. H. Auden (1907–1973)

O what is that sound which so thrills the ear
    Down in the valley drumming, drumming?
Only the scarlet soldiers, dear,
    The soldiers coming.

O what is that light I see flashing so clear   5
    Over the distance brightly, brightly?
Only the sun on their weapons, dear,
    As they step lightly.

O what are they doing with all that gear,
    What are they doing this morning, this morning?   10
Only their usual manoeuvres, dear,
    Or perhaps a warning.

O why have they left the road down there,
    Why are they suddenly wheeling, wheeling?
Perhaps a change in their orders, dear.   15
    Why are you kneeling?

O haven't they stopped for the doctor's care,
    Haven't they reined their horses, their horses?
Why, they are none of them wounded, dear,
    None of these forces.   20

O is it the parson they want, with white hair,
    Is it the parson, is it, is it?
No, they are passing his gateway, dear,
    Without a visit.

O it must be the farmer who lives so near.   25
    It must be the farmer so cunning, so cunning?
They have passed the farmyard already, dear,
    And now they are running.

O where are you going? Stay with me here!
    Were the vows you swore deceiving, deceiving?   30
No, I promised to love you, dear,
    But I must be leaving.

O it's broken the lock and splintered the door,
    O it's the gate where they're turning, turning;
Their boots are heavy on the floor   35
    And their eyes are burning.

THE BALLAD OF RUDOLPH REED
Gwendolyn Brooks (b. 1917)

Rudolph Reed was oaken.
His wife was oaken too.
And his two good girls and his good little man
Oaken as they grew.

"I am not hungry for berries.   5
I am not hungry for bread.
But hungry hungry for a house
Where at night a man in bed

"May never hear the plaster
Stir as if in pain.   10
May never hear the roaches
Falling like fat rain.

"Where never wife and children need
Go blinking through the gloom.
Where every room of many rooms   15
Will be full of room.

"Oh my home may have its east or west
Or north or south behind it.
All I know is I shall know it,
And fight for it when I find it."   20

It was in a street of bitter white
That he made his application.
For Rudolph Reed was oakener
Than others in the nation.

The agent's steep and steady stare   25
Corroded to a grin.
Why, you black old, tough old hell of a man,
Move your family in!

Nary a grin grinned Rudolph Reed,,
Nary a curse cursed he,   30
But moved in his House. With his dark little wife,
And his dark little children three.

A neighbor would look, with a yawning eye
That squeezed into a slit.
But the Rudolph Reeds and the children three   35
Were too joyous to notice it.

For were they not firm in a home of their own
With windows everywhere
And a beautiful banistered stair
And a front yard for flowers and a back yard for grass? 40

The first night, a rock, big as two fists.
The second, a rock big as three
But nary a curse cursed Rudolph Reed.
(Though oaken as man could be.)

The third night, a silvery ring of glass. 45
Patience ached to endure.
But he looked, and lo! small Mabel's blood
Was staining her gaze so pure.

Then up did rise our Rudolph Reed
And pressed the hand of his wife, 50
And went to the door with a thirty-four
And a beastly butcher knife.

He ran like a mad thing into the night.
And the words in his mouth were stinking.
By the time he had hurt his first white man 55
He was no longer thinking.

By the time he had hurt his fourth white man
Rudolph Reed was dead.
His neighbors gathered and kicked his corpse.
"Nigger—" his neighbors said. 60

Small Mabel whimpered all night long,
For calling herself the cause.
Her oak-eyed mother did no thing
But change the bloody gauze.

DOWN IN DALLAS

X. J. Kennedy (b. 1929)

Down in Dallas, down in Dallas
Where the shadow of blood lies black
Lee Oswald nailed Jack Kennedy up
With the nail of a rifle crack.

The big bright Cadillacs stomped on their brakes 5
And the man in the street fell still
When the slithering gun like a tooth of sin
Coiled back from the window sill.

In a white chrome room on a table top,
Oh, they tried all a scapel knows 10
But they couldn't spell stop to that drop-by-drop
Till it bloomed to a rigid rose.

Down on the altar, down on the altar
Christ blossoms in bread and wine
But each asphalt stone where the blood dropped down 15
Is burst to a cactus spine.

Oh down in Dallas, down in Dallas
Where a desert wind walks by night
Lee Oswald nailed Jack Kennedy up
On the cross of a rifle sight.

The Sonnet

The sonnet is the most frequently written formal poem in English. It consists of fourteen lines of iambic pentameter and employs a wide variety of rhyme schemes. The early English sonnets were adapted from Petrarch, the Italian poet (1304–1374), and they followed an *abba abba cd cd cd* rhyme scheme. However, the rhymes of the final six lines did not always keep the above pattern. Sometimes they were *cdc cde*, or *cdcdee*, or *cdeced*. Additionally, there have been three other types of sonnets in English: the Spenserian (*abab bcbc cdcd ee*), the Shakespearean (*abab cdcd efef gg*), and the Miltonic (rhymed like the Petrarchan)—which differs from the Petrarchan in the way the thought is unfolded in the poem.

A basic feature of the Petrarchan (or Italian) sonnet, commonly found in almost all sonnets that appeared in succeeding centuries, is a sharp break in the ideas presented in the poem. This break, or "turn," occurs after the eighth line. The first eight lines—the octave

—present one view, the last six lines—the sestet—offer an added perspective. Typically, a Petrarchan octave presents a situation, problem, or dilemma in the first four lines and an intensification of that situation in the next four lines. The sestet offers a conclusion, perhaps even a solution or resolution, to the problem. A version of this formal pattern is evident in John Keats's famous sonnet describing how he felt after having read a new translation of Homer's poetry. In the first stanza he says that he knows something about poetry. In the second stanza he says that, although he had heard of Homer's greatness, he had not read him until he saw Chapman's translation. The sestet concludes by describing the encounter with Homer—how it felt to travel in "the realms of gold."

ON FIRST LOOKING INTO CHAPMAN'S HOMER

John Keats (1795–1821)

Much have I traveled in the realms of gold,
   And many goodly states and kingdoms seen;
   Round many western islands have I been
Which bards in fealty to Apollo hold.
Oft of one wide expanse had I been told   5
   That deep-browed Homer ruled as his demesne;
   Yet did I never breathe its pure serene
Till I heard Chapman speak out loud and bold:
Then felt I like some watcher of the skies
   When a new planet swims into his ken;   10
Or like stout Cortez when with eagle eyes
   He stared at the Pacific—and all his men
Looked at each other with a wild surmise—
   Silent, upon a peak in Darien.

Shakespeare modified the Petrarchan sonnet by extending the turn to the final two lines. The first part of the Shakespearean (or English) sonnet consists of three quatrains rhymed *abab cdcd efef*. The thought, situation, or problem presented in the first twelve lines commonly finds its climax, solution, summary, or simply, its concluding comment in the final two lines—a couplet rhymed *gg*.

Another type of sonnet that once enjoyed some slight popularity is the Miltonic sonnet. Similar to the Petrarchan in its rhymes, the pivotal switch in the poet's thought, however, usually does not occur in the eighth line, but afterward—in the ninth line, or even later.

Modern poets have tried many variations of the sonnet. In experimenting they have sometimes dropped the crucial notion of the turn and have used a great variety of line endings—rhymed and unrhymed. Some, like Gerard Manley Hopkins, have even written poems with fewer than fourteen lines as sonnet variations. Hopkins called his ten-line poem "Pied Beauty" a "curtel" sonnet—an abbreviated sonnet. A six-line first part corresponded with the traditional octave and a four-line second part corresponded with the sestet. George Meredith wrote a "sonnet" sequence consisting of poems with sixteen lines, and critics have occasionally referred to Wallace Stevens's sixteen-line "Sunday-morning" sequence as sonnets. However, there seems to be little justification for calling such poems sonnets. Conversely, should we call every fourteen-line poem a sonnet? Although we may do so, we should be well aware that traditionally a sonnet is a fourteen-line poem with a specific rhyme scheme and a break, or turn, in the poem's thought.

The sonnets that follow demonstrate the traditional Petrarchan, Miltonic, and Shakespearean forms, as well as later innovations. Although the reader should try to ascertain whether each sonnet is successful in its own right, it is also important that he note what each selection achieves, or fails to achieve, by adhering to or ignoring the conventions of the sonnet.

SONNET 18

William Shakespeare (1564–1616)

Shall I compare thee to a summer's day?
Thou art more lovely and more temperate:
Rough winds do shake the darling buds of May,
And summer's lease hath all too short a date:
Sometimes too hot the eye of heaven shines,   5
And often is his gold complexion dimmed;
And every fair from fair sometimes declines,
By chance or natures' changing course untrimmed;
But thy eternal summer shall not fade,
Nor lose possession of that fair thou ow'st;   10
Nor shall death brag thou wander'st in his shade,
When in eternal lines to time thou grow'st:

So long as men can breathe, or eyes can see,
So long lives this, and this gives life to thee.

SONNET 30

William Shakespeare

When to the sessions of sweet silent thought
I summon up remembrance of things past,
I sigh the lack of many a thing I sought,
And with old woes new wail my dear time's waste:
Then can I drown an eye, unused to flow,   5
For precious friends hid in death's dateless night,
And weep afresh love's long since canceled woe,
And moan the expense of many a vanished sight:
Then can I grieve at grievances foregone,
And heavily from woe to woe tell o'er   10
The sad account of fore-bemoaned moan,
Which I new pay as if not paid before.
But if the while I think on thee, dear friend,
All losses are restored and sorrows end.

SONNET 73

William Shakespeare

That time of year thou mayst in me behold
When yellow leaves, or none, or few, do hang
Upon those boughs which shake against the cold,
Bare ruined choirs, where late the sweet birds sang.
In me thou see'st the twilight of such day   5
As after sunset fadeth in the west;
Which by and by black night doth take away,
Death's second self, that seals up all in rest.
In me thou see'st the glowing of such fire,
That on the ashes of his youth doth lie,   10
As the deathbed whereon it must expire,
Consumed with that which it was nourished by.
This thou perceiv'st, which makes thy love more strong,
To love that well which thou must leave ere long.

SONNET 97

William Shakespeare

How like a winter hath my absence been
From thee, the pleasure of the fleeting year!
What freezings have I felt, what dark days seen!
What old December's bareness everywhere!
And yet this time removed was summer's time,   5
The teeming autumn, big with rich increase,
Bearing the wanton burthen of the prime,
Like widowed wombs after their lords' decease;
Yet this abundant issue seemed to me
But hope of orphans and unfathered fruit;   10
For summer and his pleasures wait on thee,
And, thou away, the very birds are mute;
Or, if they sing, 'tis with so dull a cheer
That leaves look pale, dreading the winter's near.

SONNET 116

William Shakespeare

Let me not to the marriage of true minds
Admit impediments. Love is not love
Which alters when it alteration finds,
Or bends with the remover to remove:
Oh, no! it is an ever-fixed mark,   5
That looks on tempests and is never shaken;
It is the star to every wandering bark,
Whose worth's unknown, although his height be taken.
Love's not Time's fool, though rosy lips and cheeks
Within his bending sickle's compass come;   10
Love alters not with his brief hours and weeks,
But bears it out even to the edge of doom.
If this be error and upon me proved,
I never writ, nor no man ever loved.

SONNET 129

William Shakespeare

Th' expense of spirit in a waste of shame
Is lust in action; and till action, lust
Is perjured, murderous, bloody, full of blame,
Savage, extreme, rude, cruel, not to trust;
Enjoyed no sooner but despised straight: 5
Past reason hunted; and no sooner had,
Past reason hated, as a swallowed bait,
On purpose laid to make the taker mad:
Mad in pursuit, and in possession so;
Had, having, and in quest to have, extreme;   10
A bliss in proof, and proved, a very woe;
Before, a joy proposed; behind, a dream.
All this the world well knows; yet none knows well
To shun the heaven that leads men to this hell.

SONNET 147

William Shakespeare

My love is as a fever, longing still
For that which longer nurseth the disease;
Feeding on that which doth preserve the ill,
Th' uncertain sickly appetite to please.
My reason, the physician to my love,   5
Angry that his prescriptions are not kept,
Hath left me, and I desperate now approve
Desire is death, which physic did except.
Past cure I am, now reason is past care,
And frantic-mad with evermore unrest;   10
My thoughts and my discourse as madmen's are,
At random from the truth vainly expressed;
For I have sworn thee fair, and thought thee bright,
Who art as black as hell, as dark as night.

HOLY SONNET 5

John Donne (1572?–1631)

I am a little world made cunningly
Of elements, and an angelic sprite;
But black sin hath betrayed to endless night
My world's both parts, and O, both parts must die.
You which beyond that heaven which was most high   5
Have found new spheres, and of new lands can write,
Pour new seas in mine eyes, that so I might
Drown my world with my weeping earnestly,
Or wash it if it must be drowned no more.
But O, it must be burnt! Alas, the fire   10
Of lust and envy'have burnt it heretofore,
And made it fouler; let their flames retire,
And burn me, O Lord, with a fiery zeal
Of Thee'and Thy house, which doth in eating heal.

HOLY SONNET 7

John Donne

At the round earth's imagined corners, blow
Your trumpets, angels; and arise, arise
From death, you numberless infinities
Of souls, and to your scattered bodies go;
All whom the flood did, and fire shall, o'erthrow,   5
All whom war, dearth, age, agues, tyrannies,
Despair, law, chance hath slain, and you whose eyes
Shall behold God, and never taste death's woe.
But let them sleep, Lord, and me mourn a space;
For, if above all these, my sins abound,   10
'Tis late to ask abundance of Thy grace
When we are there. Here on this lowly ground,
Teach me how to repent; for that's as good
As if Thou'hadst sealed my pardon with Thy blood.

HOLY SONNET 10

John Donne

Death, be not proud, though some have called thee
Mighty and dreadful, for thou are not so;
For those whom thou think'st thou dost overthrow
Die not, poor Death, nor yet canst thou kill me.
From rest and sleep, which but thy pictures be,   5
Much pleasure; then from thee much more must flow,
And soonest our best men with thee do go,
Rest of their bones, and soul's delivery.
Thou'art slave to fate, chance, kings, and desperate men,
And dost with poison, war, and sickness dwell,   10
And poppy'or charms can make us sleep as well
And better than thy stroke; why swell'st thou then?
One short sleep past, we wake eternally
And death shall be no more; Death, thou shalt die.

HOLY SONNET 14

John Donne

Batter my heart, three-personed God; for You
As yet but knock, breathe, shine, and seek to mend;
That I may rise and stand, o'erthrow me,'and bend
Your force to break, blow, burn, and make me new.
I, like an usurped town, to'another due,   5
Labor to'admit You, but O, to no end;
Reason, Your viceroy'in me, me should defend,
But is captíved, and proves weak or untrue.
Yet dearly'I love You,' and would be lovéd fain,
But am betrothed unto Your enemy.   10
Divorce me,'untie or break that knot again;
Take me to You, imprison me, for I,
Except You'enthrall me, never shall be free,
Nor ever chaste, except You ravish me.

HOW SOON HATH TIME
John Milton (1608–1674)

How soon hath Time, the subtle thief of youth,
  Stolen on his wing my three and twentieth year!
  My hasting days fly on with full career,
  But my late spring no bud or blossom shewith,
Perhaps my semblance might deceive the truth   5
  That I to manhood am arrived so near,
  And inward ripeness doth much less appear,
  That some more timely-happy spirits indueth.
Yet be it less or more, or soon or slow,
  It shall be still in strictest measure even   10
  To that same lot, however mean or high,
Toward which Time leads me, and the will of Heaven;
  All is, if I have grace to use it so,
  As ever in my great Taskmaster's eye.

ON SHAKESPEARE
John Milton

  What needs my Shakespeare for his honored bones
  The labor of an age in piléd stones?
  Or that his hallowed reliques should be hid
  Under a star-ypointing pyramid?
  Dear son of Memory, great heir of Fame,   5
  What need'st thou such weak witness of thy name?
  Thou in our wonder and astonishment
  Hast built thyself a livelong monument.
  For whilst, to th' shame of slow-endeavoring art,
  Thy easy numbers flow, and that each heart   10
  Hath from the leaves of thy unvalued book
  Those Delphic lines with deep impression took,
  Then thou, our fancy of itself bereaving,
  Dost make us marble with too much conceiving,
  And so sepúlchred in such pomp dost lie   15
  That kings for such a tomb would wish to die.

---

8. **indueth:** endoweth.

WHEN I CONSIDER HOW MY LIGHT IS SPENT

John Milton

When I consider how my light is spent
  Ere half my days, in this dark world and wide,
  And that one talent which is death to hide
  Lodged with me useless, though my soul more bent
To serve therewith my Maker, and present   5
  My true account, lest he returning chide;
  "Doth God exact day-labor, light denied?"
  I fondly ask; but Patience to prevent
That murmur, soon replies, "God doth not need
  Either man's work or his own gifts; who best   10
  Bear his mild yoke, they serve him best. His state
Is kingly. Thousands at his bidding speed
  And post o'er land and ocean without rest:
  They also serve who only stand and wait."

IT IS A BEAUTEOUS EVENING

William Wordsworth (1770–1850)

It is a beauteous evening, calm and free,
The holy time is quiet as a Nun
Breathless with adoration; the broad sun
Is sinking down in its tranquility;
The gentleness of heaven broods o'er the Sea: 5
Listen! the mighty Being is awake,
And doth with his eternal motion make
A sound like thunder—everlastingly.
Dear Child! dear Girl! that walkest with me here,
If thou appear untouched by solemn thought,   10
Thy nature is not therefore less divine:
Thou liest in Abraham's bosom all the year,
And worship'st at the Temple's inner shrine,
God being with thee when we know it not.

LONDON, 1802

William Wordsworth

Milton! thou shouldst be living at this hour:
England hath need of thee: she is a fen
Of stagnant waters: altar, sword, and pen,
Fireside, the heroic wealth of hall and bower,
Have forfeited their ancient English dower   5
Of inward happiness. We are selfish men;
Oh! raise us up, return to us again;
And give us manners, virtue, freedom power.
Thy soul was like a Star, and dwelt apart;
Thou hadst a voice whose sound was like the sea: 10
Pure as the naked heavens, majestic, free,
So didst thou travel on life's common way,
In cheerful godliness; and yet thy heart
The lowliest duties on herself did lay.

COMPOSED UPON WESTMINSTER BRIDGE, SEPTEMBER 3, 1802

William Wordsworth

Earth has not anything to show more fair:
Dull would he be of soul who could pass by
A sight so touching in its majesty;
This City now doth, like a garment, wear
The beauty of the morning; silent, bare,   5
Ships, towers, domes, theaters, and temples lie
Open unto the fields, and to the sky;
All bright and glittering in the smokeless air.
Never did sun more beautifully steep
In his first splendor, valley, rock, or hill;   10
Ne'er saw I, never felt, a calm so deep!
The river glideth at his own sweet will:
Dear God! the very houses seem asleep;
And all that mighty heart is lying still!

THE WORLD IS TOO MUCH WITH US

William Wordsworth

The world is too much with us; late and soon,
Getting and spending, we lay waste our powers;
Little we see in Nature that is ours;
We have given our hearts away, a sordid boon!
This Sea that bares her bosom to the moon,   5
The winds that will be howling at all hours,
And are up-gathered now like sleeping flowers,
For this, for everything, we are out of tune;
It moves us not.—Great God! I'd rather be
A Pagan suckled in a creed outworn;   10
So might I, standing on this pleasant lea,
Have glimpses that would make me less forlorn;
Have sight of Proteus rising from the sea;
Or hear old Triton blow his wreathèd horn.

MUTABILITY

William Wordsworth

From low to high doth dissolution climb,
And sink from high to low, along a scale
Of awful notes, whose concord shall not fail;
A musical but melancholy chime,
Which they can hear who meddle not with crime,   5
Nor avarice, nor over-anxious care.
Truth fails not; but her outward forms that bear
The longest date do melt like frosty rime,
That in the morning whitened hill and plain
And is no more; drop like the tower sublime   10
Of yesterday, which royally did wear
His crown of weeds, but could not even sustain
Some casual shout that broke the silent air,
Or the unimaginable touch of Time.

AFTER-THOUGHT

William Wordsworth

I thought of Thee, my partner and my guide
As being past away.—Vain sympathies!
For, backward, Duddon! as I cast my eyes,
I see what was, and is, and will abide;
Still glides the Stream, and shall for ever glide;   5
The Form remains, the Function never dies;
While we, the brave, the mighty, and the wise,
We Men, who in our morn of youth defied
The elements, must vanish;—be it so!
Enough, if something from our hands have power   10
To live, and act, and serve the future hour;
And if, as toward the silent tomb we go,
Through love, through hope, and faith's transcendent dower,
We feel that we are greater than we know.

THE DEAD

Jones Very (1813–1880)

I see them—crowd on crowd they walk the earth,
Dry leafless trees no autumn wind laid bare;
And in their nakedness find cause for mirth,
And all unclad would winter's rudeness dare;
No sap doth through their clattering branches flow,   5
Whence springing leaves and blossoms bright appear;
Their hearts the living God have ceased to know
Who gives the spring-time to th' expectant year.
They mimic life, as if from Him to steal
His glow of health to paint the livid cheek;   10
They borrow words for thoughts they cannot feel,
That with a seeming heart their tongue may speak;
And in their show of life more dead they live
Than those that to the earth with many tears they give.

IN AN ARTIST'S STUDIO

Christina Rossetti (1830–1894)

One face looks out from all his canvases,
   One selfsame figure sits or walks or leans:
   We found her hidden just behind those screens,
That mirror gave back all her loveliness.
A queen in opal or in ruby dress,   5
   A nameless girl in freshest summer-greens,
   A saint, an angel—every canvas means
The same one meaning, neither more nor less.
He feeds upon her face by day and night,
   And she with true kind eyes looks back on him,   10
Fair as the moon and joyful as the light:
   Not wan with waiting, not with sorrow dim;
Not as she is, but was when hope shone bright;
   Not as she is, but as she fills his dream.

GOD'S GRANDEUR

Gerard Manley Hopkins (1844–1889)

The world is charged with the grandeur of God.
   It will flame out, like shining from shook foil;
   It gathers to a greatness, like the ooze of oil
Crushed. Why do men then now not reck his rod?
Generations have trod, have trod, have trod;   5
   And all is seared with trade; bleared, smeared with toil;
   And wears man's smudge and shares man's smell: the soil
Is bare now, nor can foot feel, being shod.

And for all this, nature is never spent;
   There lives the dearest freshness deep down things;   10
And though the last lights off the black West went
   Oh, morning, at the brown brink eastward, springs—
Because the Holy Ghost over the bent
   World broods with warm breast and with ah! bright wings.

LEDA AND THE SWAN

William Butler Yeats (1865–1939)

A sudden blow: the great wings beating still
Above the staggering girl, her thighs caressed
By the dark webs, her nape caught in his bill,
He holds her helpless breast upon his breast.

How can those terrified vague fingers push   5
The feathered glory from her loosening thighs?
And how can body, laid in that white rush,
But feel the strange heart beating where it lies?

A shudder in the loins engenders there
The broken wall, the burning roof and tower   10
And Agamemnon dead.
                    Being so caught up,
So mastered by the brute blood of the air,
Did she put on his knowledge with his power
Before the indifferent beak could let her drop?

NEW ENGLAND

Edwin Arlington Robinson (1869–1935)

Here where the wind is always north-north-east
And children learn to walk on frozen toes,
Wonder begets an envy of all those
Who boil elsewhere with such a lyric yeast
Of love that you will hear them at a feast   5
Where demons would appeal for some repose,
Still clamoring where the chalice overflows
And crying wildest who have drunk the least.

Passion is here a soilure of the wits,
We're told, and Love a cross for them to bear;   10
Joy shivers in the corner where she knits
And Conscience always has the rocking-chair,
Cheerful as when she tortured into fits
The first cat that was ever killed by Care.

MT. LYKAION

Trumbull Stickney (1874–1904)

Alone on Lykaion since man hath been
Stand on the height two columns, where at rest
Two eagles hewn of gold sit looking East
Forever; and the sun goes up between.
Far down around the mountain's oval green   5
An order keeps the falling stones abreast.
Below within the chaos last and least
A river like a curl of light is seen.
Beyond the river lies the even sea,
Beyond the sea another ghost of sky,—   10
O God, support the sickness of my eye
Lest the far space and long antiquity
Suck out my heart, and on this awful ground
The great wind kill my little shell with sound.

LOVE IS NOT ALL:
IT IS NOT MEAT NOR DRINK

Edna St. Vincent Millay (1892–1950)

Love is not all: it is not meat nor drink
Nor slumber nor a roof against the rain;
Nor yet a floating spar to men that sink
And rise and sink and rise and sink again;
Love can not fill the thickened lung with breath,   5
Nor clean the blood, nor set the fractured bone;
Yet many a man is making friends with death
Even as I speak, for lack of love alone.
It well may be that in a difficult hour,
Pinned down by pain and moaning for release,   10
Or nagged by want past resolution's power,
I might be driven to sell your love for peace,
Or trade the memory of this night for food.
It well may be. I do not think I would.

sonnet

e. e. cummings (1894–1962)

a wind has blown the rain away and blown
the sky away and all the leaves away,
and the trees stand.   I think i too have known
autumn too long

              (and what have you to say,
wind wind wind—did you love somebody   5
and have you the petal of somewhere in your heart
pinched from dumb summer?
                        O crazy daddy
of death dance cruelly for us and start

the last leaf whirling in the final brain
of air!) Let us as we have seen see   10
doom's integration . . . . a wind has blown the rain

away and the leaves and the sky and the
trees stand:
           the trees stand.   The trees,
suddenly wait against the moon's face.

The Ode

An ode is a complex lyric poem, lofty in tone, exalted in diction, and complex in structure. It often praises a great man or celebrates an occasion, a season, or the arts. It may also be a meditation on a serious subject. The model for the intense and impassioned English ode originated with the Greek poet Pindar (ca. 522–442 B.C.), while the model for a more sedate and reflective ode was derived from the Latin poet Horace (65–8 B.C.). A model for a brief ode on any subject was provided by the Greek poet Anacreon (ca. 570 B.C.), but poems that might once have been called

Anacreontic odes are now indistinguishable from brief lyric poems. Some traces of the Pindaric and Horatian influence, however, are still apparent in contemporary poetry.

Pindaric odes were written as a choral part of Greek drama. Chanted by the chorus, they described feats of gods and heroes. These odes had three divisions: the *strophe* was chanted as the chorus moved across the stage; the *antistrophe* was chanted as the chorus moved back; and when the chorus stood, or danced, in the center of the stage, it recited the *epode*. In the first ode that follows, Ben Jonson translates these terms as *turn, counterturn,* and *stand*. The Greek choral movement suggested, among other things, different attitudes, or presented different kinds of information related to the drama being performed. English poets, from the Renaissance on, indicated these divisions and this sense of contrast by writing odes with irregular stanzas, changing moods, rapidly shifting images, sudden transitions, and flexible meters and rhyme schemes. In other words, the strophe, antistrophe, and epode divisions were represented by stanzas having different numbers of lines, different meters and rhyme schemes, and contrasting images. Thus, after Jonson the original triadic form disappeared in English poetry and was replaced by a variety of poetic effects. What remained of the Horatian influence in English poetry was represented by keeping the same stanza form throughout the poem.

The Pindaric ode was more exalted, impassioned, and enthusiastic, and was written to praise the gods or heroes. The Horatian ode was reflective, philosophic, more personal, and less lofty. However, in a long and uncertain evolution, these features of the Pindaric and Horatian odes merged. Horatian odes were written about public events, and Pindaric odes become philosophic and meditative. Almost all distinctions between the two have now disappeared; from the late eighteenth and early nineteenth centuries, the English ode has been a mixture of Pindaric and Horatian.

Actually, the word "ode" originally (that is, before Abraham Cowley, 1618–1667) meant something far broader than it came to mean during the late eighteenth century. By that time, an ode was, to most English poets, an elevated utterance—a sublime and impassioned kind of lyric poem in which the poet assumed a stance as a prophetic bard. Odes continued to praise men as they had in the seventeenth century (in such poems as Jonson's to Sir Lucius Cary and Sir Henry Morrison), but specific places and scenes in nature were more frequently used as starting points for personal meditations (like Thomas Gray's "Ode on a Distant Prospect of Eton College," and William Collins's "Ode to Evening"). This development continued, and the Romantic period saw the perfection of the meditative ode. In John Keats's "Ode to a Nightingale," Samuel Taylor Coleridge's "Dejection: An Ode," and William Wordsworth's "Ode: Intimations of Immortality from Recollections of Early Childhood" the transition in each instance is from nature to personal and spiritual problems. During this same time the speaker of the ode tended to drop the prophetic voice and to assume that of a man speaking to men. An exception is Shelley's "Ode to the West Wind," where the bardic voice is retained—but even here the poem is an expression of a personal crisis rather than a new encomium to the West Wind. The speaker as a troubled man rather than as a prophet becomes more and more pronounced in the twentieth-century ode, where the speaker and his dilemma constitute almost the entire subject. This may be seen in the odes of William Butler Yeats, Allen Tate, Dylan Thomas, Léonie Adams, Robert Lowell, and Sylvia Plath.

In the poems that follow, Wordsworth's two odes are of considerable interest as illustrations of the Pindaric and Horatian strains. His "Ode: Intimations of Immortality..." is in the lofty and intense style associated with the Pindaric ode, while his "Ode to Duty" is, in keeping with its theme, written in regular stanzas and in the more reserved style associated with the Horatian ode. "Ode to Duty" was, in fact, modeled on a poem of Thomas Gray's entitled "Hymn to Adversity," which in turn was based on a poem by Horace. And such a reading may also show how much or how little the odes of Coleridge, Keats, and Shelley resemble these two poems.

However, the most valuable understanding of the ode does not result from reading poems in terms of any adherence to or deviation from historical models. In order to understand the ode as a viable poetic form it is necessary to appreciate its internal coherence. The ode, especially from the time of the Romantics, is a poem of consummate metrical and verbal craftsmanship, lofty and impassioned. It is a poem in which the poet assumes importance as the speaker. It is in this sense that we can see many of Yeats's greatest poems as odes—as well as those of Thomas, Plath, and Lowell. It is difficult, probably impossible, unless we construct a philosophy of lyric form, to make valid generalizations about the intellectual and emotional qualities that produce a great ode. But a close examination of the internal structure of the following poems will provide a starting point for further study. The questions following these selections should be helpful in understanding the formal structure of these poems.

TO THE IMMORTAL MEMORY AND FRIENDSHIP OF THAT NOBLE PAIR, SIR LUCIUS CARY AND SIR HENRY MORRISON

Ben Jonson (1573–1637)

THE TURN

Brave infant of Saguntum, clear
Thy coming forth in that great year,
When the prodigious Hannibal did crown
His rage with razing your immortal town.
Thou, looking then about,   5
Ere thou wert half got out,
Wise child, didst hastily return,
And mad'st thy mother's womb thine urn.
How summed a circle didst thou leave mankind
Of deepest lore, could we the center find!   10

THE COUNTERTURN

Did wiser Nature draw thee back
From out the horror of that sack,
Where shame, faith, honor, and regard of right
Lay trampled on; the deeds of death and night
Urged, hurried forth, and hurled   15
Upon th' affrighted world;
Sword, fire, and famine, with fell fury met,
And all on utmost ruin set,
As, could they but life's miseries foresee,
No doubt all infants would return like thee?   20

THE STAND

For what is life, if measured by the space,
Not by the act?

1. **Saguntum:** a reference to a story by the Roman author Pliny. Saguntum was a town captured by Hannibal in 219 B.C.

Or maskéd man, if valued by his face
Above his fact?
Here's one outlived his peers 25
And told forth fourscore years;
He vexéd time and busied the whole state,
Troubled both foes and friends;
But ever to no ends:
What did this stirrer but die late? 30
How well at twenty had he fall'n or stood!
For three of his fourscore he did no good.

THE TURN

He entered well, by virtuous parts,
Got up and thrived with honest arts;
He purchased friends, and fame, and honors then, 35
And had his noble name advanced with men;
But weary of that flight
He stooped in all men's sight
To sordid flatteries, acts of strife,
And sunk in that dead sea of life 40
So deep, as he did then death's waters sup,
But that the cork of title buoyed him up.

THE COUNTERTURN

Alas, but Morrison fell young;
He never fell, thou fall'st, my tongue.
He stood, a soldier to the last right end, 45
A perfect patriot, and a noble friend,
But most a virtuous son.
All offices were done
By him so ample, full, and round,
In weight, in measure, number, sound, 50
As, though his age imperfect might appear,
His life was of humanity the sphere.

THE STAND

Go now, and tell out days summed up with fears,
And make them years;
Produce thy mass of miseries on the stage 55
To swell thine age;
Repeat of things a throng,

To show thou hast been long,
Not lived; for life doth her great actions spell
By what was done and wrought   60
In season, and so brought
To light: her measures are, how well
Each syllabe answered, and was formed how fair;
These make the lines of life, and that's her air.

THE TURN

It is not growing like a tree   65
In bulk doth make man better be;
Or standing long an oak, three hundred year,
To fall a log at last, dry, bald, and sere:
A lily of a day
Is fairer far in May;   70
Although it fall and die that night,
It was the plant and flower of light.
In small proportions we just beauties see,
And in short measures life may perfect be.

THE COUNTERTURN

Call, noble Lucius, then for wine,   75
And let thy looks with gladness shine;
Accept this garland, plant it on thy head,
And think, nay know, thy Morrison's not dead.
He leaped the present age,
Possessed with holy rage   80
To see that bright eternal day;
Of which we priests and poets say
Such truths as we expect for happy men,
And there he lives with memory, and Ben

THE STAND

Jonson! who sung this of him, ere he went   85
Himself to rest,
Or taste a part of that full joy he meant
To have expressed
In this bright asterism;
Where it were friendship's schism   90
(Were not his Lucius long with us to tarry)
To separate these twi-
Lights, the Dioscuri,

And keep the one half from his Harry.
But fate doth so altérnate the design,   95
Whilst that in heaven, this light on earth must shine.

THE TURN

And shine as you exalted are,
Two names of friendship, but one star:
Of hearts the union. And those not by chance
Made, or indenture, or leased out t'advance   100
The profits for a time.
No pleasures vain did chime
Of rimes, or riots, at your feasts,
Orgies of drink, or feigned protests,
But simple love of greatness and of good;   105
That knits brave minds and manners more than blood.

THE COUNTERTURN

This made you first to know the why
You liked, then after to apply
That liking, and approach so one the tother,
Till either grew a portion of the other: 110
Each styled by his end
The copy of his friend.
You lived to be the great surnames
And titles by which all made claims
Unto the virtue. Nothing perfect done,   115
But as a Cary, or a Morrison.

THE STAND

And such a force the fair example had,
As they that saw
The good, and durst not practice it, were glad
That such a law   120
Was left yet to mankind;
Where they might read and find
Friendship, indeed, was written, not in words;
And with the heart, not pen,
Of two so early men,   125
Whose lines her rolls were, and recórds,
Who, ere the first down bloomèd on the chin,
Had sowed these fruits, and got the harvest in.

A SONG FOR ST. CECILIA'S DAY, 1687

John Dryden (1631–1700)

I

From Harmony, from heav'nly Harmony
   This universal Frame began.
   When Nature underneath a heap
     Of jarring Atomes lay,
   And cou'd not heave her Head,   5
The tuneful Voice was heard from high,
   Arise ye more than dead.
Then cold, and hot, and moist, and dry,
   In order to their stations leap,
     And Musick's pow'r obey.   10
From Harmony, from heav'nly Harmony
   This universal Frame began:
     From Harmony to Harmony
Through all the compass of the Notes it ran,
   The Diapason closing full in Man.   15

II

What Passion cannot Musick raise and quell!
    When *Jubal* struck the corded Shell,
   His list'ning Brethren stood around
   And wond'ring, on their Faces fell
   To worship that Celestial Sound.   20
Less than a God they thought there cou'd not dwell
    Within the hollow of that Shell
    That spoke so sweetly and so well.
What Passion cannot Musick raise and quell!
   The Trumpets loud Clangor   25
     Excites us to Arms
   With shrill Notes of Anger
     And mortal Alarms.
   The double double double beat
     Of the thundring Drum   30
   Cryes, heark the Foes come;
Charge, Charge, 'tis too late to retreat.

. . .

IV

   The soft complaining Flute
   In dying Notes discovers

The Woes of hopeless Lovers, 35
Whose Dirge is whisper'd by the warbling LUTE.

V

Sharp VIOLINS proclaim
Their jealous Pangs, and Desperation.
Fury, frantick Indignation,
Depth of Pains, and height of Passion, 40
For the fair, disdainful Dame.

VI

But oh! what Art can teach
What human Voice can reach
The sacred ORGANS praise?
Notes inspiring holy LOVE, 45
Notes that wing their heav'nly ways
To mend the Choires above.

VII

Orpheus cou'd lead the savage race;
And Trees unrooted left their place;
Sequacious of the Lyre: 50
But bright CECILIA rais'd the wonder high'r;
When to her ORGAN, vocal Breath was giv'n
An Angel heard, and straight appear'd
Mistaking Earth for Heaven.

GRAND CHORUS

As from the pow'r of sacred Lays 55
The Spheres began to move,
And sung the great Creator's praise
To all the bless'd above;
So when the last and dreadful hour
This crumbling Pageant shall devour, 60
The TRUMPET *shall be heard on high,*
The Dead shall live, the Living die,
And MUSICK *shall untune the Sky.*

ODE ON A DISTANT PROSPECT OF ETON COLLEGE

Thomas Gray (1716–1771)

'Άνθρωπος · 'ικανὴ πρόφασις εἰς τὸ
δυστυχεῖν.—Menander

Ye distant spires, ye antique towers,
   That crown the watery glade,
Where grateful Science still adores
   Her Henry's holy shade;
And ye, that from the stately brow   5
Of Windsor's heights the expanse below
   Of grove, of lawn, of mead survey,
Whose turf, whose shade, whose flowers among
Wanders the hoary Thames along
   His silver-winding way.   10

Ah happy hills, ah pleasing shade,
   Ah fields beloved in vain,
Where once my careless childhood strayed,
   A stranger yet to pain!
I feel the gales, that from ye blow,   15
A momentary bliss bestow,
   As waving fresh their gladsome wing,
My weary soul they seem to soothe,
And, redolent of joy and youth,
   To breathe a second spring.   20

Say, Father Thames, for thou hast seen
   Full many a sprightly race
Disporting on thy margent green
   The paths of pleasure trace,
Who foremost now delight to cleave   25
With pliant arm thy glassy wave?
   The captive linnet which enthrall?
What idle progeny succeed
To chase the rolling circle's speed,
   Or urge the flying ball?   30

'Άνθρωπος ... δυστυχεῖν: I am a man and that is cause enough for being unhappy.   **3. Science:** knowledge.   **4. Her ... shade:** Eton was founded by Henry VI.

While some on earnest business bent
    Their murmuring labors ply
'Gainst graver hours, that bring constraint
    To sweeten liberty:
Some bold adventurers disdain   35
The limits of their little reign,
    And unknown regions dare descry:
Still as they run they look behind,
They hear a voice in every wind,
    And snatch a fearful joy.   40

Gay hope is theirs by fancy fed,
    Less pleasing when possessed;
The tear forgot as soon as shed,
    The sunshine of the breast:
Theirs buxom health of rosy hue,   45
Wild wit, invention ever new,
    And lively cheer of vigor born;
The thoughtless day, the easy night,
The spirits pure, the slumbers light,
    That fly the approach of morn.   50

Alas, regardless of their doom,
    The little victims play!
No sense have they of ills to come,
    Nor care beyond today.
Yet see how all around 'em wait   55
The ministers of human fate,
    And black Misfortune's baleful train!
Ah, show them where in ambush stand
To seize their prey the murderous band!
    Ah, tell them they are men!   60

These shall the fury Passions tear,
    The vultures of the mind,
Disdainful Anger, pallid Fear,
    And Shame that skulks behind;
Or pining Love shall waste their youth,   65
Or Jealousy with rankling tooth,
    That inly gnaws the secret heart,
And Envy wan, and faded Care,
Grim-visaged comfortless Despair,
    And Sorrow's piercing dart.   70

37. Descry: discover.

Ambition this shall tempt to rise,
  Then whirl the wretch from high,
To bitter Scorn a sacrifice,
  And grinning Infamy.
The stings of Falsehood those shall try,   75
And hard Unkindness' altered eye,
  That mocks the tear it forced to flow;
And keen Remorse with blood defiled,
And moody Madness laughing wild
  Amid severest woe.   80

Lo, in the vale of years beneath
  A grisly troop are seen,
The painful family of Death,
  More hideous than their queen:
This racks the joints, this fires the veins,   85
That every laboring sinew strains,
  Those in the deeper vitals rage:
Lo, Poverty, to fill the band,
That numbs the soul with icy hand,
  And slow-consuming Age.   90

To each his sufferings: all are men,
  Condemned alike to groan;
The tender for another's pain,
  The unfeeling for his own.
Yet ah! why should they know their fate?   95
Since sorrow never comes too late,
  And happiness too swiftly flies.
Thought would destroy their paradise.
No more; where ignorance is bliss,
  'Tis folly to be wise   100

ODE TO EVENING

William Collins (1721–1759)

If aught of oaten stop, or pastoral song,
May hope, chaste Eve, to soothe thy modest ear,
  Like thy own solemn springs,

1. oaten stop: a shepherd's reed.

Thy springs and dying gales,
O nymph reserved, while now the bright-haired sun   5
Sits in yon western tent, whose cloudy skirts,
　　　With brede ethereal wove,
　　　O'erhang his wavy bed:
Now air is hushed, save where the weak-eyed bat,
With short shrill shriek flits by on leathern wing,   10
　　　Or where the beetle winds
　　　His small but sullen horn,
As oft he rises 'midst the twilight path,
Against the pilgrim borne in heedless hum:
　　　Now teach me, maid composed,   15
　　　To breathe some softened strain,
Whose numbers, stealing through thy darkening vale,
May not unseemly with its stillness suit,
　　　As, musing slow, I hail
　　　Thy genial loved return!   20
For when thy folding-star arising shows
His paly circlet, at his warning lamp
　　　The fragrant Hours, and elves
　　　Who slept in flowers the day,
And many a nymph who wreaths her brows with sedge,   25
And sheds the freshening dew, and, lovelier still,
　　　The pensive Pleasures sweet,
　　　Prepare thy shadowy car.
Then lead, calm votaress, where some sheety lake
Cheers the lone heath, or some time-hallowed pile   30
　　　Or upland fallows gray
　　　Reflect its last cool gleam.
But when chill blustering winds, or driving rain,
Forbid my willing feet, be mine the hut
　　　That from the mountain's side   35
　　　Views wilds, and swelling floods,
And hamlets brown, and dim-discovered spires,
And hears their simple bell, and marks o'er all
　　　Thy dewy fingers draw
　　　The gradual dusky veil.   40
While Spring shall pour his showers, as oft he wont,
And bathe thy breathing tresses, meekest Eve;
　　　While Summer loves to sport
　　　Beneath thy lingering light;

21. folding-star: the star at whose appearance the shepherd takes his sheep to their fold.

While sallow Autumn fills thy lap with leaves; 45
Or Winter, yelling through the troublous air,
Affrights thy shrinking train,
And rudely rends thy robes;
So long, sure-found beneath the sylvan shed,
Shall Fancy, Friendship, Science, rose-lipped Health, 50
Thy gentlest influence own,
And hymn thy favorite name!

ODE: INTIMATIONS OF IMMORTALITY FROM RECOLLECTIONS OF EARLY CHILDHOOD
William Wordsworth (1770–1850)

Pauló majora canamus.

The Child is father of the Man;
And I could wish my days to be
Bound each to each by natural piety.

I

There was a time when meadow, grove, and stream,
The earth, and every common sight,
    To me did seem
  Apparelled in celestial light,
The glory and the freshness of a dream. 5
It is not now as it hath been of yore;—
    Turn whereso'er I may,
    By night or day,
The things which I have seen I now can see no more.

II

  The Rainbow comes and goes, 10
  And lovely is the Rose,
  The Moon doth with delight
Look round her when the heavens are bare;
  Waters on a starry night
  Are beautiful and fair; 15
  The sunshine is a glorious birth;
  But yet I know, where'er I go,
That there hath past away a glory from the earth.

Pauló . . . canamus: Let us sing of somewhat higher things.

III

Now, while the birds thus sing a joyous song,
    And while the young lambs bound 20
        As to the tabor's sound,
To me alone there came a thought of grief:
A timely utterance gave that thought relief,
    And I again am strong:
The cataracts blow their trumpets from the steep; 25
No more shall grief of mine the season wrong;
I hear the Echoes through the mountains throng,
The Winds come to me from the fields of sleep,
    And all the earth is gay;
        Land and sea 30
    Give themselves up to jollity,
        And with the heart of May
    Doth every Beast keep holiday;—
        Thou Child of Joy,
Shout round me, let me hear thy shouts, thou happy
        Shepherd-boy! 35

IV

Ye blessèd Creatures, I have heard the call
    Ye to each other make; I see
The heavens laugh with you in your jubilee;
    My heart is at your festival,
    My head hath its coronal, 40
The fulness of your bliss, I feel—I feel it all.
        Oh evil day! if I were sullen
        While Earth herself is adorning,
            This sweet May-morning,
        And the Children are culling 45
            On every side,
        In a thousand valleys far and wide,
        Fresh flowers; while the sun shines warm,
And the Babe leaps up on his Mother's arm:—
    I hear, I hear, with joy I hear! 50
    —But there's a Tree, of many, one,
A single Field which I have looked upon,
Both of them speak of something that is gone:
        The Pansy at my feet
        Doth the same tale repeat: 55
Whither is fled the visionary gleam?
Where is it now, the glory and the dream?

V

Our birth is but a sleep and a forgetting:
The Soul that rises with us, our life's Star,
    Hath had elsewhere its setting,   60
      And cometh from afar:
    Not in entire forgetfulness,
    And not in utter nakedness,
But trailing clouds of glory do we come
    From God, who is our home: 65
Heaven lies about us in our infancy!
Shades of the prison-house begin to close
    Upon the growing Boy,
But He beholds the light, and whence it flows,
    He sees it in his joy;   70
The Youth, who daily farther from the east
    Must travel, still is Nature's Priest,
    And by the vision splendid
    Is on his way attended;
At length the Man perceives it die away,   75
And fade into the light of common day.

VI

Earth fills her lap with pleasures of her own;
Yearnings she hath in her own natural kind,
And, even with something of a Mother's mind,
    And no unworthy aim,   80
    The homely Nurse doth all she can
To make her Foster-child, her Inmate Man,
    Forget the glories he hath known,
And that imperial palace whence he came.

VII

Behold the Child among his new-born blisses,   85
A six years' Darling of a pigmy size!
See, where 'mid work of his own hand he lies,
Fretted by sallies of his mother's kisses,
With light upon him from his father's eyes!
See, at his feet, some little plan or chart,   90
Some fragment from his dream of human life,
Shaped by himself with newly-learned art;
    A wedding or a festival,
    A mourning or a funeral;
    And this hath now his heart,   95
    And unto this he frames his song:

    Then will he fit his tongue
To dialogues of business, love, or strife;
   But it will not be long
   Ere this be thrown aside,   100
   And with new joy and pride
The little Actor cons another part;
Filling from time to time his "humorous stage"
With all the Persons, down to palsied Age,
That Life brings with her in her equipage;   105
   As if his whole vocation
   Were endless imitation.

      VIII

Thou, whose exterior semblance doth belie
   Thy Soul's immensity;
Thou best Philosopher, who yet dost keep   110
Thy heritage, thou Eye among the blind,
That, deaf and silent, read'st the eternal deep,
Haunted forever by the eternal mind,—
   Mighty Prophet! Seer blest!
   On whom those truths do rest,   115
Which we are toiling all our lives to find,
In darkness lost, the darkness of the grave;
Thou, over whom thy Immortality
Broods like the Day, a Master o'er a Slave,
A Presence which is not to be put by;   120
Thou little Child, yet glorious in the might
Of heaven-born freedom on thy being's height,
Why with such earnest pains dost thou provoke
The years to bring the inevitable yoke,
Thus blindly with thy blessedness at strife?   125
Full soon thy Soul shall have her earthly freight,
And custom lie upon thee with a weight,
Heavy as frost, and deep almost as life!

      IX

   O joy! that in our embers
   Is something that doth live,   130
   That Nature yet remembers
   What was so fugitive!
The thought of our past years in me doth breed
Perpetual benediction: not indeed
For that which is most worthy to be blest;   135
Delight and liberty, the simple creed

Of Childhood, whether busy or at rest,
With new-fledged hope still fluttering in his breast:—
    Not for these I raise
    The song of thanks and praise; 140
    But for those obstinate questionings
    Of sense and outward things,
    Fallings from us, vanishings;
    Blank misgivings of a Creature
Moving about in worlds not realized, 145
High instincts before which our mortal Nature
Did tremble like a guilty Thing surprised:
    But for those first affections,
    Those shadowy recollections,
    Which, be they what they may, 150
Are yet the fountain light of all our day,
Are yet a master light of all our seeing;
    Uphold us, cherish, and have power to make
Our noisy years seem moments in the being
Of the eternal Silence: truths that wake, 155
    To perish never;
Which neither listlessness, nor mad endeavor,
    Nor Man nor Boy,
Nor all that is at enmity with joy,
Can utterly abolish or destroy! 160
    Hence in a season of calm weather
    Though inland far we be,
Our Souls have sight of that immortal sea
    Which brought us hither,
    Can in a moment travel thither, 165
And see the Children sport upon the shore,
And hear the mighty waters rolling evermore.

X

Then sing, ye Birds, sing, sing a joyous song!
    And let the young Lambs bound
    As to the tabor's sound! 170
We in thought will join your throng,
    Ye that pipe and ye that play,
    Ye that through your hearts to-day
    Feel the gladness of the May!
What though the radiance which was once so bright 175
Be now for ever taken from my sight,
    Though nothing can bring back the hour
Of splendor in the grass, of glory in the flower;

We will grieve not, rather find
Strength in what remains behind; 180
In the primal sympathy
Which having been must ever be;
In the soothing thoughts that spring
Out of human suffering;
In the faith that looks through death, 185
In years that bring the philosophic mind.

XI

And O, ye Fountains, Meadows, Hills, and Groves,
Forbode not any severing of our loves!
Yet in my heart of hearts I feel your might;
I only have relinquished one delight 190
To live beneath your more habitual sway.
I love the Brooks which down their channels fret,
Even more than when I tripped lightly as they;
The innocent brightness of a new-born Day
    Is lovely yet; 195
The Clouds that gather round the setting sun
Do take a sober coloring from an eye
That hath kept watch o'er man's mortality;
Another race hath been, and other palms are won.
Thanks to the human heart by which we live, 200
Thanks to its tenderness, its joys, and fears,
To me the meanest flower that blows can give
Thoughts that do often lie too deep for tears.

ODE TO DUTY

William Wordsworth

Jam non consilio bonus, sed more eo perductus, ut non tantum recte facere possim, sed nisi recte facere non possim.—Seneca

Stern Daughter of the Voice of God!
O Duty! if that name thou love
Who are a light to guide, a rod

    Jam...possim: I am not good because of reflection but because of habit —which does not so much make me act correctly as it prevents me from acting other than correctly.

To check the erring, and reprove;
Thou, who art victory and law
When empty terrors overawe;
From vain temptations dost set free;
And calm'st the weary strife of frail humanity!

There are who ask not if thine eye
Be on them; who, in love and truth,
Where no misgiving is, rely
Upon the genial sense of youth:
Glad Hearts! without reproach or blot;
Who do thy work, and know it not:
Oh! if through confidence misplaced
They fail, thy saving arms, dread Power! around them cast.

Serene will be our days and bright,
And happy will our nature be,
When love is an unerring light,
And joy its own security.
And they a blissful course may hold
Even now, who, not unwisely bold,
Live in the spirit of this creed;
Yet seek thy firm support, according to their need.

I, loving freedom, and untried,
No sport of every random gust,
Yet being to myself a guide,
Too blindly have reposed my trust;
And oft, when in my heart was heard
Thy timely mandate, I deferred
The task, in smoother walks to stray;
But thee I now would serve more strictly, if I may.

Through no disturbance of my soul,
Or strong compunction in me wrought,
I supplicate for thy control;
But in the quietness of thought:
Me this unchartered freedom tires;
I feel the weight of chance desires:
My hopes no more must change their name,
I long for a repose that ever is the same.

Stern Lawgiver! yet thou dost wear
The Godhead's most benignant grace;
Nor know we anything so fair
As is the smile upon thy face:

Flowers laugh before thee on their beds 45
And fragrance in thy footing treads;
Thou dost preserve the stars from wrong
And the most ancient heavens, through thee, are fresh and strong.

To humbler functions, awful Power!
I call thee: I myself commend 50
Unto thy guidance from this hour;
Oh, let my weakness have an end!
Give unto me, made lowly wise,
The spirit of self-sacrifice;
The confidence of reason give; 55
And in the light of truth thy Bondman let me live!

DEJECTION: AN ODE

Samuel Taylor Coleridge (1772–1834)

Late, late yestreen I saw the new Moon,
With the old Moon in her arms;
And I fear, I fear, my master dear!
We shall have a deadly storm.
    Ballad of Sir Patrick Spence

1

Well! If the bard was weather-wise, who made
 The grand old ballad of Sir Patrick Spence,
 This night, so tranquil now, will not go hence
Unroused by winds, that ply a busier trade
Than those which mold yon cloud in lazy flakes, 5
Or the dull sobbing draft, that moans and rakes
Upon the strings of this Aeolian lute,
 Which better far were mute.
 For lo! the New-moon winter-bright!
 And overspread with phantom light, 10
 (With swimming phantom light o'erspread
 But rimmed and circled by a silver thread)
I see the old Moon in her lap, foretelling
 The coming-on of rain and squally blast.
And oh! that even now the gust were swelling, 15
 And the slant night shower driving loud and fast!

Formal Contexts

> Those sounds which oft have raised me, whilst they awed,
>   And sent my soul abroad,
> Might now perhaps their wonted impulse give,
> Might startle this dull pain, and make it move and live!   20

[Margin note: *Directs our expectations to a limited resolution*]

2

> A grief without a pang, void, dark, and drear,
>   A stifled, drowsy, unimpassioned grief,
>   Which finds no natural outlet, no relief,
>   In word, or sigh, or tear—
> O Lady! in this wan and heartless mood,   25
> To other thoughts by yonder throstle wooed,
>   All this long eve, so balmy and serene,
> Have I been gazing on the western sky,
>   And its peculiar tint of yellow green:
> And still I gaze—and with how blank an eye!   30
> And those thin clouds above, in flakes and bars,
> That give away their motion to the stars;
> Those stars, that glide behind them or between,
> Now sparkling, now bedimmed, but always seen:
> Yon crescent Moon, as fixed as if it grew   35
> In its own cloudless, starless lake of blue;
> I see them all so excellently fair,
> I see, not feel, how beautiful they are!

3

>   My genial spirits fail;
>   And what can these avail   40
> To lift the smothering weight from off my breast?
>   It were a vain endeavor,
>   Though I should gaze forever
> On that green light that lingers in the west:
> I may not hope from outward forms to win   45
> The passion and the life, whose fountains are within.

4

> O Lady! we receive but what we give, [Margin note: *blessing in the end*]
> And in our life alone does Nature live:
> Ours is her wedding garment, ours her shroud!
>   And would we aught behold, of higher worth,   50
>   Than that inanimate cold world allowed
> To the poor loveless ever-anxious crowd,

Ah! from the soul itself must issue forth
A light, a glory, a fair luminous cloud
    Enveloping the Earth—   55
And from the soul itself must there be sent
  A sweet and potent voice, of its own birth,
Of all sweet sounds the life and element!

5

O pure of heart! thou need'st not ask of me
What this strong music in the soul may be!   60
What, and wherein it doth exist,
This light, this glory, this fair luminous mist,
This beautiful and beauty-making power.
  Joy, virtuous Lady! Joy that ne'er was given,
Save to the pure, and in their purest hour,   65
Life, and Life's effluence, cloud at once and shower,
Joy, Lady! is the spirit and the power,
Which wedding Nature to us gives in dower
    A new Earth and new Heaven,
Undreamt of by the sensual and the proud—   70
Joy is the sweet voice, Joy the luminous cloud—
    We in ourselves rejoice!
And thence flows all that charms or ear or sight,
  All melodies the echoes of that voice,
All colors a suffusion from that light.   75

6

There was a time when, though my path was rough,
  This joy within me dallied with distress,
And all misfortunes were but as the stuff
  Whence Fancy made me dreams of happiness:
For hope grew round me, like the twining vine,   80
And fruits, and foliage, not my own, seemed mine.
But now afflictions bow me down to earth:
Nor care I that they rob me of my mirth;
  But oh! each visitation
Suspends what nature gave me at my birth,   85
  My shaping spirit of Imagination.

For not to think of what I needs must feel,
  But to be still and patient, all I can;
And haply by abstruse research to steal
  From my own nature all the natural man—   90
  This was my sole resource, my only plan:

Till that which suits a part infects the whole,
And now is almost grown the habit of my soul.

7

Hence, viper thoughts, that coil around my mind,
   Reality's dark dream! 95
I turn from you, and listen to the wind,
   Which long has raved unnoticed. What a scream
Of agony by torture lengthened out
That lute sent forth! Thou Wind, that rav'st without,
   Bare crag, or mountain tairn, or blasted tree, 100
Or pine grove whither woodman never clomb,
Or lonely house, long held—the witches' home,
   Methinks were fitter instruments for thee,
Mad lutanist! who in this month of showers,
Of dark-brown gardens, and of peeping flowers, 105
Mak'st devils' yule, with worse than wintry song,
The blossoms, buds, and timorous leaves among.
   Thou actor, perfect in all tragic sounds!
Thou mighty poet, e'en to frenzy bold!
   What tell'st thou now about? 110
'Tis of the rushing of an host in rout,
   With groans, of trampled men, with smarting wounds—
At once they groan with pain, and shudder with the cold!
But hush! there is a pause of deepest silence!
And all that noise, as of a rushing crowd, 115
With groans, and tremulous shudderings—all is over—
   It tells another tale, with sounds less deep and loud!
     A tale of less affright,
     And tempered with delight,
As Otway's self had framed the tender lay— 120
   'Tis of a little child
   Upon a lonesome wild,
Not far from home, but she hath lost her way:
And now moans low in bitter grief and fear,
And now screams loud, and hopes to make her mother hear. 125

8

'Tis midnight, but small thoughts have I of sleep:
Full seldom may my friend such vigils keep!

106. devils' yule: a violent spring storm that makes the season seem unnatural. **120. Otway:** Thomas Otway, a seventeenth-century English dramatist.

Visit her, gentle Sleep! with wings of healing,
   And may this storm be but a mountain birth,
May all the stars hang bright above her dwelling,
   Silent as though they watched the sleeping Earth!
      With light heart may she rise,
      Gay fancy, cheerful eyes,
Joy lift her spirit, joy attune her voice;
To her may all things live, from pole to pole,
Their life the eddying of her living soul!
O simple spirit, guided from above,
Dear Lady! friend devoutest of my choice,
Thus mayest thou ever, evermore rejoice.

ODE TO THE WEST WIND

Percy Bysshe Shelley (1792–1822)

I

O wild West Wind, thou breath of Autumn's being,
Thou, from whose unseen presence the leaves dead
Are driven, like ghosts from an enchanter fleeing,

Yellow, and black, and pale, and hectic red,
Pestilence-stricken multitudes: O thou,
Who chariotest to their dark wintry bed

The wingéd seeds, where they lie cold and low,
Each like a corpse within its grave, until
Thine azure sister of the Spring shall blow

Her clarion o'er the dreaming earth, and fill
(Driving sweet buds like flocks to feed in air)
With living hues and odors plain and hill:

Wild Spirit, which art moving everywhere;
Destroyer and preserver; hear, oh hear!

II

Thou on whose stream, 'mid the steep sky's commotion,
Loose clouds like earth's decaying leaves are shed,
Shook from the tangled boughs of Heaven and Ocean,

Angels of rain and lightning: there are spread
On the blue surface of thine airy surge,
Like the bright hair uplifted from the head

Of some fierce Maenad, even from the dim verge
Of the horizon to the zenith's height
The locks of the approaching storm. Thou dirge

Of the dying year, to which this closing night
Will be the dome of a vast sepulcher, 25
Vaulted with all thy congregated might

Of vapors, from whose solid atmosphere
Black rain, and fire, and hail will burst: Oh hear!

III

Thou who didst waken from his summer dreams
The blue Mediterranean, where he lay, 30
Lulled by the coil of his crystálline streams,

Beside a pumice isle in Baiae's bay,
And saw in sleep old palaces and towers
Quivering within the wave's intenser day,

All overgrown with azure moss and flowers 35
So sweet, the sense faints picturing them! Thou
For whose path the Atlantic's level powers

Cleave themselves into chasms, while far below
The sea-blooms and the oozy woods which wear
The sapless foliage of the ocean, know 40

Thy voice, and suddenly grow gray with fear,
And tremble and despoil themselves: Oh hear!

IV

If I were a dead leaf thou mightest bear;
If I were a swift cloud to fly with thee;
A wave to pant beneath thy power, and share 45

The impulse of thy strength, only less free
Than thou, O uncontrollable! If even
I were as in my boyhood, and could be

The comrade of thy wanderings over heaven,
As then, when to outstrip thy skyey speed 50
Scarce seemed a vision, I would ne'er have striven

32. **Baiae:** an Italian town near Naples.

As thus with thee in prayer in my sore need.
Oh! lift me as a wave, a leaf, a cloud!
I fall upon the thorns of life! I bleed!

A heavy weight of hours has chained and bowed 55
One too like thee: tameless, and swift, and proud.

V

Make me thy lyre, even as the forest is:
What if my leaves are falling like its own!
The tumult of thy mighty harmonies

Will take from both a deep, autumnal tone, 60
Sweet though in sadness. Be thou, spirit fierce,
My spirit! Be thou me, impetuous one!

Drive my dead thoughts over the universe
Like withered leaves to quicken a new birth;
And, by the incantation of this verse, 65

Scatter, as from an unextinguished hearth
Ashes and sparks, my words among mankind!
Be through my lips to unawakened earth

The trumpet of a prophecy! O Wind,
If Winter comes, can Spring be far behind? 70

TO AUTUMN

John Keats (1795–1821)

1

Season of mists and mellow fruitfulness,
  Close bosom-friend of the maturing sun;
Conspiring with him how to load and bless
  With fruit the vines that round the thatch-eaves run;
To bend with apples the mossed cottage-trees, 5
  And fill all fruit with ripeness to the core;
    To swell the gourd, and plump the hazel shells
  With a sweet kernel; to set budding more,
And still more, later flowers for the bees,
Until they think warm days will never cease, 10
    For Summer has o'er-brimmed their clammy cells.

2

Who hath not seen thee oft amid thy store?
  Sometimes whoever seeks abroad may find
  Thee sitting careless on a granary floor,
    Thy hair soft-lifted by the winnowing wind;   15
  Or on a half-reaped furrow sound asleep,
  Drowsed with the fume of poppies, while thy hook
    Spares the next swath and all its twinéd flowers:
And sometimes like a gleaner thou dost keep
    Steady thy laden head across a brook;   20
  Or by a cider-press, with patient look,
    Thou watchest the last oozings hours by hours.

3

Where are the songs of Spring? Aye, where are they?
  Think not of them, thou hast thy music too—
While barréd clouds bloom the soft-dying day,   25
  And touch the stubble-plains with rosy hue;
Then in a wailful choir the small gnats mourn
  Among the river sallows, borne aloft
    Or sinking as the light wind lives or dies;
And full-grown lambs loud bleat from hilly bourn;   30
  Hedge crickets sing; and now with treble soft
  The redbreast whistles from a garden-croft;
    And gathering swallows twitter in the skies.

ODE TO A NIGHTINGALE

John Keats

1

My heart aches, and a drowsy numbness pains
  My sense, as though of hemlock I had drunk,
Or emptied some dull opiate to the drains
    One minute past, and Lethe-wards had sunk:
'Tis not through envy of thy happy lot,   5
    But being too happy in thine happiness—
      That thou, light-wingéd Dryad of the trees,

4. **Lethe:** river of forgetfulness in Hades.

        In some melodious plot
    Of beechen green, and shadows numberless,
        Singest of summer in full-throated ease.

2

O, for a draught of vintage! that hath been
    Cooled a long age in the deep-delvéd earth,
Tasting of Flora and the country green,
    Dance, and Provençal song, and sunburnt mirth!
O for a beaker full of the warm South,
    Full of the true, the blushful Hippocrene,
        With beaded bubbles winking at the brim,
           And purple-stainéd mouth;
    That I might drink, and leave the world unseen,
        And with thee fade away into the forest dim:

3

Fade far away, dissolve, and quite forget
    What thou among the leaves hast never known,
The weariness, the fever, and the fret
    Here, where men sit and hear each other groan;
Where palsy shakes a few, sad, last gray hairs,
    Where youth grows pale, and specter-thin, and dies,
        Where but to think is to be full of sorrow
           And leaden-eyed despairs,
    Where Beauty cannot keep her lustrous eyes,
        Or new Love pine at them beyond tomorrow.

4

Away! away! for I will fly to thee,
    Not charioted by Bacchus and his pards,
But on the viewless wings of Poesy,
    Though the dull brain perplexes and retards:
Already with thee! tender is the night,
    And haply the Queen-Moon is on her throne,
        Clustered around by all her starry Fays;
           But here there is no light,
    Save what from heaven is with the breezes blown
        Through verdurous glooms and winding mossy ways.

16. Hippocrene: the fountain of the Muses, its waters inspire the poet.
32. Bacchus: god of wine.

5

I cannot see what flowers are at my feet,
  Nor what soft incense hangs upon the boughs,
But, in embalmèd darkness, guess each sweet
  Wherewith the seasonable month endows
The grass, the thicket, and the fruit tree wild;   45
  White hawthorn, and the pastoral eglantine;
    Fast fading violets covered up in leaves;
      And mid-May's eldest child,
  The coming musk-rose, full of dewy wine,
    The murmurous haunt of flies on summer eves.   50

6

Darkling I listen; and for many a time
  I have been half in love with easeful Death,
Called him soft names in many a musèd rhyme,
  To take into the air my quiet breath;
Now more than ever seems it rich to die,   55
  To cease upon the midnight with no pain,
    While thou art pouring forth thy soul abroad
      In such an ecstasy!
  Still wouldst thou sing, and I have ears in vain—
    To thy high requiem become a sod.   60

7

Thou wast not born for death, immortal Bird!
  No hungry generations tread thee down;
The voice I hear this passing night was heard
  In ancient days by emperor and clown:
Perhaps the selfsame song that found a path   65
  Through the sad heart of Ruth, when, sick for home,
    She stood in tears amid the alien corn;
      The same that ofttimes hath
  Charmed magic casements, opening on the foam
    Of perilous seas, in faery lands forlorn.   70

8

Forlorn! the very word is like a bell
  To toll me back from thee to my sole self!
Adieu! the fancy cannot cheat so well
  As she is famed to do, deceiving elf.
Adieu! adieu! thy plaintive anthem fades   75

Past the near meadows, over the still stream,
   Up the hill side; and now 'tis buried deep
     In the next valley-glades:
Was it a vision, or a waking dream?
Fled is that music:—Do I wake or sleep?   80

ODE ON MELANCHOLY

John Keats

1

No, no, go not to Lethe, neither twist
   Wolfsbane, tight-rooted, for its poisonous wine;
Nor suffer thy pale forehead to be kissed
   By nightshade, ruby grape of Proserpine;
Make not your rosary of yew-berries,   5
   Nor let the beetle, nor the death-moth be
      Your mournful Psyche, nor the downy owl
A partner in your sorrow's mysteries;
   For shade to shade will come too drowsily,
      And drown the wakeful anguish of the soul.   10

2

But when the melancholy fit shall fall
   Sudden from heaven like a weeping cloud,
That fosters the droop-headed flowers all,
   And hides the green hill in an April shroud;
Then glut thy sorrow on a morning rose,   15
   Or on the rainbow of the salt sand-wave,
      Or on the wealth of globèd peonies;
Or if thy mistress some rich anger shows,
   Imprison her soft hand, and let her rave,
      And feed deep, deep upon her peerless eyes.   20

3

She dwells with Beauty—Beauty that must die;
   And Joy, whose hand is ever at his lips
Bidding adieu; and aching Pleasure nigh,

7. **Psyche:** the soul, symbolized here as a moth.

Turning to Poison while the bee-mouth sips:
Aye, in the very temple of Delight 25
Veiled Melancholy has her sov'reign shrine,
Though seen of none save him whose strenuous tongue
Can burst Joy's grape against his palate fine;
His soul shall taste the sadness of her might,
And be among her cloudy trophies hung. 30

AMONG SCHOOL CHILDREN

William Butler Yeats (1865–1939)

1

I walk through the long schoolroom questioning;
A kind old nun in a white hood replies;
The children learn to cipher and to sing,
To study reading-books and histories,
To cut and sew, be neat in everything 5
In the best modern way—the children's eyes
In momentary wonder stare upon
A sixty-year-old smiling public man.

2

I dream of a Ledaean body, bent
Above a sinking fire, a tale that she 10
Told of a harsh reproof, or trivial event
That changed some childish day to tragedy—
Told, and it seemed that our two natures blent
Into a sphere from youthful sympathy,
Or else, to alter Plato's parable, 15
Into the yolk and white of the one shell.

3

And thinking of that fit of grief or rage
I look upon one child or t'other there
And wonder if she stood so at that age—

9. Ledaean: a beautiful woman—like Leda.   **10. she:** Maud Gonne. (See page 363.)   **16. Into ... shell:** male and female, according to one of Plato's speakers in the *Symposium*, were originally a unity—like the yolk and white of an egg.

For even daughters of the swan can share   20
Something of every paddler's heritage—
And had that color upon cheek or hair,
And thereupon my heart is driven wild:
She stands before me as a living child.

4

Her present image floats into the mind—   25
Did Quattrocento finger fashion it
Hollow of cheek as though it drank the wind
And took a mess of shadows for its meat?
And I though never of Ledaean kind
Had pretty plumage once—enough of that,   30
Better to smile on all that smile, and show
There is a comfortable kind of old scarecrow.

5

What youthful mother, a shape upon her lap
Honey of generation had betrayed,
And that must sleep, shriek, struggle to escape 35
As recollection or the drug decide,
Would think her son, did she but see that shape
With sixty or more winters on its head,
A compensation for the pang of his birth,
Or the uncertainty of his setting forth?   40

6

Plato thought nature but a spume that plays
Upon a ghostly paradigm of things;
Solider Aristotle played the taws
Upon the bottom of a king of kings;
World-famous golden-thighed Pythagoras   45
Fingered upon a fiddle-stick or strings
What a star sang and careless Muses heard:
Old clothes upon old sticks to scare a bird.

42. **Upon ... things:** Plato's philosophy held the material world was mere appearance—the *real* world existed in a noumenal world of Ideas, an ideal world of prototypes. 44. **Upon ... kings:** Aristotle, as tutor to Alexander the Great, probably spanked that "king of kings." 47. **What ... heard:** Pythagoras related the mathematics of musical harmony to the harmony of the spheres. (See "A Song for St. Cecilia's Day, 1687" page 168.)

7

Both nuns and mothers worship images,
But those the candles light are not as those   50
That animate a mother's reveries,
But keep a marble or a bronze repose.
And yet they too break hearts—O Presences
That passion, piety or affection knows,
And that all heavenly glory symbolize—   55
O self-born mockers of man's enterprise;

8

Labor is blossoming or dancing where
The body is not bruised to pleasure soul,
Nor beauty born out of its own despair,
Nor blear-eyed wisdom out of midnight oil.   60
O chestnut-tree, great-rooted blossomer,
Are you the leaf, the blossom or the bole?
O body swayed to music, O brightening glance,
How can we know the dancer from the dance?

COUNTRY SUMMER

Léonie Adams (1899–1970)

Now the rich cherry whose sleek wood
And top with silver petals traced,
Like a strict box its gems encased,
Has split from out that cunning lid,
All in an innocent green round,   5
Those melting rubies which it hid;
With moss ripe-strawberry-encrusted,
So birds get half, and minds lapse merry
To taste that deep-red lark's-bite berry,
And blackcap-bloom is yellow-dusted.   10

The wren that thieved it in the eaves
A trailer of the rose could catch
To her poor droopy sloven thatch,
And side by side with the wren's brood,—
O lovely time of beggars' luck—   15
Opens the quaint and hairy bud.

And full and golden is the yield
Of cows that never have to house.
But all night nibble under boughs,
Or cool their sides in the moist field.   20

Into the rooms flow meadow airs,
The warm farm-baking smell blows round;
Inside and out and sky and ground
Are much the same; the wishing star,
Hesperus, kind and early-born,   25
Is risen only finger-far.
All stars stand close in summer air,
And tremble, and look mild as amber;
When wicks are lighted in the chamber
You might say stars were settling there.   30

Now straightening from the flowery hay,
Down the still light the mowers look;
Or turn, because their dreaming shook,
And they waked half to other days,
When left alone in yellow-stubble,   35
The rusty-coated mare would graze.
Yet thick the lazy dreams are born;
Another thought can come to mind,
But like the shivering of the wind,
Morning and evening in the corn.   40

ODE TO THE CONFEDERATE DEAD

Allen Tate (b. 1899)

Row after row with strict impunity
The headstones yield their names to the element,
The wind whirrs without recollection;
In the riven troughs the splayed leaves
Pile up, of nature the casual sacrament   5
To the seasonal eternity of death;
Then driven by the fierce scrutiny
Of heaven to their election in the vast breath,
They sough the rumor of mortality.

Autumn is desolation in the plot   10
Of a thousand acres where these memories grow

From the inexhaustible bodies that are not
Dead, but feed the grass row after rich row.
Think of the autumns that have come and gone!
Ambitious November with the humors of the year, 15
With a particular zeal for every slab,
Staining the uncomfortable angels that rot
On the slabs, a wing chipped here, an arm there:
The brute curiosity of an angel's stare
Turns you, like them, to stone, 20
Transforms the heaving air
Till plunged to a heavier world below
You shift your sea-space blindly
Heaving, turning like the blind crab.

    Dazed by the wind, only the wind 25
    The leaves flying, plunge

You know who have waited by the wall
The twilight certainty of an animal,
Those midnight restitutions of the blood
You know—the immitigable pines, the smoky frieze 30
Of the sky, the sudden call: you know the rage,
The cold pool left by the mounting flood,
Of muted Zeno and Parmenides.
You who have waited for the angry resolution
Of those desires that should be yours tomorrow, 35
You know the unimportant shrift of death
And praise the vision
And praise the arrogant circumstance
Of those who fall
Rank upon rank, hurried beyond decision— 40
Here by the sagging gate, stopped by the wall.

    Seeing, seeing only the leaves
    Flying, plunge and expire

Turn your eyes to the immoderate past,
Turn to the inscrutable infantry rising 45
Demons out of the earth—they will not last.
Stonewall, Stonewall, and the sunken fields of hemp,
Shiloh, Antietam, Malvern Hill, Bull Run.
Lost in that orient of the thick and fast
You will curse the setting sun. 50

33. Zeno and Parmenides: Greek philosophers.

    Cursing only the leaves crying
    Like an old man in a storm

You hear the shout, the crazy hemlocks point
With troubled fingers to the silence which
Smothers you, a mummy, in time.   55
    The hound bitch
Toothless and dying, in a musty cellar
Hears the wind only.

    Now that the salt of their blood
Stiffens the saltier oblivion of the sea,   60
Seals the malignant purity of the flood,
What shall we who count our days and bow
Our heads with a commemorial woe
In the ribboned coats of grim felicity,
What shall we say of the bones, unclean,   65
Whose verdurous anonymity will grow?

The ragged arms, the ragged heads and eyes
Lost in these acres of the insane green?
The gray lean spiders come, they come and go;
In a tangle of willows without light   70
The singular screech-owl's tight
Invisible lyric seeds the mind
With the furious murmur of their chivalry.

    We shall say only the leaves
    Flying, plunge and expire   75

We shall say only the leaves whispering
In the improbable mist of nightfall
That flies on multiple wing:
Night is the beginning and the end
And in between the ends of distraction   80
Waits mute speculation, the patient curse
That stones the eyes, or like the jaguar leaps
For his own image in a jungle pool, his victim.

What shall we say who have knowledge
Carried to the heart? Shall we take the act   85
To the grave? Shall we, more hopeful, set up the grave
In the house? The ravenous grave?

    Leave now
The shut gate and the decomposing wall:

The gentle serpent, green in the mulberry bush, 90
Riots with his tongue through the hush—
Sentinel of the grave who counts us all!

POEM IN OCTOBER

Dylan Thomas (1914–1953)

It was my thirtieth year to heaven
Woke to my hearing from harbor and neighbor wood
And the mussel pooled and the heron
    Priested shore
      The morning beckon 5
With water praying and call of seagull and rook
And the knock of sailing boats on the net webbed wall
    Myself to set foot
      That second
In the still sleeping town and set forth. 10

My birthday began with the water-
Birds and the birds of the winged trees flying my name
Above the farms and the white horses
    And I rose
      In rainy autumn 15
And walked abroad in a shower of all my days.
High tide and the heron dived when I took the road
    Over the border
      And the gates
Of the town closed as the town awoke. 20

A springful of larks in a rolling
Cloud and the roadside bushes brimming with whistling
    Blackbirds and the sun of October
      Summery
        On the hill's shoulder, 25
Here were fond climates and sweet singers suddenly
Come in the morning where I wandered and listened
    To the rain wringing
      Wind blow cold
In the wood faraway under me. 30

Pale rain over the dwindling harbor
And over the sea wet church the size of a snail
    With its horns through mist and the castle
        Brown as owls
          But all the gardens   35
Of spring and summer were blooming in the tall tales
Beyond the border and under the lark full cloud.
        There could I marvel
           My birthday
      Away but the weather turned around.   40

    It turned away from the blithe country
And down the other air and the blue altered sky
      Streamed again a wonder of summer
          With apples
            Pears and red currants   45
And I saw in the turning so clearly a child's
Forgotten mornings when he walked with his mother
        Through the parables
          Of sun light
        And the legends of the green chapels   50

      And the twice told fields of infancy
That his tears burned my cheeks and his heart moved in mine.
      These were the woods the river and sea
          Where a boy
            In the listening   55
Summertime of the dead whispered the truth of his joy
To the trees and the stones and the fish in the tide.
        And the mystery
          Sang alive
      Still in the water and singingbirds.   60

    And there could I marvel my birthday
Away but the weather turned around. And the true
      Joy of the long dead child sang burning
          In the sun.
            It was my thirtieth   65
Year to heaven stood there then in the summer noon
Though the town below lay leaved with October blood.
        O may my heart's truth
          Still be sung
      On this high hill in a year's turning.   70

FOR THE UNION DEAD

Robert Lowell (b. 1917)

Relinquunt Omnia Servare Rem Publicam.

The old South Boston Aquarium stands
in a Sahara of snow now. Its broken windows are boarded.
The bronze weathervane cod has lost half its scales.
The airy tanks are dry.

Once my nose crawled like a snail on the glass; 5
my hand tingled
to burst the bubbles
drifting from the noses of the cowed, compliant fish.

My hand draws back. I often sigh still
for the dark downward and vegetating kingdom 10
of the fish and reptile. One morning last March,
I pressed against the new barbed and galvanized

fence on the Boston Common. Behind their cage,
yellow dinosaur steamshovels were grunting
as they cropped up tons of mush and grass 15
to gouge their underworld garage.

Parking spaces luxuriate like civic
sandpiles in the heart of Boston.
A girdle of orange, Puritan-pumpkin colored girders
braces the tingling Statehouse, 20

shaking over the excavations, as it faces Colonel Shaw
and his bell-cheeked Negro infantry
on St. Gaudens' shaking Civil War relief,
propped by a plank splint against the garage's earthquake.

Two months after marching through Boston, 25
half the regiment was dead;
at the dedication,
William James could almost hear the bronze Negroes breathe.

Their monument sticks like a fishbone
in the city's throat. 30

Relinquunt ... Publicam: They leave all to serve the Republic.

Its Colonel is as lean
as a compass-needle.

He has an angry wrenlike vigilance,
a greyhound's gentle tautness;
he seems to wince at pleasure, 35
and suffocate for privacy.

He is out of bounds now. He rejoices in man's lovely,
peculiar power to choose life and die—
when he leads his black soldiers to death,
he cannot bend his back. 40

On a thousand small town New England greens,
the old white church holds their air
of sparse, sincere rebellion; frayed flags
quilt the graveyards of the Grand Army of the Republic

The stone statues of the abstract Union Soldier 45
grow slimmer and younger each year—
wasp-waisted, they doze over muskets
and muse through their sideburns . . .

Shaw's father wanted no monument
except the ditch, 50
where his son's body was thrown
and lost with his "niggers."

The ditch is nearer.
There are no statutes for the last war here;
on Boylston Street, a commercial photograph 55
shows Hiroshima boiling

over a Mosler Safe, the "Rock of Ages"
that survived the blast. Space is nearer.
When I crouch to my television set,
the drained faces of Negro school-children rise like balloons. 60

Colonel Shaw
is riding on his bubble,
he waits
for the blesséd break.

The Aquarium is gone. Everywhere, 65
giant finned cars nose forward like fish;
a savage servility
slides by on grease.

POINT SHIRLEY

Sylvia Plath (1932–1963)

From Water-Tower Hill to the brick prison
The shingle booms, bickering under
The sea's collapse.
Snowcakes break and welter. This year
The gritted wave leaps   5
The seawall and drops onto a bier
Of quahog chips,
Leaving a salty mash of ice to whiten

In my grandmother's sand yard. She is dead,
Whose laundry snapped and froze here, who   10
Kept house against
What the sluttish, rutted sea could do.
Squall waves once danced
Ship timbers in through the cellar window;
A thresh-tailed, lanced   15
Shark littered in the geranium bed—

Such collusion of mulish elements
She wore her broom straws to the nub.
Twenty years out
Of her hand, the house still hugs in each drab   20
Stucco socket
The purple egg-stones: from Great Head's knob
To the filled-in Gut
The sea in its cold gizzard ground those rounds.

Nobody wintering now behind   25
The planked-up windows where she set
Her wheat loaves
And apple cakes to cool. What is it
Survives, grieves
So, over this battered, obstinate spit   30
Of gravel? The waves'
Spewed relics clicker masses in the wind,

Gray waves the stub-necked eiders ride.
A labor of love, and that labor lost.
Steadily the sea   35
East at Point Shirley. She died blessed,

And I come by
Bones, bones only, pawed and tossed,
A dog-faced sea.
The sun sinks under Boston, bloody red.   40
I would get from these dry-papped stones
The milk your love instilled in them.
The black ducks dive.
And though your graciousness might stream,
And I contrive,   45
Grandmother, stones are nothing of home
To that spumiest dove.
Against both bar and tower the black sea runs.

QUESTIONS

1. Ben Jonson "To the Immortal Memory and Friendship of that Noble Pair, Sir Lucius Cary and Sir Henry Morrison"

    (Ben Jonson, a learned classicist, adapted some aspects of the pattern of the Pindaric ode to the English ode in this poem. Notice that the poem moves in groups of three stanzas (or strophes). Pindaric odes are composed of several of these three-stanza groups; the patterns and lengths of stanzas vary from ode to ode, but in a given ode, as in this one, all turns and counterturns are uniform in number of lines, lengths of lines, and rhyme schemes, and all stands are uniform and different from the turns and counterturns. The important point to notice is that Jonson uses the Greek pattern of the poem, but not for the same reason as the Greeks.)
    The two chief subjects of the poem are the early death (about twenty years old) of Sir Henry Morrison and his close friendship with Sir Lucius Cary. Morrison, however, is not directly referred to until line 43 or Cary until line 75. Consider the first forty-two lines—the first four stanzas.

(1) In the first stanza Jonson addresses the "brave infant of Saguntum," referring to a strange episode related by the ancient Roman natural historian Pliny—an episode that supposedly happened when the Carthaginian general Hannibal besieged Saguntum in 219 B.C. What was the episode? What philosophic question does it suggest to Jonson in the first two stanzas?
(2) How does Jonson use the infant, the horrors of war, and "wiser Nature" (line 11) to create an image of life's value?
(3) In lines 21–24 Jonson sets up a contrast between "space" and "act," and between "face" and "fact" (that is, between life's *extent* and *deed* and between man's *appearance* and *deed*). What answer is implied to the questions raised in these lines?
(4) In the remaining lines of stanzas three and four (lines 25–42), Jonson presents a portrait of an unnamed man. What are the facts about this man? What opinions about his value are expressed? What makes this portrait scornful or satirical? Examine especially the climactic image in lines 40–42.

Consider stanzas 5–7, lines 43–74.
(1) The fifth stanza presents an image of Morrison. Notice particularly the kind of language used. Is it specific or general? What effect is achieved by the language? What is implied in lines 43–45 by the words "fell," "fell," "fall'st" (a pun), and "stood"? In what ways does the image of Morrison created by this stanza—and particularly in lines 51–52—resolve the extreme contrasts of the first four stanzas between the "brave infant of Saguntum" and the old man of "fourescore years"?
(2) So far the poem has made important use of contrasts between several sets of concepts and images. In the sixth stanza, lines 58–59, these contrasting sets focus on a distinction between merely being ("thou hast been long") and effective living ("lived"). How does stanza six organize and explain this distinction? Who is being addressed in this stanza?
(3) Stanza seven has often been printed as a separate poem. The images and the metrical pattern of the stanza work together to make this an effective statement. Examine the structure of the stanza. Considered

in context, the stanza is both a climax of the first phase of the poem, and a consolation leading into the next stanza. Show this, noting particularly the importance of the diction in lines 73–74.

Consider the last five stanzas, lines 75–128.

(1) The second man, Lucius Cary, is addressed in line 75 and is, generally, the object of address in lines 75–116. However, what evidence indicates, that "Lucius" is being addressed in a public manner instead of a private and intimate one?

(2) In lines 75–116, note the following: the use of the poet's own name (lines 84–85) and the peculiar way the name appears—"Ben" as the last word of a line and a stanza, and "Jonson" as the first word of the next line and stanza; the word "asterism" (line 89), with its reference to the constellation Dioscuri (Castor and Pollux or Gemini); and the curious breaking of "twi-light" (lines 92–93). Why does the poet, by his manner of dividing his name, emphasize both the personal and private friend—Ben—and the more public poet—Jonson? Why is the role of the poet important? How does Jonson make clear that a poet is both a man like other men and a special kind of man?

(3) Look up the etymology of "twilight." Jonson's use of the word emphasizes the possibility of the idea of *twin*. Is there any authority for that meaning in the etymology? Why is it useful to Jonson to suggest that meaning? Is the usual meaning of the word "twilight" important in Jonson's poem?

(4) To follow the argument of lines 89–99 you should consult a mythology handbook for information about the Dioscuri. How does Jonson use this allusion to offer consolation for Morrison's death and to celebrate his friendship with Cary?

(5) In the tenth stanza (lines 97–106), how does Jonson link his image of the two friends with the idea developed in the first half of the poem?

(6) In the eleventh stanza (lines 107–16), how does Jonson epitomize the relationship between the two men? What conceit, or extravagant image, does he conclude with?

(7) In the last stanza Jonson ceases a direct address to Cary and brings together the chief themes and images

of his ode into one final statement for his audience. In addition to showing how this stanza brings these themes and images together, show how Jonson's basically skeptical view of human society, introduced by his reference to the "brave infant of Saguntum," is brought out in lines 118–21.

2. John Dryden   "A Song for St. Cecilia's Day, 1687"

Analyze the meter and rhyme scheme of this poem. What significant irregularities do you find? How are the opening lines and the concluding line related? Essentially the poem consists of enumerating the accomplishments of music. What are these accomplishments?

3. Thomas Gray   "Ode on a Distant Prospect of Eton College"

(1) Gray's first stanza seems to be addressing the spires and towers of Eton. What is the meaning of such an address? What is the emotional effect of the opening stanza? What associations does Eton College have for Gray?
(2) The third stanza of the poem asks a question of the river Thames. What is the question? What three sports are described in lines 25–30?
(3) What class of men does the fourth stanza describe?
(4) In the fifth stanza Gray seems to express sympathy for those trying to escape life's vicissitudes, yet he would have them informed of their inescapable fate. Then he vividly and passionately lists the evils that prey on men (lines 51–90). After listing these evils he returns to the idea that man should be made aware of his impending doom. What is his final attitude?

4. William Collins   "Ode to Evening"

Collins's ode is a poem of praise to evening. How does he use personification to express his feeling for evening?

What specific characteristics does he thus impart to this time of day? What role do the seasons play in this poem?

5. William Wordsworth   "Ode: Intimations of Immortality from Recollections of Early Childhood"

This ode is carefully organized into three major parts: stanzas I–IV, V–VIII, and IX–XI. Trace the major ideas presented in each part, show how these ideas are varied from part to part, and indicate the change or development they undergo. Study the stanzaic structure of the poem. How does Wordsworth vary his meter and rhyme scheme from stanza to stanza? Is this variation related to the thematic structure of the poem?

"Ode to Duty"

How is the epigraph from Seneca relevant to Wordsworth's poem? What does Wordsworth mean by "Duty"? As with Collins's poem, the "Ode to Duty" makes extensive use of personification. How does Wordsworth personify duty? Compare his personification with Collins's. Who are those who do duty's bidding and do not know they do the will of duty? What are some of the rewards that follow from fulfilling one's obligations to duty? What personal testimony does the poet give us regarding his own response to duty? Wordsworth makes duty "stern" and "awful," but nonetheless appealing. How does he do this? What does the last line of the poem mean? Compare this line with the first line of Donne's fourteenth Holy Sonnet ("Batter my heart, three-personed God"; page 152).

6. Samuel Taylor Coleridge   "Dejection: An Ode"

In this ode the speaker's thought is correlated with, or defined by, the moon, the wind, and the menace to beauty of the gathering storm. How are these effects of nature used to clarify the speaker's dejection? There are several references to a woman in this poem. In what sense is the poem addressed to her? What role do these references play in our understanding of the poem?

7. Percy Bysshe Shelley   "Ode to the West Wind"

Shelley's "Ode to the West Wind" is divided into five parts. Account for this division. What is the connection between each part? What development of thought occurs in the poem? Examine Shelley's imagery. What use is made of the leaf, the cloud, and the wave? Paraphrase the poet's prayer in the last stanza. This prayerful wish is not unlike Thomas's in "Poem in October" (page 198). Compare the two utterances.

8. John Keats   "To Autumn"

Each of the three stanzas of this poem presents a different view of autumn. What are these views? Keats addresses Autumn as a person throughout the poem. Specifically describe how this is done. What kinds of insect and animal life does Keats bring into the last seven lines of his poem? What is the effect of this? Compare the use of personification in Keats's "To Autumn" and Collins's "To Evening."

"Ode to a Nightingale"

What is the emotional state of the poet at the opening of this ode? What caused this condition? What are his feelings in the last stanza? What changes do his feelings undergo during the course of the poem? Can you account for these alterations of emotion? What kinds of imagery does Keats use in this poem? How are his images related to one another? How are they related to the thoughts expressed in the poem? Is the movement of imagery logical or purely emotional? Keats makes the nightingale immortal—an obvious impossibility. Why does Keats do this for the nightingale? How is the reader supposed to react to it?

"Ode on Melancholy"

The speaker in this poem seems to be saying, rather perversely, that the melancholy mood should be welcomed, cultivated, and brought to perfection. What arguments does he offer to support his view? One of the characteristics of Keats's odes is the way he develops several image clusters to present his thoughts and feelings. Trace the imagery in this poem. Show how it is connected to the themes of the poem.

9. William Butler Yeats   "Among School Children"

In "Among School Children," a sixty-year-old poet visits a classroom and is reminded by one of the little girls in the classroom of a woman he loved. This memory triggers a series of reflections concerning the nature and purposes of life itself. The conclusion to these reflections is that man is mocked by his ideals and dreams, but that beauty and pleasure are possible even in such a world. Find the precise stanzas that treat these steps in the poet's thought. Locate other ideas that the poet touches on. Account for the transitions of thought from stanza to stanza. Why is there no period at the end of the next-to-last stanza? What is the meaning of the tree and dance imagery of the last stanza? In the fifth stanza Yeats asks whether life is worth living —whether the pain of bearing of a child is too much when one considers the anguish of old age. What is his answer? The stanzaic form of this poem is ottava rima. What is the meter and rhyme scheme of this form?

10. Léonie Adams   "Country Summer"

The achievement of this poem rests primarily on its detailed descriptions. These require careful attention, especially in the first stanza. Give as accurate a paraphrase as possible of the opening stanza. How are these descriptions ordered? What do the final four lines mean? How is this poem like one of Keats's odes? How does it differ?

11. Allen Tate   "Ode to the Confederate Dead"

Allen Tate once wrote that his ode is " 'about' solipsism, a philosophical doctrine which says that we create the world in the act of perceiving it, or about narcissim, or any other *ism* that denotes the failure of the human personality to function objectively in nature and society." How does this fit with your view of the poem's meaning?

Tate further describes the overall structure of his ode in this manner: It begins with a man possessed by a feeling of desolation "stopping at the gate of a confederate graveyard" as leaves are falling. This beginning is the background for a meditation on "the ravages of time," which concludes with the "blind crab" image (line 24). (The crab is one symbol, according to Tate, for "the looked-in ego," the jaguar is another.) Tate says the next long section (he calls it "strophe"), beginning with line 27, declares "The other term of the conflict"—the theme of heroism. Tate sees the structure of his poem turning on "the tension between the two themes, 'active faith' which has decayed, and the fragmentary cosmos which surrounds us." Expand on this interpretation.

Compare the speaker's attitudes toward the leaves with the elements of nature present in Shelley's "Ode to the West Wind" and Keats's "Ode to a Nightingale." Comment on the serpent at the conclusion of Tate's ode (line 91). Tate himself called it "the ancient symbol of time."

The author says he called this poem an ode because it is metrically irregular, like the English imitation of the Pindaric ode. Tate also said, "I suppose in so calling it I intended an irony: The scene of the poem is not a public celebration, it is a lone man by a gate." What is the point of the irony?

12. Dylan Thomas "Poem in October"

This poem recounts the thirtieth birthday of the poet. It begins with his setting out in the morning, climbing a hill, and, at the height of his climb, being moved to utter a prayerful wish. Recount precisely the manner of his setting forth, what happens during his climb, and exactly what his wish is at the poem's end. Count the syllables in each line of any two or three stanzas. Do you find any apparent pattern (allowing for exceptions here and there)? What is the aesthetic effect of such a poetic form? Compare the autumn imagery in this poem with that of Keats's "To Autumn."

13. Robert Lowell   "For the Union Dead"

   This poem celebrates the past by a series of contrasts with the present. The chief element of the past is the Civil War as embodied in Colonel Shaw—his heroism, puritanical determination, and fatalism. However, there are several other aspects of the past that also are defined by being juxtaposed to the present. What are these? Account for the movement of thought in the poem. How does one stanza lead into another?

14. Sylvia Plath   "Point Shirley"

   Like Jonson's, Tate's, and Lowell's odes, Sylvia Plath's poem is concerned with paying tribute to the dead. Who is the dead person Plath eulogizes? How does she praise this person? What is Plath's attitude toward this person? "Point Shirley's" meaning turns on a handful of images that have symbolic import: the sea, the house by the sea, the stones, the sea ducks (eiders). What do these things mean in the poem? Compare Plath's use of nature to that of Wordsworth, Coleridge, or Keats. Plath's language occasionally becomes obscure. One of the reasons for this is that she is using words in unusual ways. For example, where is the verb in line 32? What is the meaning of "masses" in the same line? Account for the unusual positioning of "ride" in line 33. Find similar examples of uncommon word use and explain the aesthetic purpose of Plath's use of those words.

Stylistic Contexts

Diction

In poems, the phrase "poetic diction" refers to words that call attention to themselves. Many of the words that poets use do not interest us as words. Ordinarily, any curiosity about them can be satisfied by grasping the grammatical and referential context in which they are used. There are, however, words that demand attention either because we are uncertain of exactly what they mean or because there is something curious or exciting about how they are used. In this latter case we are concerned with the way they are used and the way their meaning is conveyed by the poet.

We can, simply for convenience, divide poetic diction into two categories: (1) words that strike us as strange because they are difficult, archaic, or rare, and (2) words that seem particularly precise or vivid. It is very possible that a single word may be archaic, difficult, rare, and vivid. These categories are not mutually exclusive, and a word that attracts attention in several ways is an ideal example of poetic diction.

Poets collect rare words the way some people collect stamps, coins, or matchbooks, and they exhibit this fondness for words by using the most unusual ones frequently. Each poet and, to some extent, each poem possesses a special character because of the words the poet uses. Some of these words attract our attention simply because they appear so frequently in a particular poet's work. Others attract us because they are curiosities. Thus the poet's words provide the first context in which to view poems. Here are some examples of "verbal signatures." As you read the following words, reflect on their general qualities: Gerard Manley Hopkins—minion, achieve (as a nominal rather than verbal), wimpling, stipple, stooks, brickish, brauchy, scanted, abeles, towery, mealed; e. e. cummings—mud-luscious, wee, blueeyed, kiddo, Lydia E. Pinkham, B.V.D., merds, crepuscular, throstles, tenstendoned, doidee (dirty), highfalootin, splendiferous, scrumptious, gimme (give me), triglyph's, kumrads (comrades), senecktie (necktie); Lewis Carroll—brillig, slithy, gimble, mimsy, mome, raths, frumious, Bandersnatch, manxome, whiffling, tulgey, galumphing, frabjous, chortled, mumblingly. Poets use such words to convey a particular verbal texture. In some instances though—with "Jabberwocky," for example—we will not even be able to find most of the words in the dictionary. We have to cope with such terms by absorbing the context of the poem. Although the following poems often send readers to the dictionary, one must also grasp the total circumstance in which the words are being used.

THE WINDHOVER

TO CHRIST OUR LORD

Gerard Manley Hopkins (1844–1889)

I caught this morning morning's minion, king-
   dom of daylight's dauphin, dapple-dawn-drawn Falcon, in his
   riding
Of the rolling level underneath him steady air, and striding
High there, how he rung upon the rein of a wimpling wing
In his ecstasy! then off, off forth on swing,   5
   As a skate's heel sweeps smooth on a bow-bend: the hurl and
   gliding
Rebuffed the big wind. My heart in hiding
Stirred for a bird,—the achieve of, the mastery of the thing!

Brute beauty and valour and act, oh, air, pride, plume, here
   Buckle! and the fire that breaks from thee then, a billion   10
Times told lovelier, more dangerous, O my chevalier!

   No wonder of it: shéer plód makes plough down sillion
Shine, and blue-bleak embers, ah my dear,
   Fall, gall themselves, and gash gold-vermillion.

in Just—

e. e. cummings (1894–1963)

in Just—
spring   when the world is mud-
luscious the little
lame balloonman

whistles   far   and wee   5

and eddieandbill come
running from marbles and
piracies and it's
spring

when the world is puddle-wonderful   10

the queer
old balloonman whistles
far   and   wee
and bettyandisbel come dancing

from hop-scotch and jump-rope and   15

it's
spring
and
    the

        goat-footed   20

balloonMan   whistles
far
and
wee

JABBERWOCKY

Lewis Carroll (1832–1898)

'Twas brillig, and the slithy toves
  Did gyre and gimble in the wabe:
All mimsy were the borogoves,
  And the mome raths outgrabe.

"Beware the Jabberwock, my son! 5
 The jaws that bite, the claws that catch!
Beware the Jubjub bird, and shun
 The frumious Bandersnatch!"

He took his vorpal sword in hand:
 Long time the manxome foe he sought— 10
So rested he by the Tumtum tree,
 And stood awhile in thought.

And, as in uffish thought he stood,
 The Jaberwock, with eyes of flame,
Came whiffling through the tulgey wood, 15
 And burbled as it came!

One, two! One, two! And through and through
 The vorpal blade went snicker-snack!
He left it dead, and with its head
 He went galumphing back. 20

"And, hast thou slain the Jabberwock?
 Come to my arms, my beamish boy!
O frabjous day! Callooh! Callay!"
 He chortled in his joy.

'Twas brillig, and the slithy toves 25
 Did gyre and gimble in the wabe:
All mimsy were the borogoves,
 And the mome raths outgrabe.

The above poem comes from *Through the Looking Glass* by Lewis Carroll. Alice picks up a book and opens it to "Jabberwocky," which is printed backward and must be placed before a mirror in order to be read. Later she is talking with Humpty Dumpty:

> "You seem very clever at explaining words, Sir," said Alice. "Would you kindly tell me the meaning of the poem called 'Jabberwocky'?"
> "Let's hear it," said Humpty Dumpty. "I can explain all the poems that ever were invented—and a good many that haven't been invented just yet."
> This sounded very hopeful, so Alice repeated the first verse:—
>> " 'Twas brillig, and the slithy toves
>> Did gyre and gimble in the wabe:

All mimsy were the borogoves,
And the mome raths outgrabe."

"That's enough to begin with," Humpty Dumpty interrupted: "there are plenty of hard words there. *'Brillig'* means four o'clock in the afternoon—the time when you begin *broiling* things for dinner."
"That'll do very well," said Alice "and *'slithy'*?"
"Well, *'slithy'* means 'lithe and slimy.' 'Lithe' is the same as 'active.' You see it's like a portmanteau—there are two meanings packed up into one word."
"I see it now," Alice remarked thoughtfully: "and what are *'toves'*?"
"Well, *'toves'* are something like badgers—they're something like lizards—and they're something like corkscrews."
"They must be very curious-looking creatures."
"They are that," said Humpty Dumpty; "also they make their nests under sun-dials—also they live on cheese."
"And what's to *'gyre'* and to *'gimble'*?"
"To *'gyre'* is to go round and round like a gyroscope. To *'gimble'* is to make holes like a gimlet."
"And *'the wabe'* is the grass-plot round a sun-dial, I suppose?" said Alice, surprised at her own ingenuity.
"Of course, it is. It's called *'wabe'* you know, because it goes a long way before it, and a long way behind it—"
"And a long way beyond it on each side," Alice added.
"Exactly so. Well, then, *'mimsy'* is 'flimsy and miserable' (there's another portmanteau for you). And a *'borogove'* is a thin shabby-looking bird with its feathers sticking out all round—something like a live mop."
"And then *'mome raths'*?" said Alice. "I'm afraid I'm giving you a great deal of trouble."
"Well, a *'rath'* is a sort of green pig: but *'mome'* I'm not certain about. I think it's short for 'from home'—meaning that they'd lost their way, you know."
"And what does *'outgrabe'* mean?"
"Well, *'outgribing'* is something between bellowing and whistling, with a kind of sneeze in the middle; however, you'll hear it done, maybe—down in the wood yonder—and, when you've once heard it, you'll be *quite* content. Who's been repeating all that hard stuff to you?"
"I read it in a book," said Alice.

Stylistic Contexts

In the following two poems archaic words are used to express, among other things, a sense of antiquity and ageless values. Try to determine what ideas of the past and what values are conveyed by the poet's word choices. In the first poem, Ezra Pound uses a four-stress line reminiscent of Old English poetry, along with a number of rare words, in retelling the story of Odysseus's journey to Hades. (The excerpt describes Odysseus's voyage and his visit with the prophet, Tiresias. Tiresias will tell him how to return home. But before Tiresias can speak, a sacrifice must be offered. When the animals are slaughtered, all the dead gather hoping to drink of the blood.) In the second poem John Milton includes many ancient place names. Consider the effect achieved by the use of these names. (This passage describes Satan offering Christ all the Kingdoms of this world.)

from CANTO I

Ezra Pound (1885–1972)

And then went down to the ship,
Set keel to breakers, forth on the godly sea, and
We set up mast and sail on that swart ship,
Bore sheep aboard her, and our bodies also
Heavy with weeping, and winds from sternward   5
Bore us out onward with bellying canvas,
Circe's this craft, the trim-coifed goddess.
Then sat we amidships, wind jamming the tiller,
Thus with stretched sail, we went over sea till day's end.
Sun to his slumber, shadows o'er all the ocean,   10
Came we then to the bounds of deepest water,
To the Kimmerian lands, and peopled cities
Covered with close-webbed mist, unpierced ever
With glitter of sun-rays
Nor with stars stretched, nor looking back from heaven   15
Swartest night stretched over wretched men there.
The ocean flowing backward, came we then to the place
Aforesaid by Circe.
Here did they rites, Perimedes and Eurylochus,
And drawing sword from my hip   20
I dug the ell-square pitkin;
Poured we libations unto each the dead,

First mead and then sweet wine, water mixed with white flour.
Then prayed I many a prayer to the sickly death's-heads;
As set in Ithaca, sterile bulls of the best 25
For sacrifice, heaping the pyre with goods,
A sheep to Tiresias only, black and a bell-sheep.
Dark blood flowed in the fosse,
Souls out of Erebus, cadaverous dead, of brides
Of youths and of the old who had borne much; 30
Souls stained with recent tears, girls tender,
Men many, mauled with bronze lance heads,
Battle spoil, bearing yet dreory arms,
These many crowded about me; with shouting,
Pallor upon me, cried to my men for more beasts; 35
Slaughtered the herds, sheep slain of bronze;
Poured ointment, cried to the gods,
To Pluto the strong, and praised Proserpine;
Unsheathed the narrow sword,
I sat to keep off the impetuous impotent dead, 40
Till I should hear Tiresias.
But first Elpenor came, our friend Elpenor,
Unburied, cast on the wide earth,
Limbs that we left in the house of Circe,
Unwept, unwrapped in sepulchre, since toils urged other. 45
Pitiful spirit. And I cried in hurried speech:
"Elpenor, how art thou come to this dark coast?
Cam'st thou afoot, outstripping seamen?"

from PARADISE REGAINED

John Milton (1608–1674)

Here thou beholdest
Assyria and her empire's ancient bounds,
Araxes and the *Caspian* lake, thence on
As far as *Indus* east, *Euphrates* west,
And oft beyond; to south the *Persian* Bay, 5
And inaccessible the *Arabian* drouth:
Here *Ninevah,* of length within her wall
Several days' journey, built by *Ninus* old,
Of that first golden monarchy the seat,
And seat of *Salmanassar,* whose success 10

Israel in long captivity still mourns;
There *Babylon* the wonder of all tongues,
As ancient, but rebuilt by him who twice
Judah and all thy Father *David's* house
Led captive, and *Jerusalem* laid waste, 15
Till *Cyrus* set them free; *Persepolis*
His city there thou seest, and *Bactra* there;
Ecbatana her structure vast there shews,
And *Hecatampylos* her hunderd gates,
There *Susa* by *Choaspes,* amber stream, 20
The drink of none but kings; of later fame
Built by *Emathian,* or by *Parthian* hands,
The great *Seleucia, Nisibis,* and there
Artaxata, Teredon, Tesiphon,
Turning with easy eye thou mayst behold. 25

In first reading a poem it is helpful to mark in some way those words (perhaps by circling them) that are not immediately clear. No one can be expected to know everything, but neither should one admit defeat too easily. Getting to know a poem is partly a matter of filling in the blanks.

THE MOCKERS

William Blake (1757–1827)

Mock on, mock on, Voltaire, Rousseau;
Mock on, mock on; 'tis all in vain!
You throw the sand against the wind,
And the wind blows it back again.

And every sand becomes a gem 5
Reflected in the beams divine;
Blown back they blind the mocking eye,
But still in Israel's paths they shine.

The Atoms of Democritus
And Newton's Particles of Light 10
Are sands upon the Red Sea shore,
Where Israel's tents do shine so bright.

QUESTIONS

1. Who were Voltaire and Rousseau? In what way can they be called "mockers"? Consult a reference book if the names are new to you.
2. What were the theories of Democritus and Newton? Again, if these theories are unknown, check a reference book.
3. Look up the story of the dividing of the waters of the Red Sea in the Bible (Exodus 14). What is the point of Blake's identification of atoms and particles of light with the sand of the desert?

In addition to using archaic words and references to the past in order to connote attitudes and values, poets use contemporary words and slang.

MEMORIES OF WEST STREET AND LEPKE

Robert Lowell (b. 1917)

Only teaching on Tuesdays, book-worming
in pajamas fresh from the washer each morning,
I hog a whole house on Boston's
"hardly passionate Marlborough Street,"
where even the man   5
scavenging filth in the back alley trash cans,
has two children, a beach wagon, a helpmate,
and is a "young Republican."
I have a nine months' daughter
young enough to be my granddaughter.   10
Like the sun she rises in her flame-flamingo infants' wear.

These are the tranquillized *Fifties*,
and I am forty. Ought I to regret my seedtime?

I was a fire-breathing Catholic C.O.,
and had made my manic statement,   15
telling off the state and president, and then
sat waiting sentence in the bull pen
beside a Negro boy with curlicues
of marijuana in his hair.

> Given a year, 20
> I walked on the roof of the West Street Jail, a short
> enclosure like my school soccer court,
> and saw the Hudson River once a day
> through sooty clothesline entanglements
> and bleaching khaki tenements. 25
> Strolling, I yammered metaphysics with Abramowitz,
> a jaundice-yellow ("it's really tan")
> and flyweight pacifist,
> so vegetarian
> he wore rope shoes and preferred fallen fruit. 30
> He tried to convert Bioff and Brown,
> the Hollywood pimps, to his diet.
> Hairy, muscular, suburban,
> wearing chocolate double-breasted suits,
> they blew their tops and beat him black and blue. 35
>
> I was so out of things, I'd never heard
> of the Jehovah's Witnesses.
> "Are you a C.O.?" I asked a fellow jailbird.
> "No," he answered, "I'm a J.W."
> He taught me the "hospital tuck," 40
> and pointed out the T shirted back
> of *Murder Incorporated's* Czar Lepke,
> there piling towels on a rack,
> or dawdling off to his little segregated cell full
> of things forbidden the common man: 45
> a portable radio, a dresser, two toy American
> flags tied together with a ribbon of Easter palm.
> Flabby, bald, lobotomized,
> he drifted in a sheepish calm,
> where no agonizing reappraisal 50
> jarred his concentration on the electric chair—
> hanging like an oasis in his air
> of lost connections. . . .

Certain words carry dates almost as visible as the date on a coin. In the preceding poem, at the end of the first stanza and the beginning of the second, Lowell states precisely the time of his recollections. Indeed, certain words in the poem could hardly have appeared much earlier. A few are older than they look, as a check in the OED will reveal. "Hog" (line 3), for example, goes back to

1899—and it is probably older. "Yammered" (line 26) with a direct object does not look old, but it goes back to 1786. And how long have people been talking about suntan as "tan" (line 27)? The OED's educated guess is 1827.

But many more words in the poem appear only in the most recent dictionaries—*Webster's Third New International Dictionary*, for example. Anyone the poet's age or older can remember when everyone said "washing machine" instead of "washer" (line 2). It seems likely that the new word "washer" came into use as more people installed washer-dryer combinations. It is not, of course, the word that is new but the meaning. Thus, "tranquillized" (line 12) is not a particularly new word. It has been around a long time in the sense of "made tranquil, as by a cooling breeze, a peaceful sunset, a soothing piece of music." The new element is the existence, since the 1950s, of "tranquillizers"—that is, certain drugs that have the effect of soothing the patient. A similar word is "lobotomized" (line 48). It has long been possible, as with drugs, to destroy or impair the mental faculty that perceives the relationship between cause and effect, but in the 1940s physicians began to do this surgically, with an operation called a lobotomy, and this is what is referred to in the poem.

Generally, when we speak of diction we mean the poet's aesthetic use of language. Out of a number of possible choices the poet selects the precise word he needs. Consider the word choices made in the poem below.

ROOT CELLAR

Theodore Roethke (1908–1963)

Nothing would sleep in that cellar, dank as a ditch,
Bulbs broke out of boxes hunting for chinks in the dark,
Shoots dangled and drooped,
Lolling obscenely from mildewed crates,
Hung down long yellow evil necks, like tropical snakes.   5
And what a congress of stinks!—
Roots ripe as old bait,
Pulpy stems, rank, silo-rich,
Leaf-mould, manure, lime, piled against slippery planks.
Nothing would give up life: 10
Even the dirt kept breathing a small breath.

In the left-hand column below are fourteen of the poet's actual word choices. The right-hand column lists certain alternatives that, for one reason or another, are not as vivid and precise. Discuss the poet's choice of words, using a dictionary if necessary.

line		
1	sleep	rest
	cellar	basement
	dank	damp
	ditch	sewer
2	broke out of	came out of
	hunting for	looking for
	chinks	cracks
4	obscenely	vulgarly
6	congress	meeting
7	ripe	odorous
8	rank	smelly
9	manure	fertilizer
11	dirt	soil
	small	slight

Below are five pairs of poems. Each pair has the same general subject, but each poem is vastly different. Study these differences —especially in word usage.

Both of the following poems are translations of the same Chinese poem.

A SONG OF CH'ANG-KAN

Li Po (Rihaku) (701–762)

My hair had hardly covered my forehead.
I was picking flowers, playing by my door,   *sense of culture*
When you, my lover, on a bamboo horse,
Came trotting in circles and throwing green plums.
We lived near together on a lane in Ch'ang-kan,   5
Both of us young and happy-hearted.   *conceptual*
... At fourteen I became your wife,   *flat phrase*
So bashful that I dared not smile,   *syntactic device*
And I lowered my head toward a dark corner
And would not turn to your thousand calls;   10
But at fifteen I straightened my brows and laughed,

Learning that no dust could ever seal our love,
That even unto death I would await you by my post
And would never lose heart in the tower of silent watching.
... Then when I was sixteen, you left on a long journey. 15
Through the Gorges of Ch'u-t'ang, of rock and whirling water.
And then came the Fifth month, more than I could bear,
And I tried to hear the monkeys in your lofty far-off sky.
Your foot-prints by our door, where I had watched you go,
Were hidden, every one of them, under green moss, 20
Hidden under moss too deep to sweep away.
And the first autumn wind added fallen leaves.
And now, in the Eighth-month, yellowing butterflies
Hover, two by two, in our west-garden grasses. ...
And, because of all this, my heart is breaking, 25
And I fear for my bright cheeks, lest they fade.
... Oh, at last, when you return through the three Pa districts,
Send me a message home ahead!
And I will come and meet you and will never mind the distance,
All the way to Ch'ang f'eng Sha. 30

Translated by Witter Bynner

THE RIVER-MERCHANT'S WIFE: A LETTER

Ezra Pound (1885–1972)

While my hair was still cut straight across my forehead
Played I about the front gate, pulling flowers.
You came by on bamboo stilts, playing horse,
You walked about my seat, playing with blue plums,
And we went on living in the village of Chokan: 5
Two small people, without dislike or suspicion.

At fourteen I married My Lord you.
I never laughed, being bashful.
Lowering my head, I looked at the wall.
Called to, a thousand times, I never looked back. 10

At fifteen I stopped scowling,
I desired my dust to be mingled with yours
Forever and forever and forever.
Why should I climb the lookout?

At sixteen you departed, 15
You went into far Ku-to-yen, by the river of swirling eddies,
And you have been gone five months.
The monkeys make sorrowful noise overhead. *doesn't want to get into girl's grief*
You dragged your feet when you went out.
By the gate now, the moss is grown, the different mosses, 20
Too deep to clear them away!
The leaves fall early this autumn, in wind.
The paired butterflies are already yellow with August
Over the grass in the West garden;
They hurt me. I grow older. 25
If you are coming down through the narrows of the river Kiang,
Please let me know beforehand,
And I will come out to meet you.
          As far as Cho-fu-Sa.

          by Ribaku. (Li T'ai Po)

QUESTIONS

Line references apply to both poems.
1. Compare the titles of the two poems. What effect does the notion of a letter add to Pound's poem?
2. Which opening line do you find more precise visually?
3. Note the inversion in Pound's line. This is an archaic touch. What does it add? (line 2)
4. Why might Pound have omitted the phrase "my lover"? (line 3)
5. Is there some confusion about the plums? (line 4)
6. Compare line 6 in both poems.
7. Again, note the inversion in Pound's line, along with the expression "My Lord." Are these effective? (line 7)
8. Comment on the visual precision of line 8 in the poems.
9. Compare the usage of the word "dust" in each poem. (line 12)
10. The terseness in Pound's poem and its avoidance of such predictable phrases as "tower of silent watching" and

"whirling water" are deliberate. Why? What purpose is served? (lines 14–16)
11. Compare the uses of the monkey and footprint images. Can you account for the similarity of the moss imagery? (lines 18–21)
12. Compare the relative economy of lines 25.
13. Why do you think Pound concentrates on the river and the narrows? (line 26)
14. From the numerous comparisons between the two poems, choose two or three important words or phrases that most clearly illustrate the importance of the poet's word choices.

David Daiches, a British critic, composed the following poem in a conventional nineteenth-century style to contrast with Dylan Thomas's "A Refusal to Mourn. . . ." Compare the two ways of saying much the same thing.

NOT UNTIL DOOMSDAY'S ...

Not until doomsday's final call
And all the earth returns once more
To that primaeval home of all,
When on that insubstantial shore
The tumbling primal waters foam   5
And silence rules her lonely home,

And I return to whence I came,
The sacramental child of earth,
Joining with nature to proclaim
A death that is a second birth—   10
No, not until that final sleep
Will I for this dead infant weep.

She lies with her ancestral dead,
The child of London, home at last
To earth from whence all life is bred   15
And present mingles with the past.
The unmourning waters lap her feet:
She has no second death to meet.

A REFUSAL TO MOURN THE DEATH, BY FIRE, OF A CHILD IN LONDON

Dylan Thomas (1914–1953)

Never until the mankind making *everything created*
Bird beast and flower *out of darkness*
Fathering and all humbling darkness
Tells with silence the last light breaking *end of world*
And the still hour   5
Is come of the sea tumbling in harness

And I must enter again the round
Zion of the water bead
And the synagogue of the ear of corn
Shall I let pray the shadow of a sound   10
Or sow my salt seed
In the least valley of sackcloth to mourn

The majesty and burning of the child's death.
I shall not murder
Everyone must The mankind of her going with a grave truth *Stations of* 15
die. Sentiment Nor blaspheme down the stations of the breath *the Cross*
would obscure With any further
this fact. Elegy of innocence and youth.

Deep with the first dead lies London's daughter,
Robed in the long friends,   20
The grains beyond age, the dark veins of her mother, *Earth*
Secret by the unmourning water
Of the riding Thames.
After the first death, there is no other.

* * *

A PRAYER FOR MY DAUGHTER

William Butler Yeats (1865–1939)

Once more the storm is howling, and half hid
Under this cradle-hood and coverlid
My child sleeps on. There is no obstacle

But Gregory's wood and one bare hill
Whereby the haystack- and roof-levelling wind,   5
Bred on the Atlantic, can be stayed;
And for an hour I have walked and prayed
Because of the great gloom that is in my mind.

I have walked and prayed for this young child an hour
And heard the sea-wind scream upon the tower,   10
And under the arches of the bridge, and scream
In the elms above the flooded stream;
Imagining in excited reverie
That the future years had come,
Dancing to a frenzied drum,   15
Out of the murderous innocence of the sea.

May she be granted beauty and yet not
Beauty to make a stranger's eye distraught,
Or hers before a looking-glass, for such,
Being made beautiful overmuch,   20
Consider beauty a sufficient end,
Lose natural kindness and maybe
The heart-revealing intimacy
That chooses right, and never find a friend.

Helen being chosen found life flat and dull   25
And later had much trouble from a fool,
While that great Queen, that rose out of the spray,
Being fatherless could have her way
Yet chose a bandy-legged smith for man.
It's certain that fine women eat   30
A crazy salad with their meat
Whereby the Horn of Plenty is undone.

In courtesy I'd have her chiefly learned;
Hearts are not had as a gift but hearts are earned
By those that are not entirely beautiful;   35
Yet many, that have played the fool
For Beauty's very self, has charm made wise,
And many a poor man that has roved,
Loved and thought himself beloved,
From a glad kindness cannot take his eyes.   40

May she become a flourishing hidden tree
That all her thoughts may like the linnet be,

27. **Queen:** Venus.   29. **smith:** Vulcan.

And have no business but dispensing round
Their magnanimities of sound,
Nor but in merriment begin a chase, 45
Nor but in merriment a quarrel,
O may she live like some green laurel
Rooted in one dear perpetual place.

My mind, because the minds that I have loved,
The sort of beauty that I have approved, 50
Prosper but little, has dried up of late,
Yet knows that to be choked with hate
May well be of all evil chances chief.
If there's no hatred in a mind
Assault and battery of the wind 55
Can never tear the linnet from the leaf.

An intellectual hatred is the worst,
So let her think opinions are accursed.
Have I not seen the loveliest woman born
Out of the mouth of Plenty's horn, 60
Because of her opinionated mind
Barter that horn and every good
By quiet natures understood
For an old bellows full of angry wind?

Considering that, all hatred driven hence, 65
The soul recovers radical innocence
And learns at last that it is self-delighting,
Self-appeasing, self-affrighting,
And that its own sweet will is Heaven's will;
She can, though every face should scowl 70
And every windy quarter howl
Or every bellows burst, be happy still.

And may her bridegroom bring her to a house
Where all's accustomed, ceremonious;
For arrogance and hatred are the wares 75
Peddled in the thoroughfares.
How but in custom and in ceremony
Are innocence and beauty born?
Ceremony's a name for the rich horn,
And custom for the spreading laurel tree. 80

59. **loveliest woman born**: Maud Gonne.

THE FORTRESS

Anne Sexton (b. 1928)

<pre>   while taking a nap with Linda</pre>

Under the pink quilted covers
I hold the pulse that counts your blood.
I think the woods outdoors
are half asleep,
left over from summer   5
like a stack of books after a flood,
left over like those promises I never keep.
On the right, the scrub pine tree
waits like a fruit store
holding up bunches of tufted broccoli.   10

We watch the wind from your square bed.
I press down my index finger—
half in jest, half in dread—
on the brown mole
under your left eye, inherited   15
from my right cheek: a spot of danger
where a bewitched worm ate its way through our soul
in search of beauty. My child, since July
the leaves have been fed
secretly from a pool of beet-red dye.   20

And sometimes they are battle green
with trunks as wet as hunters' boots,
smacked hard by the wind, clean
as oilskins. No,
the wind's not off the ocean.   25
Yet, it cried in your room like a wolf
and your pony tail hurt you. That was a long time ago.
The wind rolled the tide like a dying
woman. She wouldn't sleep,
she rolled there all night, grunting and sighing.   30

Darling, life is not in my hands;
life with its terrible changes
will take you, bombs or glands,
your own child at

your breast, your own house on your own land. 35
Outside the bittersweet turns orange.
Before she died, my mother and I picked those fat
branches, finding orange nipples
on the gray wire strands.
We weeded the forest, curing trees like cripples. 40
Your feet thump-thump against my back
and you whisper to yourself. Child,
what are you wishing? What pact
are you making?
What mouse runs between your eyes? What ark 45
can I fill for you when the world goes wild?
The woods are underwater, their weeds are shaking
in the tide; birches like zebra fish
flash by in a pack.
Child, I cannot promise that you will get your wish. 50

I cannot promise very much.
I give you the images I know.
Lie still with me and watch.
A pheasant moves
by like a seal, pulled through the mulch 55
by his thick white collar. He's on show
like a clown. He drags a beige feather that he removed,
one time, from an old lady's hat.
We laugh and we touch.
I promise you love. Time will not take away that. 60

* * *

A NOISELESS PATIENT SPIDER

Walt Whitman (1819–1892)

A noiseless patient spider,
I mark'd where on a little promontory it stood isolated,
Mark'd how to explore the vacant vast surrounding,
It launch'd forth filament, filament, filament, out of itself,
Ever unreeling them, ever tirelessly speeding them. 5

And you O my soul where you stand,
Surrounded, detached, in measureless oceans of space,
Ceaselessly musing, venturing, throwing, seeking the spheres to
    connect them,
Till the bridge you will need be form'd, till the ductile anchor hold,
Till the gossamer thread you fling catch somewhere, O my soul.   10

MR. EDWARDS AND THE SPIDER

Robert Lowell (b. 1917)

I saw the spiders marching through the air,
Swimming from tree to tree that mildewed day
  In latter August when the hay
    Came creaking to the barn. But where
      The wind is westerly,   5
    Where gnarled November makes the spiders fly
    Into the apparitions of the sky,
  They purpose nothing but their ease and die
Urgently beating east to sunrise and the sea;

  What are we in the hands of the great God?   10
  It was in vain you set up thorn and briar
    In battle array against the fire
      And treason crackling in your blood;
      For the wild thorns grow tame
    And will do nothing to oppose the flame;   15
    Your lacerations tell the losing game
  You play against a sickness past your cure.
How will the hands be strong? How will the heart endure?

  A very little thing, a little worm,
  Or hourglass-blazoned spider, it is said,   20
    Can kill a tiger. Will the dead
    Hold up his mirror and affirm
      To the four winds the smell
    And flash of his authority? It's well
    If God who holds you to the pit of hell,   25
    Much as one holds a spider, will destroy,
  Baffle and dissipate your soul. As a small boy

On Windsor Marsh, I saw the spider die
When thrown into the bowels of fierce fire:
  There's no long struggle, no desire   30
  To get up on its feet and fly—
    It stretches out its feet
And dies. This is the sinner's last retreat;
Yes, and no strength exerted on the heat
Then sinews the abolished will, when sick   35
And full of burning, it will whistle on a brick.

But who can plumb the sinking of that soul?
Josiah Hawley, picture yourself cast
  Into a brick-kiln where the blast
  Fans your quick vitals to a coal—   40
    If measured by a glass,
How long would it seem burning! Let there pass
A minute, ten, ten trillion, but the blaze
Is infinite, eternal; this is death,
To die and know it. This is the Black Widow, death.   45

* * *

THE HAWK IN THE RAIN

Ted Hughes (b. 1930)

I drown in the drumming ploughland, I drag up
Heel after heel from the swallowing of the earth's mouth,
From clay that clutches my each step to the ankle
With the habit of the dogged grave, but the hawk

Effortlessly at height hangs his still eye.   5
His wings hold all creation in a weightless quiet,
Steady as a hallucination in the streaming air.
While banging wind kills these stubborn hedges,

Thumbs my eyes, throws my breath, tackles my heart,
And rain hacks my head to the bone, the hawk hangs   10
The diamond point of will that polestars
The sea drowner's endurance: and I,

Bloodily grabbed dazed last-moment-counting
Morsel in the earth's mouth, strain towards the master-
Fulcrum of violence where the hawk hangs still.   15
That maybe in his own time meets the weather

Coming the wrong way, suffers the air, hurled upside down,
Fall from his eye, the ponderous shires crash on him,
The horizon trap him; the round angelic eye
Smashed, mix his heart's blood with the mire of the land. 20

OVER SIR JOHN'S HILL

Dylan Thomas (1914–1953)

Over Sir John's hill,
The hawk on fire hangs still;
In a hoisted cloud, at drop of dusk, he pulls to his claws
And gallows, up the rays of his eyes the small birds of the bay
And the shrill child's-play   5
Wars
Of the sparrows and such who swansing, dusk, in wrangling hedges.
And blithely they squawk
To fiery tyburn over the wrestle of elms until
The flash the noosed hawk   10
Crashes, and slowly the fishing holy stalking heron
In the river Towy below bows his tilted headstone.

Flash, and the plumes crack,
And a black cap of jack-
Daws Sir John's just hill dons, and again the gulled birds hare 15
To the hawk on fire, the halter height, over Towy's fins,
In a whack of wind.
There
Where the elegiac fisherbird stabs and paddles
In the pebbly dab-filled   20
Shallow and sedge and "dilly dilly" calls the loft hawk,
"Come and be killed,"
I open the leaves of the water at a passage
Of psalms and shadows among the pincered sandcrabs prancing

And read, in a shell,   25
Death clear as a buoy's bell;
All praise of the hawk on fire in hawk-eyed dusk be sung,
When his viperish fuse hangs looped with flames under the brand
Wing, and blest shall
Young   30
Green chickens of the bay and bushes cluck "dilly dilly,"

"Come let us die."
We grieve as the green birds, never again leave shingle and elm,
The heron and I:
I young Aesop fabling to the near night by the dingle   35
Of eels, saint heron hymning in the shell-hung distant

Crystal harbour vale
Where the sea cobbles sail,
And wharves of water where the walls dance and the white
     crane tilt.
It is the heron and I, under judging Sir John's elmed   40
Hill, tell-tale the knelled
Guilt
Of the led-astray birds whom God, from their breast of whistles,
Have mercy on,
God in his whirlwind save, who marks the sparrows hail,   45
For their souls' song.
Now the heron grieves in the weeded verge. Through windows
Of dusk and water I see the tilting whispering

Heron, mirrored, go,
As the snapt feathers snow,   50
Fishing in the tear of the Towy. Only a hoot owl
Hollows, a grassblade blown in cupped hands, in the looted elms,
And no green cocks or hens
Shout
Now on Sir John's hill. The heron, ankling the scaly   55
Lowlands of the waves,
Makes all the music; and I who hear the tune of the slow
Near-willow river, grave,
Before the lunge of the night, the notes on this time-shaken
Stone for the sake of the souls of the slain birds sailing.   60

Rhythm and Meter

Rhythm and meter are two different things, but they are so closely related that, at times, they become one in a poem. Rhythm has to do with the movement of a poem—whether it is fast, slow, or a bit of both. It also refers to changes of pace in a poem—moments when the poem stops and then begins again. Rhythm, in other words, has to do with the dynamics of a poem as it is performed.

Meter is, on the other hand, a measurement of each line of a poem. In this section, however, we are only going to stress the measurement of accented and unaccented syllables. Traditional poetry established a pattern of stress for each line of the poem, then varied that pattern somewhat for effect. The important thing was that the reader or hearer of the poem had a sense of the norm of the meter to refer to. For instance, if the poem was a sonnet, the reader knew automatically that each line would have ten syllables and every other syllable would be stressed. When the line did not fit into this pattern, it was received as a novelty or surprise by the listener. The following line has its metrical stresses marked by an / and the unstressed syllables marked by ⌣:

⌣ / ⌣ / ⌣ / ⌣ / ⌣ /
They also serve who only stand and wait.

This pattern consists of five units of: ⌣ /, or iambs. When there are five iambs, the line is called iambic pentameter—penta- is the prefix for five. All sonnets have the metrical norm of iambic pentameter, so the reader is in no way surprised to find that this last line of Milton's sixteenth sonnet is metrically regular. In fact, it is useful to be able to identify iambic pentameter in poetry, since all the great English poets used that meter, and most great English poetry is characterized by it.

The metrical feet
The most important metrical feet in English are:

iamb: ⌣ /
trochee: / ⌣

Lines composed of these feet are called iambic and trochaic. The next most important metrical feet are:

anapest: ⌣ ⌣ /
dactyl: / ⌣ ⌣

Lines composed of these feet are called anapestic and dactylic. Finally, there are a few other useful feet that appear much less frequently and are therefore less important:

pyrrhic: ⌣ ⌣
spondee: / /
amphibrach: / ⌣ /
amphimach: ⌣ / ⌣

Having determined the type of feet possible in the line, it is now necessary to know the number of feet in the line. Depending on the number of feet, each line has a name. Greek terminology is normally used for such names. The names are:

Number of feet	Name of line
one	monometer
two	dimeter
three	trimeter
four	tetrameter
five	pentameter
six	hexameter
seven	heptameter
eight	octameter
nine	nonameter
ten	decameter

How to scan a line for its meter

The best source of help in learning to scan is the dictionary, in which every word is broken into syllables, with the accented syllable clearly marked: ac′-cent; sur-prise′; in-ter′-pre-ta′-tion, and so forth. When in doubt about a word, check the dictionary. Few poets ever tamper with the normal pronunciation of a word, so you will be on safe ground.

The next best source of help is reading a line aloud. Although with very difficult lines, reading aloud will not always fully clarify the position of the accents, usually you will be able to hear yourself accent the normally accented syllables. In difficult situations, ask a friend to read aloud and check him carefully, marking the accented syllables as he reads. Do this, too, every time your instructor reads, until you can do it yourself.

The importance of a word in context will help with lines that are primarily monosyllabic. Good poets rarely accent the unimportant words or syllables at the expense of the meaningful and important words and syllables. Consider the following line from "Kubla Khan" by Coleridge:

> And drunk the milk of Paradise

"And," "the," and "of" are clearly of vastly less importance than the other words in the line. Thus, "drunk," "milk," and "Paradise" receive the accents. "Paradise" is accented as it is in the dictionary: par'-a-dise'. That is an easy line. Another line from the same poem is much more difficult:

> Amid whose swift half-intermitted burst

If we apply the above principles, we would agree at once that "burst" is a highly important word and should be accented. "Swift" would also be easy to agree upon. But then we need to proceed to another element, the dictionary. According to the dictionary, "a-mid'" is accented on the second syllable and "in'-ter-mit'-ted" on the first and third syllables. If we simply put those marks down, we have:

$$\smile \ / \ ? \ / \ ? \ / \ \smile \ / \ \smile \ /$$

The question marks must be solved by reading the line aloud. A normal reader would probably not accent "whose," but it is highly possible that he might emphasize "half." It depends on how one reads it. However, it is also obvious, from what we have done so far, that the line is iambic pentameter. Therefore, the "norm" would be for both questionable words to receive no accent. Try reading the line aloud to see which is more natural for you.

It would be useful for you to apply the methods we have been discussing to a few lines in the poems in this chapter. If you apply them carefully, they will work. If you run into a snag, ask help from someone whose reading of poems you like.

Determining the foot

We have been discussing means by which we determine the accented syllables in a line. Once that process is completed we usually also want to know what the overall meter of the line is. Iambic pentameter lines are relatively easy to identify, but some other lines are much more troublesome. The following line, from Browning's "The Heretic's Tragedy," is a useful example:

$$/ \smile \smile / \smile \smile / \smile /$$
John of the Temple, whose fame so bragged,

The only tricky thing about finding the accents is the last word, which visually seems two syllables, but is aurally one (the dictionary agrees). Now, the question is: how many metrical feet are there here? And what is the name of the overall line? The best advice is to *begin at the end of the line.*

Starting at the end of the line, looking for the simplest metrical foot, we find an iamb: $\smile /$. The next simplest foot is an iamb: $\smile /$; then a trochee: $/ \smile$; then a dactyl: $/ \smile \smile$. Thus the line scans:

$/ \smile \smile$	$/ \smile$	$\smile /$	$\smile /$
dactyl	trochee	iamb	iamb

We count four metrical feet, hence the line is tetrameter. Two of the feet are iambic, but since the line has other metrical feet, it is considered irregular (regular iambic would be *all* iambs). Therefore, the line is irregular iambic tetrameter.

You might ask why, in counting from the end of the line, we did not begin with the amphibrach: $/ \smile /$. As we indicated, this foot is not very common. We suggested finding the simplest foot, and as we have shown, the simplest and most common foot is the iamb. However, the above line might be seen as dactyl-dactyl-amphibrach. How do we know it is not dactyllic trimeter? The answer is that we cannot be sure if the line is taken in isolation. But the line does not appear alone, so we can use the rest of the stanza to help us establish the norm. The next line is more "normal" than the first we quoted:

Is burning alive in Paris square!

We would scan that:

$$\smile / \mid \smile \smile / \mid \smile / \mid \smile /$$

This line is unambiguously iambic tetrameter. The basic iambic pattern of the poem now begins to show up.

The basic rule in finding the metrical character of a line is to look for the simplest, most common forms. Read the line in the most natural, unstrained fashion. Resort to feet like the amphimach or the spondee only when more common options do not seem possible. Then, read the line in the context of the surrounding lines before making a final judgment about its metrical character.

Rhythm as a contrast to meter
When we talk about ==rhythm== we are usually talking about ==the dynamics of a poem.== Often the dynamics happen because the movement of the line's phrases contrasts with the basic meter. The meter seems to be like the floor against which a ball is bounced, in the sense that it offers the resistance against which the rhythm functions.

When we talk about rhythm and dynamics we use a number of relatively simple technical terms. When a line stops it is called end-stopped and is usually marked by a period or other punctuation mark. When it does not stop, but goes on to the next line, it is called run-on or enjambed. An example of the enjambed line is given in John Keats's "Fall of Hyperion."

> Fanatics have their dreams, wherewith they weave
> A paradise for a sect;

Keats does not permit us to stop at the end of the line. Pope, in the following example from "To a Lady," demands that we stop at the end of each line:

> See Sin in state, majestically drunk;
> Proud as a peeress, prouder as a punk;
> Chaste to her husband, frank to all beside,
> A teeming mistress, but a barren bride.

The end-stopped lines of Pope demand that we read, then stop, read, then stop, as if each line were a statement that had to be absorbed separately because of its significance. The pauses that are noted at each of the commas—in both examples—are usually called caesuras, or breaks. Some scanners of poetry prefer only to call such breaks pauses, however, and reserve the term "caesura" for absolute breaks that occur at the end of a sentence.

==The pause is a very important feature of poetic rhythm, since it demarks movement of many kinds; it offers contrast and control to the rapidity of movement that often characterizes much verse.==
In addition to the pause, or caesura, there are a number of other devices with rhythmic functions that should be taken into

consideration when an assessment of a poem's rhythmic and metrical achievement is desired. One obvious device is rhyme—both end rhyme and internal rhyme (rhyme within the line). In the example from "To a Lady," rhyme emphasizes the stopping of the lines. Rhymes like "punk" and "bride" are vastly more emphatic because they fulfill the anticipation of the rhyme word that ends the previous line. One favorite device in later poetry is setting up the anticipation of rhyme and relaxing the end-stopping, then giving the rhyme word, but forcing the reader to enjamb the line into the next. The result is anxiety or uneasiness that builds up tension in the reader that the poet, hopefully, wants to put to good poetic use.

Another device that contributes to motion in the poem is alliteration—a term that describes the repetition of sounds in words. An example is the title of John Skelton's poem—the first in this section—"Mannerly Margery Milk and Ale." Because of the repetition of the "M's," the line has to move in a specific way, with the accents on the syllables controlled by the "M's." There are three kinds of alliteration: initial, at the beginning of words (the title of Skelton's poem), medial, in the middle of words, and terminal, at the end of words.

In the following example from Algernon Charles Swinburne's "Poeta Loquitur" ("The Poet Speaks"), the alliteration is marked by one of three initials to identify it: I, M, or T.

>   In a maze of monotonous murmur
>   T   I T   I M M T I M
>   Where reason roves ruined by rhyme,
>   M I M   I   T I   I
>   In a voice neither graver nor firmer
>   I   T   M T   T M T
>   Than the bells on a fool's cap chime,
>   M   M
>   A party pretentiously pensive,
>   I M I   M   I
>   With a Muse that deserves to be skinned,
>   T   M   T   I
>   Makes language and metre offensive
>   I   I
>   With rhymes on the wind.
>   I   I

The point of this example is that Swinburne is using subtle techniques to accomplish a rather brilliant sense of movement and rhythm in the stanza. If you reread the stanza you will see that the alliterated syllables receive extra emphasis because of the alliteration, and the movement of the stanza is most emphatic in the lines that are most densely alliterated. The openness of the last lines is effective because of the contrast with those densely alliterated lines.

Why worry about rhythm and meter?

Sooner or later everyone asks why any reader of poetry should bother with rhythm and meter. Even though many poets feel rhythm and meter is at the core of their work, and poems establish norms of rhythm from age to age—and therefore constitute a relationship or a context in which we can read the poems—most readers have been able to enjoy poetry without having to know any of the technical material offered here. Why, then, is it useful?

The standard answer has to do with increasing one's perceptual contact with a poem. Rhythm and meter have to be understood for a poem to be read well, either aloud or silently. In many poems, a general intuitive understanding will do. But in more difficult poems, a careful analysis is essential if every nuance of the poem is to be brought out. Most of us will agree that nuances are important in poetry, and we should be sensitive to those that are at the heart of the poem's structure.

Associated with this is the fact that some poems have a kind of mystery that is difficult for readers to pin down. Readers are sometimes reduced to saying little about the poem, other than that it is great, or appeals to them. As a personal response, this is often adequate. But many readers want more than a personal response. In the discussion that follows, the mysterious qualities of William Blake's famous poem "The Tyger" are shown to derive at first, if not at last, from some rather interesting metrical experiments. The metrical scansion is marked, and you will see that the method we have suggested earlier proves that the poem is probably iambic. However, you will also see that the power of the opening lines derives from the fact that they *appear* at first to be trochaic because of the intense emphasis on the first syllable of "Tyger." The emotional adjustment we must make in shifting from trochaic to iambic is such that it creates a dimension of inexplicability that matches the inexplicability of the poem itself, which asks if the same god (or man?) that made the lamb also made the tiger. In a way, the poem forces us unconsciously to ask if the same poet who made the trochaic also made the iambic metrical order of the poem.

THE TYGER

William Blake (1757–1827)

/ ˘ / ˘ / ˘ /
Tyger, tyger, burning bright,

/ ˘ / ˘ / ˘ /
In the forests of the night;

/ ˘ / ˘ / ˘ /
What immortal hand or eye,

˘ / ˘ / ˘ / ˘ /
Could frame thy fearful symmetry?

/ ˘ / ˘ / ˘ /
In what distant deeps of skies 5

/ ˘ / ˘ / ˘ /
Burnt the fire of thine eyes!

/ ˘ / ˘ / ˘ /
On what wings dare he aspire?

/ ˘ / ˘ / ˘ /
What the hand, dare seize the fire?

/ ˘ / ˘ / ˘ /
And what shoulder, and what art,

˘ / ˘ / ˘ / ˘ /
Could twist the sinews of thy heart? 10

˘ / ˘ / ˘ / ˘ /
And when thy heart began to beat,

/ / / ˘ / / /
What dread hand? and what dread feet?

    / ˘ / ˘ / ˘ /
What the hammer? what the chain?
    ˘ / / ˘ / ˘ /
In what furnace was thy brain?
    / ˘ / ˘ / ˘ /
What the anvil? what dread grasp,   15
    / ˘ / ˘ / ˘ /
Dare its deadly terrors clasp?

    / ˘ / ˘ / ˘ /
When the stars threw down their spears
    ˘ / ˘ / ˘ / ˘ /
And water'd heaven with their tears:
    / ˘ / ˘ / ˘ /
Did he smile his work to see?
    ˘ / ˘ / ˘ / ˘ /
Did he who made the Lamb make thee?   20

    / ˘ / ˘ / ˘ /
Tyger, Tyger, burning bright,
    / ˘ / ˘ / ˘ /
In the forests of the night:
    / ˘ / ˘ / ˘ /
What immortal hand or eye
    ˘ / ˘ / ˘ / ˘ /
Dare frame thy fearful symmetry?

The virgule (|), which marks the ending of a foot, has been deliberately left out here so you can experiment with the scansion. If you begin with the feeling that the poem is trochaic, you can verify it by counting the trochees; you will see them as greater in number than any other foot. However, if you begin with the assumptions that the poem is regular instead of irregular, and that the last lines of the first and last stanzas represent the general iambic norm, then you will see more iambic feet in the poem. Thus, the trochaic lines are seen as beginning with a half-iamb; otherwise the same lines will be seen as ending with a half-trochee. Of course, we could say such lines begin with an amphibrach and end with an amphimach, but this is not supported by the metrical pattern we feel instinctively from reading the poem. The important thing is not that we absolutely identify the poem as either trochaic or iambic but that we see that Blake uses the ambiguity (first perceived intuitively, later intellectually) both to unsettle us and to help us respond on a deep emotional level to the poem's statements about the lamb and the tiger—as literal animals and as the symbols he perceives them to be.

This poem is also worth looking at for its rhythmic qualities. It relies on the rhetorical question—the question that expects no answer and gets none—for much of its movement. Stanza four, for example, is totally made up of rhetorical questions. Caesuras mark the end of each question, whether at the end or in the middle of a line. This may be the most striking technique in the poem. Who, for instance, will answer these questions? To whom are they addressed? The very fact that we hardly know is of first importance to the success of the poem—to gauging its impact on us.

Alliteration abounds in the poem. And, with a tight metrical pattern of the sort we noted above, the poem tends to have a nursery-rhyme quality: tight rhyme, tight meter, tight alliteration. The nursery-rhyme effect is one that most readers have observed about the poem, and their observation suggests that this disarming quality helps Blake begin to raise serious issues—the existence of good and evil (lamb and tiger), charity and wrath, love and hate, and innocence and experience in a world created by one god. How such opposites can cohere without the world's falling apart is enacted in the heart of the poem itself, with the opposites of stopping and going, of trochee and iamb, straining against one another all the time. The structure of the poem dramatizes its theme.

A last word

The poems that follow are contextually related to all other poems in terms of rhythm and meter, since no poem can exist without rhythm and stress (which are built into language). But they also represent a context of virtuoso performances in terms of rhythm and meter. For this reason you will find that they have a great deal in common. The poems tend to reveal their meanings in terms of their movement. You may be as profoundly or as lightly technical as you wish. But you will find that even the slightest attention to the qualities we have been describing will uncover unsuspected levels of interest and meaning in most good poems.

POEMS FOR FURTHER STUDY

MANNERLY MARGERY MILK AND ALE

John Skelton (1460?–1529)

Ay, beshrew you! by my fay,
These wanton clerks be nice alway!
Avaunt, avaunt, my popinjay!
What, will you do nothing but play?
Tilly vally straw, let be I say!   5
Gup, Christian Clout, gup, Jack of the Vale!
With Mannerly Margery Milk and Ale.

By God, ye be a pretty pode,
And I love you an whole cart-load.
Straw, James Foder, ye play the fode,   10
I am no hackney for your rode:
Go watch a bull, your back is broad!
Gup, Christian Clout, gup, Jack of the Vale!
With Mannerly Margery Milk and Ale.

Ywis ye deal uncourteously;   15
What, would ye frumple me? now fy!
What, and ye shall be my pigesnye?
By Christ, ye shall not, no hardely:
I will not be japéd bodily!
Gup, Christian Clout, gup, Jack of the Vale!   20
With Mannerly Margery Milk and Ale.

Walk forth your way, ye cost me nought;
Now have I found that I have sought:
The best cheap flesh that ever I bought.
Yet, for His love that all hath wrought,   25
Wed me, or else I die for thought.
Gup, Christian Clout, your breath is stale!
Go, Mannerly Margery Milk and Ale!
Gup, Christian Clout, gup, Jack of the Vale!
With Mannerly Margery Milk and Ale.   30

1. beshrew you: to wish one ill will. **fay:** faith. **2. nice:** ignorant or lewd. **6. gup:** go up. **8. pode:** possibly a frog or toad. **10. fode:** seducer. **11. hackney:** whore. **rode:** rod. **16. frumple:** tumble. **19. japéd:** used, fooled with.

A LITANY IN TIME OF PLAGUE

Thomas Nashe (1567–1601)

Adieu, farewell, earth's bliss;
This world uncertain is;
Fond are life's lustful joys;
Death proves them all but toys;
None from his darts can fly;   5
I am sick, I must die.
    Lord, have mercy on us!

Rich men, trust not in wealth,
Gold cannot buy you health;
Physic himself must fade.   10
All things to end are made,
The plague full swift goes by;
I am sick, I must die.
    Lord, have mercy on us!

Beauty is but a flower   15
Which wrinkles will devour;
Brightness falls from the air;
Queens have died young and fair;
Dust hath closed Helen's eye.
I am sick, I must die.   20
    Lord, have mercy on us!

Strength stoops unto the grave,
Worms feed on Hector brave;
Swords may not fight with fate,
Earth still holds ope her gate.   25
"Come, come!" the bells do cry.
I am sick, I must die.
    Lord, have mercy on us.

Wit with his wantonness
Tasteth death's bitterness;   30
Hell's executioner
Hath no ears for to hear
What vain art can reply.
I am sick, I must die.
    Lord, have mercy on us.   35

Haste, therefore, each degree,
To welcome destiny;
Heaven is our heritage,
Earth but a player's stage;
Mount we unto the sky.   40
I am sick, I must die.
   Lord, have mercy on us.

STILL TO BE NEAT, STILL TO BE DREST

Ben Jonson (1573–1637)

Still to be neat, still to be drest,
As you were going to a feast;
Still to be pou'dred, still perfum'd:
Lady, it is to be presum'd,
Though arts hid causes are not found,   5
All is not sweet, all is not sound.

Give me a looke, give me a face,
That makes simplicitie a grace;
Robes loosely flowing, haire as free:
Such sweet neglect more taketh me,   10
Then all th'adulteries of art.
They strike mine eyes, but not my heart.

DELIGHT IN DISORDER

Robert Herrick (1591–1674)

A sweet disorder in the dress
Kindles in clothes a wantonness:
A lawn about the shoulders thrown
Into a fine distraction,
An erring lace, which here and there   5
Enthralls the crimson stomacher,
A cuff neglectful, and thereby
Ribbands to flow confusedly,

A winning wave (deserving note)
In the tempestuous petticoat,   10
A careless shoe-string, in whose tie
I see a wild civility,
Do more bewitch me, than when art
Is too precise in every part.

AND DID THOSE FEET IN ANCIENT TIME

William Blake (1757–1827)

And did those feet in ancient time
  Walk upon England's mountains green?
And was the holy Lamb of God
  On England's pleasant pastures seen?

And did the Countenance Divine   5
  Shine forth upon our clouded hills?
And was Jerusalem builded here
  Among these dark Satanic mills?

Bring me my Bow of burning gold!
  Bring me my Arrows of desire!   10
Bring me my Spear: O clouds, unfold!
  Bring me my Chariot of fire!

I will not cease from Mental Fight,
  Nor shall my Sword sleep in my hand,
Till we have built Jerusalem   15
  In England's green and pleasant land.

ULYSSES

Alfred, Lord Tennyson (1809–1892)

It little profits that an idle king,
By this still hearth, among these barren crags,
Matched with an aged wife, I mete and dole

Ulysses. Ulysses is the hero of Homer's *Odyssey.* He is cast as one of the damned in Dante's *Inferno,* Canto 26, for his guile and cunning. Tennyson is thinking of both references in his effort to revive our good opinion of Ulysses. **3. aged wife:** Penelope, whose faithfulness to Ulysses is legendary.

Unequal laws unto a savage race,
That hoard, and sleep, and feed, and know not me. 5
I cannot rest from travel: I will drink
Life to the lees; all times I have enjoyed
Greatly, have suffered greatly, both with those
That loved me, and alone; on shore, and when
Through scudding drifts the rainy Hyades 10
Vext the dim sea: I am become a name;
For always roaming with a hungry heart
Much have I seen and known; cities of men
And manners, climates, councils, governments,
Myself not least, but honoured of them all; 15
And drunk delight of battle with my peers,
Far on the ringing plains of windy Troy.
I am a part of all that I have met;
Yet all experience in an arch wherethrough
Gleams that untravelled world, whose margin fades 20
For ever and for ever when I move.
How dull it is to pause, to make an end,
To rust unburnished, not to shine in use!
As though to breathe were life. Life piled on life
Were all too little, and of one to me 25
Little remains; but every hour is saved
From that eternal silence, something more,
A bringer of new things; and vile it were
For some three suns to store and hoard myself,
And this grey spirit yearning in desire 30
To follow knowledge like a sinking star,
Beyond the utmost bound of human thought.
    This is my son, mine own Telemachus,
To whom I leave the sceptre and the isle—
Well-loved of me, discerning to fulfil 35
This labour, by slow prudence to make mild
A rugged people, and through soft degrees
Subdue them to the useful and the good.
Most blameless is he, centered in the sphere
Of common duties, decent not to fail 40
In offices of tenderness, and pay
Meet adoration to my household gods,

---

10. Hyades: stars whose appearance in the sky signaled the oncoming spring rains.

When I am gone. He works his work, I mine.
There lies the port; the vessel puffs her sail:
There gloom the dark broad seas. My mariners, 45
Souls that have toiled, and wrought, and thought with me—
That ever with a frolic welcome took
The thunder and the sunshine, and opposed
Free hearts, free foreheads—you and I are old;
Old age hath yet his honour and his toil: 50
Death closes all; but something ere the end,
Some work of noble note, may yet be done,
Not unbecoming men that strove with Gods.
The lights begin to twinkle from the rocks:
The long day wanes: the slow moon climbs: the deep 55
Moans round with many voices. Come, my friends,
'Tis not too late to seek a newer world.
Push off, and sitting well in order smite
The sounding furrows; for my purpose holds
To sail beyond the sunset, and the baths 60
Of all the western stars, until I die.
It may be that the gulfs will wash us down:
It may be we shall touch the Happy Isles,
And see the great Achilles, whom we knew.
Though much is taken, much abides; and though 65
We are not now that strength which in old days
Moved earth and heaven; that which we are, we are;
One equal temper of heroic hearts,
Made weak by time and fate, but strong in will
To strive, to seek, to find, and not to yield. 70

LOVE AMONG THE RUINS

Robert Browning (1812–1889)

Where the quiet-colored end of evening smiles
    Miles and miles
On the solitary pastures where our sheep
    Half-asleep

63. **Happy Isles:** Greek equivalent of heaven. 64. **Achilles:** a hero at Troy; the hero of Homer's *Iliad*.

Tinkle homeward through the twilight, stray or stop 5
    As they crop—
Was the site once of a city great and gay,
    (So they say)
Of our country's very capital, its prince
    Ages since 10
Held his court in, gathered councils, wielding far
    Peace or war.

Now,—the country does not even boast a tree,
    As you see,
To distinguish slopes of verdure, certain rills 15
    From the hills
Intersect and give a name to, (else they run
    Into one,)
Where the domed and daring palace shot its spires
    Up like fires 20
O'er the hundred-gated circuit of a wall
    Bounding all,
Made of marble, men might march on nor be pressed,
    Twelve abreast.

And such plenty and perfection, see, of grass 25
    Never was!
Such a carpet as, this summer-time, o'erspreads
    And embeds
Every vestige of the city, guessed alone,
    Stock or stone— 30
Where a multitude of men breathed joy and woe
    Long ago;
Lust of glory pricked their hearts up, dread of shame
    Struck them tame;
And that glory and that shame alike, the gold 35
    Bought and sold.

Now,—the single little turret that remains
    On the plains,
By the caper overrooted, by the gourd
    Overscored, 40
While the patching houseleek's head of blossom winks
    Through the chinks—
Marks the basement whence a tower in ancient time
    Sprang sublime,

And a burning ring, all round, the chariots traced 45
 As they raced,
And the monarch and his minions and his dames
 Viewed the games.
And I know, while thus the quiet-colored eve
 Smiles to leave 50
To their folding, all our many-tinkling fleece
 In such peace,
And the slopes and rills in undistinguished gray
 Melt away—
That a girl with eager eyes and yellow hair 55
 Waits me there
In the turret whence the charioteers caught soul
 For the goal,
When the king looked, where she looks now, breathless, dumb
 Till I come. 60

But he looked upon the city, every side,
 Far and wide,
All the mountains topped with temples, all the glades'
 Colonnades,
All the causeys, bridges, aqueducts,—and then, 65
 All the men!
When I do come, she will speak not, she will stand,
 Either hand
On my shoulder, give her eyes the first embrace
 Of my face, 70
Ere we rush, ere we extinguish sight and speech
 Each on each.

In one year they sent a million fighters forth
 South and North,
And they built their gods a brazen pillar high 75
 As the sky,
Yet reserved a thousand chariots in full force—
 Gold, of course.
Oh heart! oh blood that freezes, blood that burns!
 Earth's returns 80
For whole centuries of folly, noise and sin!
 Shut them in,
With their triumphs and their glories and the rest!
 Love is best.

THE GARDEN OF PROSERPINE

Algernon Charles Swinburne (1837–1909)

Here, where the world is quiet;
 Here, where all trouble seems
Dead winds' and spent waves' riot
 In doubtful dreams of dreams;
I watch the green field growing 5
For reaping folk and sowing,
For harvest-time and mowing,
 A sleepy world of streams.

I am tired of tears and laughter,
 And men that laugh and weep; 10
Of what may come hereafter
 For men that sow to reap:
I am weary of days and hours,
Blown buds of barren flowers,
Desires and dreams and powers 15
 And everything but sleep.

Here life has death for neighbour,
 And far from eye or ear
Wan waves and wet winds labour,
 Weak ships and spirits steer; 20
They drive adrift, and whither
They wot not who make thither;
But no such winds blow hither,
 And no such things grow here.

No growth of moor or coppice, 25
 No heather-flower or vine,
But bloomless buds of poppies,
 Green grapes of Proserpine,
Pale beds of blowing rushes,
Where no leaf blooms or blushes 30

The Garden of Proserpine. Proserpine was stolen by Pluto and made his queen. She was permitted to live six months of the year above ground—in Sicily—and the remainder of the year with Pluto in Hades. **14. Blown:** blossomed. **22. wot:** know. **25. moor or coppice:** moor is a heath, coppice a shrubby undergrowth.

Save this whereout she crushes
For dead men deadly wine.

Pale, without name or number,
    In fruitless fields of corn,
They bow themselves and slumber   35
    All night till light is born;
And like a soul belated,
In hell and heaven unmated,
By cloud and mist abated
    Comes out of darkness morn.   40

Though one were strong as seven,
    He too with death shall dwell,
Nor wake with wings in heaven,
    Nor weep for pains in hell;
Though one were fair as roses,   45
    His beauty clouds and closes;
And well though love reposes,
    In the end it is not well.

Pale, beyond porch and portal,
    Crowned with calm leaves, she stands   50
Who gathers all things mortal
    With cold immortal hands;
Her languid lips are sweeter
Than love's who fears to greet her,
To men that mix and meet her   55
    From many times and lands.

She waits for each and other,
    She waits for all men born;
Forgets the earth her mother,
    The life of fruits and corn;   60
And spring and seed and swallow
Take wing for her and follow
Where summer song rings hollow
    And flowers are put to scorn.

There go the loves that wither,   65
    The old loves with wearier wings;
And all dead years draw thither,
    And all disastrous things;
Dead dreams of days forsaken,
Blind buds that snows have shaken,   70

Wild leaves that winds have taken,
Red strays of ruined springs.

We are not sure of sorrow,
   And joy was never sure;
Today will die tomorrow;   75
   Time stoops to no man's lure;
And love, grown faint and fretful,
With lips but half regretful
Sighs, and with eyes forgetful
   Weeps that no loves endure.   80

From too much love of living,
   From hope and fear set free,
We thank with brief thanksgiving
   Whatever gods may be
That no life lives for ever;   85
That dead men rise up never;
That even the weariest river
   Winds somewhere safe to sea.

Then star nor sun shall waken,
   Nor any change of light: 90
Nor sound of waters shaken,
   Nor any sound or sight:
Nor wintry leaves nor vernal,
Nor days nor things diurnal;
Only the sleep eternal   95
   In an eternal night.

FIRE AND ICE

Robert Frost (1874–1963)

Some say the world will end in fire,
Some say in ice.
From what I've tasted of desire
I hold with those who favor fire.
But if it had to perish twice,   5
I think I know enough of hate

---

93. vernal: pertaining to summer.   **94. diurnal:** pertaining to day.

To say that for destruction ice
Is also great
And would suffice.

THE LOVE SONG OF J. ALFRED PRUFROCK

T. S. Eliot (1888–1965)

*S'io credessi che mia risposta fosse
A persona che mai tornasse al mondo,
Questa fiamma staria senza più scosse.
Ma per ciò che giammai de questo fondo
Non tornò vivo alcun, s'i'odo il vero
Senza tema d'infamia ti rispondo.*

Let us go then, you and I,
When the evening is spread out against the sky
Like a patient etherized upon a table;
Let us go, through certain half-deserted streets,
The muttering retreats   5
Of restless nights in one-night cheap hotels
And sawdust restaurants with oyster-shells:
Streets that follow like a tedious argument
Of insidious intent
To lead you to an overwhelming question....   10
Oh, do not ask, "What is it?"
Let us go and make our visit.

In the room the women come and go
Talking of Michelangelo.

The yellow fog that rubs its back upon the window-panes,   15
The yellow smoke that rubs its muzzle on the window-panes,
Licked its tongue into the corners of the evening,

S'io credessi...rispondo. If I believed that my answer were to a person who should ever return to the world, this flame would stand without further movement; but since never one returns alive from this deep, if I hear true, I answer you without fear of infamy. *Inferno,* xxvii, 61–66.   **1. you and I:** Prufrock is talking to himself.   **3–9. Like...intent:** the environment is a strange one for the aristocratic Prufrock, which underscores the unusualness of his facing up to certain questions.

Lingered upon the pools that stand in drains,
Let fall upon its back the soot that falls from chimneys,
Slipped by the terrace, made a sudden leap, 20
And seeing that it was a soft October night,
Curled once about the house, and fell asleep.

And indeed there will be time
For the yellow smoke that slides along the street
Rubbing its back upon the window-panes; 25
There will be time, there will be time
To prepare a face to meet the faces that you meet;
There will be time to murder and create,
And time for all the works and days of hands
That lift and drop a question on your plate; 30
Time for you and time for me,
And time yet for a hundred indecisions,
And for a hundred visions and revisions,
Before the taking of a toast and tea.

In the room the women come and go 35
Talking of Michelangelo.

And indeed there will be time
To wonder, "Do I dare?" and, "Do I dare?"
Time to turn back and descend the stair,
With a bald spot in the middle of my hair— 40
(They will say: "How his hair is growing thin!")
My morning coat, my collar mounting firmly to the chin,
My necktie rich and modest, and asserted by a simple pin—
(They will say: "But how his arms and legs are thin!")
Do I dare 45
Disturb the universe?
In a minute there is time
For decisions and revisions which a minute will reverse.

For I have known them all already, known them all—
Have known the evenings, mornings, afternoons, 50
I have measured out my life with coffee spoons;
I know the voices dying with a dying fall

23–34. And...tea: the weightiness of line 26, along with the seriousness of the entire issue of time, devolves into "tea-time" at the end of the stanza, thus representing much that is of importance in Prufrock's life. It drains away into insignificance and meaninglessness, as in line 51, when he measures out his life in coffee spoons.

>   Beneath the music from a farther room.
>   So how should I presume?
>
> And I have known the eyes already, known them all—   55
> The eyes that fix you in a formulated phrase,
> And when I am formulated, sprawling on a pin,
> When I am pinned and wriggling on the wall,
> Then how should I begin
> To spit out all the butt-ends of my days and ways?   60
>   And how should I presume?
>
> And I have known the arms already, known them all—
> Arms that are braceleted and white and bare
> (But in the lamplight, downed with light brown hair!)
> Is it perfume from a dress   65
> That makes me so digress?
> Arms that lie along a table, or wrap about a shawl.
>   And should I then presume?
>   And how should I begin?
>   *   *   *
>
> Shall I say, I have gone at dusk through narrow streets   70
> And watched the smoke that rises from the pipes
> Of lonely men in shirt-sleeves, leaning out of windows? . . .
>
> I should have been a pair of ragged claws
> Scuttling across the floors of silent seas.
>   *   *   *
>
> And the afternoon, the evening, sleeps so peacefully!
> Smoothed by long fingers,   75
> Asleep . . . tired . . . or it malingers,
> Stretched on the floor, here beside you and me.
> Should I, after tea and cakes and ices,
> Have the strength to force the moment to its crisis?   80
> But though I have wept and fasted, wept and prayed,
> Though I have seen my head (grown slightly bald) brought in
>   upon a platter,

55–61. And . . . presume: these lines reveal his concerns for what "society" thinks of him. In order to escape from their gaze he has to go to "certain half-deserted streets." **79–80. Should . . . crisis:** the rhyme of "ices" and "crisis" is effective in making them seem equivalent—like "time" and tea-time. **82. Though . . . platter:** the reference is to the head of St. John the Baptist—prophet for Christ—which was brought in upon a platter as a reward for Salome, who had danced before Herod.

I am no prophet—and here's no great matter;
I have seen the moment of my greatness flicker,
And I have seen the eternal Footman hold my coat, and snicker, 85
And in short, I was afraid.

And would it have been worth it, after all,
After the cups, the marmalade, the tea,
Among the porcelain, among some talk of you and me,
Would it have been worth while, 90
To have bitten off the matter with a smile,
To have squeezed the universe into a ball
To roll it toward some overwhelming question,
To say: "I am Lazarus, come from the dead,
Come back to tell you all, I shall tell you all"— 95
If one, settling a pillow by her head,
    Should say: "That is not what I meant at all.
    That is not it, at all."

And would it have been worth it, after all,
Would it have been worth while, 100
After the sunsets and the dooryards and the sprinkled streets,
After the novels, after the teacups, after the skirts that trail
    along the floor—
And this, and so much more?—
It is impossible to say just what I mean!
But as if a magic lantern threw the nerves in patterns on a
    screen: 105
Would it have been worth while
If one, settling a pillow or throwing off a shawl,
And turning toward the window, should say:
    "That is not it at all,
    That is not what I meant, at all." 110

    *   *   *

No! I am not Prince Hamlet, nor was meant to be;
Am an attendant lord, one that will do
To swell a progress, start a scene or two,
Advise the prince; no doubt, an easy tool,
Deferential, glad to be of use, 115
Politic, cautious, and meticulous;
Full of high sentence, but a bit obtuse;
At times, indeed, almost ridiculous—
Almost, at times, the Fool.

94. Lazarus: Christ brought Lazarus back from the dead (John 11).

I grow old.... I grow old....   120
I shall wear the bottoms of my trousers rolled.

Shall I part my hair behind? Do I dare to eat a peach?
I shall wear white flannel trousers, and walk upon the beach.
I have heard the mermaids singing, each to each.

I do not think that they will sing to me.   125

I have seen them riding seaward on the waves
Combing the white hair of the waves blown back
When the wind blows the water white and black.

We have lingered in the chambers of the sea
By sea-girls wreathed with seaweed red and brown   130
Till human voices wake us, and we drown.

anyone lived in a pretty how town

e. e. cummings (1894–1962)

anyone lived in a pretty how town
(with up so floating many bells down)
spring summer autumn winter
he sang his didn't he danced his did.

Women and men(both little and small)   5
cared for anyone not at all
they sowed their isn't they reaped their same
sun moon stars rain

children guessed(but only a few
and down they forgot as up they grew   10
autumn winter spring summer)
that noone loved him more by more

when by now and tree by leaf
she laughed his joy she cried his grief

121. bottoms...rolled: Prufrock can at least decide he wants cuffs on his trousers. 124–131. I...drown: these lines suggest Prufrock knows about heroic possibilities for others, but cannot hope to participate in greatness. His knowledge is what makes his position such a painful one for him.
  anyone lived in a pretty how town. "anyone" and "noone" can be considered the principal characters of the poem.

bird by snow and stir by still 15
anyone's any was all to her

someones married their everyones
laughed their cryings and did their dance
(sleep wake hope and then)they
said their nevers they slept their dream 20

stars rain sun moon
(and only the snow can begin to explain
how children are apt to forget to remember
with up so floating many bells down)

one day anyone died i guess 25
(and noone stooped to kiss his face)
busy folk buried them side by side
little by little and was by was

all by all and deep by deep
and more by more they dream their sleep 30
noone and anyone earth by april
wish by spirit and if by yes.

Women and men(both dong and ding)
summer autumn winter spring
reaped their sowing and went their came 35
sun moon stars rain

HARLEM SWEETIES

Langston Hughes (1902–1967)

Have you dug the spill
Of Sugar Hill?
Cast your gims
On this sepia thrill:
Brown sugar lassie, 5
Caramel treat,
Honey-gold baby
Sweet enough to eat.
Peach-skinned girlie,
Coffee and cream, 10
Chocolate darling
Out of a dream.

Walnut tinted
Or cocoa brown,
Pomegranate lipped 15
Pride of the town.
Rich cream colored
To plum-tinted black,
Feminine sweetness
In Harlem's no lack. 20
Glow of the quince
To blush of the rose.
Persimmon bronze
To cinnamon toes.
Blackberry cordial, 25
Virginia Dare wine—
All those sweet colors
Flavor Harlem of mine!
Walnut or cocoa,
Let me repeat: 30
Caramel, brown sugar,
A chocolate treat,
Molasses taffy,
Coffee and cream,
Licorice, clove, cinnamon 35
To a honey-brown dream.
Ginger, wine-gold,
Persimmon, blackberry,
All though the spectrum
Harlem girls vary— 40
So if you want to know beauty's
Rainbow-sweet thrill,
Stroll down luscious,
Delicious, *fine* Sugar Hill.

INVITATION TO MISS MARIANNE MOORE

Elizabeth Bishop (b. 1911)

From Brooklyn, over the Brooklyn Bridge, on this fine morning,
   please come flying.
In a cloud of fiery pale chemicals,
   please come flying,

to the rapid rolling of thousands of small blue drums   5
descending out of the mackerel sky
over the glittering grandstand of harbor-water,
   please come flying.

Whistles, pennants and smoke are blowing. The ships
are signaling cordially with multitudes of flags   10
rising and falling like birds all over the harbor.
Enter: two rivers, gracefully bearing
countless little pellucid jellies
in cut-glass epergnes dragging with silver chains.
The flight is safe; the weather is all arranged.   15
The waves are running in verses this fine morning.
   Please come flying.

Come with the pointed toe of each black shoe
trailing a sapphire highlight,
with a black capeful of butterfly wings and bon-mots,   20
with heaven knows how many angels all riding
on the broad black brim of your hat,
   please come flying.

Bearing a musical inaudible abacus,
a slight censorious frown, and blue ribbons,   25
   please come flying.
Facts and skyscrapers glint in the tide; Manhattan
is all awash with morals this fine morning,
   so please come flying.

Mounting the sky with natural heroism,   30
above the accidents, above the malignant movies,
the taxicabs and injustices at large,
while horns are resounding in your beautiful ears
that simultaneously listen to
a soft uninvented music, fit for the musk deer,   35
   please come flying.

For whom the grim museums will behave
like courteous male bower-birds,
for whom the agreeable lions lie in wait
on the steps of the Public Library,   40
eager to rise and follow through the doors
up into the reading rooms,
   please come flying.

We can sit down and weep; we can go shopping,
or play at a game of constantly being wrong   45
with a priceless set of vocabularies,
or we can bravely deplore, but please
  please come flying.

With dynasties of negative constructions
darkening and dying around you,   50
with grammar that suddenly turns and shines
like flocks of sandpipers flying,
  please come flying.

Come like a light in the white mackerel sky,
come like a daytime comet   55
with a long unnebulous train of words,
from Brooklyn, over the Brooklyn Bridge, on this fine morning,
  please come flying.

FERN HILL

Dylan Thomas (1914–1953)

Now as I was young and easy under the apple boughs
About the lilting house and happy as the grass was green,
   The night above the dingle starry,
     Time let me hail and climb
   Golden in the heydays of his eyes,   5
And honoured among wagons I was prince of the apple towns
And once below a time I lordly had the trees and leaves
     Trail with daisies and barley
   Down the rivers of the windfall light.

And as I was green and carefree, famous among the barns   10
About the happy yard and singing as the farm was home,
   In the sun that is young once only,
     Time let me play and be
   Golden in the mercy of his means,
And green and golden I was huntsman and herdsman, the calves   15
Sang to my horn, the foxes on the hills barked clear and cold,

Fern Hill. This is a farm Thomas's aunt owned and which he visited as a child. **3. dingle:** a valley.

   And the sabbath rang slowly
  In the pebbles of the holy streams.

All the sun long it was running, it was lovely, the hay
Fields high as the house, the tunes from the chimneys, it was air 20
   And playing, lovely and watery
    And fire green as grass.
  And nightly under the simple stars
As I rode to sleep the owls were bearing the farm away,
All the moon long I heard, blessed among stables, the night-jars 25
   Flying with the ricks, and the horses
    Flashing into the dark.

And then to awake, and the farm, like a wanderer white
With the dew, come back, the cock on his shoulder: it was all
   Shining, it was Adam and maiden,   30
    The sky gathered again
  And the sun grew round that very day.
So it must have been after the birth of the simple light
In the first, spinning place, the spellbound horses walking warm
   Out of the whinnying green stable   35
    On to the fields of praise.

And honoured among foxes and pheasants by the gay house
Under the new made clouds and happy as the heart was long,
   In the sun born over and over,
    I ran my heedless ways,   40
   My wishes raced through the house high hay
And nothing I cared, at my sky blue trades, that time allows
In all his tuneful turning so few and such morning songs
    Before the children green and golden
     Follow him out of grace,   45

Nothing I cared, in the lamb white days, that time would take me
Up to the swallow thronged loft by the shadow of my hand,
   In the moon that is always rising,
    Nor that riding to sleep
   I should hear him fly with the high fields   50
And wake to the farm forever fled from the childless land.
Oh as I was young and easy in the mercy of his means,
    Time held me green and dying
   Though I sang in my chains like the sea.

25. **night-jars**: birds. 26. **ricks**: haystacks.

A SUPERMARKET IN CALIFORNIA

Allen Ginsberg (b. 1926)

What thoughts I have of you tonight, Walt Whitman, for I walked down the sidestreets under the trees with a headache self-conscious looking at the full moon.
    In my hungry fatigue, and shopping for images, I went into the neon fruit supermarket, dreaming of your enumerations!   5
    What peaches and what penumbras! Whole families shopping at night! Aisles full of husbands! Wives in the avocados, babies in the tomatoes!—and you, Garcia Lorca, what were you doing down by the watermelons?
    I saw you, Walt Whitman, childless, lonely old grubber,   10
poking among the meats in the refrigerator and eyeing the grocery boys.
    I heard you asking questions of each: Who killed the pork chops? What price bananas? Are you my Angel?
    I wandered in and out of the brilliant stacks of cans following 15
you, and followed in my imagination by the store detective.
    We strode down the open corridors together in our solitary fancy tasting artichokes, possessing every frozen delicacy, and never passing the cashier.
    Where are we going, Walt Whitman? The doors close in an   20
hour. Which way does your beard point tonight?
    (I touch your book and dream of our odyssey in the supermarket and feel absurd.)
    Will we walk all night through solitary streets? The trees add shade to shade, lights out in the houses, we'll both be lonely. 25
    Will we stroll dreaming of the lost America of love past blue automobiles in driveways, home to our silent cottage?
    Ah, dear father, graybeard, lonely old courage-teacher, what America did you have when Charon quit poling his ferry and you got out on a smoking bank and stood watching the boat   30
disappear on the black waters of Lethe?
                                          Berkeley 1955

A Supermarket in California. The setting, with Ginsberg talking to himself, is reminiscent of "The Love Song of J. Alfred Prufrock." The rhythm imparted by the rhetorical questions also alludes to that poem.   **8. Garcia Lorca:** a Spanish poet murdered by the Falangists. *The Poet in New York* by Lorca is a modern classic.   **29. Charon:** the boatman who carries the dead across the river Styx into the underworld. Here, the Styx is represented by the Lethe, the river of forgetfulness (see Keats's "Ode to a Nightingale," page 188).

RINGING THE BELLS

Anne Sexton (b. 1928)

    And this is the way they ring
the bells in Bedlam
and this is the bell-lady
who comes each Tuesday morning
to give us a music lesson   5
and because the attendants make you go
and because we mind by instinct,
like bees caught in the wrong hive,
we are the circle of the crazy ladies
who sit in the lounge of the mental house   10
and smile at the smiling woman
who passes us each a bell,
who points at my hand
that holds my bell, E flat,
and this is the gray dress next to me   15
who grumbles as if it were special
to be old, to be old,
and this is the small hunched squirrel girl
on the other side of me
who picks at the hairs over her lip,   20
who picks at the hairs over her lip all day,
and this is how the bells really sound,
as untroubled and clean
as a workable kitchen,
and this is always my bell responding   25
to my hand that responds to the lady
who points at me, E flat;
and although we are not better for it,
they tell you to go. And you do.

FASTBALL

Jonathan Williams (b. 1929)

(FOR WW, HOT FOR HONORARY INSTALLATION AT COOPERSTOWN)

not just folklore, or
                a tall can of corn (or *Grass* on Cranberry Street)—

>   to point at the wall and win
>   the whole ball of wax ...
> yet
>   Walt Whitman
> struck out, singing: 'rambled
>   all around,
>   in & out the town, ram-
>   bled til the butchers
>   cut him down'
> hard from the heels, swung,
>   took a notion, had a hankering,
>   had good wood, but
>   came out—
>   a ripple
>   in the breeze
> bingo!—
>   old solitary Whiff-Beard

ARIEL

Sylvia Plath (1932–1963)

> Stasis in darkness.
> Then the substanceless blue
> Pour of tor and distances.
>
> God's lioness,
> How one we grow,
> Pivot of heels and knees!—The furrow
>
> Splits and passes, sister to
> The brown arc
> Of the neck I cannot catch,
>
> Nigger-eye
> Berries cast dark
> Hooks——
>
> Black sweet blood mouthfuls,
> Shadows.
> Something else

Hauls me through air——
Thighs, hair;
Flakes from my heels.

White
Godiva, I unpeel—— 20
Dead hands, dead stringencies.

And now I
Foam to wheat, a glitter of seas.
The child's cry

Melts in the wall. 25
And I
Am the arrow,

The dew that flies
Suicidal, at one with the drive
Into the red 30

Eye, the cauldron of morning.

IN MEMORY OF RADIO

Imamu Amiri Baraka (LeRoi Jones) (b. 1934)

Who has ever stopped to think of the divinity of Lamont Cranston?
(Only Jack Kerouac, that I know of: & me.
The rest of you probably had on WCBS and Kate Smith,
Or something equally unattractive.)

What can I say? 5
It is better to have loved and lost
Than to put linoleum in your living rooms?

Am I a sage or something?
Mandrake's hypnotic gesture of the week?
(Remember, I do not have the healing powers of Oral Roberts . . . 10
I cannot, like F. J. Sheen, tell you how to get saved & rich!

   1. Lamont Cranston: the name of "The Shadow," a radio series of the 1940s.   **2. Jack Kerouac**: a writer of the 1950s' "Beat Generation."   **3. Kate Smith**: a singer famous on radio for her rendition of "God Bless America."   **9. Mandrake**: "Mandrake the Magician," a front-page-featured comic strip in the *Newark Evening News* in the 1940s and 1950s.   **10–11. Oral Roberts and F[ulton] J. Sheen**: religious evangelists who projected strong radio-television personalities.

I cannot even order you to gaschamber satori like Hitler or Goody
    Knight

& Love is an evil word.
Turn it backwards/see, see what I mean?
An evol word. & besides   15
who understands it?
I certainly wouldn't like to go out on that kind of limb.

Saturday mornings we listened to *Red Lantern* & his undersea folk.
At 11, *Let's Pretend*/& we did/& I, the poet, still do, Thank God!

What was it he used to say (after the transformation, when he was
    safe   20
& invisible & the unbelievers couldn't throw stones?) "Heh, heh, heh,

Who knows what evil lurks in the hearts of men? The Shadow
    knows."

O, yes he does
O, yes he does.
An evil word it is,   25
This Love.

QUESTIONS

1. In order to more fully develop the ability to scan poetry, choose some lines at random from the selected poems and try scanning them. Have them checked by someone who knows something about scansion. If you have lines that offer unusual problems, discuss them in class.
2. In a brief class presentation or essay, discuss the rhythmic features of one poem that seems to you to be especially successful. How much of the poem's success is dependent on rhythm and meter?
3. Select a poem from another section of this book and sug-

---

12. Goody Knight: Goodwin Knight, governor of California in the 1950s. **21–22.** "**Heh, heh, heh...knows**": the closing rubric of each of "The Shadow" installments.

gest reasons that would justify its inclusion in this section as well.
4. Choose a poem that, in your opinion, has the most outstanding use of one of the following: alliteration, the caesura, end-stopped and/or enjambed lines, rhyme. Explain why this feature is so important to the poem.
5. Choose the poetry of one historical period: the metaphysical, the romantic, the imagistic, or a period not represented in this book, and look closely at the uses of rhythm and meter. Is there any basic rhythmic and metrical similarity in the poems of a given period? Would this constitute an important element of style?
6. Look closely at the rhythmic and metrical features of the poems by Whitman, Yeats, or Dickinson (pages 337–92). Do most of their poems have similar tendencies regarding rhythm and meter? Discuss this in detail, give examples, and suggest what your findings might mean for someone looking for a more sensitive way of reading these poems.
7. Examine the rhythm and meter of the work of a contemporary poet. How do his attitudes differ from those observable in the poems here? How are they similar?

Historical Contexts

An historical context is one of the most clear-cut and traditional in poetry. In all the arts, certain styles or stylistic influences seem to "catch on" and dominate at certain times. The three periods illustrated here—metaphysical, romantic, and imagistic—are familiar to most readers of English and American poetry, though the styles are not limited by nationality. The Metaphysicals had their counterparts in Italy and France. The English Romantics had other nineteenth- and even twentieth-century followers in both those countries as well as America, Germany, and Russia, to name only the most prominent nations where their influence was felt. The Imagists also had their own following in most nations where a romance or romance-influenced language was spoken. However, the poems here are not by non-English-speaking poets; they are from the heart of the English-language movements that they illustrate. When dealing closely with style, one must deal with it in a given language, not in the abstract. It is natural, indeed essential, that our attention be drawn closely to poems in our own language when we are concerned with period and style. This does not mean that the effects of the metaphysical style cannot be seen in poems in translation. They can. But they are neither as sharply defined nor as easy to identify.

Metaphysical Poetry: Early Seventeenth Century

Metaphysical implies a going beyond the physical world into an ideal or spiritual world that is only shadowed or suggested by the "real" world of the senses. The followers of seventeenth-century poet John Donne (1572?–1631) shared some of his concerns for the other-worldly potential of immediate human experience, and, in particular, they concerned themselves with the potential that human sexual love had for leading one into the divine ecstasy of the love of God. Thus, this section begins with poems on sexual love and ends with poems discussing the love of God or platonic love.

Movement from one kind of experience to another, such as the shift from sex to God, is always a creative act of the imagination, and, as such, often needs a technique as effective or dramatic as the act it creates. The technique that is most associated with the Metaphysicals is the conceit. "Conceit" is a term that comes from the same root as the word "concept," and in many ways it must be thought of in relation to that word. The conceit has nothing to do with the modern idea of being conceited or proud. It means conceiving of something in a given way that gives it a new perspective or freshness. Generally the conceit has not only a freshness but a considerable amount of surprise as well. When Richard Crashaw refers to Mary Magdalene's weeping eyes (she is crying for Jesus), he calls them "two portable and compendious oceans." The comparison is overwhelming for most of us and delightful for many of us. It puts Mary Magdalene's crying in an entirely new context for us, one we are unfamiliar with and that we can think about.

Usually, a conceit is basically a comparison, like a metaphor. It is distinguished from a metaphor in that the comparison is really a stretching of comparative norms; it compares things in a way that seems both striking and odd, particularly at first. We do not think of eyes as portable, yet we carry them with us. We do not think of them as compendious, yet they can view the universe at a glance. We do not think of them as oceans, yet they are filled with salt tears. Thus the conceit seems unexpectedly reasonable. The surprise and the ingenuity of the conceit are its prime sources of power.

Beneath the surprise, however, is the link between the paradox of the conceit as it is applied to any situation and the entire idea of paradox in life. This is particularly strong in the poetry of the Metaphysicals because of their sustained interest in religion and religious affairs. The poets whose works follow were all Christians and most were Anglican Catholics. Most, since they had university degrees, were actually preachers and divines. They saw the conventional paradoxes of Christianity as enriching human experience. For instance, the son of God became man and died in order to give Christians eternal life. Such a concept is difficult to accept, if only because it is so paradoxical. Instead of having been born to a grand queen, Christ was born to a humble woman; instead of having seen first human light in a palace befitting God, Christ was born in a stable; instead of having been proud, Christ was humble. The paradoxes are almost endless. As Milton insisted, the ways of God are just and justifiable to man. All one has to do is understand them. The Metaphysicals sought, in a way, to imitate the ways of God in their own paradoxes and their own difficult conceits.

THE FLEA

John Donne (1572?–1631)

Marke but this flea, and marke in this,
How little that which thou deny'st me is;
It suck'd me first, and now sucks thee,
And in this flea, our two bloods mingled bee;
Thou know'st that this cannot be said   5
A sinne, nor shame, nor losse of maidenhead,
    Yet this enjoyes before it wooe,
    And pamper'd swells with one blood made of two,
And this, alas, is more then wee would doe.

Oh stay, three lives in one flea spare,   10
Where wee almost, yea more then maryed are.
This flea is you and I, and this
Our mariage bed, and mariage temple is;
Though parents grudge, and you, w'are met,
And cloysterd in these living walls of Jet.   15

Though use make you apt to kill mee,
Let not to that, selfe murder added bee,
And sacrilege, three sinnes in killing three.
Cruell and sodaine, hast thou since
Purpled thy naile, in blood of innocence? 20
Wherein could this flea guilty bee,
Except in that drop which it suckt from thee?
Yet thou triumph'st, and saist that thou
Find'st not thy selfe, nor mee the weaker now;
'Tis true, then learne how false, feares bee; 25
Just so much honor, when thou yeeld'st to mee,
Will wast, as this flea's death tooke life from thee.

SONG

John Donne

Goe, and catche a falling starre,
   Get with child a mandrake roote,
Tell me, where all past yeares are,
   Or who cleft the Divels foot,
Teach me to heare Mermaides singing, 5
Or to keep off envies stinging,
      And finde
      What winde
Serves to'advance an honest minde.

If thou beest borne to strange sights, 10
   Things invisible to see,
Ride ten thousand daies and nights,
   Till age snow white haires on thee,
Thou, when thou retorn'st, will tell mee
All strange wonders that befell thee, 15
      And sweare
      No where
Lives a woman true, and faire.

1–9. Goe ... minde: The instructions are proverbial impossibilities. **2. Mandrake:** the mandrake plant was thought to have the shape of a human. **5. Mermaides singing:** compare this with the last lines of "The Love Song of J. Alfred Prufrock" (page 258).

>   If thou findst one, let mee know,
>   Such a Pilgrimage were sweet,   20
>   Yet doe not, I would not goe,
>   Though at next doore wee might meet,
>   Though shee were true, when you met her,
>   And last, till you write your letter,
>   Yet shee   25
>   Will bee
>   False, ere I come, to two, or three.

A VALEDICTION FORBIDDING MOURNING

John Donne

>   As virtuous men passe mildly'away,
>   And whisper to their soules, to goe,
>   Whilst some of their sad friends doe say,
>   The breath goes now, and some say, no.
>
>   So let us melt, and make no noise,   5
>   No teare-floods, nor sigh-tempests move,
>   T'were prophanation of our joyes
>   To tell the layetie our love.
>
>   Moving of th'earth brings harmes and feares,
>   Men reckon what it did and meant,   10
>   But trepidation of the spheares,
>   Though greater farre, is innocent.
>
>   Dull sublunary lovers love
>   (Whose soule is sense) cannot admit
>   Absence, because it doth remove   15
>   Those things which elemented it.

27. to two, or three: refers to two or three men.

A Valediction Forbidding Mourning. In 1611 Donne was leaving for the Continent on an expedition. The opening stanzas ask that he and his wife not make a tearful scene at their parting, but that they act like virtuous men who, because they are virtuous, do not lament even when they die.   **8. layetie:** makes Donne and his wife priests of their own religion—love.   **11. trepidation of the spheares:** refers to the unpredictable movement of the planets; compared with the less cosmically significant earthquake, "moving of th' earth" (line 9), such huge tremors are innocent.   **13. sublunary:** beneath the moon—thus earth-bound and given to the ebb and flow familiar to us on earth.

But we by'a love, so much refin'd,
That our selves know not what it is,
Inter-assured of the mind,
Care lesse, eyes, lips, and hands to misse.   20

Our two soules therefore, which are one,
Though I must goe, endure not yet
A breach, but an expansion,
Like gold to ayery thinnesse beate.

If they be two, they are two so   25
As stiffe twin compasses are two,
Thy soule the fixt foot, makes no show
To move, but doth, if the'other doe.

And though it in the center sit,
Yet when the other far doth rome,   30
It leanes, and hearkens after it,
And growes erect, as that comes home.

Such wilt thou be to mee, who must
Like th'other foot, obliquely runne.
Thy firmnes makes my circle just,   35
And makes me end, where I begunne.

ELEGIE: GOING TO BED

John Donne

Come, Madam, come, all rest my powers defie,
Until I labour, I in labour lie.
The foe oft-times having the foe in sight,
Is tir'd with standing though he never fight.
Off with that girdle, like heavens Zone glittering,   5
But a far fairer world incompassing.

24. **gold ... beate:** refers to the proverbially malleability of gold, which can be hammered to incredible thinness.   26. **compasses:** instruments used in navigation; now used by schoolchildren (and others) for drawing circles. This conceit is the most famous in the poem and one of the best examples of an unusual metaphor extended in this fashion.
    5. **girdle:** belt.

Unpin that spangled breastplate which you wear,
That th'eyes of busie fooles may be stopt there.
Unlace your self, for that harmonious chyme,
Tells me from you, that now it is bed time. 10
Off with that happy busk, which I envie,
That still can be, and still can stand so nigh.
Your gown going off, such beautious state reveals,
As when from flowry meads th'hills shadowe steales.
Off with that wyerie Coronet and shew 15
The haiery Diadem which on you doth grow:
Now off with those shooes, and then softly tread
In this loves hallow'd temple, this soft bed.
In such white robes, heaven's Angels us'd to be
Receavd by men: thou Angel bringst with thee 20
A heaven like Mahomets Paradice, and though
Ill spirits walk in white, we easly know,
By this these Angels from an evil sprite,
Those set our hairs, but these our flesh upright.
  Licence my roaving hands, and let them go, 25
Behind, before, above, between, below.
O my America! my new-found-land,
My kingdome, safeliest when with one man man'd,
My Myne of precious stones: My Emperie,
How blest am I in this discovering thee! 30
To enter in these bonds, is to be free;
Then where my hand is set, my seal shall be.
  Full nakedness! All joyes are due to thee,
As souls unbodied, bodies uncloth'd must be,
To taste whole joyes. Jems which you women use 35
Are like Atlanta's balls, cast in mens views,
That when a fools eye lighteth on a Jem,
His earthly soul may covet theirs, not them:
Like pictures or like books gay coverings made
For lay-men, are all women thus array'd. 40
Themselves are mystick books, which only wee
(Whom their imputed grace will dignifie)
Must see reveal'd. Then since that I may know;
As liberally, as to a Midwife shew

---

11. busk: corset.   **27. America:** a frequent image for any kind of discovery or exploration.   **36. Atlanta's balls:** three glittering apples whose golden brilliance brought Atalanta to a stop in a crucial race. They symbolize the way men and women can be distracted from important things by trivialities.

Thy self: cast all, yea, this white lynnen hence, 45
There is no pennance due to innocence:
To teach thee I am naked first; why than
What needst thou have more covering then a man?

A FLY THAT FLEW INTO MY MISTRESS HER EYE

Lord Herbert of Cherbury (1580–1630)

When this fly liv'd, she us'd to play
In the sunshine all the day;
Till, coming near my Celia's sight,
She found a new and unknown light,
So full of glory as it made 5
The noonday sun a gloomy shade.
Then this amorous fly became
My rival, and did court my flame;
She did from hand to bosom skip,
And from her breath, her cheek, and lip, 10
Suck'd all the incense and the spice,
And grew a bird of paradise.
At last into her eye she flew,
There scorch'd in flames and drown'd in dew,
Like Phaëton from the sun's sphere, 15
She fell, and with her dropp'd a tear,
Of which a pearl was straight compos'd,
Wherein her ashes lie enclos'd.
Thus she receiv'd from Celia's eye
Funeral, flame, tomb, obsequy. 20

SONNET OF BLACK BEAUTY

Lord Herbert of Cherbury

Black beauty, which, above that common light,
Whose power can no colours here renew

---

15. Phaëton: a god who guided the sun's chariot in a disastrous turn around the sky. If Jupiter had not intervened and cast Phaëton from the chariot into a river, the world would have been set afire.

But those which darkness can again subdue,
Dost still remain unvari'd to the sight,
And like an object equal to the view, 5
Art neither chang'd with day, nor hid with night;
When all these colours which the world call bright,
And which old poetry doth so pursue,
Are with the night so perished and gone
That of their being there remains no mark, 10
Thou still abidest so entirely one,
That we may know thy blackness is a spark
Of light inaccessible, and alone
Our darkness which can make us think it dark.

EASTER-WINGS

George Herbert (1593–1633)

Lord, who createdst man in wealth and store,
Though foolishly he lost the same,
Decaying more and more,
Till he became
Most poore: 5
With thee
O let me rise
As larks, harmoniously,
And sing this day thy victories:
Then shall the fall further the flight in me. 10

My tender age in sorrow did beginne:
And still with sicknesses and shame
Thou didst so punish sinne,
That I became
Most thinne. 15
With thee
Let me combine
And feel this day thy victorie:
For, if I imp my wing on thine,
Affliction shall advance the flight in me. 20

Easter-wings. This is a shaped poem—one of many Herbert wrote. It was originally published "on its side," and the wings then appeared more soaring. **10. the fall:** Adam and Eve's fall, or the sin all men bear. **19. imp:** a term from falconry referring to implantation of feathers in the falcon's wings to help it fly better.

THE COLLAR

George Herbert

I struck the board, and cry'd, No more.
    I will abroad.
What? shall I ever sigh and pine?
My lines and life are free; free as the rode,
    Loose as the winde, as large as store.   5
        Shall I be still in suit?
Have I no harvest but a thorn
To let me bloud, and not restore
What I have lost with cordiall fruit?
        Sure there was wine   10
Before my sighs did drie it: there was corn
    Before my tears did drown it.
Is the yeare onely lost to me?
        Have I no bayes to crown it?
No flowers, no garlands gay? all blasted?   15
        All wasted?
Not so, my heart: but there is fruit,
    And thou hast hands.
Recover all thy sigh-blown age
On double pleasures: leave thy cold dispute   20
Of what is fit, and not. Forsake thy cage,
    Thy rope of sands,
Which pettie thoughts have made, and made to thee
    Good cable, to enforce and draw,
        And be thy law,   25

The Collar. For more than two hundred years, the collar was assumed to be the minister's collar; and the board (line 1), the communion board of the Anglican church. Herbert was a minister, so it did not seem necessary to search further. In the late 1960s, however, scholars observed the many references to nautical images—"rode" (line 4), the sea; being "in suit" (line 6), waiting to sail; "good cable" (line 24) just to name a few—including the word "collar." On the mainmast of ships of the time, the collar was the ring that held the mast aloft and true. The board, then, is the railing one touches when going aboard a ship. Both the religious and the nautical comparisons are effective in this poem.

    While thou didst wink and wouldst not see.
                Away; take heed;
                I will abroad.
    Call in thy deaths head there: tie up thy fears.
                He that forbears   30
          To suit and serve his need,
              Deserves his load.
    But as I rav'd and grew more fierce and wilde
                At every word,
    Me thoughts I heard one calling, *Child!*   35
           And I reply'd, *My Lord.*

OF THE LAST VERSES IN THE BOOK

Edmund Waller (1606–1687)

When we for age could neither read nor write,
The subject made us able to indite;
The soul, with nobler resolutions decked,
The body stooping, does herself erect.
No mortal parts are requisite to raise   5
Her that, unbodied, can her Maker praise.
    The seas are quiet when the winds give o'er;
So, calm are we when passions are no more!
For then we know how vain it was to boast
Of fleeting things, so certain to be lost.   10
Clouds of affection from our younger eyes
Conceal that emptiness which age descries.
    The soul's dark cottage, battered and decayed,
Lets in new light through chinks that time has made;
Stronger by weakness, wiser men become,   15
As they draw near to their eternal home.
Leaving the old, both worlds at once they view,
That stand upon the threshold of the new.

2. indite: write.   **12. descries:** observes, sees.

SAINTE MARY MAGDALENE
OR
THE WEEPER

Richard Crashaw (1613?–1649)

Loe where a WOUNDED HEART with Bleeding EYES conspire.
Is she a FLAMING Fountain, or a Weeping fire?

I

Hail, sister springs!
   Parents of sylver-footed rills!
   Ever bubling things!
   Thawing crystall! snowy hills,
Still spending, never spent! I mean   5
Thy fair eyes, sweet MAGDALENE!

II

Heavens thy fair eyes be;
Heavens of ever-falling starres.
'Tis seed-time still with thee
And starres thou sow'st, whose harvest dares   10
Promise the earth to counter shine
Whatever makes heavn's forhead fine.

III

But we'are deceived all.
Starres indeed they are too true;
For they but seem to fall,   15
As Heavn's other spangles doe.
It is not for our earth and us
To shine in Things so pretious.

Sainte Mary Magdalene. This is one of the most extreme moments in metaphysical poetry. The tears of Mary Magdalene travel an almost epic journey—which to some readers is comic. For Crashaw, the more extreme the conceit, the more intense the feeling. Many contemporary readers agreed with him.

IV

Upwards thou dost weep.
Heavn's bosome drinks the gentle stream.
Where th' milky rivers creep,
Thine floates above; and is the cream.
Waters above th'Heavns, what they be
We'are taught best by thy Teares and thee.

V

Every morn from hence
A brisk Cherub somthing sippes
Whose sacred influence
Addes sweetnes to his sweetest Lippes.
Then to his musick. And his song
Tasts of this Breakfast all day long.

VI

Not in the evening's eyes
When they Red with weeping are
For the Sun that dyes,
Sitts sorrow with a face so fair,
No where but here did ever meet
Sweetnesse so sad, sadnesse so sweet.

VII

When sorrow would be seen
In her brightest majesty
(For she is a Queen)
Then is she drest by none but thee.
Then, and only then, she weares
Her proudest pearles; I mean, thy Teares.

VIII

The deaw no more will weep
The primrose's pale cheek to deck,
The deaw no more will sleep
Nuzzel'd in the lilly's neck;
Much reather would it be thy Tear,
And leave them Both to tremble here.

IX

There's no need at all
That the balsom-sweating bough 50
So coyly should let fall
His med'cinable teares; for now
Nature hath learn't to'extract a deaw
More soveraign and sweet from you.

X

Yet let the poore drops weep 55
(Weeping is the ease of woe)
Softly let them creep,
Sad that they are vanquish't so.
They, though to others no releife,
Balsom maybe, for their own greife. 60

XI

Such the maiden gemme
By the purpling vine put on,
Peeps from her parent stemme
And blushes at the bridegroome sun.
This watry Blossom of thy eyn, 65
Ripe, will make the richer wine.

XII

When some new bright Guest
Takes up among the starres a room,
And Heavn will make a feast,
Angels with crystall violls come 70
And draw from these full eyes of thine
Their master's Water: their own Wine.

XIII

Golden though he be,
Golden Tagus murmures tho;
Were his way by thee, 75
Content and quiet he would goe.
So much more rich would he esteem
Thy sylver, then his golden stream.

65. **eyn**: eyes.   74. **Tagus**: a river whose sand gave it a golden hue.

XIV

    Well does the May that lyes
    Smiling in thy cheeks, confesse
    The April in thine eyes.
    Mutuall sweetnesse they expresse.
No April ere lent kinder showres,
Nor May return'd more faithfull flowres.

XV

    O cheeks! Bedds of chast loves
    By your own showres seasonably dash't;
    Eyes! nests of milky doves
    In your own wells decently washt,
O wit of love! that thus could place
Fountain and Garden in one face.

XVI

    O sweet Contest; of woes
    With loves, of teares with smiles disputing!
    O fair, and Freindly Foes,
    Each other kissing and confuting!
While rain and sunshine, Cheekes and Eyes
Close in kind contrarietyes.

XVII

    But can these fair Flouds be
    Freinds with the bosom fires that fill thee!
    Can so great flames agree
    Æternall Teares should thus distill thee!
O flouds, o fires! o suns o showres!
Mixt and made freinds by loue's sweet powres.

XVIII

    Twas his well-pointed dart
    That digg'd these wells, and drest this Vine;
    And taught the wounded HEART
    The way into these weeping Eyn.
Vain loves avant; bold hands forbear!
The lamb hath dipp't his white foot here.

107. avant: go away.

XIX

And now where're he strayes,
Among the Galilean mountaines,   110
Or more unwellcome wayes,
He's follow'd by two faithfull fountaines;
Two walking baths; two weeping motions;
Portable, and compendious oceans.

XX

O Thou, thy lord's fair store!   115
In thy so rich and rare expenses,
Even when he show'd most poor,
He might provoke the wealth of Princes.
What Prince's wanton'st pride e're could
Wash with Sylver, wipe with Gold.   120

XXI

Who is that King, but he
Who calls't his Crown to be call'd thine,
That thus can boast to be
Waited on by a wandring mine,
A voluntary mint, that strowes   125
Warm sylver shoures where're he goes!

XXII

O pretious Prodigall!
Fair spend-thrift of thy self! thy measure
(Mercilesse love!) is all.
Even to the last Pearle in thy treasure. 130
All places, Times, and objects be
Thy teare's sweet opportunity.

XXIII

Does the day-starre rise?
Still thy starres doe fall and fall.
Does day close his eyes?   135
Still the FOUNTAIN weeps for all.
Let night or day doe what they will,
Thou hast thy task; thou weepest still.

XXIV

Does thy song lull the air?
Thy falling teares keep faithfull time. 140
Does thy sweet-breath'd praire
Up in clouds of incense climb?
Still at each sigh, that is, each stop,
A bead, that is, A Tear, does drop.

XXV

At these thy weeping gates, 145
(Watching their watry motion)
Each winged moment waits,
Takes his Tear, and gets him gone.
By thine Ey's tinct enobled thus
Time layes him up; he's pretious. 150

XXVI

Not, so long she lived,
Shall thy tomb report of thee;
But, so long she greived,
Thus must we date thy memory.
Others by moments, months, and yeares 155
Measure their ages; thou, by Teares.

XXVII

So doe perfumes expire.
So sigh tormented sweets, opprest
With proud unpittying fire.
Such Teares the suffring Rose that's vext 160
With ungentle flames does shed,
Sweating in a too warm bed.

XXVIII

Say, ye bright brothers,
The fugitive sons of those fair Eyes
Your fruitfull mothers! 165
What make you here? what hopes can tice
You to be born? what cause can borrow
You from Those nests of noble sorrow?

XXIX

Whither away so fast?
For sure the sordid earth   170
Your Sweetnes cannot tast
Nor does the dust deserve your birth.
Sweet, whither hast you then? ô say
Why you trip so fast away?

XXX

We goe not to seek,   175
The darlings of Auroras bed,
The rose's modest Cheek
Nor the violet's humble head.
Though the Feild's eyes too WEEPERS be
Because they want such TEARES as we.   180

XXXI

Much lesse mean we to trace
The Fortune of inferior gemmes,
Preferr'd to some proud face
Or pertch't upon fear'd Diadems.
Crown'd Heads are toyes. We goe to meet   185
A worthy object, our lord's FEET.

ON OUR CRUCIFIED LORD NAKED, AND BLOODY

Richard Crashaw

Th' have left thee naked Lord, O that they had;
This Garment too I would they had deny'd.
Thee with thy selfe they have too richly clad,
Opening the purple wardrobe of thy side.
    O never could bee found Garments too good   5
    For thee to weare, but these, of thine owne blood.

THE WORLD
Henry Vaughan (1622–1695)

I Saw Eternity the other night
Like a great *Ring* of pure and endless light,
    All calm, as it was bright,
And round beneath it, Time in hours, days, years
    Drivn' by the spheres   5
Like a vast shadow mov'd, In which the world
    And all her train were hurl'd;
The doting Lover in his queintest strain
    Did their Complain,
Neer him, his Lute, his fancy, and his flights,   10
    Wits sour delights,
With gloves, and knots the silly snares of pleasure
    Yet his dear Treasure
All scatter'd lay, while he his eys did pour
    Upon a flowr.   15

2

The darksome States-man hung with weights and woe
Like a thick midnight-fog mov'd there so slow
    He did nor stay, nor go;
Condemning thoughts (like sad Ecclipses) scowl
    Upon his soul,   20
And Clouds of crying witnesses without
    Pursued him with one shout.
Yet dig'd the Mole, and lest his ways be found
    Workt under ground,
Where he did Clutch his prey, but one did see   25
    That policie,
Churches and altars fed him, Perjuries
    Were gnats and flies,
It rain'd about him bloud and tears, but he
    Drank them as free.   30

3

The fearfull miser on a heap of rust
Sate pining all his life there, did scarce trust

8. **queintest strain:** the most carefully crafted style.

His own hands with the dust,
Yet would not place one peece above, but lives
    In feare of theeves.   35
Thousands there were as frantick as himself
    And hug'd each one his pelf,
The down-right Epicure plac'd heav'n in sense
    And scornd pretence
While others slipt into a wide Excesse   40
    Said little lesse;
The weaker sort slight, triviall wares Inslave
    Who think them brave,
And poor, despised truth sate Counting by
    Their victory.   45

4

Yet some, who all this while did weep and sing,
And sing, and weep, soar'd up into the *Ring,*
    But most would use no wing.
O fools (said I,) thus to prefer dark night
    Before true light,   50
To live in grots, and caves, and hate the day
    Because it shews the way,
The way which from this dead and dark abode
    Leads up to God,
A way where you might tread the Sun, and be   55
    More bright than he.
But as I did their madnes so discusse
    One whisper'd thus,
This Ring the Bride-groome did for none provide
    But for his bride.   60

THE LAMPE

Henry Vaughan

'Tis dead night round about: Horrour doth creepe
And move on with the shades; stars nod, and sleepe,

---

37. pelf: worldly goods.   **38. Epicure:** a follower of Epicurus, who placed pleasure as the highest good.

And through the dark aire spin a firie thread
Such as doth gild the lazie glow-worms bed.
  Yet, burn'st thou here, a full day; while I spend   5
My rest in Cares, and to the dark world lend
These flames, as thou dost thine to me; I watch
That houre, which must thy life, and mine dispatch;
But still thou doest out-goe me, I can see
Met in thy flames, all acts of piety;   10
Thy light, is *Charity;* Thy heat, is *Zeale;*
And thy aspiring, active fires reveale
Devotion still on wing; Then, thou dost weepe
Still as thou burn'st, and the warme droppings creepe
To measure out thy length, as if thou'dst know   15
What stock, and how much time were left thee now;
Nor dost thou spend one teare in vain, for still
As thou dissolv'st to them, and they distill,
They're stor'd up in the socket, where they lye,
When all is spent, thy last, and sure supply,   20
And such is true repentance, ev'ry breath
Wee spend in sighes, is treasure after death;
Only, one point escapes thee; That thy Oile
Is still out with thy flame, and so both faile;
But whensoe're I'm out, both shalbe in,   25
And where thou mad'st an end, there I'le begin.

THE DEDICATION

Henry Vaughan

My God, thou that didst dye for me,
These thy deaths fruits I offer thee.
Death that to me was life, and light
But darke, and deep pangs to thy sight.
Some drops of thy all-quickning bloud   5
Fell on my heart, these made it bud
And put forth thus, though, Lord, before
The ground was curs'd, and void of store.
  Indeed, I had some here to hire
Which long resisted thy desire,   10

That ston'd thy Servants, and did move
To have thee murther'd for thy Love,
But, Lord, I have expell'd them, and so bent
Begge thou wouldst take thy Tenants Rent.

QUESTIONS

1. Critics usually point to the conceit as one of the most important devices of the Metaphysicals. As we said in the introductory discussion, the conceit is a metaphor in which the comparisons are extremely far-fetched at first glance, but which become more reasonable as one considers them. The "stiffe twin compasses" (line 26) in Donne's "A Valediction Forbidding Mourning" is one of the most famous examples. Examine these poems to find other instances of the conceit. Are they plentiful? How are they used in the poem? Are they successful?
2. Find a poem that uses no conceits and compare it with poems that use the device. How does the poem compare in use of language, attitudes toward rhythm and meter, and thematic interests? Is it profoundly different from poems that rely on the conceit, or is it only moderately different?
3. Another feature of metaphysical poetry is its tendency to establish arguments and to construct logical patterns that are designed to convince a listener of a given point. Which poems in this selection are of this type? Examine the argument of the poem you feel is most successful. What makes it successful? Does the tightness of the argument make it less interesting than a prose version of the same idea would be?
4. Examine the themes of these poems. What themes seem most common to all? What themes might be inappropriate for the Metaphysicals?
5. A high degree of intelligence and a cerebral quality are often cited as hallmarks of the Metaphysicals. Is such a judgment warranted? Are most of these poems unusually thoughtful or intellectual? Explain. Are any of them not thoughtful or intellectual?

Romantic Poetry:
Early Nineteenth Century

The style of the Romantics is much less complex than that of the Metaphysicals. The Romantics used simpler language. They lacked interest in knotty and ingenious wit. They were not so much interested in intellectualization as in feeling and responding to nature and to man. Where the Metaphysicals were God-centered, the Romantics were man-centered. Such generalizations, naturally, are much too simple to account for the enormous variety of romantic poetry, but testing them in light of the poems that follow can be instructive.

The romantic poets concerned themselves with many of the things that still excite our interest: psychology, human freedom, and the potential for revolution in Europe and in other parts of the world. The imagination, or the inner recesses of the mind, was of consummate interest to them. Drugs were not unknown to these poets, and Coleridge's famous "Kubla Khan" is said to have been influenced by an opium dream. The power of the imagination was largely unexplored by earlier poets, with the very notable exception of Shakespeare, for reasons that are not entirely clear. One reason was that the imagination—or fancy—was thought to be unreliable and to offer visions that were impossible—hence unreal. Such visions would be no help, except under extraordinary circumstances, for discovering the truth about the world and about God. The Romantics, however, made the inner world their discovery and explored it without worrying whether the visions were real or not. The visions were interesting and in some ways exciting. That was enough. The visions also gave them fresh new territory for exploration, and that was good reason for pursuing such experiments as writing down dreams and recreating the antique worlds of the past, as Keats did in "La Belle Dame sans Merci."

Haunted castles, the dim past, witches, magic, and the lament for a lost love are all standard ingredients of romantic poems. And the fact seems to be that, like the highly intellectual and abstract techniques of the Metaphysicals, the interests of the Romantics have continued to excite modern writers. Once the romantic attitude has been perceived in all its variety and energy, one begins to see that the Romantics actually defined a mode of thought—

which all of us tend to use at various times—as well as a literary style. What is hard for us to understand is that such a way of thinking was largely unknown to people before the time of Blake and Wordsworth. Or at least it is reasonable to say that it was unknown to a large number of people. Perhaps the geniuses of any age would have had much in common with the Romantics. But the proletarian character of the romantic movement, the effort to make art, poetry, and the inner world available to all who might want them, was something very new in poetry. And it is still respected by many readers even today, despite the fact that the most modern of poets have explored the use of obscurity and very "difficult" verse.

ELEGY
WRITTEN IN A COUNTRY CHURCH YARD

Thomas Gray (1716–1771)

The Curfew tolls the knell of parting day,
The lowing herd wind slowly o'er the lea,
The plowman homeward plods his weary way,
And leaves the world to darkness and to me.

Now fades the glimmering landscape on the sight,   5
And all the air a solemn stillness holds,
Save where the beetle wheels his droning flight,
And drowsy tinklings lull the distant folds;

Save that from yonder ivy-mantled tow'r
The mopeing owl does to the moon complain   10
Of such, as wand'ring near her secret bow'r,
Molest her ancient solitary reign.

Beneath those rugged elms, that yew-tree's shade,
Where heaves the turf in many a mould'ring heap,
Each in his narrow cell for ever laid,   15
The rude Forefathers of the hamlet sleep.

The breezy call of incense-breathing Morn,
The swallow twitt'ring from the straw-built shed,

The cock's shrill clarion, or the ecchoing horn,
No more shall rouse them from their lowly bed.   20

For them no more the blazing hearth shall burn,
Or busy houswife ply her evening care:
No children run to lisp their sire's return,
Or climb his knees the envied kiss to share.

Oft did the harvest to their sickle yield,   25
Their furrow oft the stubborn glebe has broke;
How jocund did they drive their team afield!
How bow'd the woods beneath their sturdy stroke!

Let not Ambition mock their useful toil,
Their homely joys, and destiny obscure;   30
Nor Grandeur hear with a disdainful smile,
The short and simple annals of the poor.

The boast of heraldry, the pomp of pow'r,
And all that beauty, all that wealth e'er gave,
Awaits alike th' inevitable hour.   35
The paths of glory lead but to the grave.

Nor you, ye Proud, impute to These the fault,
If Mem'ry o'er their Tomb no Trophies raise,
Where thro' the long-drawn isle and fretted vault
The pealing anthem swells the note of praise.   40

Can storied urn or animated bust
Back to its mansion call the fleeting breath?
Can Honour's voice provoke the silent dust,
Or Flatt'ry sooth the dull cold ear of Death?

Perhaps in this neglected spot is laid   45
Some heart once pregnant with celestial fire,
Hands, that the rod of empire might have sway'd,
Or wak'd to extasy the living lyre.

But Knowledge to their eyes her ample page
Rich with the spoils of time did ne'er unroll;   50
Chill Penury repress'd their noble rage,
And froze the genial current of the soul.

Full many a gem of purest ray serene,
The dark unfathom'd caves of ocean bear:

Full many a flower is born to blush unseen, 55
And waste its sweetness on the desert air.

Some village-Hampden, that with dauntless breast
The little Tyrant of his fields withstood;
Some mute inglorious Milton here may rest,
Some Cromwell guiltless of his country's blood. 60

Th' applause of list'ning senates to command,
The threats of pain and ruin to despise,
To scatter plenty o'er a smiling land,
And read their hist'ry in a nation's eyes

Their lot forbad: nor circumscrib'd alone 65
Their growing virtues, but their crimes confin'd;
Forbad to wade through slaughter to a throne,
And shut the gates of mercy on mankind,

The struggling pangs of conscious truth to hide,
To quench the blushes of ingenuous shame, 70
Or heap the shrine of Luxury and Pride
With incense kindled at the Muse's flame.

Far from the madding crowd's ignoble strife,
Their sober wishes never learn'd to stray;
Along the cool sequester'd vale of life 75
They kept the noiseless tenor of their way.

Yet ev'n these bones from insult to protect
Some frail memorial still erected nigh,
With uncouth rhimes and shapeless sculpture deck'd,
Implores the passing tribute of a sigh. 80

Their name, their years, spelt by th' unletter'd muse,
The place of fame and elegy supply:
And many a holy text around she strews,
That teach the rustic moralist to die.

For who to dumb Forgetfulness a prey, 85
This pleasing anxious being e'er resign'd,

57. Hampden: John Hampden, who refused to submit to King Charles I's demand for a tax he thought illegal.   **60. Cromwell:** Oliver Cromwell, head of state after King Charles I was defeated in the English Civil War and subsequently beheaded.

Left the warm precincts of the chearful day,
Nor cast one longing ling'ring look behind?

On some fond breast the parting soul relies,
Some pious drops the closing eye requires; 90
Ev'n from the tomb the voice of Nature cries,
Ev'n in our Ashes live their wonted Fires.

For thee, who mindful of th' unhonour'd Dead
Dost in these lines their artless tale relate;
If chance, by lonely contemplation led, 95
Some kindred Spirit shall inquire thy fate,

Haply some hoary-headed Swain may say,
"Oft have we seen him at the peep of dawn
"Brushing with hasty steps the dews away
"To meet the sun upon the upland lawn. 100

"There at the foot of yonder nodding beech
"That wreathes its old fantastic roots so high,
"His listless length at noontide wou'd he stretch,
"And pore upon the brook that babbles by.

"Hard by yon wood, now smiling as in scorn, 105
"Mutt'ring his wayward fancies he wou'd rove,
"Now drooping, woeful wan, like one forlorn,
"Or craz'd with care, or cross'd in hopeless love.

"One morn I miss'd him on the custom'd hill,
"Along the heath and near his fav'rite tree; 110
"Another came; nor yet beside the rill,
"Nor up the lawn, nor at the wood was he,

"The next with dirges due in sad array
"Slow thro' the church-way path we saw him born[e].
"Approach and read (for thou can'st read) the lay, 115
"Grav'd on the stone beneath yon aged thorn."

THE EPITAPH

Here rests his head upon the lap of Earth
A Youth to Fortune and to Fame unknown,
Fair Science frown'd not on his humble birth,
And Melancholy mark'd him for her own. 120

Large was his bounty, and his soul sincere,
Heav'n did a recompence as largely send:

He gave to Mis'ry all he had, a tear,
He gain'd from Heav'n ('twas all he wish'd) a friend.

No farther seek his merits to disclose, 125
Or draw his frailties from their dread abode,
(There they alike in trembling hope repose)
The bosom of his Father and his God.

THE GARDEN OF LOVE

William Blake (1757–1827)

I went to the Garden of Love,
And saw what I never had seen:
A Chapel was built in the midst,
Where I used to play on the green.

And the gates of this Chapel were shut, 5
And Thou shalt not. writ over the door;
So I turn'd to the Garden of Love,
That so many sweet flowers bore,

And I saw it was filled with graves,
And tomb-stones where flowers should be: 10
And Priests in black gowns, were walking their rounds,
And binding with briars, my joys & desires.

MAD SONG

William Blake

The wild winds weep,
 And the night is a-cold;
Come hither, Sleep,
 And my griefs infold:
But lo! the morning peeps 5
 Over the eastern steeps,
And the rustling birds of dawn
The earth do scorn.

Lo! to the vault
   Of paved heaven,   10
With sorrow fraught
   My notes are driven:
They strike the ear of night,
   Make weep the eyes of day;
They make mad the roaring winds,   15
   And with tempests play.

Like a fiend in a cloud
   With howling woe,
After night I do croud,
   And with night will go;   20
I turn my back to the east,
From whence comforts have increas'd;
For light doth seize my brain
With frantic pain.

LONDON

William Blake

I wander thro' each charter'd street,
Near where the charter'd Thames does flow.
And mark in every face I meet
Marks of weakness, marks of woe.

In every cry of every Man,   5
In every Infants cry of fear,
In every voice: in every ban,
The mind-forg'd manacles I hear

How the Chimney-sweepers cry
Every blackning Church appalls,   10
And the hapless Soldiers sigh,
Runs in blood down Palace walls

---

1. charter'd: implies imprisoned, or fixed in its bounds.

But most thro' midnight streets I hear
How the youthful Harlots curse
Blasts the new-born Infants tear   15
And blights with plagues the Marriage hearse

TO MY SISTER

William Wordsworth (1770–1850)

It is the first mild day of March:
Each minute sweeter than before,
The redbreast sings from the tall larch
That stands beside our door.

There is a blessing in the air,   5
Which seems a sense of joy to yield
To the bare trees, and mountains bare,
And grass in the green field.

My sister! ('tis a wish of mine)
Now that our morning meal is done,   10
Make haste, your morning task resign;
Come forth and feel the sun.

Edward will come with you;—and, pray,
Put on with speed your woodland dress;
And bring no book: for this one day   15
We'll give to idleness.

No joyless forms shall regulate
Our living calendar:
We from to-day, my Friend, will date
The opening of the year.   20

Love, now a universal birth,
From heart to heart is stealing,
From earth to man, from man to earth:
—It is the hour of feeling.

To My Sister. Dorothy Wordsworth was William's constant companion and a constant concern and inspiration to him.   **13. Edward:** Edward Montagu, a five-year-old boy staying with the Wordsworths.

One moment now may give us more 25
Than years of toiling reason:
Our minds shall drink at every pore
The spirit of the season.

Some silent laws our hearts will make,
Which they shall long obey: 30
We for the year to come may take
Our temper from to-day.

And from the blessed power that rolls
About, below, above,
We'll frame the measure of our souls: 35
They shall be tuned to love.

Then come, my Sister! come, I pray,
With speed put on your woodland dress;
And bring no book: for this one day
We'll give to idleness. 40

TO TOUSSAINT L'OUVERTURE

William Wordsworth

Toussaint, the most unhappy man of men!
Whether the whistling Rustic tend his plough
Within thy hearing, or thy head be now
Pillowed in some deep dungeon's earless den;—
O miserable Chieftain! where and when 5
Wilt thou find patience! Yet die not; do thou
Wear rather in thy bonds a cheerful brow:
Though fallen thyself, never to rise again,
Live, and take comfort. Thou hast left behind
Powers that will work for thee; air, earth, and skies; 10
There's not a breathing of the common wind
That will forget thee; thou hast great allies;
Thy friends are exultations, agonies,
And love, and man's unconquerable mind.

To Toussaint L'Ouverture. Toussaint L'Ouverture led a daring slave revolt in Haiti. He freed Haiti, stood up to Napoleon when he tried to reintroduce slavery to the island, and died in France after his ultimate capture.

KUBLA KHAN

Samuel Taylor Coleridge (1772–1834)

In Xanadu did Kubla Khan
A stately pleasure-dome decree:
Where Alph, the sacred river, ran
Through caverns measureless to man
    Down to a sunless sea. 5
So twice five miles of fertile ground
With walls and towers were girdled round:
And there were gardens bright with sinuous rills,
Where blossomed many an incense-bearing tree;
And here were forests ancient as the hills, 10
Enfolding sunny spots of greenery.

But oh! that deep romantic chasm which slanted
Down the green hill athwart a cedarn cover!
A savage place! as holy and enchanted
As e'er beneath a waning moon was haunted 15
By woman wailing for her demon-lover!
And from this chasm, with ceaseless turmoil seething,
As if this earth in fast thick pants were breathing,
A mighty fountain momently was forced:
Amid whose swift half-intermitted burst 20
Huge fragments vaulted like rebounding hail,
Or chaffy grain beneath the thresher's flail:
And 'mid these dancing rocks at once and ever
It flung up momently the sacred river.
Five miles meandering with a mazy motion 25
Through wood and dale the sacred river ran,
Then reached the caverns measureless to man,
And sank in tumult to a lifeless ocean:
And 'mid this tumult Kubla heard from far
Ancestral voices prophesying war! 30
    The shadow of the dome of pleasure
    Floated midway on the waves;
    Where was heard the mingled measure
    From the fountain and the caves.

Kubla Khan. Kubla Khan was the grandson of Genghis Khan. In the 1200s he founded the Mongol dynasty in China. Coleridge considered this poem a "fragment," saying that it was induced as a "kind of reverie" by two grains of opium. Both possibilities are questionable.

It was a miracle of rare device,   35
A sunny pleasure-dome with caves of ice!

A damsel with a dulcimer
In a vision once I saw:
It was an Abyssinian maid,
And on her dulcimer she played,   40
Singing of Mount Abora.
Could I revive within me
Her symphony and song,
To such a deep delight 'twould win me,
That with music loud and long,   45
I would build that dome in air,
That sunny dome! those caves of ice!
And all who heard should see them there,
And all should cry, Beware! Beware!
His flashing eyes, his floating hair!   50
Weave a circle round him thrice,
And close your eyes with holy dread,
For he on honey-dew hath fed,
And drunk the milk of Paradise.

SONNET

Samuel Taylor Coleridge

COMPOSED ON A JOURNEY HOMEWARD; THE AUTHOR HAVING RECEIVED INTELLIGENCE OF THE BIRTH OF A SON, SEPT. 20, 1796

Oft o'er my brain does that strange fancy roll
  Which makes the present (while the flash doth last)
  Seem a mere semblance of some unknown past,
Mixed with such feelings, as perplex the soul
Self-questioned in her sleep; and some have said   5
  We liv'd, ere yet this robe of flesh we wore.
  O my sweet baby! when I reach my door,
If heavy looks should tell me thou art dead,
(As sometimes, through excess of hope, I fear)
I think that I should struggle to believe   10
  Thou wert a spirit, to this nether sphere
Sentenc'd for some more venial crime to grieve;

Did'st scream, then spring to meet Heaven's quick reprieve,
While we wept idly o'er thy little bier!

STANZAS FOR MUSIC

THERE BE NONE OF BEAUTY'S DAUGHTERS

George Gordon, Lord Byron (1788–1824)

> There be none of Beauty's daughters
>   With a magic like thee;
> And like music on the waters
>   Is thy sweet voice to me:
> When, as if its sounds were causing   5
> The charméd Ocean's pausing,
> The waves lie still and gleaming,
> And the lulled winds seem dreaming:
>
> And the midnight Moon is weaving
>   Her bright chain o'er the deep;   10
> Whose breast is gently heaving,
>   As an infant's asleep:
> So the spirit bows before thee,
> To listen and adore thee;
> With a full but soft emotion,   15
> Like the swell of Summer's ocean.

STANZAS FOR MUSIC

THERE'S NOT A JOY THE WORLD CAN GIVE LIKE THAT IT TAKES AWAY

George Gordon, Lord Byron

There's not a joy the world can give like that it takes away,
When the glow of early thought declines in Feeling's dull decay;
'Tis not on Youth's smooth cheek the blush alone, which fades so fast,
But the tender bloom of heart is gone, ere Youth itself be past.

Then the few whose spirits float above the wreck of happiness 5
Are driven o'er the shoals of guilt or ocean of excess:
The magnet of their course is gone, or only points in vain
The shore to which their shivered sail shall never stretch again.

Then the mortal coldness of the soul like Death itself comes down;
It cannot feel for others' woes, it dare not dream its own; 10
That heavy chill has frozen o'er the fountain of our tears,
And though the eye may sparkle still, 'tis where the ice appears.

Though wit may flash from fluent lips, and mirth distract the breast,
Through midnight hours that yield no more their former hope of rest;
'Tis but as ivy-leaves around the ruined turret wreath, 15
All green and wildly fresh without, but worn and grey beneath.

Oh, could I feel as I have felt,—or be what I have been,
Or weep as I could once have wept, o'er many a vanished scene;
As springs in deserts found seem sweet, all brackish though they be,
So, midst the withered waste of life, those tears would flow to me. 20

SONNET: ENGLAND IN 1819

Percy Bysshe Shelley (1792–1822)

An old, mad, blind, despised, and dying king,—
Princes, the dregs of their dull race, who flow
Through public scorn,—mud from a muddy spring,—
Rulers who neither see, nor feel, nor know,
But leech-like to their fainting country cling, 5
Till they drop, blind in blood, without a blow,—
A people starved and stabbed in the untilled field,—
An army, which liberticide and prey
Makes as a two-edged sword to all who wield,—
Golden and sanguine laws which tempt and slay; 10
Religion Christless, Godless—a book sealed;
A Senate,—Time's worst statute unrepealed,—
Are graves, from which a glorious Phantom may
Burst, to illumine our tempestuous day.

1. An old ... king: George III, who died after bouts with insanity in 1820.
7. a people starved: refers to the Peterloo Massacre in 1819 when a peaceful assembly of citizens was dispersed violently by cavalry.

OZYMANDIAS

Percy Bysshe Shelley

I met a traveller from an antique land
Who said: Two vast and trunkless legs of stone
Stand in the desert... Near them, on the sand,
Half sunk, a shattered visage lies, whose frown,
And wrinkled lip, and sneer of cold command,   5
Tell that its sculptor well those passions read
Which yet survive, stamped on these lifeless things,
The hand that mocked them, and the heart that fed:
And on the pedestal these words appear:
"My name is Ozymandias, king of kings: 10
Look on my works, ye Mighty, and despair!"
Nothing beside remains. Round the decay
Of that colossal wreck, boundless and bare
The lone and level sands stretch far away.

TO——

John Keats (1795–1821)

What can I do to drive away
Remembrance from my eyes? for they have seen,
Aye, an hour ago, my brilliant Queen!
Touch has a memory. O say, love, say,
What can I do to kill it and be free   5
In my old liberty?
When every fair one that I saw was fair,
Enough to catch me in but half a snare,
Not keep me there:
When, howe'er poor or particolour'd things,   10
My muse had wings,
And ever ready was to take her course
Whither I bent her force,
Unintellectual, yet divine to me;—
Divine, I say!—What sea-bird o'er the sea   15
Is a philosopher the while he goes
Winging along where the great water throes?

How shall I do
  To get anew
Those moulted feathers, and so mount once more
  Above, above
  The reach of fluttering Love,
And make him cower lowly while I soar?
Shall I gulp wine? No, that is vulgarism,
A heresy and schism,
  Foisted into the canon law of love;—
No,—wine is only sweet to happy men;
  More dismal cares
  Seize on me unawares,—

Where shall I learn to get my peace again?
To banish thoughts of that most hateful land,
Dungeoner of my friends, that wicked strand
Where they were wreck'd and live a wrecked life;
That monstrous region, whose dull rivers pour,
Ever from their sordid urns unto the shore,
Unown'd of any weedy-haired gods;
Whose winds, all zephyrless, hold scourging rods,
Iced in the great lakes, to afflict mankind;
Whose rank-grown forests, frosted, black, and blind,
Would fright a Dryad; whose harsh herbag'd meads
Make lean and lank the starv'd ox while he feeds;
There bad flowers have no scent, birds no sweet song,
And great unerring Nature once seems wrong.

O, for some sunny spell
To dissipate the shadows of this hell!
Say they are gone,—with the new dawning light
Steps forth my lady bright!
O, let me once more rest
My soul upon that dazzling breast!
Let once again these aching arms be plac'd,
The tender gaolers of thy waist!
And let me feel that warm breath here and there
To spread a rapture in my very hair,—
O, the sweetness of the pain!
Give me those lips again!
Enough! Enough! it is enough for me
To dream of thee!

LA BELLE DAME SANS MERCI

John Keats

O what can ail thee, knight-at-arms,
    Alone and palely loitering?
The sedge has wither'd from the lake,
    And no birds sing.

O what can ail thee, knight-at-arms,   5
    So haggard and so woe-begone?
The squirrel's granary is full,
    And the harvest's done.

I see a lily on thy brow
    With anguish moist and fever dew,   10
And on thy cheek a fading rose
    Fast withereth too.

I met a lady in the meads,
    Full beautiful—a faery's child,
Her hair was long, her foot was light,   15
    And her eyes were wild.

I made a garland for her head,
    And bracelets too, and fragrant zone;
She look'd at me as she did love,
    And made sweet moan.   20

I set her on my pacing steed,
    And nothing else saw all day long,
For sidelong would she bend, and sing
    A faery's song.

She found me roots of relish sweet,   25
    And honey wild, and manna dew,
And sure in language strange she said—
    "I love thee true."

She took me to her elfin grot,
    And there she wept, and sigh'd full sore.   30
And there I shut her wild wild eyes
    With kisses four.

And there she lulled me asleep,
   And there I dream'd—Ah! woe betide!
The latest dream I ever dream'd
   On the cold hill side.

I saw pale kings and princes too,
   Pale warriors, death-pale were they all;
They cried—"La Belle Dame sans Merci
   Hath thee in thrall!"

I saw their starved lips in the gloam,
   With horrid warning gaped wide,
And I awoke and found me here,
   On the cold hill's side.

And this is why I sojourn here,
   Alone and palely loitering,
Though the sedge is wither'd from the lake,
   And no birds sing.

ON SEEING THE ELGIN MARBLES

John Keats

My spirit is too weak—mortality
   Weighs heavily on me like unwilling sleep,
   And each imagin'd pinnacle and steep
Of godlike hardship tells me I must die
Like a sick Eagle looking at the sky.
   Yet 'tis a gentle luxury to weep
   That I have not the cloudy winds to keep
Fresh for the opening of the morning's eye.
Such dim-conceived glories of the brain
   Bring round the heart an undescribable feud;
So do these wonders a most dizzy pain,
   That mingles Grecian grandeur with the rude
Wasting of old Time—with a billowy main—
   A sun—a shadow of a magnitude.

QUESTIONS

1. Emphasis on subtle rhythmic and metrical effects is common to romantic poetry. Do you find examples of such subtlety in these poems? Select the poem you feel is most interesting for its use of rhythm and meter and explain the way it achieves its effect.
2. The Romantics are often said to be poets of feeling rather than of thought. Can you verify or contradict such a statement on the basis of the poems you have read?
3. What themes seem most important to the romantic poets? From what we know of their thematic interests, how might some of these poets feel about current social and political problems? Do you think that they are old-fashioned or up-to-date in their thinking?
4. After reading all of the selections in this section, choose the poet who you feel is most typically romantic. Defend your choice by a careful discussion of that poet's work. You may discuss poems not included in this collection.
5. Select several poems by a contemporary poet whose work you feel is romantic in character. By pointing out similarities of theme, technique, and attitude, show how the poet you have chosen could rightly find a place beside those represented here.
6. Select several poems by a contemporary poet who you feel is distinctly opposed to the romantic view of the world. Indicate clearly what makes him or her an antiromantic. Do others agree with your choice?

Imagistic Poetry: Early Twentieth Century

The many relationships between poetry and painting were well summarized by the ancient Greek philosopher Simonides when he defined poetry as "a speaking picture." But a narrower and more precise similarity between painting and poetry is summed up in the phrase "word paintings." The belief that a poem should be a painting in words has seldom, if ever, been completely subscribed to, but many poems have come close to it. Ancient Chinese poetry and the ideogram, the Japanese haiku, nineteenth-century French symbolist poetry, and most important for our purpose, the American and British imagistic poetry (ca. 1910) have all put great stress on word painting.

The Imagists sought an exact equivalent in rhythm and image for the experience that moved the poet to write his poem. Many of their most successful poems consisted entirely of images. The first poems of this kind appeared in France, but shortly before the First World War, English and American poets began writing imagist poems.

For the Imagists any natural object presented an image. Being representations of natural objects, images are perceived by all the senses—sight, hearing, smell, touch, taste. Thus the ordinary definition of poetic image is the presentation in language of a sense experience. Sometimes critics speak of visual, auditory, olfactory, tactile, and gustatory images, although single images often appeal to several senses at once. Of the numerous visual images, those of motion are most often referred to by a special term. They are called *kinesthetic*. Another word referring to images, and sometimes confused with kinesthetic, is *synesthetic*. A synesthetic image deliberately renders one sense experience in terms of another. For example, it speaks of a sound in terms of a color, "purple cries"; or a color in terms of a sound, "crackling purple."

Amy Lowell, one of the first American imagist poets, demonstrated in a number of her poems how an experience can be conveyed entirely through images:

THE POND

Amy Lowell (1874–1925)

Cold, wet leaves
Floating on moss-colored water,
And the croaking of frogs—
Cracked bell-notes in the twilight.

The poem consists of four images: the opening tactile image, the visual image of the second line, and the aural images of the last two lines. The first three images build to, or equate with, "cracked bell-notes," and all four are intended to re-create the mood that seized the poet as she looked at the pond.

The fact that there is really no verb in "The Pond" is significant; it shows the extent to which the image is given full power over everything else that the poet might use to convey an experience—even a grammatically correct sentence. Adding a verb would make a slight difference, of course, but even in an imagistic poem with a verb we can see the poet exerting control over the images. We can see the movement toward a statement in the following poem:

Oread

H. D. (1886–1961)

[handwritten: forested mountains]

Whirl up sea—
whirl your pointed pines,
splash your great pines
on our rocks,
hurl your green over us, 5
cover us with your pools of fir.

We might reconstruct the poem without any verbs:

> sea
> pointed pines
> great pines
> on rocks
> green over us
> pools of fir

We thus reduce it to its bare images and also eliminate the strong presence of the speaker, the voice uttering the imperatives. Actually, in "Oread" there is a playing-off of the imagistic and the dramatic statement, making the poem neither pure image nor quite a drama. Perhaps it should also be mentioned that the shaping impulse of rhyme is incipiently present here, most apparently in the double use of "whirl," which is picked up in the "hurl" in the fifth line.

The following poem sums up the view that images should dominate a poem.

ARS POETICA

Archibald MacLeish (b. 1892)

A poem should be palpable and mute
As a globed fruit,

Dumb
As old medallions to the thumb,

Silent as the sleeve-worn stone 5
Of casement ledges where the moss has grown—

A poem should be wordless
As the flight of birds.

A poem should be motionless in time
As the moon climbs, 10

Leaving, as the moon releases
Twig by twig the night-entangled trees,

Leaving, as the moon behind the winter leaves,
Memory by memory the mind—

A poem should be motionless in time 15
As the moon climbs.

A poem should be equal to:
Not true.

For all the history of grief
An empty doorway and a maple leaf. 20

For love
The leaning grasses and two lights above the sea—

A poem should not mean
But be.

In presenting its case for the preeminence of the image, this poem gives us almost a compendium of possible images. MacLeish uses both taste and touch in the first stanza, touch and sight in the second, sight and sound in the third, sight in the next four stanzas; employs a colon in what amounts to an image of a mathematical equal sign; then gives us two imagistic equations. The poem as a whole is a brilliant demonstration of the mixture of the poetry of statement (didactic poetry) with the most nondidactic elements of poetry—the autonomous images.

As "Ars Poetica" illustrates, imagery is a way of saying something. Imagery is closely connected with other poetic devices, such as simile, metaphor, figure of speech, symbol, and archetype. While imagism may be seen as a distinct historical movement, the use of imagery is no more restricted to any period of history than the use of any other poetic technique. Poetic techniques are so closely related to one another that most may be found in almost any poetic utterance. Imagism should be understood as a new emphasis on poetic elements that all poets have used to greater and lesser degrees throughout the history of poetry. In fact when MacLeish says

> A poem should be palpable and mute
> As a globed fruit,
>
> Dumb
> As old medallions to the thumb,

he is using similes as well as images. "Globed fruit" is one image, "old medallions" another. As students are taught in grade school, a simile is a comparison between things not usually regarded as similar, using "like," "as," or "than." Thus take "as" out of each stanza and you have metaphors, as in Wallace Stevens's definition of poetry (from "Adagia O.P."):

> A poem is a pheasant
> The body is a great poem
> Poems are new subjects.

All the images of the first seven stanzas of "Ars Poetica" are used as similes, but in stanzas ten and eleven the images are used as metaphors, and in the final stanza there is no image—only a straightforward, declarative statement: "A poem should not mean/ But be."

In order to see the metaphors in stanzas ten and eleven more clearly, we should perhaps supply a verb: ". . . the history of grief/

[is] An empty doorway and a maple leaf." "... love/[is] The leaning grasses and two lights above the sea." Robert Frost was fond of saying, "Poetry ... is metaphor, saying one thing and meaning another, saying one thing in terms of another ... Poetry is simply made of metaphor ... Every poem is a new metaphor inside or it is nothing." (Edward C. Lathem and Lawrance Thompson, *Robert Frost: Poetry and Prose* [New York, 1972], pp. 400–01.) Broadly speaking, of course, he was right. A great majority of other terms used by rhetoricians to distinguish figurative ways of writing (and there are hundreds of such terms) are basically ways of distinguishing kinds of metaphors—that is, ways of saying one thing in terms of another.

The essential point to keep in mind is that poetry constantly says one thing in terms of another. Frost put his finger on this basic method of poetry in another way when he asked young people to take "poetry as the first form of understanding." Relating one thing to another is at the beginning of all intellectual comprehension.

In life, as in poetry, one of our first inclinations is to compare the nonhuman world to the human, to see everything in anthropomorphic terms—nature, abstract qualities, ideas are all described in terms applicable to humankind. Such is the impulse behind personification, which sees truth balancing her scales, trees lifting their leafy arms, and fear walking the land by night. (The exaggerated or unwarranted attribution of manlike characteristics to nature—as when the poet speaks of the sea's "cruel crawling foam" —was labeled the *pathetic fallacy* by John Ruskin in the late nineteenth century. The term, however, does not always mean defective poetic technique.)

The great figures of myth—Hercules, Apollo, and the like— spring from much the same impulse as personification, that is, the impulse to understand the world by translating it into human terms. A myth is a story, often depending on a number of interrelated images, that holds significance for a large group of people. Anthropologists have sometimes explained the significance of myths for primitive people in practical terms—an account of a brave hunter, together with appropriate pantomime, song, and dance, helps assure a successful hunt. But some psychologists have held that the events in myths symbolize man's wishes, desires, and fears—the whole of his unconscious life. The Swiss psychiatrist Carl Gustav Jung (1875–1961) theorized that common social experiences over hundreds of thousands of years have created certain patterns in the unconscious mind of man. Patterns of experience, he held, are formed from centuries of witnessing birth, growth, and decay; traveling over land and water; and being exposed to sun and season. Jung labeled these patterns archetypes. Literary critics have been quick to apply this notion of psychological archetype to literature, and archetype has come to mean any significant image, idea, or action that is repeated over a long period. In literature, the less pretentious *conventional symbol* means much the same thing as an over-generalized use of archetype. A conventional symbol, however, should be distinguished from archetype on the basis of complexity. The setting sun is first of all an image from nature, then a conventional symbol of an ending. The accumulated use not only of this symbol but of seasonal rituals (G. S. Fraser's *The Golden Bough* is a good place to find examples of these) and such stories as that of Phaëton and Icarus expand in sun imagery and its ordinary uses to provide us with archetypes.

Related to image-personification-myth and archetype is allegory—a story in which the main characters stand for something else, usually abstractions. Stereotypical Westerns tend to be allegorical, with "Badman" on the black horse and "Law" on the white horse. But allegory is not always so banal; it is simply saying two things with one story.

An image that means more than itself is a symbol, but not all symbols are images. Images are concrete; symbols are both concrete and abstract. In "My love is like a radish," radish is both image and symbol. But what is symbolized by radish—perhaps smallness, hotness, sharpness—could be symbolized by action, character, or even the abstractions "hotness" and "sharpness."

It is impossible to say how much meaning an image must have before one can legitimately call it a symbol. An "empty doorway" and "a maple leaf" are by themselves simply images. But in the lines "For all the history of grief/An empty doorway and a maple leaf," MacLeish has packed meaning into them. For him and for the reader they probably have a private symbolism—the doorway standing for a farewell; an old house in the neighborhood; a death familiar only to oneself. If MacLeish had established the season and made the leaf, say, yellow, we could call the image a conventional symbol. And if the poem heavily depended on this symbol, or the symbol was more fully developed, we might say he was using a seasonal archetype. In brief, to know what we should call an image requires close examination of the context of the poem, informed sensitivity, and experience in reading. Here is a poem to practice on.

SPEAKING OF POETRY

John Peale Bishop (1892–1944)

The ceremony must be found
that will wed Desdemona to the huge Moor.

It is not enough—
to win the approval of the Senator
or to outwit his disapproval; honest Iago
can manage that: it is not enough. For then,
though she may pant again in his black arms
(his weight resilient as a Barbary stallion's)
she will be found
when the ambassadors of the Venetian state arrive
again smothered. These things have not been changed,
not in three hundred years.

    (Tupping is still tupping
though that particular word is obsolete.
Naturally, the ritual would not be in Latin.)

For though Othello had his blood from kings
his ancestry was barbarous, his ways African,
his speech uncouth. It must be remembered
that though he valued an embroidery—
three mulberries proper on a silk like silver—
it was not for the subtlety of the stitches,
but for the magic in it. Whereas, Desdemona
once contrived to imitate in needlework
her father's shield, and plucked it out
three times, to begin again, each time
with diminished colors. This is a small point
but indicative.

    Desdemona was small and fair,
delicate as a grasshopper
at the tag-end of summer: a Venetian
to her noble finger tips.

    O, it is not enough
that they should meet, naked, at dead of night
in a small inn on a dark canal. Procurers
less expert than Iago can arrange as much.

>   The ceremony must be found
>   Traditional, with all its symbols
>   ancient as the metaphors in dreams;
>   strange, with never before heard music; continuous
>   until the torches deaden at the bedroom door.   40

NOTES AND QUESTIONS

Line 1   Define ceremony in light of the poem's title.

Line 2   Desdemona, the wife of Othello, and Othello ("the huge Moor") are both characters from Shakespeare's *Othello*. They, and their marriage, are metaphors, or symbols, for the essential elements of poetry. The rest of the poem explains their metaphoric or symbolic meaning in detail.

Lines 3–12   The metaphor of marriage is extended, and each term, such as "Senator," has meaning not only in terms of Shakespeare's play but also in terms of the poetic process. Thus, besides its obvious meaning, Senator also implies something comparable to Editor of *The New Yorker* or *The Atlantic Monthly*. Carefully work out the meanings of the terms involved in the extended metaphor.

Line 13   "Tupping" can be found in a dictionary. Guess first, but look it up to be sure of its meaning.

Line 15   Ritual is related to ceremony. Why should it *not* be in Latin?

Lines 16–22   These lines are the clearest revelations of Othello's character.

Line 20   This is a visual and tactile image symbolic of Othello's character. The symbolism is explained by the statement "he valued an embroidery . . . not for the subtlety of the stitches,/but for the magic in it."

Lines 22–27   These lines are symbolic of Desdemona's character.

Lines 28–31   A physical description of Desdemona turns on a simile and an image.

Lines 32–35   Note the repetition of the phrase "it is not enough" (line 3). As an affair is not enough to make a marriage, so the simple bringing together of poetic elements—word and image, idea and sound—is not enough to make a poem. The phrase "in a small inn on a dark canal" is one of the most concrete parts of the poem. How does this concreteness serve the meaning of these lines?

Line 36 What effect does repeating this line serve?

Lines 37–40 Notice the words "traditional," "ancient," and "strange" in the final stanza. Why are they placed where they are? The final image is one of an ancient wedding procession where the bride and bridegroom are escorted by torch bearers to the nuptial chamber.

Line 40 "Torches deaden" is a synesthetic image. Why has it been used? What is its effect?

POEMS AND PAINTINGS

Critics often refer to poems as word paintings. It is, however, as instructive to note the differences between painting and poetry as it is to note the similarities. Below are two reproductions from the work of the Flemish painter Pieter Brueghel (1520–1569). Examine the paintings closely and note the details. Then read each poem, noting what parts of the paintings it comments on, what parts it ignores. Finally, you might wish to compare the poems not only in terms of their relative selectiveness but also in terms of how each poet developed his basic experience—the encounter with the Brueghel painting.

HUNTERS IN THE SNOW: BRUEGHEL

Joseph Langland (b. 1917)

Quail and rabbit hunters with tawny hounds,
Shadowless, out of late afternoon
Trudge toward the neutral evening of indeterminate form.
Done with their blood-annunciated day
Public dogs and all the passionless mongrels   5
Through deep snow
Trail their deliberate masters
Descending from the upper village home in lowering light.
Sooty lamps
Glow in the stone-carved kitchens.   10

This is the fabulous hour of shape and form
When Flemish children are gray-black-olive
And green-dark-brown
Scattered and skating informal figures
On the mill ice pond.   15
Moving in stillness
A hunched dame struggles with her bundled sticks,
Letting her evening's comfort cudgel her
While she, like jug or wheel, like a wagon cart
Walked by lazy oxen along the old snowlanes,   20

Creeps and crunches down the dusky street.
High in the fire-red dooryard
Half unhitched the sign of the Inn
Hangs in wind
Tipped to the pitch of the roof.   25
Near it anonymous parents and peasant girl,
Living like proverbs carved in the alehouse walls,
Gather the country evening into their arms
And lean to the glowing flames.

Now in the dimming distance fades 30
The other village; across the valley
Imperturbable Flemish cliffs and crags
Vaguely advance, close in, loom
Lost in nearness. Now
The night-black raven perched in branching boughs 35
Opens its early wing and slipping out
Above the gray-green valley
Weaves a net of slumber over the snow-capped homes.
And now the church, and then the walls and roofs
Of all the little houses are become 40
Close kin to shadow with small lantern eyes.
And now the bird of evening
With shadows streaming down from its gliding wings
Circles the neighboring hills
Of Hertogenbosch, Brabant. 45

Darkness stalks the hunters,
Slowly sliding down,
Falling in beating rings and soft diagonals.
Lodged in the vague vast valley the village sleeps.

III THE HUNTERS IN THE SNOW

William Carlos Williams (1883–1963)

The over-all picture is winter
icy mountains
in the background the return

from the hunt it is toward evening
from the left 5
sturdy hunters lead in

their pack the inn-sign
hanging from a
broken hinge is a stag a crucifix

between his antlers the cold 10
inn yard is
deserted but for a huge bonfire

that flares wind-driven tended by
women who cluster
about it to the right beyond 15

the hill is a pattern of skaters
Brueghel the painter
concerned with it all has chosen

a winter-struck bush for his
foreground to 20
complete the picture . . .

WINTER LANDSCAPE

John Berryman (1914–1972)

The three men coming down the winter hill
In brown, with tall poles and a pack of hounds
At heel, through the arrangement of the trees
Past the five figures at the burning straw,
Returning cold and silent to their town, 5

Returning to the drifted snow, the rink
Lively with children, to the older men,
The long companions they can never reach,
The blue light, men with ladders, by the church
The sledge and shadow in the twilit street, 10

Are not aware that in the sandy time
To come, the evil waste of history
Outstretched, they will be seen upon the brow
Of that same hill: when all their company
Will have been irrecoverably lost, 15

These men, this particular three in brown
Witnessed by birds will keep the scene and say
By their configuration with the trees,
The small bridge, the red houses and the fire,
What place, what time, what morning occasion 20
Sent them into the wood, a pack of hounds
At heel and the tall poles upon their shoulders,
Thence to return as now we see them and
Ankle-deep in snow down the winter hill
Descend, while three birds watch and the fourth flies. 25

II LANDSCAPE WITH THE FALL OF ICARUS
William Carlos Williams

According to Brueghel
when Icarus fell
it was spring

a farmer was ploughing
his field   5
the whole pageantry

of the year was
awake tingling
near

the edge of the sea   10
concerned
with itself

sweating in the sun
that melted
the wings' wax   15

unsignificantly
off the coast
there was

a splash quite unnoticed
this was   20
Icarus drowning

MUSÉE DES BEAUX ARTS

W. H. Auden (1907–1973)

About suffering they were never wrong,
The Old Masters: how well they understood
Its human position; how it takes place
While someone else is eating or opening a window or just walking
    dully along;
How, when the aged are reverently, passionately waiting   5
For the miraculous birth, there always must be
Children who did not specially want it to happen, skating
On a pond at the edge of the wood:
They never forgot
That even the dreadful martyrdom must run its course   10
Anyhow in a corner, some untidy spot
Where the dogs go on with their doggy life and the torturer's horse
Scratches its innocent behind on a tree.

In Brueghel's Icarus, for instance: how everything turns away
Quite leisurely from the disaster; the ploughman may   15
Have heard the splash, the forsaken cry,
But for him it was not an important failure; the sun shone
As it had to on the white legs disappearing into the green
Water; and the expensive delicate ship that must have seen
Something amazing, a boy falling out of the sky,   20
Had somewhere to get to and sailed calmly on.

POEMS FOR FURTHER STUDY

A few of the imagistic poems that follow depend on a single image; others depend on two or more images. Study the poems to discover the uses they make of images, metaphors, and symbols.

VENUS TRANSIENS
Amy Lowell (1874–1925)

Tell me,
Was Venus more beautiful
Than you are,
When she topped
The crinkled waves,   5
Drifting shoreward
On her plaited shell?
Was Boticelli's vision
Fairer than mine;
And were the painted rosebuds   10
He tossed his lady,
Of better worth
Than the words I blow about you
To cover your too great loveliness
As with a gauze   15
Of misted silver?
For me,
You stand poised
In the blue and buoyant air,
Cinctured by bright winds,   20
Treading the sunlight.
And the waves which precede you
Ripple and stir
The sands at my feet.

DISILLUSIONMENT OF TEN O'CLOCK
Wallace Stevens (1879–1955)

The houses are haunted
By white night-gowns.
None are green,
Or purple with green rings,
Or green with yellow rings,   5
Or yellow with blue rings.
None of them are strange,
With socks of lace

And beaded ceintures.
People are not going 10
To dream of baboons and periwinkles.
Only, here and there, an old sailor,
Drunk and asleep in his boots,
Catches tigers
In red weather. 15

STUDY OF TWO PEARS

Wallace Stevens

I

Opusculum paedagogum.
The pears are not viols,
Nudes or bottles.
They resemble nothing else.

II

They are yellow forms 5
Composed of curves
Bulging toward the base.
They are touched red.

III

They are not flat surfaces
Having curved outlines. 10
They are round
Tapering toward the top.

IV

In the way they are modeled
They are bits of blue.
A hard dry leaf hangs 15
From the stem.

V

The yellow glistens.
It glistens with various yellows,
Citrons, oranges and greens
Flowering over the skin. 20

VI

The shadows of the pears
Are blobs on the green cloth.
The pears are not seen
As the observer wills.

THE RED WHEELBARROW

William Carlos Williams

so much depends
upon

a red wheel
barrow

glazed with rain   5
water

beside the white
chickens.

NANTUCKET

William Carlos Williams

Flowers through the window
lavender and yellow

changed by white curtains—
Smell of cleanliness—

Sunshine of late afternoon—   5
On the glass tray

a glass pitcher, the tumbler
turned down, by which

a key is lying—And the
immaculate white bed   10

DAISY

William Carlos Williams

The dayseye hugging the earth
In August, ha! Spring is
gone down in purple,
weeds stand high in the corn,
the rainbeaten furrow   5
is clotted with sorrel
and crabgrass, the
branch is black under
the heavy mass of the leaves—
The sun is upon a   10
slender green stem
ribbed lengthwise.
He lies on his back—
it is a woman also—
he regards his former   15
majesty and
round the yellow center,
split and creviced and done into
minute flowerheads, he sends out
his twenty rays—a little   20
and the wind is among them
to grow cool there!

One turns the thing over
in his hand and looks
at it from the rear: brownedged,   25
green and pointed scales
armor his yellow.

But turn and turn,
the crisp petals remain
brief, translucent, greenfastened,   30
barely touching at the edges:
blades of limpid seashell.

DAWN
William Carlos Williams

Ecstatic bird songs pound
the hollow vastness of the sky
with metallic clinkings—
beating color up into it
at a far edge,—beating it, beating it   5
with rising, triumphant ardor,—
stirring it into warmth,
quickening in it a spreading change,—
bursting wildly against it as
dividing the horizon, a heavy sun   10
lifts himself—is lifted—
bit by bit above the edge
of things,—runs free at last
out into the open—! lumbering
glorified in full release upward—   15
          songs cease.

IN A STATION OF THE METRO
Ezra Pound (1885–1972)

The apparition of these faces in the crowd;
Petals on a wet, black bough.

DORIA
Ezra Pound

Be in me as the eternal moods
    of the bleak wind, and not
As transient things are—
    gaiety of flowers.
Have me in the strong loneliness   5
    of sunless cliffs
And of grey waters.
    Let the gods speak softly of us
In days hereafter,
    The shadowy flowers of Orcus   10
Remember thee.

IMERRO

Ezra Pound

Thy soul
Grown delicate with satieties,
Atthis.
O Atthis,
I long for thy lips.   5
I long for thy narrow breasts,
Thou restless, ungathered.

HEAT

H. D.

O wind, rend open the heat,
cut apart the heat,
rend it to tatters.

Fruit cannot drop
through this thick air—   5
fruit cannot fall into heat
that presses up and blunts
the points of pears
and rounds the grapes.

Cut the heat—   10
plough through it,
turning it on either side
of your path.

EVENING

Richard Aldington (1892–1962)

The chimneys, rank on rank,
Cut the clear sky;
The moon
With a rag of gauze about her loins
Poses among them, an awkward Venus—   5

And here am I looking wantonly at her
Over the kitchen sink.

OCTOBER

Denise Levertov (b. 1923)

Certain branches cut
certain leaves fallen
the grapes
        cooked and put up
for winter 5

mountains without one
shrug of cloud
no feint of blurred
wind-willow leaf-light

their chins up 10
in blue of the eastern sky
their red cloaks
wrapped tight to the bone

Biographical Contexts

All poems are written by human beings whose lives are sometimes reflected to a considerable degree and sometimes to a slight degree in their work. The fashion of the last two decades of poetic criticism has been to ignore or underplay the importance of a poet's life in his work. The life the poet leads, the reasoning goes, is separate from the work, and the work must be evaluated independently on the basis of what is "really" there rather than on the basis of what we know about the author. The fact that we can work fairly well without referring to the author's life is clear in our critical evaluations of Shakespeare's plays—since we know relatively little about him. In discussing modern writers, about whom more is usually known, we find that some critics overload slight poems with biographical information, sometimes making them crack and split under the load. There are dangers, to be sure, in suggesting a relationship between poetry and the poet, and one of our purposes here will be to warn that biographical claims may be too strong. But we suggest that it is unwise to demand a total accounting of any poem without looking for biographical information that could illuminate it.

Biographical information, like all information, should not be used thoughtlessly by the critic. The critic must have good cause, must see a relationship that we, as observers, can concur on, and must make no more claim for advancing "meaning" than someone who supplies us the meaning of a word from a dictionary. The poet's life can be seen as a lexicon of experiences, images, thoughts, and feelings that is drawn on (in many instances) for the construction of a poem. Were we to consider a poem that had as its subject the history of a city, such as William Carlos Williams's "Paterson," we would not feel it unproductive to read about the early days of

New Jersey as a way of gaining insight into the poem. We look at Dante's *Divine Comedy* as a preparation for reading Pound's *Cantos*, just as we would want to read Homer's *Odyssey* before James Joyce's *Ulysses*. These modern works actually allude to something other than themselves, and thus they depend on some contextual knowledge—a knowledge of places and works that the poet has before he begins writing.

In much the same fashion, the poet who treats his own experience as central to his poetry will allude to his life (in some extreme cases the poet will actually try to elude his life). Some poems can be understood more completely if we have the information the poet himself had. If we know, for instance, something about the relationship he enjoyed with those figures he makes direct reference to, or the way he felt about places he describes, our ability to understand the poem will increase. The poetry of some poets is simply a collection of moments in a long and varied life. The poems are of value, certainly, but so is the life. The poems existed in the context of that life; once the author is dead they still exist in the context of a biography, even if we do not have much biographical information. A more thorough biographical knowledge of Catullus or Donne could help us immensely in knowing how to treat the tone of their love poems: Were they serious or were they ironic? The poem itself cannot tell us. Irony is a mode that needs a context for its existence; for these poets the context necessary is a biographical one.

The first thing we should admit is that every biographical situation is unique. No two poets will write about their experiences in the same way, even if they profess to be recording their lives in their works. Also, it is not always useful to relate a poet's life to his poetry. A great deal of unfruitful work has been carried on in trying to see Milton in Milton's work. *Paradise Lost* and *Paradise Regained* are not autobiographical in any usual sense, and to treat them so is to do their real character an injustice. Even *Samson Agonistes*, the story of a blind hero made slave by his captors, cannot be happily connected to Milton's life, despite outward appearances. Some critical common sense is needed to realize that forcing the biographical issue is by no means useful when the works are as rich as these are.

On the other hand, writers such as Walt Whitman, Emily Dickinson, and William Butler Yeats tended to see themselves in relation to their own poems in a way that many older poets did not. Their experiences often find a home in their work, and they sometimes work out their own personal problems or make personal observations in the texture of their poems. In Yeats's writing, some poems are virtually incomprehensible unless we have biographical information, particularly about his relationship with the woman who constantly spurned him in the prime of his life: Maud Gonne. The development of the poems that have Maud Gonne at their center is better understood when paralleled with the development of Yeats's relationship. These poems become even clearer when we view them against the background of the history of Ireland during those years.

Emily Dickinson led a withdrawn life that is shrouded in mystery. Recent efforts have been made by scholars to connect her poetry with the details of her life, but none have been entirely satisfactory. Thus, to treat Dickinson's poems in the context of biography presents some difficulties. In one sense, there is little or no enlightenment to be derived from her biography. The essential facts of her life we know—where she was born and died, her relatives, her readings, her friends, her letters, her journeys—and such things are useful. Concerning her beliefs—her emotional life, her precise involvement with others—we have little factual information. The poems, rather than the biography, provide us with our best knowledge of Emily Dickinson. In fact, what they offer us is an "inner biography" of her feelings and her sense of the world. And it is from this "inner biography" of her poems that we seek to construct the biographical context.

Walt Whitman (1819-1892)

Whitman's *Leaves of Grass* chronicles a spiritual and personal growth, and Whitman is not being facetious when he says he becomes his poem. "Song of Myself" is clearly biographical in intent. It may be seen partly as a record of a life, but it also must be seen as a projection of a life. The distinction is serious, since Whitman cannot *be* his poem, except artistically; he must craft both life and poem at the same time. Consequently, reading *Leaves of Grass* gives us access to the imprint of a living personality—living and changing right before our eyes.

A chronological chart of Whitman's life would not reveal much to us about his work; his work, however, reveals what Whitman feels is important—even when it distorts a fact we have some knowledge about. But it is interesting to know some of the larger details of his life—details that did not seem to interest him directly in his writing. He was born on Long Island in 1819, lived in Brooklyn for a while and later became a printer, and was involved in politics as a campaigner for Martin Van Buren. In the 1840s he edited a number of newspapers, including the *Brooklyn Daily Eagle*, from which he was probably fired. While he was writing the first edition of *Leaves of Grass*, he lived with his family and worked as a carpenter, not as a newspaperman. Tradition has it that his book of poems was published on July 4, 1855. Before that time he had published almost no poetry of promise. He seemed to have sprung out of nowhere with a brand new way of writing poems. It was not until the 1860s that major writers in Europe took notice of him, although Ralph Waldo Emerson had recognized his genius earlier. When Whitman became a government clerk in 1865, his authorship of the book was the cause of his being fired: the moral tone of *Leaves of Grass*, with explicit talk about sex, was not high enough for the government. He traveled very little—only to the American West in the late 1870s, never to Europe—and the nature of his involvement in the American Civil War centered on his brother's having been wounded and on his own participation as a nurse on the battlefield. His experiences as a nurse are recorded in some detail in his poems. Yet, we do not find much about his work as a newspaperman, his life as a famous man of letters, or his personal difficulties with family and lovers. He chose to show us a life that was only part of his life, and it is clear that, when he considered becoming his poem, he also had in mind that his poem would become him—that when we knew his poem we would know all of him he wished us to know.

To gain a clear understanding of the problems in criticism that are involved here, you may refer to Whitman's biography *The Solitary Singer* by Gay Wilson Allen (New York, 1955). The poems that appear in the following pages can easily be supplemented by a full reading of *Leaves of Grass*, or at least all of "Song of Myself." Reference to these two works represents a beginning in understanding the life Whitman led and the life he wished to project. These do not always agree, and when this is so, we find ourselves critically involved with the texture of the poems that might actually contradict the knowledge we have of his actual life.

If nothing else, we gain sensitivity to the subject of the poems in a unique and significant way.

The biographical problem Whitman offers us is not itself unique. Many poets project another self into their poems, and since Whitman's time, many have tried to use their poetry to explore their own feelings—to present, examine, and find a value for them. Whitman does this in a serious, single-minded fashion that has become a model for other poets. His poetry can be thought of as a portrait in much the same way a photograph or painting represents a figure. They are not the figure, yet they depend on the figure for their identity. They may be faithful, distorted, honest, frank, covert, flattering, or unflattering. Whitman's poetry is of this order. And his poetry has taken on aesthetic significance of its own, just as great portraits do. The poetry is important even without our knowledge of its subject, but *with* that knowledge its importance deepens and our awareness of its achievement grows. It may not be necessary actually to see Mont Ste.-Victoire to understand Cézanne's paintings of it, but seeing it cannot fail to illuminate us on several counts. It may alter our interpretation of Cézanne and give us a different ground for observing what is "really" in the paintings. Much the same is true for Whitman's self-portrait.

from SONG OF MYSELF

1

I celebrate myself, and sing myself,
And what I assume you shall assume,
For every atom belonging to me as good belongs to you.

I loafe and invite my soul,
I lean and loafe at my ease observing a spear of summer grass.   5

My tongue, every atom of my blood, form'd from this soil, this air,
Born here of parents born here from parents the same, and their
    parents the same,
I, now thirty-seven years old in perfect health begin,
Hoping to cease not till death.

Creeds and schools in abeyance,   10
Retiring back a while sufficed at what they are, but never forgotten,

I harbor for good or bad, I permit to speak at every hazard,
Nature without check with original energy.

2

Houses and rooms are full of perfumes, the shelves are crowded
    with perfumes,
I breathe the fragrance myself and know it and like it,   15
The distillation would intoxicate me also, but I shall not let it.

The atmosphere is not a perfume, it has no taste of the distillation,
    it is odorless,
It is for my mouth forever, I am in love with it,
I will go to the bank by the wood and become undisguised and
    naked,
I am mad for it to be in contact with me.   20
The smoke of my own breath,
Echoes, ripples, buzz'd whispers, love-root, silk-thread, crotch and
    vine,
My respiration and inspiration, the beating of my heart, the passing
    of blood and air through my lungs,
The sniff of green leaves and dry leaves, and of the shore and
    dark-color'd sea-rocks, and of hay in the barn,
The sound of the belch'd words of my voice loos'd to the eddies
    of the wind,   25
A few light kisses, a few embraces, a reaching around of arms,
The play of shine and shade on the trees as the supple boughs wag,
The delight alone or in the rush of the streets, or along the fields
    and hill-sides,
The feeling of health, the full-noon trill, the song of me rising from
    bed and meeting the sun.

Have you reckon'd a thousand acres much? have you reckon'd
    the earth much?   30
Have you practis'd so long to learn to read?
Have you felt so proud to get at the meaning of poems?

Stop this day and night with me and you shall possess the origin
    of all poems,
You shall possess the good of the earth and sun, (there are millions
    of suns left,)
You shall no longer take things at second or third hand, nor look
    through the eyes of the dead, nor feed on the spectres in books,   35
You shall not look through my eyes either, nor take things from me,
You shall listen to all sides and filter them from your self.

3

I have heard what the talkers were talking, the talk of the beginning
    and the end,
But I do not talk of the beginning or the end.

There was never any more inception than there is now,   40
Nor any more youth or age than there is now,
And will never be any more perfection than there is now,
Nor any more heaven or hell than there is now.

Urge and urge and urge,
Always the procreant urge of the world.   45

Out of the dimness opposite equals advance, always substance and
    increase, always sex,
Always a knit of identity, always distinction, always a breed of life.

To elaborate is no avail, learn'd and unlearn'd feel that it is so.

Sure as the most certain sure, plumb in the uprights, well entretied,
    braced in the beams,
Stout as a horse, affectionate, haughty, electrical,   50
I and this mystery here we stand.

Clear and sweet is my soul, and clear and sweet is all that is not
    my soul.

Lack one lacks both, and the unseen is proved by the seen,
Till that becomes unseen and receives proof in its turn.

Showing the best and dividing it from the worst age vexes age,   55
Knowing the perfect fitness and equanimity of things, while they
    discuss I am silent, and go bathe and admire myself.

Welcome is every organ and attribute of me, and of any man
    hearty and clean,
Not an inch nor a particle of an inch is vile, and none shall be
    less familiar than the rest.

I am satisfied—I see, dance, laugh, sing;
As the hugging and loving bed-fellow sleeps at my side through
    the night, and withdraws at the peep of the day with
    stealthy tread,   60
Leaving me baskets cover'd with white towels swelling the house
    with their plenty,

    49. **Sure ... beams:** carpenter's terms for details of good building.

Shall I postpone my acceptation and realization and scream at my eyes,
That they turn from gazing after and down the road,
And forthwith cipher and show me to a cent,
Exactly the value of one and exactly the value of two, and which
    is ahead? 65

4

Trippers and askers surround me,
People I meet, the effect upon me of my early life or the ward
    and city I live in, or the nation,
The latest dates, discoveries, inventions, societies, authors old and
    new,
My dinner, dress, associates, looks, compliments, dues,
The real or fancied indifference of some man or woman I love, 70
The sickness of one of my folks or of myself, or ill-doing or loss or
    lack of money, or depressions or exaltations,
Battles, the horrors of fratricidal war, the fever of doubtful news,
    the fitful events;
These come to me days and nights and go from me again,
But they are not the Me myself.

Apart from the pulling and hauling stands what I am, 75
Stands amused, complacent, compassionating, idle, unitary,
Looks down, is erect, or bends an arm on an impalpable certain rest,
Looking with side-curved head curious what will come next,
Both in and out of the game and watching and wondering at it.

Backward I see in my own days where I sweated through fog with
    linguists and contenders, 80
I have no mockings or arguments, I witness and wait.

5

I believe in you my soul, the other I am must not abase itself to you,
And you must not be abased to the other.

Loafe with me on the grass, loose the stop from your throat,
Not words, not music or rhyme I want, not custom or lecture, not
    even the best, 85
Only the lull I like, the hum of your valvèd voice.

I mind how once we lay such a transparent summer morning,
How you settled your head athwart my hips and gently turn'd over
    upon me,

And parted the shirt from my bosom-bone, and plunged your
    tongue to my bare-stript heart,
And reach'd till you felt my beard, and reach'd till you held my feet.   90

Swiftly arose and spread around me the peace and knowledge that
    pass all the argument of the earth,
And I know that the hand of God is the promise of my own,
And I know that the spirit of God is the brother of my own,
And that all the men ever born are also my brothers, and the
    women my sisters and lovers,
And that a kelson of the creation is love,   95
And limitless are leaves stiff or drooping in the fields,
And brown ants in the little wells beneath them,
And mossy scabs of the worm fence, heap'd stones, elder, mullein
    and poke-weed.

6

A child said *What is the grass?* fetching it to me with full hands;
How could I answer the child? I do not know what it is any more
    than he.   100

I guess it must be the flag of my disposition, out of hopeful green
    stuff woven.

Or I guess it is the handkerchief of the Lord,
A scented gift and remembrancer designedly dropt,
Bearing the owner's name someway in the corners, that we may
    see and remark, and say *Whose?*

Or I guess the grass is itself a child, the produced babe of the
    vegetation.   105

Or I guess it is a uniform hieroglyphic,
And it means, Sprouting alike in broad zones and narrow zones,
Growing among black folks as among white,
Kanuck, Tuckahoe, Congressman, Cuff, I give them the same, I
    receive them the same.

And now it seems to me the beautiful uncut hair of graves.   110

Tenderly will I use you curling grass,
It may be you transpire from the breasts of young men,
It may be if I had known them I would have loved them,

109. **Kanuck:** French Canadian.   **Tuckahoe:** Virginian.   **Cuff:** a black.

It may be you are from old people, or from offspring taken soon
    out of their mothers' laps,
And here you are the mothers' laps. 115

This grass is very dark to be from the white heads of old mothers,
Darker than the colorless beards of old men,
Dark to come from under the faint red roofs of mouths.

O I perceive after all so many uttering tongues,
And I perceive they do not come from the roofs of mouths for
    nothing. 120

I wish I could translate the hints about the dead young men and
    women,
And the hints about old men and mothers, and the offspring taken
    soon out of their laps.

What do you think has become of the young and old men?
And what do you think has become of the women and children?

They are alive and well somewhere, 125
The smallest sprout shows there is really no death,
And if ever there was it led forward life, and does not wait at the
    end to arrest it,
And ceas'd the moment life appear'd.

All goes onward and outward, nothing collapses,
And to die is different from what any one supposed, and luckier. 130

7

Has any one supposed it lucky to be born?
I hasten to inform him or her it is just as lucky to die, and I know it.

I pass death with the dying and birth with the new-wash'd babe,
    and am not contain'd between my hat and boots,
And peruse manifold objects, no two alike and every one good,
The earth good and the stars good, and their adjuncts all good. 135

I am not an earth nor an adjunct of an earth,
I am the mate and companion of people, all just as immortal and
    fathomless as myself,
(They do not know how immortal, but I know.)

Every kind for itself and its own, for me mine male and female,
For me those that have been boys and that love women, 140
For me the man that is proud and feels how it stings to be slighted,
For me the sweet-heart and the old maid, for me mothers and the
    mothers of mothers,

For me lips that have smiled, eyes that have shed tears,
For me children and the begetters of children.

Undrape! you are not guilty to me, nor stale nor discarded,
I see through the broadcloth and gingham whether or no,
And am around, tenacious, acquisitive, tireless, and cannot be shaken away.

8

The little one sleeps in its cradle,
I lift the gauze and look a long time, and silently brush away flies with my hand.

The youngster and the red-faced girl turn aside up the bushy hill,
I peeringly view them from the top.

The suicide sprawls on the bloody floor of the bedroom,
I witness the corpse with its dabbled hair, I note where the pistol has fallen.

The blab of the pave, tires of carts, sluff of boot-soles, talk of the promenaders,
The heavy omnibus, the driver with his interrogating thumb, the clank of the shod horses on the granite floor,
The snow-sleighs, clinking, shouted jokes, pelts of snow-balls,
The hurrahs for popular favorites, the fury of rous'd mobs,
The flap of the curtain'd litter, a sick man inside borne to the hospital,
The meeting of enemies, the sudden oath, the blows and fall,
The excited crowd, the policeman with his star quickly working his passage to the centre of the crowd,
The impassive stones that receive and return so many echoes,
What groans of over-fed or half-starv'd who fall sunstruck or in fits,
What exclamations of women taken suddenly who hurry home and give birth to babes,
What living and buried speech is always vibrating here, what howls restrain'd by decorum,
Arrests of criminals, slights, adulterous offers made, acceptances, rejections with convex lips,
I mind them or the show or resonance of them—I come and I depart.

9

The big doors of the country barn stand open and ready,
The dried grass of the harvest-time loads the slow-drawn wagon,
The clear light plays on the brown gray and green intertinged,
The armfuls are pack'd to the sagging mow.

I am there, I help, I came stretch'd atop of the load,
I felt its soft jolts, one leg reclined on the other,
I jump from the cross-beams and seize the clover and timothy,
And roll head over heels and tangle my hair full of wisps.

10

Alone far in the wilds and mountains I hunt,   175
Wandering amazed at my own lightness and glee,
In the late afternoon choosing a safe spot to pass the night,
Kindling a fire and broiling the fresh-kill'd game,
Falling asleep on the gather'd leaves with my dog and gun by my
    side.

The Yankee clipper is under her sky-sails, she cuts the sparkle and
    scud,   180
My eyes settle the land, I bend at her prow or shout joyously from
    the deck.

The boatmen and clam-diggers arose early and stopt for me,
I tuck'd my trowser-ends in my boots and went and had a good
    time;
You should have been with us that day round the chowder-kettle.

I saw the marriage of the trapper in the open air in the far west,
    the bride was a red girl,   185
Her father and his friends sat near cross-legged and dumbly
    smoking, they had moccasins to their feet and large thick
    blankets hanging from their shoulders,
On a bank lounged the trapper, he was drest mostly in skins, his
    luxuriant beard and curls protected his neck, he held his
    bride by the hand,
She had long eyelashes, her head was bare, her coarse straight
    locks descended upon her voluptuous limbs and reach'd to
    her feet.

The runaway slave came to my house and stopt outside,
I heard his motions crackling the twigs of the woodpile,   190
Through the swung half-door of the kitchen I saw him limpsy and
    weak,
And went where he sat on a log and led him in and assured him,
And brought water and fill'd a tub for his sweated body and bruis'd
    feet,

175–198. Alone . . . corner: Whitman did not have these experiences himself.
He projects them as fiction.

And gave him a room that enter'd from my own, and gave him
    some coarse clean clothes,
And remember perfectly well his revolving eyes and his
    awkwardness, 195
And remember putting plasters on the galls of his neck and ankles;
He staid with me a week before he was recuperated and pass'd
    north,
I had him sit next me at table, my fire-lock lean'd in the corner.

11

Twenty-eight young men bathe by the shore,
Twenty-eight young men and all so friendly; 200
Twenty-eight years of womanly life and all so lonesome.

She owns the fine house by the rise of the bank,
She hides handsome and richly drest aft the blinds of the window.

Which of the young men does she like the best?
Ah the homeliest of them is beautiful to her. 205

Where are you off to, lady? for I see you,
You splash in the water there, yet stay stock still in your room.

Dancing and laughing along the beach came the twenty-ninth bather,
The rest did not see her, but she saw them and loved them.

The beards of the young men glisten'd with wet, it ran from their
    long hair, 210
Little streams pass'd all over their bodies.

An unseen hand also pass'd over their bodies,
It descended tremblingly from their temples and ribs.

The young men float on their backs, their white bellies bulge to
    the sun, they do not ask who seizes fast to them,
They do not know who puffs and declines with pendant and
    bending arch, 215
They do not think whom they souse with spray.

* * *

42

A call in the midst of the crowd,
My own voice, orotund sweeping and final. 1055

Come my children,
Come my boys and girls, my women, household and intimates,

Now the performer launches his nerve, he has pass'd his prelude on the reeds within.

Easily written loose-finger'd chords—I feel the thrum of your climax and close.

My head slues round on my neck, 1060
Music rolls, but not from the organ,
Folks are around me, but they are no household of mine.

Ever the hard unsunk ground,
Ever the eaters and drinkers, ever the upward and downward sun, ever the air and the ceaseless tides,
Ever myself and my neighbors, refreshing, wicked, real, 1065
Ever the old inexplicable query, ever that thorn'd thumb, that breath of itches and thirsts,
Ever the vexer's *hoot! hoot!* till we find where the sly one hides and bring him forth,
Ever love, ever the sobbing liquid of life,
Ever the bandage under the chin, ever the trestles of death.

Here and there with dimes on the eyes walking, 1070
To feed the greed of the belly the brains liberally spooning,
Tickets buying, taking, selling, but in to the feast never once going,
Many sweating, ploughing, thrashing, and then the chaff for payment receiving,
A few idly owning, and they the wheat continually claiming.

This is the city and I am one of the citizens, 1075
Whatever interests the rest interests me, politics, wars, markets, newspapers, schools,
The mayor and councils, banks, tariffs, steamships, factories, stocks, stores, real estate and personal estate.

The little plentiful manikins skipping around in collars and tail'd coats,
I am aware who they are, (they are positively not worms or fleas,)
I acknowledge the duplicates of myself, the weakest and shallowest is deathless with me, 1080
What I do and say the same waits for them,
Every thought that flounders in me the same flounders in them.

I know perfectly well my own egotism,
Know my omnivorous lines and must not write any less,
And would fetch you whoever you are flush with myself. 1085

Not words of routine this song of mine,
But abruptly to question, to leap beyond yet nearer bring;
This printed and bound book—but the printer and the printing-
    office boy?
The well-taken photographs—but your wife or friend close and
    solid in your arms?
The black ship mail'd with iron, her mighty guns in her turrets—
    but the pluck of the captain and engineers?   1090
In the houses the dishes and fare and furniture—but the host and
    hostess, and the look out of their eyes?
The sky up there—yet here or next door, or across the way?
The saints and sages in history—but you yourself?
Sermons, creeds, theology—but the fathomless human brain,
And what is reason? and what is love? and what is life?   1095

43

I do not despise you priests, all time, the world over,
My faith is the greatest of faiths and the least of faiths,
Enclosing worship ancient and modern and all between ancient
    and modern,
Believing I shall come again upon the earth after five thousand
    years,
Waiting responses from oracles, honoring the gods, saluting the
    sun,   1100
Making a fetich of the first rock or stump, powowing with sticks
    in the circle of obis,
Helping the llama or brahmin as he trims the lamps of the idols,
Dancing yet through the streets in a phallic procession, rapt and
    austere in the woods a gymnosophist,
Drinking mead from the skull-cup, to Shastas and Vedas admirant,
    minding the Koran,
Walking the teokallis, spotted with gore from the stone and knife,
    beating the serpent-skin drum,   1105
Accepting the Gospels, accepting him that was crucified, knowing
    assuredly that he is divine,
To the mass kneeling or the puritan's prayer rising, or sitting
    patiently in a pew,
Ranting and frothing in my insane crisis, or waiting dead-like till
    my spirit arouses me,
Looking forth on pavement and land, or outside of pavement and
    land,
Belonging to the winders of the circuit of circuits.   1110

One of that centripetal and centrifugal gang I turn and talk like a
    man leaving charges before a journey.
Down-hearted doubters dull and excluded,
Frivolous, sullen, moping, angry, affected, dishearten'd, atheistical,
I know every one of you, I know the sea of torment, doubt,
    despair and unbelief.

How the flukes splash! 1115
How they contort rapid as lightning, with spasms and spouts of
    blood!

Be at peace bloody flukes of doubters and sullen mopers,
I take my place among you as much as among any,
The past is the push of you, me, all, precisely the same,
And what is yet untried and afterward is for you, me, all, precisely
    the same. 1120

I do not know what is untried and afterward,
But I know it will in its turn prove sufficient, and cannot fail.

Each who passes is consider'd, each who stops is consider'd, not
    a single one can it fail.

It cannot fail the young man who died and was buried,
Nor the young woman who died and was put by his side, 1125
Nor the little child that peep'd in at the door, and then drew back
    and was never seen again,
Nor the old man who has lived without purpose, and feels it with
    bitterness worse than gall,
Nor him in the poor house tubercled by rum and the bad disorder,
Nor the numberless slaughter'd and wreck'd, nor the brutish koboo
    call'd the ordure of humanity,
Nor the sacs merely floating with open mouths for food to slip in, 1130
Nor any thing in the earth, or down in the oldest graves of the
    earth,
Nor any thing in the myriads of spheres, nor the myriads of
    myriads that inhabit them,
Nor the present, nor the least wisp that is known.

44

It is time to explain myself—let us stand up.

What is known I strip away, 1135
I launch all men and women forward with me into the Unknown.

1129. **koboo:** a Sumatran.

The clock indicates the moment—but what does eternity indicate?

We have thus far exhausted trillions of winters and summers,
There are trillions ahead, and trillions ahead of them.

Births have brought us richness and variety,
And other births will bring us richness and variety.

I do not call one greater and one smaller,
That which fills its period and place is equal to any.

Were mankind murderous or jealous upon you, my brother, my sister?
I am sorry for you, they are not murderous or jealous upon me,
All has been gentle with me, I keep no account with lamentation,
(What have I to do with lamentation?)

I am an acme of things accomplish'd, and I am encloser of things to be.

My feet strike an apex of the apices of the stairs,
On every step bunches of ages, and larger bunches between the steps,
All below duly travel'd, and still I mount and mount.

Rise after rise bow the phantoms behind me,
Afar down I see the huge first Nothing, I know I was even there,
I waited unseen and always, and slept through the lethargic mist,
And took my time, and took no hurt from the fetid carbon.

Long I was hugg'd close—long and long.

Immense have been the preparations for me,
Faithful and friendly the arms that have help'd me.

Cycles ferried my cradle, rowing and rowing like cheerful boatmen,
For room to me stars kept aside in their own rings,
They sent influences to look after what was to hold me.

Before I was born out of my mother generations guided me,
My embryo has never been torpid, nothing could overlay it.

For it the nebula cohered to an orb,
The long slow strata piled to rest it on,
Vast vegetables gave it sustenance,
Monstrous sauroids transported it in their mouths and deposited it with care.

All forces have been steadily employ'd to complete and delight me,
Now on this spot I stand with my robust soul.

45

O span of youth! ever-push'd elasticity!
O manhood, balanced, florid and full.

My lovers suffocate me,
Crowding my lips, thick in the pores of my skin,
Jostling me through streets and public halls, coming naked to me
    at night,
Crying by day *Ahoy!* from the rocks of the river, swinging and
    chirping over my head,
Calling my name from flower-beds, vines, tangled underbrush,
Lighting on every moment of my life,
Bussing my body with soft balsamic busses,
Noiselessly passing handfuls out of their hearts and giving them
    to be mine.

Old age superbly rising! O welcome, ineffable grace of dying days!

Every condition promulges not only itself, it promulges what grows
    after and out of itself,
And the dark hush promulges as much as any.

I open my scuttle at night and see the far-sprinkled systems,
And all I see multiplied as high as I can cipher edge but the rim
    of the farther systems.

Wider and wider they spread, expanding, always expanding,
Outward and outward and forever outward.

My sun has his sun and round him obediently wheels,
He joins with his partners a group of superior circuit,
And greater sets follow, making specks of the greatest inside them.

There is no stoppage and never can be stoppage,
If I, you, and the worlds, and all beneath or upon their surfaces,
    were this moment reduced back to a pallid float, it would
    not avail in the long run,
We should surely bring up again where we now stand,
And surely go as much farther, and then farther and farther.

1181. promulges: makes known.

A few quadrillions of eras, a few octillions of cubic leagues, do not
    hazard the span or make it impatient,
They are but parts, any thing is but a part. 1195

See ever so far, there is limitless space outside of that,
Count ever so much, there is limitless time around that.

My rendezvous is appointed, it is certain,
The Lord will be there and wait till I come on perfect terms,
The great Camerado, the lover true for whom I pine will be there. 1200

46

I know I have the best of time and space, and was never measured
    and never will be measured.

I tramp a perpetual journey, (come listen all!)
My signs are a rain-proof coat, good shoes, and a staff cut from
    the woods,
No friend of mine takes his ease in my chair,
I have no chair, no church, no philosophy, 1205
I lead no man to a dinner-table, library, exchange,
But each man and each woman of you I lead upon a knoll,
My left hand hooking you round the waist,
My right hand pointing to landscapes of continents and the public
    road.

Not I, not any one else can travel that road for you, 1210
You must travel it for yourself.

It is not far, it is within reach,
Perhaps you have been on it since you were born and did not know,
Perhaps it is everywhere on water and on land.

Shoulder your duds dear son, and I will mine, and let us hasten
    forth, 1215
Wonderful cities and free nations we shall fetch as we go.

If you tire, give me both burdens, and rest the chuff of your hand
    on my hip,
And in due time you shall repay the same service to me,
For after we start we never lie by again.

This day before dawn I ascended a hill and look'd at the crowded
    heaven, 1220
And I said to my spirit *When we become the enfolders of those*

orbs, and the pleasure and knowledge of every thing in
them, shall we be fill'd and satisfied then?
And my spirit said No, we but level that lift to pass and continue
    beyond.

You are also asking me questions and I hear you,
I answer that I cannot answer, you must find out for yourself.

Sit a while dear son, 1225
Here are biscuits to eat and here is milk to drink,
But as soon as you sleep and renew yourself in sweet clothes, I
    kiss you with a good-by kiss and open the gate for your
    egress hence.

Long enough have you dream'd contemptible dreams,
Now I wash the gum from your eyes,
You must habit yourself to the dazzle of the light and of every
    moment of your life. 1230

Long have you timidly waded holding a plank by the shore,
Now I will you to be a bold swimmer,
To jump off in the midst of the sea, rise again, nod to me, shout,
    and laughingly dash with your hair.

47

I am the teacher of athletes,
He that by me spreads a wider breast than my own proves the
    width of my own, 1235
He most honors my style who learns under it to destroy the
    teacher.

The boy I love, the same becomes a man not through derived
    power, but in his own right,
Wicked rather than virtuous out of conformity or fear,
Fond of his sweetheart, relishing well his steak,
Unrequited love or a slight cutting him worse than sharp steel cuts, 1240
First-rate to ride, to fight, to hit the bull's eye, to sail a skiff, to
    sing a song or play on the banjo,
Preferring scars and the beard and faces pitted with small-pox
    over all latherers,
And those well-tann'd to those that keep out of the sun.

I teach straying from me, yet who can stray from me?
I follow you whoever you are from the present hour, 1245
My words itch at your ears till you understand them.

I do not say these things for a dollar or to fill up the time while I
    wait for a boat,
(It is you talking just as much as myself, I act as the tongue of you,
Tied in your mouth, in mine it begins to be loosen'd.)

I swear I will never again mention love or death inside a house,
And I swear I will never translate myself at all, only to him or her
    who privately stays with me in the open air.

If you would understand me go to the heights or water-shore,
The nearest gnat is an explanation, and a drop or motion of waves
    a key,
The maul, the oar, the hand-saw, second my words.

No shutter'd room or school can commune with me,
But roughs and little children better than they.

The young mechanic is closest to me, he knows me well,
The woodman that takes his axe and jug with him shall take me
    with him all day,
The farm-boy ploughing in the field feels good at the sound of my
    voice,
In vessels that sail my words sail, I go with fishermen and seamen
    and love them.

The soldier camp'd or upon the march is mine,
On the night ere the pending battle many seek me, and I do not
    fail them,
On that solemn night (it may be their last) those that know me
    seek me.

My face rubs to the hunter's face when he lies down alone in his
    blanket,
The driver thinking of me does not mind the jolt of his wagon,
The young mother and old mother comprehend me,
The girl and the wife rest the needle a moment and forget where
    they are,
They and all would resume what I have told them.

48

I have said that the soul is not more than the body,
And I have said that the body is not more than the soul,
And nothing, not God, is greater to one than one's self is,
And whoever walks a furlong without sympathy walks to his own
    funeral drest in his shroud,

And I or you pocketless of a dime may purchase the pick of the
    earth,
And to glance with an eye or show a bean in its pod confounds
    the learning of all times,
And there is no trade or employment but the young man following
    it may become a hero,   1275
And there is no object so soft but it makes a hub for the wheel'd
    universe,
And I say to any man or woman, Let your soul stand cool and
    composed before a million universes.

And I say to mankind, Be not curious about God,
For I who am curious about each am not curious about God,
(No array of terms can say how much I am at peace about God
    and about death.)   1280

I hear and behold God in every object, yet understand God not
    in the least,
Nor do I understand who there can be more wonderful than
    myself.

Why should I wish to see God better than this day?
I see something of God each hour of the twenty-four, and each
    moment then,
In the faces of men and women I see God, and in my own face in
    the glass,   1285
I find letters from God dropt in the street, and every one is sign'd
    by God's name,
And I leave them where they are, for I know that wheresoe'er I go,
Others will punctually come for ever and ever.

49

And as to you Death, and you bitter hug of mortality, it is idle to
    try to alarm me.

To his work without flinching the accoucheur comes,   1290
I see the elder-hand pressing receiving supporting,
I recline by the sills of the exquisite flexible doors,
And mark the outlet, and mark the relief and escape.

And as to you Corpse I think you are good manure, but that does
    not offend me,

1290. accoucheur: male midwife.

I smell the white roses sweet-scented and growing, 1295
I reach to the leafy lips, I reach to the polish'd breasts of melons.

And as to you Life I reckon you are the leavings of many deaths,
(No doubt I have died myself ten thousand times before.)

I hear you whispering there O stars of heaven,
O suns—O grass of graves—O perpetual transfers and
  promotions, 1300
If you do not say any thing how can I say any thing?

Of the turbid pool that lies in the autumn forest,
Of the moon that descends the steeps of the soughing twilight,
Toss, sparkles of day and dusk—toss on the black stems that
  decay in the muck,
Toss to the moaning gibberish of the dry limbs. 1305

I ascend from the moon, I ascend from the night,
I perceive that the ghastly glimmer is noonday sunbeams reflected,
And debouch to the steady and central from the offspring great or
  small.

50

There is that in me—I do not know what it is—but I know it is
  in me.
Wrench'd and sweaty—calm and cool then my body becomes, 1310
I sleep—I sleep long.

I do not know it—it is without name—it is a word unsaid,
It is not in any dictionary, utterance, symbol.

Something it swings on more than the earth I swing on,
To it the creation is the friend whose embracing awakes me. 1315

Perhaps I might tell more. Outlines! I plead for my brothers
  and sisters.

Do you see O my brothers and sisters?
It is not chaos or death—it is form, union, plan—it is eternal
  life—it is Happiness.

51

The past and present wilt—I have fill'd them, emptied them,
And proceed to fill my next fold of the future. 1320

1308. debouch: come out.

Listener up there! what have you to confide to me?
Look in my face while I snuff the sidle of evening,
(Talk honestly, no one else hears you, and I stay only a minute longer.)

Do I contradict myself?
Very well then I contradict myself, 1325
(I am large, I contain multitudes.)
I concentrate toward them that are nigh, I wait on the door-slab.

Who has done his day's work? who will soonest be through with his supper?
Who wishes to walk with me?
Will you speak before I am gone? will you prove already too late? 1330

52

The spotted hawk swoops by and accuses me, he complains of my gab and my loitering.

I too am not a bit tamed, I too am untranslatable,
I sound my barbaric yawp over the roofs of the world.

The last scud of day holds back for me,
It flings my likeness after the rest and true as any on the shadow'd wilds, 1335
It coaxes me to the vapor and the dusk.

I depart as air, I shake my white locks at the runaway sun,
I effuse my flesh in eddies, and drift it in lacy jags.

I bequeath myself to the dirt to grow from the grass I love,
If you want me again look for me under your boot-soles. 1340

You will hardly know who I am or what I mean,
But I shall be good health to you nevertheless,
And filter and fibre your blood.

Failing to fetch me at first keep encouraged,
Missing me one place search another, 1345
I stop somewhere waiting for you.

A WOMAN WAITS FOR ME

A woman waits for me, she contains all, nothing is lacking,
Yet all were lacking if sex were lacking, or if the moisture of the right man were lacking.

Sex contains all, bodies, souls,
Meanings, proofs, purities, delicacies, results, promulgations,
Songs, commands, health, pride, the maternal mystery, the seminal
    milk,
All hopes, benefactions, bestowals, all the passions, loves, beauties,
    delights of the earth,
All the governments, judges, gods, follow'd persons of the earth,
These are contain'd in sex as parts of itself and justifications of
    itself.

Without shame the man I like knows and avows the deliciousness
    of his sex,
Without shame the woman I like knows and avows hers.

Now I will dismiss myself from impassive women,
I will go stay with her who waits for me, and with those women
    that are warm-blooded and sufficient for me,
I see that they understand me and do not deny me,
I see that they are worthy of me, I will be the robust husband
    of those women.

They are not one jot less than I am,
They are tann'd in the face by shining suns and blowing winds,
Their flesh has the old divine suppleness and strength,
They know how to swim, row, ride, wrestle, shoot, run, strike,
    retreat, advance, resist, defend themselves,
They are ultimate in their own right—they are calm, clear, well-
    possess'd of themselves.

I draw you close to me, you women,
I cannot let you go, I would do you good,
I am for you, and you are for me, not only for our own sake, but
    for others' sakes,
Envelop'd in you sleep greater heroes and bards,
They refuse to awake at the touch of any man but me.

It is I, you women, I make my way,
I am stern, acrid, large, undissuadable, but I love you,
I do not hurt you any more than is necessary for you,
I pour the stuff to start sons and daughters fit for these States, I
    press with slow rude muscle,
I brace myself effectually, I listen to no entreaties,
I dare not withdraw till I deposit what has so long accumulated
    within me.

Through you I drain the pent-up rivers of myself,
In you I wrap a thousand onward years,

On you I graft the grafts of the best-loved of me and America,
The drops I distil upon you shall grow fierce and athletic girls,
    new artists, musicians, and singers,
The babes I beget upon you are to beget babes in their turn, 35
I shall demand perfect men and women out of my love-spendings,
I shall expect them to interpenetrate with others, as I and you
    interpenetrate now,
I shall count on the fruits of the gushing showers of them, as I
    count on the fruits of the gushing showers I give now,
I shall look for loving crops from the birth, life, death, immortality,
    I plant so lovingly now.

FULL OF LIFE NOW

Full of life now, compact, visible,
I, forty years old the eighty-third year of the States,
To one a century hence or any number of centuries hence,
To you yet unborn these, seeking you.

When you read these I that was visible am become invisible, 5
Now it is you, compact, visible, realizing my poems, seeking me,
Fancying how happy you were if I could be with you and become
    your comrade;
Be it as if I were with you. (Be not too certain but I am now with
    you.)

QUESTIONS

1. How do these selections reveal Whitman's efforts to make a poetic biography? Does reading them give you any insight into the way in which poems can represent a life? Can poetry represent a life? a personality?
2. Do you think it can be fairly argued that the poems in this group have no real bearing on the life of their author? Is it possible that they have only a limited bearing? Compare your answer to other answers based, first, on no outside knowledge about Whitman's life, and second, on at least one biography. Are the responses different?

3. Are some of these poems more dependent on biographical information than others? In what ways are they dependent? How important is that dependence?
4. Read a biography of Whitman and then read *Leaves of Grass*. What particular effects in the poetry are you more sensitive to because you have read the biography? Did the biography dull you to any aspects of the poetry you feel you might otherwise have been able to respond to?
5. What does Whitman's poetry offer apart from the biographical? What is its achievement?
6. In what important ways do these poems avoid autobiography? Do they avoid it entirely?

William Butler Yeats (1865-1939)

THE MAUD GONNE POEMS

In February 1889, when William Butler Yeats was twenty-three, Maud Gonne called at the Yeats home to speak with John Yeats, the poet's father and a well-known portrait painter. But while there she also met the son and told him that she had wept over some lines in his recently published volume *The Wanderings of Oisin*.

Maud Gonne was one of the most remarkable women of her time. The daughter of a colonel in the British Army who had been stationed in Dublin, she was tall (six-feet), statuesque, vivacious, and beautiful. Of his meeting with Maud, Yeats's biographer writes: "What he was best to remember . . . was her figure as she stood by the window with a spray of flowers, the light on her golden brown hair and delicate face." He thought she seemed "like a classical impersonation of the spring." The apple trees were in bloom when Yeats first saw Maud, and he ever afterward associated apple blossom with her. He brought some of these feelings together in such lines as these:

> newly grown to be a woman
> Tall and noble but with face and bosom
> Delicate in colour as apple blossom.

That first evening in 1889, Maud Gonne and William Butler Yeats dined together. Thus began one of the longest and most unusual love affairs recorded in literature. Maud was, at twenty-five, not only a celebrated beauty but also an actress and, more important, a passionate revolutionary dedicated to the overthrow of British rule in Ireland. Her presence demanded attention. She was surrounded not only by songbirds—which she carried with her wherever she went—but also by admirers, and from 1889 to practically the end of his life in 1939, Yeats's imagination was full of Maud Gonne.

Yeats catalogues in his poems the misery and frustration of nearly fifty years of devotion to Maud. In the beginning it is a story of unrequited love. Yeats once said that his devotion to this woman "might as well have been offered to an image in a milliner's window or to a statue in a museum." Those days of youthful melancholy and frustration are reflected in such poems as "The Pity of Love," and "When You Are Old."

The first turning point in the Maud Gonne poems comes shortly after 1903—the year in which Maud married a dashing army officer, Major John McBride. The marriage lasted only two years, but Maud vowed never to remarry and, instead, devoted herself more passionately to the cause of Irish independence. The effect of the marriage, and her subsequent refusal to remarry, is reflected in Yeats's poems by a new note of bitterness, a kind of worldly cynicism not previously present in the poems concerned with Maud. This new toughness is seen in such poems as "Never Give All the Heart" and "A Thought from Propertius."

A third crucial point in Yeats's relationship with Maud was his marriage in 1917. His new responsibilities brought new attitudes toward his love of earlier years. Poems concerned with Maud now began to reflect an anxiety for an aging friend who had become too deeply involved in politics. During this period he wrote to Olivia Shakespeare: "She had to choose (perhaps all women must) between broomstick and distaff, and she chose the broomstick...." Yeats at times became like a concerned parent whose child is acting unwisely and whose associates seem disreputable.

The final view of Maud is that of an extraordinary friend—almost of a superhuman figure, "perhaps a queen." She comes to be seen as the inspiration of his earliest work (see "The Circus Animals' Desertion" in his Collected Poems) and finally, in the last poem explicitly concerned with her—"The Bronze Head"—is raised above life and seen possessing immortality.

The Maud Gonne poems are fully comprehensible only when we understand Yeats's love for and long devotion to this woman. Once we have the essential biographical facts of the relationship, we not only comprehend the individual poems better and see their relationship to one another more clearly, but we are able to distinguish these poems from others like them. For Yeats wrote at least four kinds of love poem—to Maud Gonne, to Diana Vernon, to Iseult Gonne, and to his wife. A clear understanding of the Maud Gonne poems enables us to distinguish them from those other similar poems. "The Lover Mourns for the Loss of Love" is a poem about a love affair that ended when the woman saw the man was still in love with someone else. We know that such a situation seems unlikely between Maud and Yeats—and, upon further research, we find that Yeats was involved with another woman, and that the loss of love referred to in the poem is not the loss of Maud's love. Similarly, in a sequence of poems entitled "The Woman Young and Old," Yeats deals with emotional situations that we know Yeats and Maud never experienced together. Thus, we are on firm ground when we exclude these poems from the Maud Gonne group.

The following poems should be read individually as aesthetic works in their own right and then collectively as parts of a single theme—Yeats's love for Maud Gonne.

THE PITY OF LOVE

A pity beyond all telling
Is hid in the heart of love:
The folk who are buying and selling,
The clouds on their journey above,
The cold wet winds ever blowing,   5
And the shadowy hazel grove
Where mouse-grey waters are flowing,
Threaten the head that I love.

THE LOVER TELLS OF THE ROSE
IN HIS HEART

All things uncomely and broken, all things worn out and old,
The cry of a child by the roadway, the creak of a lumbering cart,
The heavy steps of the ploughman, splashing the wintry mould,
Are wronging your image that blossoms a rose in the deeps of my heart.

The wrong of unshapely things is a wrong too great to be told;   5
I hunger to build them anew and sit on a green knoll apart,
With the earth and the sky and the water, remade, like a casket of gold
For my dreams of your image that blossoms a rose in the deeps of my heart.

HE TELLS OF THE PERFECT BEAUTY

O cloud-pale eyelids, dream-dimmed eyes,
The poets labouring all their days
To build a perfect beauty in rhyme
Are overthrown by a woman's gaze
And by the unlabouring brood of the skies: 5
And therefore my heart will bow, when dew
Is dropping sleep, until God burn time,
Before the unlabouring stars and you.

HE HEARS THE CRY OF THE SEDGE

I wander by the edge
Of this desolate lake
Where wind cries in the sedge:
Until the axle break
That keeps the stars in their round,   5
And hands hurl in the deep
The banners of East and West,
And the girdle of light is unbound,
Your breast will not lie by the breast
Of your beloved in sleep.   10

WHEN YOU ARE OLD

When you are old and grey and full of sleep,
And nodding by the fire, take down this book,
And slowly read, and dream of the soft look
Your eyes had once, and of their shadows deep;

How many loved your moments of glad grace, 5
And loved your beauty with love false or true,
But one man loved the pilgrim soul in you,
And loved the sorrows of your changing face;

And bending down beside the glowing bars,
Murmur, a little sadly, how Love fled 10
And paced upon the mountains overhead
And hid his face amid a crowd of stars.

THE FOLLY OF BEING COMFORTED

One that is ever kind said yesterday:
"Your well-belovèd's hair has threads of grey,
And little shadows come about her eyes;
Time can but make it easier to be wise
Though now it seem impossible, and so 5
All that you need is patience."
                          Heart cries, "No,
I have not a crumb of comfort, not a grain.
Time can but make her beauty over again:
Because of that great nobleness of hers
The fire that stirs about her, when she stirs, 10
Burns but more clearly. O she had not these ways
When all the wild summer was in her gaze."

O heart! O heart! if she'd but turn her head,
You'd know the folly of being comforted.

NEVER GIVE ALL THE HEART

Never give all the heart, for love
Will hardly seem worth thinking of
To passionate women if it seem

Certain, and they never dream
That it fades out from kiss to kiss;   5
For everything that's lovely is
But a brief, dreamy, kind delight.
O never give the heart outright,
For they, for all smooth lips can say,
Have given their hearts up to the play.   10
And who could play it well enough
If deaf and dumb and blind with love?
He that made this knows all the cost,
For he gave all his heart and lost.

O DO NOT LOVE TOO LONG

Sweetheart, do not love too long:
I loved long and long,
And grew to be out of fashion
Like an old song.

All through the years of our youth   5
Neither could have known
Their own thought from the other's,
We were so much at one.

But O, in a minute she changed—
O do not love too long,   10
Or you will grow out of fashion
Like an old song.

AGAINST UNWORTHY PRAISE

O Heart, be at peace, because
Nor knave nor dolt can break
What's not for their applause,
Being for a woman's sake.
Enough if the work has seemed,   5
So did she your strength renew,
A dream that a lion had dreamed
Till the wilderness cried aloud,
A secret between you two,
Between the proud and the proud.   10

What, still you would have their praise!
But here's a haughtier text,
The labyrinth of her days
That her own strangeness perplexed;
And how what her dreaming gave 15
Earned slander, ingratitude,
From self-same dolt and knave;
Aye, and worse wrong than these.
Yet she, singing upon her road,
Half lion, half child, is at peace. 20

FALLEN MAJESTY

Although crowds gathered once if she but showed her face,
And even old men's eyes grew dim, this hand alone,
Like some last courtier at a gypsy camping-place
Babbling of fallen majesty, records what's gone.

The lineaments, a heart that laughter has made sweet, 5
These, these remain, but I record what's gone. A crowd
Will gather, and not know it walks the very street
Whereon a thing once walked that seemed a burning cloud.

FRIENDS

Now must I these three praise—
Three women that have wrought
What joy is in my days:
One because no thought,
Nor those unpassing cares, 5
No, not in these fifteen
Many-times-troubled years,
Could ever come between
Mind and delighted mind;
And one because her hand 10
Had strength that could unbind
What none can understand,
What none can have and thrive,
Youth's dreamy load, till she
So changed me that I live 15

Labouring in ecstasy.
And what of her that took
All till my youth was gone
With scarce a pitying look?
How could I praise that one?
When day begins to break
I count my good and bad,
Being wakeful for her sake,
Remembering what she had,
What eagle look still shows,
While up from my heart's root
So great a sweetness flows
I shake from head to foot.

THE PEOPLE

"What have I earned for all that work," I said,
"For all that I have done at my own charge?
The daily spite of this unmannerly town,
Where who has served the most is most defamed,
The reputation of his lifetime lost
Between the night and morning. I might have lived,
And you know well how great the longing has been,
Where every day my footfall should have lit
In the green shadow of Ferrara wall;
Or climbed among the images of the past—
The unperturbed and courtly images—
Evening and morning, the steep street of Urbino
To where the Duchess and her people talked
The stately midnight through until they stood
In their great window looking at the dawn;
I might have had no friend that could not mix
Courtesy and passion into one like those
That saw the wicks grow yellow in the dawn;
I might have used the one substantial right
My trade allows: chosen my company,
And chosen what scenery had pleased me best."
Thereon my phoenix answered in reproof,
"The drunkards, pilferers of public funds,
All the dishonest crowd I had driven away,
When my luck changed and they dared meet my face,

Crawled from obscurity, and set upon me
Those I had served and some that I had fed;
Yet never have I, now nor any time,
Complained of the people."

                        All I could reply
Was: "You, that have not lived in thought but deed,   30
Can have the purity of a natural force,
But I, whose virtues are the definitions
Of the analytic mind, can neither close
The eye of the mind nor keep my tongue from speech."
And yet, because my heart leaped at her words,   35
I was abashed, and now they come to mind
After nine years, I sink my head abashed.

A THOUGHT FROM PROPERTIUS

She might, so noble from head
To great shapely knees
The long flowing line,
Have walked to the altar
Through the holy images   5
At Pallas Athene's side,
Or been fit spoil for a centaur
Drunk with the unmixed wine.

A DEEP-SWORN VOW

Others because you did not keep
That deep-sworn vow have been friends of mine;
Yet always when I look death in the face,
When I clamber to the heights of sleep,
Or when I grow excited with wine,   5
Suddenly I meet your face.

PRESENCES

This night has been so strange that it seemed
As if the hair stood up on my head.
From going-down of the sun I have dreamed
That women laughing, or timid or wild,
In rustle of lace or silken stuff, 5
Climbed up my creaking stair. They had read
All I had rhymed of that monstrous thing
Returned and yet unrequited love.
They stood in the door and stood between
My great wood lectern and the fire 10
Till I could hear their hearts beating:
One is a harlot, and one a child
That never looked upon man with desire,
And one, it may be, a queen.

QUARREL IN OLD AGE

Where had her sweetness gone?
What fanatics invent
In this blind bitter town,
Fantasy or incident
Not worth thinking of, 5
Put her in a rage.
I had forgiven enough
That had forgiven old age.

All lives that has lived;
So much is certain; 10
Old sages were not deceived:
Somewhere beyond the curtain
Of distorting days
Lives that lonely thing
That shone before these eyes 15
Targeted, trod like Spring.

A BRONZE HEAD

Here at right of the entrance this bronze head,
Human, superhuman, a bird's round eye,
Everything else withered and mummy-dead.
What great tomb-haunter sweeps the distant sky
(Something may linger there though all else die;)   5
And finds there nothing to make its terror less
Hysterica passio of its own emptiness?

No dark tomb-haunter once; her form all full
As though with magnanimity of light,
Yet a most gentle woman; who can tell   10
Which of her forms has shown her substance right?
Or maybe substance can be composite,
Profound McTaggart thought so, and in a breath
A mouthful held the extreme of life and death.

But even at the starting-post, all sleek and new,   15
I saw the wildness in her and I thought
A vision of terror that it must live through
Had shattered her soul. Propinquity had brought
Imagination to that pitch where it casts out
All that is not itself: I had grown wild   20
And wandered murmuring everywhere, "My child, my child!"

Or else I thought her supernatural;
As though a sterner eye looked through her eye
On this foul world in its decline and fall;
On gangling stocks grown great, great stocks run dry,   25
Ancestral pearls all pitched into a sty,
Heroic reverie mocked by clown and knave,
And wondered what was left for massacre to save.

QUESTIONS

1. In almost every one of Yeats's poems there is an "I" who tells of his feelings. Reading the poems consecutively can

13. McTaggart: J. M. E. McTaggart, contemporary Scottish philosopher.

give us a general idea of what kind of person the "I" in these poems is. How would you describe this person? Give a composite picture of the speaker's character, concerns, and fortunes.
2. If these love poems are successful, they should convey a strong sense of a man's love for a woman. Can you describe that love in some detail?
3. Examine the diction and imagery in Yeats's poems. Which words and images seem to you most effective? Which least? Are some of the words and images archaic? Specifically cite how the imagery and diction shift from poem to poem.
4. Compare Yeats's Maud Gonne poems with some love poems from the Thematic Contexts. Does Yeats celebrate the excitement of love, the pleasures of love, or the loss of love? Make specific comparisons between the love poems in the earlier unit and one or two of Yeats's poems. What is the range of love themes covered by Yeats's poems? How does this range compare with that represented by the other poems?

Emily Dickinson (1830-1886)

Yeats's Maud Gonne poems are illuminated by a knowledge of his life. Reading the poems in a biographical context helps one to understand specific references and to see how one poem is related to another. Whitman's poems and his life are even more closely connected. *Leaves of Grass* is, in effect, a poetic autobiography, and the relationships between the life and the poetry are numerous and constant. The relationship between Emily Dickinson's life and her poems is different from either that of Yeats or Whitman. Emily Dickinson's biography rarely casts light on her poems, and her poems rarely chronicle the ordinary events of her life. The poems do, however, constitute a kind of emotional-intellectual biography —a biography of the inner life. They tell us how Emily Dickinson viewed her world in exact and minute detail.

The definite facts of Emily Dickinson's life are few and they can be summarized in a paragraph. She was born in 1830 and died in 1886. The daughter of a stern and prominent Massachusetts lawyer—a man who served a term in Congress—she lived her entire life as a well-to-do spinster in a New England college town. Although she never formally became a church communicant, the prevailing religious sensibility of her time—derived from New England's Puritan beginnings—was a formative influence in her life. From girlhood on, she made a number of strong attachments to both men and women, and her letters reveal that some of the most usual experiences of everyday life were overwhelming emotional events for her. Never married, she centered her entire life on her father's house, her family—especially her brother and his wife—a small circle of friends, and, most important, her poetry.

The scant details of her life have encouraged some of her critics and biographers to speculate about her cast of mind, her religious beliefs, and her possible (though unlikely) sexual relations with certain men and women. While the known facts of her life are too meager to tell us with certainty about any of these things, her poetry gives us an abundance of information about her religious views, about her sense of the world, and about her emotional responses to other human beings. The poems are, in fact, the only real source of information for most of the speculation about her life.

An "inner biography" does not tell us what happened in a poet's life; it tells us what the poet felt. Because the poet imagined she was a wife, it does not mean she was legally, or even physically, a wife. We do not need to know the name of her lover—or whether she really ever had a lover. The reality of an inner biography is the reality of the imagination. We learn with absolute certainty how she felt about love, or suffering, or God. That is the biographical context in which it is most useful to approach Emily Dickinson's poems.

The poems that follow reveal only a fraction of the complexity of Emily Dickinson's inner life by presenting poems dealing with four concerns: her loves, her sense of her own mind in turmoil, nature, and God. There are 1,775 poems in Emily Dickinson's *Complete Poems,* so the few selections we have been able to include here are intended only to indicate how intensely lyric poetry may reveal the inner dimensions of her life through art. A full demonstration of this inner life may be found by examining the *Complete Poems* and by reading her *Collected Letters.*

FOR EACH ECSTATIC INSTANT

For each ecstatic instant
We must an anguish pay
In keen and quivering ratio
To the ecstasy.

For each beloved hour   5
Sharp pittances of years—
Bitter contested farthings—
And Coffers heaped with Tears!

HE WAS WEAK

He was weak, and I was strong—then—
So He let me lead him in—
I was weak, and He was strong then—
So I let him lead me—Home.

'Twasn't far—the door was near—   5
'Twasn't dark—for He went—too—
'Twasn't loud, for He said nought—
That was all I cared to know.

Day knocked—and we must part—
Neither—was strongest—now—   10
He strove—and I strove—too—
We didn't do it—tho'!

I'M "WIFE"

I'm "wife"—I've finished that—
That other state—
I'm Czar—I'm "Woman" now—
It's safer so—

How odd the Girl's life looks   5
Behind this soft Eclipse—
I think that Earth feels so
To folks in Heaven—now—

This being comfort—then
That other kind—was pain— 10
But why compare?
I'm "Wife"! Stop there!

WILD NIGHTS

Wild Nights—Wild Nights!
Were I with thee
Wild Nights should be
Our luxury!

Futile—the Winds— 5
To a Heart in port—
Done with the Compass—
Done with the Chart!

Rowing in Eden—
Ah, the Sea! 10
Might I but moor—Tonight—
In Thee!

I REASON, EARTH IS SHORT

I reason, Earth is short—
And Anguish—absolute—
And many hurt,
But, what of that?

I reason, we could die— 5
The best Vitality
Cannot excel Decay,
But, what of that?

I reason, that in Heaven—
Somehow, it will be even— 10
Some new Equation, given—
But, what of that?

AFTER GREAT PAIN, A FORMAL FEELING COMES

After great pain, a formal feeling comes—
The Nerves sit ceremonious, like Tombs—
The stiff Heart questions was it He, that bore,
And Yesterday, or Centuries before?

The Feet, mechanical, go round—   5
Of Ground, or Air, or Ought—
A Wooden way
Regardless grown,
A Quartz contentment, like a stone—

This is the Hour of Lead—   10
Remembered, if outlived,
As Freezing persons, recollect the Snow—
First—Chill—then Stupor—then the letting go—

OF COURSE—I PRAYED

Of Course—I prayed—
And did God Care?
He cared as much as on the Air
A Bird—had stamped her foot—
And cried "Give Me"—   5
My Reason—Life—
I had not had—but for Yourself—
'Twere better Charity
To leave me in the Atom's Tomb—
Merry, and Nought, and gay, and numb—   10
Than this smart Misery.

THE FIRST DAY'S NIGHT HAD COME

The first Day's Night had come—
And grateful that a thing
So terrible—had been endured—
I told my Soul to sing—

She said her Strings were snapt— 5
Her Bow—to Atoms blown—
And so to mend her—gave me work
Until another Morn—

And then—a Day as huge
As Yesterdays in pairs, 10
Unrolled its horror in my face—
Until it blocked my eyes—

My Brain—begun to laugh—
I mumbled—like a fool—
And tho' 'tis Years ago—that Day— 15
My Brain keeps giggling—still.

And Something's odd—within—
That person that I was—
And this One—do not feel the same—
Could it be Madness—this? 20

MUCH MADNESS IS DIVINEST SENSE

Much Madness is divinest Sense—
To a discerning Eye—
Much Sense—the starkest Madness—
'Tis the Majority
In this, as All, prevail— 5
Assent—and you are sane—
Demur—you're straightway dangerous—
And handled with a Chain—

I RECKON—WHEN I COUNT AT ALL

I reckon—when I count at all—
First—Poets—Then the Sun—
Then Summer—Then the Heaven of God—
And then—the List is done—

But, looking back—the First so seems 5
To Comprehend the Whole—
The Others look a needless Show—
So I write—Poets—All—

Their Summer—lasts a Solid Year—
They can afford a Sun   10
The East—would deem extravagant—
And if the Further Heaven—

Be Beautiful as they prepare
For Those who worship Them—
It is too difficult a Grace—   15
To justify the Dream—

IT WOULD HAVE STARVED A GNAT

It would have starved a Gnat—
To live so small as I—
And yet I was a living Child—
With Food's necessity

Upon me—like a Claw—   5
I could no more remove
Than I could coax a Leech away—
Or make a Dragon—move—

Nor like the Gnat—had I—
The privilege to fly   10
And seek a Dinner for myself—
How mightier He—than I—

Nor like Himself—the Art
Upon the Window Pane
To gad my little Being out—   15
And not begin—again—

THEY SHUT ME UP IN PROSE

They shut me up in Prose—
As when a little Girl
They put me in the Closet—
Because they liked me "still"—

Still! Could themself have peeped—   5
And seen my Brain—go round—

They might as wise have lodged a Bird
For Treason—in the Pound—

Himself has but to will
And easy as a Star   10
Abolish his Captivity—
And laugh—No more have I—

OURSELVES WERE WED ONE SUMMER—DEAR

Ourselves were wed one summer—dear—
Your Vision—was in June—
And when Your little Lifetime failed,
I wearied—too—of mine—

And overtaken in the Dark—   5
Where You had put me down—
By Some one carrying a Light—
I—too—received the Sign.

'Tis true—Our Futures different lay—
Your Cottage—faced the sun—   10
While Oceans—and the North must be—
On every side of mine

'Tis true, Your Garden led the Bloom,
For mine—in Frosts—was sown—
And yet, one Summer, we were Queens—   15
But You—were crowned in June—

I DWELL IN POSSIBILITY

I dwell in Possibility—
A fairer House than Prose—
More numerous of Windows—
Superior—for Doors—

Of Chambers as the Cedars—   5
Impregnable of Eye—
And for an Everlasting Roof
The Gambrels of the Sky—

Of Visitors—the fairest—
For Occupation—This—
The spreading wide my narrow Hands
To gather Paradise—

AGAIN—HIS VOICE IS AT THE DOOR

Again—his voice is at the door—
I feel the old *Degree*—
I hear him ask the servant
For such an one—as me—

I take a *flower*—as I go—
My face to *justify*—
He never *saw* me—*in this life*—
I might *surprise* his eye!

I cross the Hall with *mingled* steps—
I—silent—pass the door—
I look on all this world *contains*—
Just his face—nothing more!

We talk in *careless*—and in *toss*—
A kind of *plummet* strain—
Each—sounding—shyly—
Just—how—deep—
The *other's* one—had been—

We *walk*—I leave my Dog—at home—
A *tender*—*thoughtful* Moon
Goes with us—just a little way—
And—then—we are *alone*—

Alone—if *Angels* are "alone"—
First time they *try* the *sky!*
Alone—if those "veiled faces"—be—
We cannot *count*—on High!

I'd give—to live that hour—*again*—
The *purple*—in my Vein—
But *He* must *count the drops*—*himself*—
My price for *every stain!*

ONE NEED NOT BE A CHAMBER

One need not be a Chamber—to be Haunted—
One need not be a House—
The Brain has Corridors—surpassing
Material Place—

Far safer, of a Midnight Meeting
External Ghost
Than its interior Confronting—
That Cooler Host.

Far safer, through an Abbey gallop,
The Stones a'chase—
Than Unarmed, one's a'self encounter—
In lonesome Place—

Ourself behind ourself, concealed—
Should startle most—
Assassin hid in our Apartment
Be Horror's least.

The Body—borrows a Revolver—
He bolts the Door—
O'erlooking a superior spectre—
Or More—

IT DROPPED SO LOW

It dropped so low—in my Regard—
I heard it hit the Ground—
And go to pieces on the Stones
At bottom of my Mind—

Yet blamed the Fate that flung it—*less*
Than I denounced Myself,
For entertaining Plated Wares
Upon my Silver Shelf—

BECAUSE THE BEE MAY BLAMELESS HUM

Because the Bee may blameless hum
For Thee a Bee do I become
List even unto Me.

Because the Flowers unafraid
May lift a look on thine, a Maid   5
Alway a Flower would be.

Nor Robins, Robins need not hide
When Thou upon their Crypts intrude
So Wings bestow on Me
Or Petals, or a Dower of Buzz   10
That Bee to ride, or Flower of Furze
I that way worship Thee.

HOW HAPPY I WAS IF I COULD FORGET

How happy I was if I could forget
To remember how sad I am
Would be an easy adversity
But the recollecting of Bloom

Keeps making November difficult   5
Till I who was almost bold
Lose my way like a little Child
And perish of the cold.

IF I CAN STOP ONE HEART FROM BREAKING

If I can stop one Heart from breaking
I shall not live in vain
If I can ease one Life the Aching
Or cool one Pain

Or help one fainting Robin   5
Unto his Nest again
I shall not live in Vain.

STRUCK, WAS I, NOT YET BY LIGHTNING

Struck, was I, not yet by Lightning—
Lightning—lets away
Power to perceive His Process
With Vitality.

Maimed—was I—yet not by Venture—
Stone of stolid Boy—
Nor a Sportsman's Peradventure—
Who mine Enemy?

Robbed—was I—intact to Bandit—
All my Mansion torn—
Sun—withdrawn to Recognition—
Furthest shining—done—

Yet was not the foe—of any—
Not the smallest Bird
In the nearest Orchard dwelling
Be of Me—afraid.

Most—I love the Cause that slew Me.
Often as I die
Its beloved Recognition
Holds a Sun on Me—

Best—at Setting—as is Nature's—
Neither witnessed Rise
Till the infinite Aurora
In the other's eyes.

I FELT A CLEAVING IN MY MIND

I felt a Cleaving in my Mind—
As if my Brain had split—
I tried to match it—Seam by Seam—
But could not make them fit.

The thought behind, I strove to join
Unto the thought before—
But Sequence ravelled out of Sound
Like Balls—upon a Floor.

WHEN THEY COME BACK

When they come back—if Blossoms do—
I always feel a doubt
If Blossoms can be born again
When once the Art is out—

When they begin, if Robins may,   5
I always had a fear
I did not tell, it was their last Experiment
Last Year,

When it is May, if May return,
Had nobody a pang   10
Lest in a Face so beautiful
He might not look again?

If I am there—One does not know
What Party—One may be
Tomorrow, but if I am there   15
I take back all I say—

TO WHOM THE MORNINGS STAND FOR NIGHTS

To Whom the Mornings stand for Nights,
What must the Midnights—be!

A GREAT HOPE FELL

A great Hope fell
You heard no noise
The Ruin was within
Oh cunning wreck that told no tale
And let no Witness in   5

The mind was built for mighty Freight
For dread occasion planned
How often foundering at Sea
Ostensibly, on Land

A not admitting of the wound   10
Until it grew so wide
For the suspended Candidate
There came unsummoned in—

That portion of the Vision
The World applied to fill   15
Not unto nomination
The Cherubim reveal—

LIKE RAIN IT SOUNDED TILL IT CURVED

Like Rain it sounded till it curved
And then I knew 'twas Wind—
It walked as wet as any Wave
But swept as dry as sand—
When it had pushed itself away   5
To some remotest Plain
A coming as of Hosts was heard
That was indeed the Rain—
It filled the Wells, it pleased the Pools
It warbled in the Road—   10
It pulled the spigot from the Hills
And let the Floods abroad—
It loosened acres, lifted seas
The sites of Centres stirred
Then like Elijah rode away   15
Upon a Wheel of Cloud.

I THOUGHT THAT NATURE WAS ENOUGH

I thought that nature was enough
Till Human nature came
But that the other did absorb
As Parallax a Flame—

Of Human nature just aware   5
There added the Divine
Brief struggle for capacity
The power to contain

Is always as the contents
But give a Giant room   10
And you will lodge a Giant
And not a smaller man

A LITTLE MADNESS IN THE SPRING

A little Madness in the Spring
Is wholesome even for the King,
But God be with the Clown—

Who ponders this tremendous scene—
This whole Experiment of Green—   5
As if it were his own!

MY MAKER—LET ME BE

My Maker—let me be
Enamored most of thee—
But nearer this
I more should miss—

THE FACT THAT EARTH IS HEAVEN

The Fact that Earth is Heaven—
Whether Heaven is Heaven or not
If not an Affidavit
Of that specific Spot
Not only must confirm us   5
That it is not for us
But that it would affront us
To dwell in such a place—

IT WAS A QUIET SEEMING DAY

It was a quiet seeming Day—
There was no harm in earth or sky—
Till with the closing sun
There strayed an accidental Red
A Strolling Hue, one would have said   5
To westward of the Town—

But when the Earth began to jar
And Houses vanished with a roar
And Human Nature hid
We comprehended by the Awe   10
As those that Dissolution saw
The Poppy in the Cloud

ONE JOY OF SO MUCH ANGUISH

One Joy of so much anguish
Sweet nature has for me
I shun it as I do Despair
Or dear iniquity—
Why Birds, a Summer morning   5
Before the Quick of Day
Should stab my ravished spirit
With Dirks of Melody
Is part of an inquiry
That will receive reply   10
When Flesh and Spirit sunder
In Death's Immediately—

"HEAVENLY FATHER"

"Heavenly Father"—take to thee
The supreme iniquity
Fashioned by thy candid Hand
In a moment contraband—
Though to trust us—seem to us   5
More respectful—"We are Dust"—
We apologize to thee
For thine own Duplicity—

THE BIBLE IS AN ANTIQUE VOLUME

The Bible is an antique Volume—
Written by faded Men
At the suggestion of Holy Spectres—
Subjects—Bethlehem—
Eden—the ancient Homestead—   5
Satan—the Brigadier—
Judas—the Great Defaulter—
David—the Troubadour—
Sin—a distinguished Precipice
Others must resist—   10
Boys that "believe" are very lonesome—

Other Boys are "lost"—
Had but the Tale a warbling Teller—
All the Boys would come—
Orpheus' Sermon captivated—   15
It did not condemn—

OF GOD WE ASK ONE FAVOR

Of God we ask one favor,
That we may be forgiven—
For what, he is presumed to know—
The Crime, from us, is hidden—
Immured the whole of Life   5
Within a magic Prison
We reprimand the Happiness
That too competes with Heaven.

IS IT TOO LATE TO TOUCH YOU, DEAR?

Is it too late to touch you, Dear?
We this moment knew—
Love Marine and Love terrene—
Love celestial too—

IF ALL THE GRIEFS I AM TO HAVE

If all the griefs I am to have
Would only come today,
I am so happy I believe
They'd laugh and run away.

If all the joys I am to have   5
Would only come today,
They could not be so big as this
That happens to me now.

REARRANGE A "WIFE'S" AFFECTION!

Rearrange a "Wife's" affection!
When they dislocate my Brain!
Amputate my freckled Bosom!
Make me bearded like a man!

Blush, my spirit, in thy Fastness— 5
Blush, my unacknowledged clay—
Seven years of troth have taught thee
More than Wifehood ever may!

Love that never leaped its socket—
Trust entrenched in narrow pain— 10
Constancy thro' fire—awarded—
Anguish—bare of anodyne!

Burden—borne so far triumphant—
None suspect me of the crown,
For I wear the "thorns" till *Sunset*— 15
Then my diadem put on.

Big my Secret but it's *bandaged*—
It will never get away
Till the Day its Weary Keeper
Leads it through the grave to thee. 20

LAD OF ATHENS

Lad of Athens, faithful be
To Thyself,
And Mystery—
All the rest is Perjury—

QUESTIONS

1. These poems touch on a number of subjects—such as love, pain, and God. Group the poems according to theme. Describe Emily Dickinson's sense of God—or love, or pain —as described in these poems.

2. Examine the meter of Dickinson's poems. Take particular care to determine where she appears to be observing an iambic norm and where she varies that norm.
3. All of Dickinson's poems are relatively short, and many even seem constructed on the basis of phrases rather than sentences. How does the brevity and phraseology of these poems help provide an appropriate form?
4. One of the most striking features of Emily Dickinson's poems is their figurative language—such as similes, metaphors, and personification. Make a list of some of her most striking similes and metaphors. Examine these figures as they appear in individual poems and explain how they function as part of these specific poems. Which poems are built on extended metaphors? Which depend on personification?
5. Comment as fully as possible on Emily Dickinson's ideas on poetry.
6. Compare Dickinson's love poems with Yeats's love poems in terms of style and form.

Cultural Contexts

There are more cultural contexts than even a larger book could include, but we have chosen two that we feel are representative: the limited social context that begets poems of protest, and the larger social context that develops poetic traditions differing from our own. The first has a universal quality: all societies produce protest of one form or another; most societies have experienced war and war protest; most societies have included minority groups and have had protests by those minorities. All cultures have developed their own views—with multiple outside influences, of course—about what poetry should be. In reading African and Oriental poetry, we find ourselves aware of how many basic assumptions we accept about poetry based on our western traditions. In order to read poems of other cultures—even in translation—we have to surrender some of our preconceptions.

Protest Poetry

Protest poetry is marked by a powerful rhetorical approach that is impossible for the reader to ignore. The techniques of rhetorical poetry are notably those of direct address, argument, harangue, tirade, accusation, shock, and appeals to sympathy. Its purpose is to convince the reader. It is basically argumentative: one position is being argued for and another (usually) attacked. The reader is in the balance, and the poet is pushing him to a decision. For that reason rhetorical poetry is profoundly affective. Readers can contend with it, but they rarely can be indifferent to it. Conventional criticism has tended to relegate the rhetorical poetic forms to the lower levels of poetry. This is partly because of the romantic poets of the early nineteenth century, who reacted against a rhetorical poetry that had absorbed some of the exaggerated mannerisms of the rhetorical stage. It is also a reaction against didactic poetry—poetry that teaches a lesson, usually moral. But not all rhetorical poetry is didactic, though the rhetorical poem functions as an instrument of action. One is not meant just to sit there once he reads a rhetorical poem; he is expected to *do* something. The power of rhetorical poetry to command an audience is something of a threat to more aesthetically "pure" poetry, since the latter is a contemplative form. The more "pure" poem does not do something, it *is* something.

Fortunately, we need not argue for or against either form of poetry; both are plentifully represented here. We do want to suggest, however, that there are useful critical ways of reading poems of protest. This will be true whether we agree or disagree with the poet's argument.

It is useful in the present group of poems of war protest and black protest to compare both techniques and the effectiveness of those techniques. It is also valuable to examine the poems for techniques that have a high "fatigue" value—that is, those that are effective the first time they are confronted, but grow more tolerable and, hence, less effective. For instance, the movie-going audience of 1939 was shocked and stunned when, in *Gone With the Wind*, Rhett Butler said, "I don't give a damn!" Today, increased profanity in films has lessened its effectiveness. Is this fatigue apparent in any of these poems?

Not all of the protest poems that follow are specifically rhetorical. Claude McKay, for one, would not have felt that his work was specifically an attack or an argument; he felt he was making statements like any other poet. This is true of Langston Hughes and a number of the writers of black protest poetry. It is true of much of the war protest poetry we have assembled here. Whether we consider the earliest examples of war protest poems or the latest examples, we find a multiplicity of technical approaches. Some poems, like Wilfred Owen's, are tightly metrical and tightly rhymed; others, like John William Corrington's, are free in form and approach.

All this is to say that there is no one way to write protest poetry. There are many ways, and all are good that work.

Finally, we might ask ourselves how important technique is

for poets who want to protest aspects of their culture. Should a protest poet pay close attention to technique? Should he pay no attention? Taking a middle road between these extremes is no solution, because the question really is: How important is the form of a poem that protests injustice or horror? Is there any poem, no matter what its subject or intention, for which form is of little or no consequence? These are difficult questions, and they are answerable only after some consideration of the achievement of protest poetry.

POEMS OF WAR PROTEST

DAVID'S LAMENT

from II SAMUEL

The beauty of Israel is slain upon thy high places: how are the mighty fallen!
Tell *it* not in Gath, publish *it* not in the streets of Askelon; lest the daughters of the Philistines rejoice, lest the daughters of the uncircumcised triumph. 5
Ye mountains of Gilboa, *let there be* no dew, neither *let there be* rain, upon you, nor fields of offerings: for there the shield of the mighty is vilely cast away, the shield of Saul, *as though he had* not *been* anointed with oil.
From the blood of the slain, from the fat of the mighty, 10 the bow of Jonathan turned not back, and the sword of Saul returned not empty.
Saul and Jonathan *were* lovely and pleasant in their lives, and in their death they were not divided: they were swifter than eagles, they were stronger than lions. 15
Ye daughters of Israel, weep over Saul, who clothed you in scarlet, with *other* delights, who put on ornaments of gold upon your apparel.
How are the mighty fallen in the midst of the battle! O Jonathan, *thou wast* slain in thine high places. 20
I am distressed for thee, my brother Jonathan: very pleasant hast thou been unto me: thy love to me was wonderful, passing the love of women.
How are the mighty fallen, and the weapons of war perished! 25

THE NEFARIOUS WAR

Li Po (701–762)

Last year we fought by the head-stream of the So-kan,
This year we are fighting on the Tsung-ho road.
We have washed our armor in the waves of the Chiao-chi
    lake,
We have pastured our horses on Tien-shan's snowy
    slopes.
The long, long war goes on ten thousand miles from
    home,   5
Our three armies are worn and grown old.

The barbarian does man-slaughter for plowing;
On his yellow sand-plains nothing has been seen but
    blanched skulls and bones.
Where the Chin emperor built the walls against the
    Tartars,
There the defenders of Han are burning beacon fires.   10
The beacon fires burn and never go out,
There is no end to war!—

In the battlefield men grapple each other and die;
The horses of the vanquished utter lamentable cries to
    heaven,
While ravens and kites peck at human entrails,   15
Carry them up in their flight, and hang them on the
    branches of dead trees.

So, men are scattered and smeared over the desert grass,
And the generals have accomplished nothing.

Oh, nefarious war! I see why arms
Were so seldom used by the benign sovereigns.   20

EPITAPH ON AN ARMY OF MERCENARIES

A. E. Housman (1859–1936)

    These, in the day when heaven was falling,
      The hour when earth's foundations fled,
    Followed their mercenary calling
      And took their wages and are dead.

Their shoulders held the sky suspended; 5
  They stood, and earth's foundations stay;
What God abandoned, these defended,
  And saved the sum of things for pay.

AN IRISH AIRMAN FORESEES HIS DEATH

William Butler Yeats (1865–1939)

I know that I shall meet my fate
Somewhere among the clouds above;
Those that I fight I do not hate,
Those that I guard I do not love;
My country is Kiltartan Cross, 5
My countrymen Kiltartan's poor,
No likely end could bring them loss
Or leave them happier than before.
Nor law, nor duty bade me fight,
Nor public men, nor cheering crowds, 10
A lonely impulse of delight
Drove to this tumult in the clouds;
I balanced all, brought all to mind,
The years to come seemed waste of breath,
A waste of breath the years behind 15
In balance with this life, this death.

COUNTER-ATTACK

Siegfried Sassoon (1886–1967)

We'd gained our first objective hours before
While dawn broke like a face with blinking eyes,
Pallid, unshaved and thirsty, blind with smoke.
Things seemed all right at first. We held their line,
With bombers posted, Lewis guns well placed, 5
And clink of shovels deepening the shallow trench.
The place was rotten with dead; green clumsy legs
High-booted, sprawled and grovelled along the saps;

An Irish Airman Foresees His Death. The Irish airman is Major Robert Gregory, the subject of Yeats's elegy (page 111).

And trunks, face downward in the sucking mud,
Wallowed like trodden sand-bags loosely filled;   10
And naked sodden buttocks, mats of hair,
Bulged, clotted heads, slept in the plastering slime.
And then the rain began,—the jolly old rain!

A yawning soldier knelt against the bank,
Staring across the morning blear with fog;   15
He wondered when the Allemands would get busy;
And then, of course, they started with five-nines
Traversing, sure as fate, and never a dud.
Mute in the clamour of shells he watched them burst
Spouting dark earth and wire with gusts from hell,   20
While posturing giants dissolved in drifts of smoke.
He crouched and flinched, dizzy with galloping fear
Sick for escape,—loathing the strangled horror
And butchered, frantic gestures of the dead.

An officer came blundering down the trench: 25
"Stand-to and man the fire-step!" On he went . . .
Gasping and bawling, "Fire-step . . . counter-attack!"
Then the haze lifted. Bombing on the right
Down the old sap: machine-guns on the left;
And stumbling figures looming out in front.   30
"O Christ, they're coming at us!" Bullets spat,
And he remembered his rifle . . . rapid fire . . .
And started blazing wildly . . . then a bang
Crumpled and spun him sideways, knocked him out
To grunt and wriggle: none heeded him; he choked   35
And fought the flapping veils of smothering gloom,
Lost in a blurred confusion of yells and groans . . .
Down, and down, and down, he sank and drowned,
Bleeding to death. The counter-attack had failed.

CONSCIENTIOUS OBJECTOR

Edna St. Vincent Millay (1892–1950)

I shall die, but that is all that I shall do for Death.

I hear him leading his horse out of the stall; I hear the clatter on
the barn-floor.

17. five-nines: German artillery.

He is in haste; he has business in Cuba, business in the Balkans,
    many calls to make this morning.
But I will not hold the bridle while he cinches the girth.
And he may mount by himself: I will not give him a leg up.   5

Though he flick my shoulders with his whip, I will not tell him
    which way the fox ran.
With his hoof on my breast, I will not tell him where the black
    boy hides in the swamp.
I shall die, but that is all that I shall do for Death; I am not on
    his pay-roll.

I will not tell him the whereabouts of my friends nor of my
    enemies either.
Though he promise me much, I will not map him the route to
    any man's door.   10

Am I a spy in the land of the living, that I should deliver men to
    Death?
Brother, the password and the plans of our city are safe with me;
    never through me
Shall you be overcome.

ARMS AND THE BOY

Wilfred Owen (1893–1918)

Let the boy try along this bayonet-blade
How cold steel is, and keen with hunger of blood;
Blue with all malice, like a madman's flash;
And thinly drawn with famishing for flesh.

Lend him to stroke these blind, blunt bullet-heads   5
Which long to nuzzle in the hearts of lads,
Or give him cartridges of fine zinc teeth,
Sharp with the sharpness of grief and death.

For his teeth seem for laughing round an apple.
There lurk no claws behind his fingers supple;   10
And God will grow no talons at his heels,
Nor antlers through the thickness of his curls.

SPRING OFFENSIVE

Wilfred Owen

Halted against the shade of a last hill,
They fed, and lying easy, were at ease
And, finding comfortable chests and knees,
Carelessly slept. But many there stood still
To face the stark, blank sky beyond the ridge,   5
Knowing their feet had come to the end of the world.

Marvelling they stood, and watched the long grass swirled
By the May breeze, murmurous with wasp and midge,
For though the summer oozed into their veins
Like an injected drug for their bodies' pains,   10
Sharp on their souls hung the imminent line of grass,
Fearfully flashed the sky's mysterious glass.

Hour after hour they ponder the warm field—
And the far valley behind, where the buttercup
Had blessed with gold their slow boots coming up,   15
Where even the little brambles would not yield,
But clutched and clung to them like sorrowing hands;
They breathe like trees unstirred.

Till like a cold gust thrills the little word
At which each body and its soul begird   20
And tighten them for battle. No alarms
Of bugles, no high flags, no clamorous haste—
Only a lift and flare of eyes that faced
The sun, like a friend with whom their love is done.
O larger shone that smile against the sun,—   25
Mightier than his whose bounty these have spurned.

So, soon they topped the hill, and raced together
Over an open stretch of herb and heather
Exposed. And instantly the whole sky burned
With fury against them; earth set sudden cups   30
In thousands for their blood; and the green slope
Chasmed and steepened sheer to infinite space.

Of them who running on that last high place
Leapt to swift unseen bullets, or went up
On the hot blast and fury of hell's upsurge,   35
Or plunged and fell away past this world's verge,
Some say God caught them even before they fell.

But what say such as from existence' brink
Ventured but drave too swift to sink,
The few who rushed in the body to enter hell, 40
And there out-fiending all its fiends and flames
With superhuman inhumanities,
Long-famous glories, immemorial shames—
And crawling slowly back, have by degrees
Regained cool peaceful air in wonder— 45
Why speak not they of comrades that went under?

EXPOSURE

Wilfred Owen

Our brains ache, in the merciless iced east winds that knive us . . .
Wearied we keep awake because the night is silent . . .
Low, drooping flares confuse our memory of the salient . . .
Worried by silence, sentries whisper, curious, nervous,
    But nothing happens. 5

Watching, we hear the mad gusts tugging on the wire,
Like twitching agonies of men among its brambles.
Northward, incessantly, the flickering gunnery rumbles,
Far off, like a dull rumour of some other war.
    What are we doing here? 10

The poignant misery of dawn begins to grow . . .
We only know war lasts, rain soaks, and clouds sag stormy.
Dawn massing in the east her melancholy army
Attacks once more in ranks on shivering ranks of gray,
    But nothing happens. 15

Sudden successive flights of bullets streak the silence.
Less deathly than the air that shudders black with snow,
With sidelong flowing flakes that flock, pause, and renew;
We watch them wandering up and down the wind's nonchalance,
    But nothing happens. 20

Pale flakes with fingering stealth come feeling for our faces—
We cringe in holes, back on forgotten dreams, and stare,
    snow-dazed,
Deep into grassier ditches. So we drowse, sun-dozed,
Littered with blossoms trickling where the blackbird fusses.
    Is it that we are dying? 25

Slowly our ghosts drag home: glimpsing the sunk fires, glozed
With crusted dark-red jewels; crickets jingle there;
For hours the innocent mice rejoice: the house is theirs;
Shutters and doors, all closed: on us the doors are closed,—
    We turn back to our dying.   30

Since we believe not otherwise can kind fires burn;
Nor ever suns smile true on child, or field, or fruit.
For God's invincible spring our love is made afraid;
Therefore, not loath, we lie out here; therefore were born,
    For love of God seems dying.   35

To-night, His frost will fasten on this mud and us,
Shrivelling many hands, puckering foreheads crisp.
The burying-party, picks and shovels in their shaking grasp,
Pause over half-known faces. All their eyes are ice,
    But nothing happens.   40

DULCE ET DECORUM EST

Wilfred Owen

Bent double, like old beggars under sacks,
Knock-kneed, coughing like hags, we cursed through sludge,
Till on the haunting flares we turned our backs
And towards our distant rest began to trudge.
Men marched asleep. Many had lost their boots   5
But limped on, blood-shod. All went lame; all blind;
Drunk with fatigue; deaf even to the hoots
Of tired, outstripped Five-Nines that dropped behind.

Gas! GAS! Quick, boys!—An ecstasy of fumbling,
Fitting the clumsy helmets just in time;   10
But someone still was yelling out and stumbling
And flound'ring like a man in fire or lime . . .
Dim, through the misty panes and thick green light,
As under a green sea, I saw him drowning.

In all my dreams, before my helpless sight,   15
He plunges at me, guttering, choking, drowning.

If in some smothering dreams you too could pace
Behind the wagon that we flung him in,

And watch the white eyes writhing in his face,
His hanging face, like a devil's sick of sin; 20
If you could hear, at every jolt, the blood
Come gargling from the froth-corrupted lungs,
Obscene as cancer, bitter as the cud
Of vile, incurable sores on innocent tongues,—
My friend, you would not tell with such high zest 25
To children ardent for some desperate glory,
The old Lie: Dulce et decorum est
Pro patria mori.

i sing of Olaf glad and big

e. e. cummings (1894–1962)

i sing of Olaf glad and big
whose warmest heart recoiled at war:
a conscientious object-or

his wellbelovéd colonel(trig
westpointer most succinctly bred) 5
took erring Olaf soon in hand;
but—though an host of overjoyed
noncoms(first knocking on the head
him)do through icy waters roll
that helplessness which others stroke 10
with brushes recently employed
anent this muddy toiletbowl,
while kindred intellects evoke
allegiance per blunt instruments—
Olaf(being to all intents 15
a corpse and wanting any rag
upon what God unto him gave)
responds,without getting annoyed
"I will not kiss your f.ing flag"

straightway the silver bird looked grave 20
(departing hurriedly to shave)

27. **Dulce ... mori:** It is sweet and fitting to die for one's country.

but—though all kinds of officers
(a yearning nation's blueeyed pride)
their passive prey did kick and curse
until for wear their clarion   25
voices and boots were much the worse,
and egged the firstclassprivates on
his rectum wickedly to tease
by means of skilfully applied
bayonets roasted hot with heat—   30
Olaf(upon what were once knees)
does almost ceaselessly repeat
"there is some s. I will not eat"

our president,being of which
assertions duly notified   35
threw the yellowsonofabitch
into a dungeon,where he died

Christ(of His mercy infinite)
i pray to see;and Olaf,too

preponderatingly because   40
unless statistics lie he was
more brave than me:more blond than you.

THE KNOWN SOLDIER

Kenneth Patchen (b. 1911)

The balancing spaces are not disturbed
By the yes or no of these cantering brutes.
Frequently another hate-stained robe is placed
On the unriddling skeleton of man's labor
To destroy his life-enchanted animal;   5
Then do the hordes of murder howl
On the solemn islands of death.
But these unsorrowing angels
Still hover above my city,
And they pick golden fruit   10
On the orchard slopes of our destiny.

We cannot wish to—it seems—hear confessions
That teach innocence; we are not possessed
Of mercy enough to pardon those whom evil
Has not fattened, whose use has not kissed guns.   15
What is this crazy croon of nobleness,
Of ancient human wisdom and honor?
What majesty itches on the grinning tongues
Of these who have died
That men might not live?   20

A TRIP TO OMAHA
(Normandy 6.VI.44)

John William Corrington (b. 1932)

  hamlet would have laughed
    his
      tragic socks down
    his
      byzantine eyes   5
    chips of sullen color
    crammed full of politics
  would
    have gusted sympathy

if he had seen us mincing   10
    in the surf
      like
    balletgirls armed to the
    tits
      and some shy admirers   15
    tossing roses from the wings
    that bloomed instant red and
    wonderful
scattering iron petals on the sandy
    stage ahead   20
and we thinking
    —drench krauts with poison
    truth outrage bears
    sling bulls arrow eagles
      lisp banners   25

        wave travellers to the bourn
    all the lights in the world were on
        and shattering
            above
        before us   30
            spewing hedges
        rivers mad with summer
            a too too solid
        continent ahead
                to cultivate   35
                    somehow
    and thinking finally
                —dying is a
    bitch
            and perhaps   40
                the
                    goddess
                        of
                            love

POEMS OF BLACK AMERICAN PROTEST

IF WE MUST DIE

Claude McKay (1891–1948)

If we must die, let it not be like hogs
Hunted and penned in an inglorious spot,
While round us bark the mad and hungry dogs,
Making their mock at our accursed lot.
If we must die, O let us nobly die,   5
So that our precious blood may not be shed
In vain; then even the monsters we defy
Shall be constrained to honor us though dead!
O kinsmen! we must meet the common foe!
Though far outnumbered let us show us brave,   10
And for their thousand blows deal one deathblow!
What though before us lies the open grave?
Like men we'll face the murderous, cowardly pack,
Pressed to the wall, dying, but fighting back!

THE NEGRO'S TRAGEDY

Claude McKay

It is the Negro's tragedy I feel
Which binds me like a heavy iron chain,
It is the Negro's wounds I want to heal
Because I know the keenness of his pain.
Only a thorn-crowned Negro and no white   5
Can penetrate into the Negro's ken,
Or feel the thickness of the shroud of night
Which hides and buries him from other men.

So what I write is urged out of my blood.
There is no white man who could write my book,   10
Though many think their story should be told
Of what the Negro people ought to brook.
Our statesmen roam the world to set things right.
This Negro laughs and prays to God for light!

THE LYNCHING

Claude McKay

His Spirit in smoke ascended to high heaven.
His father, by the cruelest way of pain,
Had bidden him to his bosom once again;
The awful sin remained still unforgiven.
All night a bright and solitary star   5
(Perchance the one that ever guided him,
Yet gave him up at last to Fate's wild whim)
Hung pitifully o'er the swinging char.

Day dawned, and soon the mixed crowds came to view
The ghastly body swaying in the sun.   10
The women thronged to look, but never a one
Showed sorrow in her eyes of steely blue;
And little lads, lynchers that were to be,
Danced round the dreadful thing in fiendish glee.

LET AMERICA BE AMERICA AGAIN

Langston Hughes (1902–1967)

Let America be America again.
Let it be the dream it used to be.
Let it be the pioneer on the plain
Seeking a home where he himself is free.

(America never was America to me.)

Let America be the dream the dreamers dreamed—
Let it be that great strong land of love
Where never kings connive or tyrants scheme
That any man be crushed by one above.

(It never was America to me.)

O, let my land be a land where Liberty
Is crowned with no false patriotic wreath,
But opportunity is real, and life is free,
Equality is in the air we breathe.

(There's never been equality for me,
Nor freedom in this "homeland of the free.")

Say who are you that mumbles in the dark?
And who are you that draws your veil across the stars?

I am the poor white, fooled and pushed apart,
I am the Negro bearing slavery's scars.
I am the red man driven from the land,
I am the immigrant clutching the hope I seek—
And finding only the same old stupid plan
Of dog eat dog, of mighty crush the weak.

I am the young man, full of strength and hope,
Tangled in that ancient endless chain
Of profit, power, gain, of grab the land!
Of grab the gold!
Of grab the ways of satisfying need!
Of work the men! Of take the pay!
Of owning everything for one's own greed!

I am the farmer, bondsman to the soil.
I am the worker sold to the machine.
I am the Negro, servant to you all.

I am the people, worried, hungry, mean—
Hungry yet today despite the dream.
Beaten yet today—O, Pioneers!
I am the man who never got ahead,
The poorest worker bartered through the years.

Yet I'm the one who dreamt our basic dream
In that Old World while still a serf of kings.
Who dreamt a dream so strong, so brave, so true,
That even yet its mighty daring sings
In every brick and stone, in every furrow turned
That's made America the land it has become.
O, I'm the man who sailed those early seas
In search of what I meant to be my home—
For I'm the one who left dark Ireland's shore,
And Poland's plain, and England's grassy lea,
And torn from Black Africa's strand I came
To build a "homeland of the free."

The free?

A dream—
Still beckoning to me!

O, let America be America again—
The land that never has been yet—
And yet must be—
The land where every man is free.
The land that's mine—
The poor man's, Indian's, Negro's ME—
Who made America,
Whose sweat and blood, whose faith and pain,
Whose hand at the foundry, whose plow in the rain,
Must bring back our mighty dream again.
Sure, call me any ugly name you choose—
The steel of freedom does not stain.
From those who live like leeches on the people's lives,
We must take back our land again,
America!

O, yes,
I say it plain,
America never was America to me,
And yet I swear this oath—
America will be!

An ever-living seed, 75
Its dream
Lies deep in the heart of me.

We, the people, must redeem
Our land, the mines, the plants, the rivers,
The mountains and the endless plain— 80
All, all the stretch of these great green states—
And make America again!

A BROWN GIRL DEAD

Countee Cullen (1903–1946)

With two white roses on her breasts,
   White candles at head and feet,
Dark Madonna of the grave she rests;
   Lord Death has found her sweet.

Her mother pawned her wedding ring 5
   To lay her out in white;
She'd be so proud she'd dance and sing
   To see herself tonight.

SCOTTSBORO, TOO, IS WORTH ITS SONG

A POEM TO AMERICAN POETS

Countee Cullen

I said:
   Now will the poets sing,—
   Their cries go thundering
   Like blood and tears
   Into the nation's ears, 5

Scottsboro, Too, Is Worth Its Song. The Scottsboro Boys were a group of black men accused of raping a white woman and ultimately convicted and executed. They are compared in this poem with the celebrated contemporary case of Sacco and Vanzetti, two white immigrants convicted—perhaps wrongly —of murder after a trial that had political overtones. They were both executed amid international protest—something no one provided for the Scottsboro Boys.

Like lightning dart
Into the nation's heart.
Against disease and death and all things fell,
And war,
Their strophes rise and swell 10
To jar
The foe smug in his citadel.

Remembering their sharp and pretty
Tunes for Sacco and Vanzetti,
I said: 15
Here too's a cause divinely spun
For those whose eyes are on the sun,
Here in epitome
Is all disgrace
And epic wrong, 20
Like wine to brace
The minstrel heart, and blare it into song.

Surely, I said,
Now will the poets sing.
 But they have raised no cry. 25
 I wonder why.

BETWEEN THE WORLD AND ME

Richard Wright (1908–1960)

And one morning while in the woods I stumbled suddenly
 upon the thing,
Stumbled upon it in a grassy clearing guarded by scaly oaks
 and elms.
And the sooty details of the scene rose, thrusting themselves
 between the world and me. . . .
There was a design of white bones slumbering forgottenly
 upon a cushion of ashes.
There was a charred stump of a sapling pointing a blunt
 finger accusingly at the sky. 5
There were torn tree limbs, tiny veins of burnt leaves, and a
 scorched coil of greasy hemp;

A vacant shoe, an empty tie, a ripped shirt, a lonely hat, and
a pair of trousers stiff with black blood.
And upon the trampled grass were buttons, dead matches,
butt-ends of cigars and cigarettes, peanut shells, a drained
gin-flask, and a whore's lipstick;
Scattered traces of tar, restless arrays of feathers, and the
lingering smell of gasoline.
And through the morning air the sun poured yellow surprise
into the eye sockets of a stony skull. . . .   10
And while I stood my mind was frozen with a cold pity for
the life that was gone.
The ground gripped my feet and my heart was circled by icy
walls of fear—
The sun died in the sky; a night wind muttered in the grass
and fumbled the leaves in the trees; the woods poured
forth the hungry yelping of hounds, the darkness screamed
with thirsty voices; and the witnesses rose and lived:
The dry bones stirred, rattled, lifted, melting themselves into
my bones.
The grey ashes formed flesh firm and black, entering into my
flesh.   15
The gin-flask passed from mouth to mouth; cigars and cigarettes glowed, the whore smeared the lipstick red upon
her lips,
And a thousand faces swirled around me, clamoring that my
life be burned. . . .
And then they had me, stripped me, battering my teeth into
my throat till I swallowed my own blood.
My voice was drowned in the roar of their voices, and my
black wet body slipped and rolled in their hands as they
bound me to the sapling.
And my skin clung to the bubbling hot tar, falling from me
in limp patches.   20
And the down and quills of the white feathers sank into my
raw flesh, and I moaned in my agony.
Then my blood was cooled mercifully, cooled by a baptism of
gasoline.
And in a blaze of red I leaped to the sky as pain rose like
water, boiling my limbs.
Panting, begging I clutched childlike, clutched to the hot sides
of death.
Now I am dry bones and my face a stony skull staring in
yellow surprise at the sun. . . .   25

JONATHAN'S SONG
Owen Dodson (b. 1914)

A Negro Saw the Jewish Pageant, "We Will Never Die"
For Sol Gordon

I am a part of this:
Four million starving
And six million dead:
I am flesh and bone of this.

I have starved
In the secret alleys of my heart
And died in my soul
Like Ahab at the white whale's mouth.

The twisted cross desire
For final annihilation
Of my race of sufferers:
I am Abel, too.

Because my flesh is whole
Do not think that it signifies life.
I am the husk, believe me.
The rest is dead, remember.

I am a part of this
Memorial to suffering,
Militant strength:
I am a Jew.

Jew is not a race
Any longer—but a condition.
All the desert flowers have thorns;
I am bleeding in the sand.

Take me for your own David:
My father was not cruel,
I will sing your psalms,
I have learned them by heart.

I have loved you as a child,
We pledged in blood together.
The union is not strange,
My brother and my lover.

There was a great scent of death
In the garden when I was born.
Now it is certain: 35
Love me while you can.

The wedding is powerful as battle,
Singular, dread, passionate, loud,
Ahab screaming and the screaming whale
And the destination among thorns. 40

Love is a triple desire:
Flesh, freedom, hope:
No wanton thing is allowed.
I will sing thy psalms, all thy psalms,
Take me while you can. 45

from AWARD

Ray Durem (1915–1963)

[A Gold Watch to the FBI Man (who has followed me) for 25 Years.]

Well, old spy
looks like I
led you down some pretty blind alleys,
took you on several trips to Mexico,
fishing in the high Sierras, 5
jazz at the Philharmonic.
You've watched me all your life,
I've clothed your wife,
put your two sons through college,
what good has it done? 10
Sun keeps rising every morning.
Ever see me buy an Assistant President,
Or close a school?
Or lend money to Somoza?
I bought some afterhours whiskey in L.A. 15
but the Chief got his pay.
I ain't killed no Koreans,
or fourteen-year-old boys in Mississippi,
neither did I bomb Guatemala,
or lend guns to shoot Algerians. 20

I admit I took a Negro child
to a white rest room in Texas,
but she was my daughter, only three,
and she had to pee,
and I just didn't know what to do,   25
would you?
See, I'm so light, it don't seem right
to go to the colored rest room;
my daughter's brown, and folks frown on that in Texas,
I just don't know how to go to the bathroom in the free world!   30

THE IDEA OF ANCESTRY

Etheridge Knight (b. 1933)

I

Taped to the wall of my cell are 47 pictures; 47 black
faces: my father, mother, grandmothers (1 dead), grand
fathers (both dead), brothers, sisters, uncles, aunts,
cousins (1st & 2nd), nieces, and nephews. They stare
across the space at me sprawling on my bunk.   5

I know their dark eyes, they know mine. I know their style,
they know mine. I am all of them, they are all of me;
they are farmers, I am a thief, I am me, they are thee.

I have at one time or another been in love with my mother,
1 grandmother, 2 sisters, 2 aunts (1 went to the asylum),   10
and 5 cousins. I am now in love with a 7 yr old niece
(she sends me letters written in large block print, and
her picture is the only one that smiles at me).

I have the same name as 1 grandfather, 3 cousins, 3 nephews,
and 1 uncle. The uncle disappeared when he was 15, just took 15
off and caught a freight (they say). He's discussed each year
when the family has a reunion, he causes uneasiness in
the clan, he is an empty space. My father's mother, who is 93
and who keeps the Family Bible with everybody's birth dates
(and death dates) in it, always mentions him. There is no   20
place in her Bible for "whereabouts unknown."

II

Each Fall the graves of my grandfathers call me, the brown
hills and red gullies of mississippi send out their electric
messages, galvanizing my genes. Last yr/like a salmon quitting
the cold ocean—leaping and bucking up his birthstream/I   25
hitchiked my way from L.A. with 16 caps in my pocket and a
monkey on my back. and I almost kicked it with the kinfolks.
I walked barefooted in my grandmother's backyard/I smelled the old
land and the woods/I sipped cornwhiskey from fruit jars with the
    men/
I flirted with the women/I had a ball till the caps ran out   30
and my habit came down. That night I looked at my grandmother
and split/my guts were screaming for junk/but I was almost
contented/I had almost caught up with me.
(The next day in Memphis I cracked a croaker's crib for a fix.)

This yr there is a gray stone wall damming my stream, and when   35
the falling leaves stir my genes, I pace my cell or flop on my bunk
and stare at 47 black faces across the space. I am all of them,
they are all of me, I am me, they are thee, and I have no sons
to float in the space between.

VICE

Imamu Amiri Baraka (LeRoi Jones) (b. 1934)

Sometimes I feel I have to express myself
and then, whatever it is I have to express
falls out of my mouth like flakes of ash
from a match book that the drunken guest
at the grey haired jew lady's birthday party has   5
set on fire, for fun & to ease the horrible boredom.

& when these flakes amass, I make serious collages
or empty them (feinting a gratuitous act) out the window
on the heads of the uncurious puerto rican passersby.

ACT I. The celibate bandit pees in the punch bowl.   10

34. croaker's crib: a doctor's safe for drug storage.

(curious image) occurring friday evening, a house
full of middle class women & a photogenic baker.
Baby bear has eaten her porridge, had her bath, shit
& gone to sleep. Smoke rises (strange for mid-summer)
out of a strange little shack in the middle of the   15
torn down cathedral. Everything seems to be light green.
I suppose, a color of despair or wretchedness. Anyway,
everything is light green, even the curling little hairs
on the back of my hand, and the old dog scar glinting
in the crooked (green, light green) rays of an unshaded bulb.   20

There doesn't seem to be any act 2. The process is stopped.
Functional, as a whip, a strong limb broken off in the gale
lying twisty & rotten, unnoticed in my stone back yard.
All this means nothing is happening to me (in this world).

I suppose some people are having a ball. Organized fun.   25
Pot Smokers Institute is going on an outing tomorrow; my
corny sister, in her fake bohemian pants, is borrowing something
else. (A prestige item). These incomprehensible dullards!

Asked to be special, & alive in the mornings, if they are green
& I am still alive, (& green) hovering above all the things I   30
seem to want to be a part of (curious smells, the high-noon idea
of life .... a crowded train station where they broadcast a slice,
just one green slice, of some glamourous person's life).
& I can't isolate my pleasures. All the things I can talk about
mean nothing to me.   35

This is *not* rage. (I am not that beautiful!) Only immobile coughs
& gestures towards somethings I don't understand. If I were lucky
enough to still be an adolescent, I'd just attribute these weird
singings in my intestine to sex, & slink off merrily to mastur
bate. Mosaic of disorder I own but cannot recognize. Mist in me.   40

There must be some great crash in the slinky world: MYSTIC
     CURE...
Cunning panacea of the mind. The faith of it. the singed hairs
of human trust, corrupt & physical as a disease. A glass stare.

Resolution, for the quick thrust of epee, to force your opponent
cringing against the wall, not in anger, but unfettered happiness   45
while your lady is watching from the vined balcony, your triumph.

& years after, you stand in subways watching your invincible hand
bring the metal to bear again & again, when you are old & the lady,
(o, fond memories we hide in our money belts, & will not spend)
the lady, you young bandits who have not yet stolen your first
   purse   50
the lady will be dead.

And if you are alone (if there is something in you so cruel)

You will wonder at the extravagance

of youth.

THE NEW SHERIFF

Imamu Amiri Baraka (LeRoi Jones)

There is something
in me so cruel, so
silent. It hesitates
to sit on the grass
with the young white   5
            virgins
of my time. The blood-
letter, clothed in what
it is. Elemental essence,
animal grace, not that, but   10
a rude stink of color
huger, more vast, than
this city suffocating. Red
street. Waters noise
in the ear, inside   15
the hard bone
of the brain. Inside
the soft white meat
of the feelings. Inside
your flat white stomach   20
I move my tongue

off d pig

Ishmael Reed (b. 1938)

for f duvalier who maintained d trust

background:
    a reckoning has left
some minds hard hit . they blow,
crying for help , out to sea like
dead trees & receding housetops . i   5
can sympathize . i mean , all of us
have had our dreams broken over some
body's head . those scratched phono
graph records of d soul .
we   10
    all have been zombed along
d way of a thousand eyes glowing at midnite .
    our pupils have been vacant
    our hands have been icey &
    we have walked with a d tell tale   15
    lurch
all of us have had this crisis of consciousness
which didnt do nobody no good
or a search for identity
which didnt make no never mind neither   20

at those times we got down on our knees & call
ed up the last resort . seldom do we bother him
for he is doing heavy duty for d universe . only
once has he been disturbed & this was to
    put some color into a woman's blues   25
he came like a black fire engine spun & sped
by khepera
he is very pressed for time &
do nots play

he apologises for being late   30
he rolls up his sleeves & rests his bird
he starts to say a few words to d crowd
he sees d priests are out to lunch so he
just goes on head with what he got to do

off d pig. The title means kill the cop. The references to Thoth (line 36), Osiris (line 48), and Ra (line 61)—all Egyptian deities—suggest a link with ancient black culture.

out of d night blazing from ceciltaylor pianos 35
Thoth sets down his fine black self
d first blak scribe
d one who fixes up their art
d one who draws d circle with his pen
d man who beats around d bush 40
d smeller outer of d fiend
    jehovah-apep jumpo up bad on
    d set
    but squeals as spears bring him
    down 45
a curfew is lifted on soul
friendly crowds greet one another in d streets
Osiris struts his stuff & dos d thang to words
 hidden beneath d desert
chorus—just like a legendary train that 50
 one has heard of but never seen
 broke all records in its prime
 takes you to where you want to go right fast

 i hears you woo woo o neo american hoo doo
  church 55
 i hears you woo woo o neo american hoo doo church
 i hears you woo woo o neo american hoo doo
  church
 i hears you woo woo o neo american hoo doo
  church 60
 amen-ra a-men ra a-man ra

A POEM LOOKING FOR A READER

Don L. Lee (b. 1942)

to be read with a love consciousness

black is not
all inclusive,
there are other colors,
color her warm and womanly,

color her feeling and life,
color her a gibran poem and 4
　women of simone.
children will give her color
paint her the color of her
man.

most of all color her
love
a remembrance of life
a true reflection
that we
will
move u will move with

i want
u
a fifty minute call to
　blackwomanworld:
　　hi baby,
　　how u doin?
need u.
listening to
young-holt's, *please sunrise, please.*

to give i'll give
most personal.
what about the other
scenes: children playing in vacant lots,
　　or like the first time u knowingly
　　　kissed a girl,
　　was it joy or just beautifully beautiful.
i
remember at 13
reading chester himes'
cast the first stone and
the eyes of momma when she caught me: read on,
　son.

　　6. gibran: Kalil Gibran, author of *The Prophet.*　**7. simone:** Simone de Beauvoir, author of *The Second Sex.*　**26. young-holt's:** the Young-Holt Trio, a jazz group.　**36. chester himes:** American author of *Cotton Comes to Harlem* and *Run Man Run.*

```
        how will u come:                                          40
            like a soulful strut in a two-piece beige o-rig'i-nal,
            or afro-down with a beat in yr/walk?
        how will love come:
            painless and deep like a razor cut
            or like some cheap 75¢ movie;                         45
            i think not.
        will she be the woman
        other men will want
        or
        will her beauty be                                        50
        accented with my name on it?
        she will come as she would
        want her man to come.
        she'll come,
        she'll come.                                              55
        i
        never wrote a love letter
        but
        that doesn't mean
        i                                                         60
        don't love.
```

from BACK OF THE BUS

Anonymous

NEW SOUTHERN FOLKSONG

If you miss me on the picket line
    And you can't find me nowhere
Come on over to the city jail
    I'll be rooming over there.

If you miss me in the freedom fight   5
    And you can't find me nowhere
Come on over to the graveyard
    I'll be buried over there.

QUESTIONS

1. What do the poems protesting war and the poems of black protest have in common? Do you see them as all alike or as poems whose diversity makes it impossible to link them together? Explain your reasoning.
2. In what ways, technically or otherwise, do these two kinds of protest poetry differ from one another? Are there any poetic techniques that one kind of poetry uses that the other kind could benefit from using?
3. Choose a single poem from either protest group. Explain why you feel it might be difficult or impossible to discuss it fairly outside of the context of protest. What causes the problems that might make this so?
4. Examine the war protest poems and comment on them for the attention they pay to technique. Is their attention to technique a strength or a weakness? Are there any poems that seem more consciously technical to you than others? Explain. Does their success for you depend on technical achievement?
5. What use do the poets of black protest make of established technique? Are the best of these poems successful due to their technical achievement? If not, what makes them successful?

The Poetry of Other Cultures

Since the period of the late Renaissance—the 1300s and 1400s—Africa has been colonized by a number of European countries. Portugal, France, England, and to a lesser extent, Germany, have left indelible marks on African culture. Even a good deal of African poetry has been written in non-African languages, particularly in French and English. And yet, there are profoundly African considerations in much of the poetry that follows. Images that could come only from Africa—evocations of the historical plundering of the continent, the fierce pride and independence that comes to developing nations—mark this poetry as being quite out of western traditions. The western reader must adapt to the premises of the African poet—a task he will find easier if he has been exposed to the protest poetry of black Americans, since both poetries have a great deal in common.

In general, the poetry we have selected is modern. It comes from a number of nations—principally black—in different sections of Africa. Had we included older poetry of these nations, we could have chosen from a wide range of poems, particularly narrative folk poetry—a form Africa has long been noted for. Modern poetry tends to be frank, direct, and energetic. Formally, there is nothing for which the western reader is unprepared. However, in order to appreciate these works fully, the western reader must presume what the poet presumed: a culture that has been plundered for almost a thousand years. The poets represented here are constantly aware of the cultural burden they bear, and it is always present in their work—even in the silence of those moments when they try to forget.

Chinese poetry, on the other hand, speaks across the ages from generation to generation—and with what, to the western ear, seems the same voice. It is not easy, even in translation, to tell whether a poem was written in 1925 or 1625, by Mao Tse-Tung or by Tu Fu. Experts can easily tell, of course, but most of us can hardly pretend to that expertise. For us, Li Po, Tu Fu, Tu Mu, and other masters of Chinese poetry are great, but they are not distinguishable until we have considerable familiarity with their subjects and their styles.

Luckily, and perhaps paradoxically, we are better able to talk about the character and quality of Chinese poetry because the most important school of poetry in the English language today is that of the Imagists (pages 314–35). The Imagists were heavily influenced by the translations of Ezra Pound, who found in Chinese poetry the attention to image, the calmness, and the careful articulation of theme without direct "statement" that he felt should characterize his own work. Because of this, the poetry we have selected will not look totally foreign to most western readers. Yet it may be something of a shock to see that what interested the older poets still interests the most modern ones. For the Chinese poet, the daily events of his society are only a ripple on the surface of a culture that is immeasurably deep and illimitably profound.

In Chinese poetry, both the form and the technique tend to

baffle the western reader. It is difficult for us to understand how a poet can take a simple image, state it carefully, then juxtapose it with a seemingly unrelated observation about life and expect that to be a poem. We are used to poems that are sentences—developed and polished so they say something with great economy. It is hard for us to accept the fact that a moon shining on still waters will mean something important by itself. Granted, the Imagists have helped us recognize this limitation in our cultural background, but it is still not easy to overcome it. The bafflement of the western reader when confronted with Chinese poetry can be quickly illustrated, not with a Chinese, but with a Japanese poem. Here is the most famous example of Japanese haiku—"The Old Pond," by Bashō. It was written in March 1685.

> The ancient pond!
> A frog plunged—splash!

It is not easy for the western reader to understand why this poem is known to virtually every Japanese or why Bashō himself discussed it with his disciples years after its composition and felt it to be the cornerstone of his work. Clearly, conventional critical methods cannot cope with a poem of this nature—even in its native language:

> Furuike ya/Kawazu tobikomu/Mizu no oto.

The only alternative for the western reader is to immerse himself in that particular form and style. Anyone who had read a thousand haiku would find "The Old Pond" much less baffling than a person who had read none. Also, anyone with a knowledge of Bashō's life would find the poem a different experience from a person who knows nothing of Bashō at all.

For the Chinese poets, we cannot provide much in the way of biographical information—certainly none that would be useful to a reading of the poems that follow. But we can provide the poetry itself, from the earliest times to the present, forming a continuum that would not be possible in the poetry of most other cultures. The western reader should read the poetry, then reread it. He must not expect it to be what western poetry is nor to do what western poetry does; he must take it on its own terms. And his reading of the poetry ought to aim at discovering what the terms are. Only by reading will he discover them.

AFRICAN POEMS

PRAYER WITHOUT ECHO

Tshakatumba (Modern)

Why this deafness
why this dull silence
at the mechanical Our Fathers
of my race molded
from the alloy of suffering   5
suffering as ancient as the world
Oh gray-beard God
grinding the supposedly pagan Negro
with teeth of death.

Listen to me God of Moses   10
why the extermination
of the first-born males of the country
of Ra
White Nile bloody Nile
Zambezi beaten but unsettled   15
Deaf ears blind eyes
of the Wallaces who with their hounds
trained hounds track me
throwing bowels to the sun
sun with the narcotic scent   20
in the beaks of scavengers
bowels disappear

Toward a God unmoved by pity
at the *misereres* of a race
mounting without echo at high noon   25
tropical noon poor people
your emancipation depends on you
but the spirituals, fruits born
of sad labors, could move
neither You nor Your puritans   30
and I say to my people
that the redemption of the fearful race

13. Ra: Egypt.   **17. Wallaces:** George Wallace, Governor of Alabama.
24. misereres: prayers for deliverance.

lies within itself
How many pens denounce the tormenting
how many voices raise a pure echo 35
from the black temples of the black world
how many infants die
nourishing the hope of a better day
waving the flag of deliverance
deliverance of a race betrayed 40
with Your knowledge, in Your sight, in Your name.

    Translated from the French by Lee Jacobus

NOSTALGIA

Sembène Ousmane (Modern)

Diouana
Our Sister
Born on the banks of our Casamance
Away goes the water of our river King
Toward other horizons, 5
And the thundering tidal bore lashes the flanks of our Africa.

Diouana
Our Sister
The slave-ships no longer pitch at the reef
The terror, the despair, the bewildering raid 10
The cries, the screaming are hushed
In our memories the echoes resound
Diouana,
The reef remains.
Centuries are added to centuries 15
The chains are broken
The pillories devoured by termites
On the flanks of our Mother
Africa
Stand the slave-houses 20

 1. Diouana: an exploited Senegalese maid; ultimately a suicide. **3. Casamance:** a river in Senegal.

(These houses are monuments to our history)
Diouana, proud African woman
Do you carry into the tomb
The golden rays of our setting sun
The dance of the ears of new corn   25
The waltz of the rice-cuttings

Diouana
Our Sister
Goddess of the night
The perfume of our forest   30
Our nights of rejoicing
Our rude and miserable life
Are preferable to servitude
Nostalgia for the homeland
Nostalgia for liberty   35
Diouana
Light of our coming dawns
You are a victim, like our ancestors
Of barter
You die from transplanting   40
Like the cocoa and banana trees
Decorating the sidewalks in Antibes
Those transplanted and sterile trees.

Diouana
Our Sister   45
Splendor of the mornings to come
One day—a day very soon—
We will say:
These forests
These fields   50
These rivers
This earth
Our flesh
Our bones
Belong to us   55
Image of Our Mother Africa
We grieve over your bartered body
You are our
Mother
Diouana.   60

                          Translated from the French

THE DREAM OF AFRICAN UNITY
Boevi Zankli (Modern)

O Mother Africa O,
We Africans dream a dream O,
It is a dream of African unity O.

O Mother Africa, O,
We your sons and daughters 5
Promise you O,
We will always dream of African Unity O
We will always pray for its realisation O.
We will always work assiduously, for its fulfilment O,
    Night and Day O. 10

We will always work life and death
    For its birth O,
We will always preach it O,
    From coast to coast O
    Shore to shore O 15
    And ports to ports O

From Cairo to Cape of Shaka,
From Dakar to Dar Es Salam,
    In hamlets and cities,
    In market places, 20
    In the valleys of Africa,
    In the caves of Africa,

We will always sing it aloud O,
From our various tongues O;
We will play it 25
On our gourds O,
On our balanjis O,
On our koras strings O
With the best of African
Sweet-symphonic-harmony. 30

We will always dream
Of African Unity O,
In our sleeps O,
    In our works O,
    In our plays O, 35

We will always paint it
    On canvas O,

>   We will always carve it
>   On woods O,
>   We will always mold it   40
>   In concretes O,
>   We will always cast it
>   In metals O,
>   And
>   Set it in colorful mosaic O,   45
>   Until the day of total independence,
>   For Balkanised Africa O,
>   Oh Mother Africa O,
>   Forward to the Union Government O,
>   For one Africa we dream O,   50
>
>   We promise you Mother Africa O,
>   We pledge that our dreams
>   Will not be an empty dream O,
>   We promise you that if it
>   Is a matter of spilling our   55
>   Black blood, for its realisation,
>   We are ready to go to battle O
>
>   O Mother Africa O,
>   We promise you O, we shall
>   Keep our oath to you O.   60
>   May we all live to see the birth of
>   The glorious dream of our dreams O,
>   African Unity O,
>   African Unity O,
>   African Unity for ever. O   65
>   Yah O Yah O Yah O.

THE IMAGE OF GOD

John M. Ruganda (Modern)

> It is the sweet death
> Of the God who dies

47. Balkanised Africa: refers to the way in which the Balkans—Greece, Bulgaria, Yugoslavia, Albania, and parts of Turkey—were arbitrarily broken up into countries by international agreement; for several decades early in the twentieth century the Balkans were the political hot spot of Europe.

In Man's birth,
That is the spring of Kato's freedom,
Alike in vanity and divinity; 5
And it is the victory
Of the God who is
When man dies
That impels Kato,
Not to want heaven, 10
But the eternal form of pleasure:
For God is
Because man lives.

DEATH

Ezekiel Mphahlele (Modern)

You want to know?
My mother died at 45
at 42 my brother followed.
You want to know?
She cleaned the houses of white folk, 5
and washed their bodily dirt
out of the baths.
One night a coma took her,
and he—
cancer hounded him two years 10
and rolled him in the dust.
You want to know?
My grandma left at 80,
she also washed her years away
and saw them flow 15
into the drain
with the white man's scum.
Many more from our tree have fallen—
known and unknown.

4. **Kato:** the Philippino houseboy of the Green Hornet, the hero of an old radio serial.

.....and that white colossus   20
he was butchered by a man
they say is mad.

How often do I dream
my dearest dead stand across a river—
small and still I cannot traverse   25
to join them
and I try to call to them
and they wave and smile so distantly
receding beyond the water
that pulls me in   30
and spits me out into the dawn of the living.

.....and he was butchered
like a buffalo
after overseeing many a negro's execution.

You want to know—   35
why do I say all this?
what have they to do with us
the ones across the water?
How should I know?
These past two decades   40
death has been circling closer
and beating the air about me
like a flight of vultures
in a cruel age
when instruments of torture   45
can be found with any fool and tyrant,
churchman, all alike,
all out to tame the heretic, they say.

.....and they tell us
when that colossus fell   50
he did not even have a triple-worded
Roman chance

And so to kill a bug
they set a house on fire
to kill a fire   55

20. white colossus: a white slave overseer.   **51–52. triple-worded Roman chance:** a reference to Shakespeare's *Julius Caesar*; Caesar's last words were "et tu, Brute?" ("and you, too, Brutus?").

they flood a country
to save a country
drench the land in blood
to peg the frontiers of their colour madness
they'll herd us into ghettoes
jail us
kill us slowly
because we are the Attribute
that haunts their dreams
because *they* are the blazing neon lights
that will not let us be
because we are the children of their Sin
they'll try to erase the evidence
because their deeds are howling from a fog
beyond their reach.

. . . . .*and we laughed and danced
when news came of the death of that colossus
—the death of a beast of prey.*

What can we do with the ashes of a tyrant?
who will atone?
whose blood will pay for those of us who went
down under the tanks of fire?
And voices cried It's not enough,
a tyrant dead is not enough!
Vengeance is mine and yours and his,
says the testament of man
nailed to the boulder of pain.

. . . . .*and they say the butcher's mad
who sank the knife into the tyrant's neck
while the honourable men
who rode his tanks of fire
looked on
as if they never heard of giants die
as they had lived,
and all about the frog who burst
when he pushed his energy
beyond the seams of his own belly.*

What if I go as the unknown soldier
or attended by a buzzing fly?
what if my carcass were soaked in organ music,
or my ancestors had borne me home?

I hear already
echoes from a future time of voices
coming from a wounded bellowing multitude
cry Who will atone   100
Who will atone?

You want to know?—
because I nourish
a deadly life within
my madness shall have blood.   105

UNCLE TOM'S BLACK HUMOUR

Taban Lo Liyong (Modern)

For Michael Dennis Browne

let us now praise famous men
                  our past masters
and why not

after all there are many sides to the same thing   5
               were beneficial side effects
and we can now afford to laugh

we cost many the heads the crowns
shaky french cabinets stumbled and fell   10

i was taught a tongue
with which to curse prospero and woo miranda
since ariel was so airy
he had no room for a heart

well mr I admired your gun   15
but you could not my magic
now i can make your gun make
but do you know my magic
to your one I have two

12, 13. prospero, miranda, ariel: characters from *The Tempest* by Shakespeare.

summers come
you go for tan
from eating you divert oil for rubbing
you strive to get as dark as i am
but can you
my blackness is original
inimitable desirable but induplicable
i will never go to sunbathe
youll never catch me exposing myself to snow
in order to become white
as far as color is concerned
i am content

now about hair
short hair is best
and thats what i have
as any navy man
my teeth are just as white
as mungo found them
as strong as
livingstones wife's were

now ive taken to growing cocoa
for chocolate
and sugar cane
for sugar and candies
with these to cause a decay
of your teeth
the dentist collects them
and i give him gold
to fill the gaps
sweets or gold
i fill my purse

you may praise blue eyes
yes as color blue is blue
what about visibility

because i labored hard in the fields
now i am the best boxer
mohamed ali or no mohamed ali
we keep the championships

37, 39. mungo, livingstone: Mungo Park and Dr. David Livingstone are famous explorers of Africa.

in other sports too
the blacks are to the fore
with better coaching 60
to monopolise the medals
you brought great/dads here
few arrived
but we are many now
because of pleasure 65
or vigor
or ignorance of birth curb
we shall populate the earth

sexually
my prowess is proverbial 70
and you want your women spared
or deprived
perhaps
to save your grandsons
from seasonal sunexposure 75
let me coal black
mate your daughter lily white
and beget a merger race suitably tanned
and sink our oversights
and let nature adjust things 80

caliban smelled like fish
quoth trinculo
but a beast of burden has to smell something
if not fish he will smell food

man to man othello beat iago 85
in direct confrontation
it is the underhanded acts that derange the world

i hollered a lot under the yoke
and in revival meetings
by songs and dances and sways and handclappings 90
i can exorcise hoggish demons
but

81. caliban: a nonhuman character in *The Tempest;* disinherited from his island by Prospero, he is regarded by some as a model for the "native."
82. trinculo: a European who is in league with Caliban against Prospero.
85. othello: a black man; the hero of Shakespeare's *Othello.*   **Iago:** a white man; the villain of *Othello.*

now i can sing very well
and cut records
and act roles
and write
my big lips
are good for kissing
they are substantial
not diminutive

yes whitey i know what you have always wanted to
be black like me what with all my excellence in
baseball in football in basketball in jazz in boxing
and now even in westmorelands viet nam game how
could you look at me and not envy me

do what you may you will never become like me
you may bask in the suns or even go to the moon
to be nearer the sun but to be black like me you
will never be

have you known a confirmed culprit who is always
reprieved and then condoned thats UNCLE TOM have
you known of the freedom of nonregulation of your
own life you would if you were UNCLE TOM always
receiving orders and directions ever pondered the
lightness of possessing little to nothing see it
from me ever watched lions fighting all their days
in order to be one inch beyond the other and you
yourself never caring a damn about that race thats
my art if you have seen masters rise and fall in
the pursuit of an artificial life you would know
why i stay pat no butler ever served a hero the hero
is actually the butler himself thats me baby UNCLE
TOM

from the look of things too i am humble enough
to inherit heaven and when i inherit it i will
keep all of it to myself and my chillun and
we shall wear shoes and walk shoulder straight

you see i am not mean with gods heaven or
sumthin the trouble with the other people is that
they are so rich or mean they cant pass through

---

104. **westmoreland**: General William Westmoreland, the commander of United States troops in Vietnam.

the needless eye in the gate
me with my few aims and scanty possessions and little
vice (a little cursing is welcomed even in heaven
getting drunk on weekends too is not so bad since
it keeps one off major offenses borrowing from
the cellar or store or missus cupboard is not
bad at all since master can afford more easily)
i travel light and thats heavenly quality
jesuss apostles except judas knew that as well as
me

and one thing more i am not going to pitch for
the presidency of the united states either no sir
the spirit tells me i would make the best and thats
where the trouble lies i dont want to be shot at
no sir i dont want to have abdominal problems
or sleep in the walter reeds hospital

anyway i am a free man i dont want to ride in a
harmored car i want a big cadillac a convertible
in which to breeze and listen to a blaring duke
ellington jazz a big car makes all the difference
to a mistress who has to make a choice between
candidates moreover it has room for doing you know
what

some of my haunts arent even safe for hoover i
dont want my activities noted down no sir i just
want to be responsible to my appetites first
next my whimses third the defence of my master
and mistress

each public show of concern for their welfare endears
me more and more moreover miss sarah pays
me to keep from master her own secrets and master
doles me to keep missus in the dark thus i get
two bonus payments besides the threat of blackmail
i have retained the best team of permanent defence
my faults enjoy the rare state of everlasting
excuses and reprieves
AUNT JEMIMA she done teach young master how to be
man yes sir she done it yes maam he gone done it
never mind them talks about integration and other
shits and me i know my way around

154. **hoover:** J. Edgar Hoover, the former head of the FBI.

and master does all the worrying for us miss sarah
the children AUNT and UNCLE the undergrowth is
too good to be left i am a permanent parasite in
permanent dependence sheltered from the overhead
struggles by our towering master 175

after hes made billions from oil
or ford cars
he still eats through his mouth
like i do
goes to the toilet 180
like i do
get drunk
like i do
fuck missus
less than i do 185
so what the hell have i to worry about

THE LIMITS OF SUBMISSION

Faarah Nuur (?–1930)

Over and over again to people
I show abundant kindness.

If they are not satisfied,
I spread out bedding for them
And invite them to sleep. 5

If they are still not satisfied,
The milk of the camel whose name is Suub
I milk three times for them,
And tell them to drink it up.

If they are still not satisfied, 10
The homestead's ram
And the fat he-goat I kill for them.

If they are still not satisfied,
The plate from Aden
I fill with ghee for them. 15

The Limits of Submission. The poet may be thinking of a specific situation, since Nuur's group had been in submission to another group for generations. **15. ghee:** a delicacy made from butter; it is boiled and strained through cloth.

If they are still not satisfied,
A beautiful girl
And her bridal house I offer them.

If they are still not satisfied,
I select livestock also   20
And add them to the tribute.

If they are still not satisfied,
"Oh, brother-in-law, O Sultan, O King!"—
These salutations I lavish upon them.

If they are still not satisfied,   25
At the time of early morning prayers I prepare
The dark grey horse with black tendons,
And with the words "Praise to the Prophet" I take
The iron-shafted spear
And drive it through their ribs   30
So that their lungs spew out.
Then they are satisfied!

PRAYER TO THE MASKS

Léopold Sédar Senghor (b. 1906)

Masks! O Masks!
Black mask red mask, you black and white masks
Masks with the four points from which the Spirit blows
I greet you in the silence!
And not you the last, lion-headed Ancestor   5
You guard this place forbidden to all laughter of woman, to every
    smile that fades
You give forth this air of eternity wherein I breathe the breath
    of my Fathers.
Masks with maskless faces, bereft of every dimple as of every
    wrinkle
Who have fashioned this image, this face of mine leaning over
    the altar of white paper
In your image, hear me!   10

1. **Masks:** symbolize the past and the poet's ancestors (line 9).

Behold, Africa of the empires is dying—it is the agony of a
 pitiable princess
And also Europe to whom we are bound by the navel.
Fix your immutable eyes upon your children who are commanded
Who give their lives like the poor man his last garment.
May we answer Present at the rebirth of the World   15
As the leaven which is necessary to the white flour.
For who would teach rhythm to the dead world of machines and
 of cannons?
Who would raise the cry of joy to awaken the dead and the
 orphans at dawn?
Speak, who would restore the memory of life to the man with
 gutted hopes?
They call us the men of cotton, of coffee, of oil   20
They call us the men of death.
We are the men of dance, whose feet regain vigor in striking
 the hard earth.

Translated from the French

BREATH

Birago Diop (b. 1906)

Listen more to things
Than to words that are said.
The water's voice sings
And the flame cries
And the wind that brings   5
The woods to sighs
Is the breathing of the dead.

Those who are dead have never gone away.
They are in the shadows darkening around,
They are in the shadows fading into day,   10
The dead are not under the ground.
They are in the trees that quiver,
They are in the woods that weep,
They are in the waters of the rivers,

12. navel: suggests the rebirth of Africa out of the death throes of an older civilization; the same theme also figures in line 15.

They are in the waters that sleep. 15
They are in the crowds, they are in the homestead.
The dead are never dead.

    Listen more to things
    Than to words that are said.
    The water's voice sings 20
    And the flame cries
    And the wind that brings
    The woods to sighs
    Is the breathing of the dead.
    Who have not gone away 25
    Who are not under the ground
    Who are never dead.

Those who are dead have never gone away.
They are at the breast of the wife.
They are in the child's cry of dismay 30
And the firebrand bursting into life.
The dead are not under the ground.
They are in the fire that burns low
They are in the grass with tears to shed,
In the rock where whining winds blow 35
They are in the forest, they are in the homestead.
The dead are never dead.

    Listen more to things
    Than to words that are said.
    The water's voice sings 40
    And the flame cries
    And the wind that brings
    The woods to sighs
    Is the breathing of the dead.

And repeats each day 45
The Covenant where it is said
That our fate is bound to the law,
And the fate of the dead who are not dead
To the spirits of breath who are stronger than they.
We are bound to Life by this harsh law 50
And by this Covenant we are bound
To the deeds of the breathings that die
Along the bed and the banks of the river,
To the deeds of the breaths that quiver

In the rock that whines and the grasses that cry 55
To the deeds of the breathings that lie
In the shadow that lightens and grows deep
In the tree that shudders, in the woods that weep,
In the waters that flow and the waters that sleep,
To the spirits of breath which are stronger than they 60
That have taken the breath of the deathless dead
Of the dead who have never gone away
Of the dead who are not now under the ground.

    Listen more to things
    Than to words that are said. 65
    The water's voice sings
    And the flame cries
    And the wind that brings
    The woods to sighs
    Is the breathing of the dead. 70

              Translated from the French

AFRICA

David Diop (Modern)

Africa my Africa
Africa of proud warriors in the ancestral savannahs
Africa my grandmother sings of
Beside her distant river
I have never seen you 5
But my gaze is full of your blood
Your black blood spilt over the fields
The blood of your sweat
The sweat of your toil
The toil of slavery 10
The slavery of your children
Africa, tell me Africa,
Are you the back that bends
Lies down under the weight of humbleness?
The trembling back striped red 15
That says yes to the sjambok on the roads of noon?
Solemnly a voice answers me

"Impetuous child, that young and sturdy tree
That tree that grows
There splendidly alone among white and faded flowers   20
Is Africa, your Africa. It puts forth new shoots
With patience and stubbornness puts forth new shoots
Slowly its fruits grow to have
The bitter taste of liberty."

                              Translated from the French

THE LINES OF OUR HANDS
Bernard B. Dadié (b. 1916)

The lines of our hands
Are not parallel lines
Nor roads through the mountains
Nor fissures on tree trunks
Nor the scars of homeric fights.   5

The lines of our hands
Are not longitude lines

Nor furrows in the plains
Nor partings in the hair
Nor paths through the bush   10

No they are not
    gutters for grief
    channels for tears
    drainage for hate
    ropes for the hanged   15
    nor portions
    nor parts
    nor pieces
        of this . . . and that . . .

The lines of our hands   20
    not Yellow
    Black
    White
No they are not frontiers
Ditches between our villages   25
Cords to bind faggots of bitterness

The lines of our hands
Are the lines of Life,
　of Fate,
　of Heart,　　　　　　　　　　　　　　　30
　of Love.

Gentle bonds
To bind us
To one another
The living to the dead.　　　　　　　　　35

The lines of our hands
　not white
　not black
　not yellow

The lines of our hands　　　　　　　　　40
Bind the nosegays of our dreams.

　　　　　　　Translated from the French

PIANO AND DRUMS

Gabriel Okara (b. 1921)

When at break of day at a riverside
I hear jungle drums telegraphing
the mystic rhythm, urgent, raw
like bleeding flesh, speaking of
primal youth and the beginning,　　　　5
I see the panther ready to pounce,
the leopard snarling about to leap
and the hunters crouch with spears poised;

And my blood ripples, turns torrent,
topples the years and at once I'm　　　10
in my mother's lap a suckling;
at once I'm walking simple
paths with no innovations,

Piano and Drums. The piano and the drums symbolize European and African cultures respectively. Okara is bicultural and examines his indebtedness to each culture in this poem. His confusion—being between two cultures—is representative of that of many modern Africans.

    rugged, fashioned with the naked
    warmth of hurrying feet and groping hearts   15
    in green leaves and wild flowers pulsing.

    Then I hear a wailing piano
    solo speaking of complex ways
    in tear-furrowed concerto;
    of far-away lands   20
    and new horizons with
    coaxing diminuendo, counterpoint,
    crescendo. But lost in the labyrinth
    of its complexities, it ends in the middle
    of a phrase at a daggerpoint.   25

    And I lost in the morning mist
    of an age at a riverside keep
    wandering in the mystic rhythm
    of jungle drums and the concerto.

ANCESTRAL FACES

Kwesi Brew (b. 1928)

They sneaked into the limbo of time.
But could not muffle the gay jingling
Bells on the frothy necks
Of the sacrificial sheep that limped and nodded after them;
They could not hide the moss on the bald pate   5
Of their reverent heads;
And the gnarled barks of the *wawa* trees;
Nor the rust on the ancient state-swords;
Nor the skulls studded with grinning cowries;
They could not silence the drums,   10
The fibre of their souls and ours—
The drums that whisper to us behind black sinewy hands.
They gazed,
And sweeping like white locusts through the forests
Saw the same men, slightly wizened,   15
Shuffle their sandalled feet to the same rhythms,
They heard the same words of wisdom uttered
Between puffs of pale blue smoke:
They saw us,
And said: They have not changed!   20

NIGHT RAIN

John Pepper Clark (b. 1935)

What time of night it is
I do not know
Except that like some fish
Doped out of the deep
I have bobbed up bellywise   5
From stream of sleep
And no cocks crow.
It is drumming hard here
And I suppose everywhere
Droning with insistent ardour upon   10
Our roof thatch and shed
And thro' sheaves slit open
To lightning and rafters
I can not quite make out overhead
Great water drops are dribbling   15
Falling like orange or mango
Fruits showered forth in the wind
Or perhaps I should say so
Much like beads I could in prayer tell
Them on string as they break   20
In wooden bowls and earthenware
Mother is busy now deploying
About our roomlet and floor.
Although it is so dark
I know her practised step as   25
She moves her bins, bags and vats
Out of the run of water
That like ants filing out of the wood
Will scatter and gain possession
Of the floor. Do not tremble then   30
But turn, brothers, turn upon your side
Of the loosening mats
To where the others lie.
We have drunk tonight of a spell
Deeper than the owl's or bat's   35
That wet of wings may not fly.
Bedraggled up on the iroko, they stand
Emptied of hearts, and
Therefore will not stir, no, not

Even at dawn for then 40
They must scurry in to hide.
So let us roll over on our back
And again roll to the beat
Of drumming all over the land
And under its ample soothing hand 45
Joined to that of the sea
We will settle to sleep of the innocent and free.

CHINESE POEMS

A CONFUCIAN ODE: BLESSINGS

(800–600 B.C.)

On the southern hills grows the nutgrass;
On the northern hills the goosefoot.
Happiness to our lord
That is the groundwork of land and home!
Happiness to our lord! 5
May he live for evermore.

On the southern hills the mulberry;
On the northern hills the willow.
Happiness to our lord,
That is the light of land and home. 10
Happiness to our lord!
May he live for ever and ever.

On the southern hills the aspen;
On the northern hills the plum-tree.
Happiness to our lord 15
That is the father and mother of his people.
Happiness to our lord!
May his fair fame be for ever.

On the southern hills the cedrela;
On the northern hills the privet. 20
Happiness to our lord,
Yes, and life long-lasting!
Happiness to our lord!
May his fair fame never droop.

On the southern hills the box-thorn; 25
On the northern hills the catalpa.
Happiness to our lord,
Yes, till locks are seer and face is grey!
Happiness to you, our lord!
To your descendants, safety and peace! 30

                Translated by Arthur Waley

A CONFUCIAN ODE: THE LEGEND OF SHANG

(800–600 B.C.)

Deep and wise was Shang,
Always furthering its good omens.
The waters of the Flood spread wide.
Yü ranged lands and realms on earth below;
Beyond, great kingdoms were his frontier, 5
And when this far-flung power had been made lasting
The clan of Sung was favoured;
God appointed its child to bear Shang.

The dark king valiantly ruled;
The service of small states everywhere he received, 10
The service of great States everywhere he received.
He followed the precepts of ritual and did not overstep them;
He obeyed the showings of Heaven and carried them out.
Hsiang-t'u was very glorious;
Beyond the seas he ruled. 15

God's appointment did not fail;
In the time of T'ang it was fulfilled.
T'ang came down in his due time,
Wise warnings daily multiplied,
Magnificent was the radiance that shone below. 20
God on high gazed down;
God appointed him to be a model to all the lands.
He received the big statutes, the little statutes,
He became a mark and signal to the lands below.

He bore the blessing of Heaven, 25
Neither violent nor slack,
Neither hard nor soft.
He spread his ordinances in gentle harmony,
A hundred blessings he gathered upon himself.

Great laws and little laws he received, 30
He became great protector of the lands below.
He bore the favour of Heaven.
Far and wide he showed his valour,
Was never shaken or moved,
Never feared nor trembled; 35
A hundred blessings he united in himself.

The warlike king gave the signal;
Firmly he grasped his battle-axe,
His wrath blazed like a fire.
None dare do us injury. 40
The stem had three sprouts;
None prospered nor grew.
All the regions were subdued;
Wei and Ku were smitten,
K'un-wu, and Chieh of Hsia. 45

Of old, in the middle time,
There were tremblings and dangers.
But truly Heaven cherished us;
It gave us a minister,
A true "holder of the balance," 50
Who succoured the King of Shang.

Translated by Arthur Waley

A CONFUCIAN ODE: MINISTER OF WAR

(800–600 B.C.)

Minister of War,
We are the king's claws and fangs.
Why should you roll us on from misery to misery,
Giving us no place to stop in or take rest?

Minister of War,   5
We are the king's claws and teeth.
Why should you roll us from misery to misery,
Giving us no place to come to and stay?

Minister of War,
Truly you are not wise.   10
Why should you roll us from misery to misery?
We have mothers who lack food.

Translated by Arthur Waley

DÉJEUNER SUR L'HERBE

Tu Fu (712–770)

It's pleasant to board the ferry in the sunscape
As the late light slants into afternoon;
The faint wind ruffles the river, rimmed with foam.
We move through the aisles of bamboo
Towards the cool water-lilies.   5

The young dandies drop ice into the drinks,
While the girls slice the succulent lotus root.
Above us, a patch of cloud spreads, darkening
Like a water-stain on silk.
Write this down quickly, before the rain!   10

Don't sit there! The cushions were soaked by the shower.
Already the girls have drenched their crimson skirts.
Beauties, their powder streaked with mascara,
                  lament their ruined faces.

The wind batters our boat, the mooring-line   15
Has rubbed a wound in the willow bark.
The edges of the curtains are embroidered by river foam.
Like a knife in a mango, Autumn slices Summer.
It will be cold, going back.

Translated by Carolyn Kizer

   Déjeuner Sur L'Herbe. The French means luncheon on the grass, or, more colloquially, picnic. This is the same poem as that which follows, though it is a different translation.

THE EXCURSION

Tu Fu

How delightful, at sunset, to loosen the boat!
A light wind is slow to raise waves.
Deep in the bamboo grove, the guests linger;
The lotus-flowers are pure and bright in the cool evening air.
The young nobles stir the ice-water;   5
The Beautiful Ones wash the lotus-roots, whose fibers are like
    silk threads.
A layer of clouds above our heads is black.
It will certainly rain, which impels me to write this poem.

The rain comes, soaking the mats upon which we are sitting.
A hurrying wind strikes the bow of the boat.   10
The rose-red rouge of the ladies from Yueh is wet;
The Yen beauties are anxious about their kingfisher-eyebrows.
We throw out a rope and draw in to the sloping bank.
    We tie the boat to the willow-trees.

We roll up the curtains and watch the floating wave-flowers.   15
Our return is different from our setting out. The wind whistles
    and blows in great gusts.
By the time we reach the shore, it seems as though the
    Fifth Month were Autumn.

> Translated by Amy Lowell and Florence Ayscough

THE EMPEROR

Tu Fu

On a throne of new gold the Son of the Sky
    is sitting among his Mandarins. He shines
    with jewels and is like a sun surrounded by stars.

The Mandarins speak gravely of grave things;
    but the Emperor's thought has flown out by   5
    the open window.

In her pavilion of porcelain the Empress is
    sitting among her women. She is like a bright
    flower among leaves.

She dreams that her beloved stays too long   10
    at council, and wearily she moves her fan.

A breathing of perfumed air kisses the face
    of the Emperor.

"My beloved moves her fan, and sends me a
    perfume from her lips."   15

Towards the pavilion of porcelain walks the
    Emperor, shining with his jewels; and leaves his
    grave Mandarins to look at each other in silence.

                  Translated by E. Powys Mathers

THE AUTUMN WASTES

Tu Fu

The autumn wastes are each day wilder:
Cold in the river the blue sky stirs.
I have tied my boat to the Well Rope Star of barbarians,
Sited my house in a village of Ch'u.
Though the dates are ripe let others cut them down,   5
I'll hoe for myself where the mallows run to seed.
From the old man's dinner on my plate
I'll scatter my alms to the fish in the brook.

Easy to sense the trend in the drift of life,
Hard to compel one creature out of its course.   10
In the deepest water is the fish's utmost joy,
In the leafiest wood the bird will find its home.
Age and decline are content to be poor and sick,
Praise and blame belong to youth and glory.
Though the autumn wind blows on my staff and pillow   15
I shall not weary of the North Mountain's ferns.

Music and rites to conquer my failings,
Mountains and woods to prolong my zest.
On my twitching head the silk cap slants,
I sun my back in the shine of bamboo books,   20
Pick up the pine cones dropped by the wind,
Split open the hive when the sky is cold
By scattered and tiny red and blue
Halt pattened feet close to the faint perfume.

The autumn sands are white on the far shore,   25
The glow of evening reddens the mountain range.
Submerged scales push startled ripples,
Returning wings veer with the high wind.
The pounding of washing blocks echoes from house to house,
Woodcutters' voices sing the same tune.   30
The frost flies down in the care of the Dark Maid,
But the blanket she gives parts me from the Southern Palace.

My ambition, to be pictured in Unicorn Hall:
But my years decline where the ducks and herons troop.
On the great river autumn is soon in spate,   35
In the empty gorge the night is full of noises.
The by-paths hide in a thousand piling stones:
The sail has come to a stop, one streak of cloud.
My children too have learned a barbarous tongue,
Though it's not so sure they will rise to high command.   40

Translated by A. C. Graham

AT THE CORNER OF THE WORLD

Tu Fu

By Yangtse and Han the mountains pile their barriers.
A cloud in the wind, at the corner of the world.
Year in, year out, there's no familiar thing,
And stop after stop is the end of my road.
In ruin and discord, the Prince of Ch'in-ch'uan: 5
Pining in exile, the courtier of Ch'u.
My heart in peaceful times had cracked already,
And I walk a road each day more desolate.

Translated by A. C. Graham

from THE SOUTH MOUNTAINS

Han Yu (768–824)

(*Three extracts from a poem of 102 couplets, all ending on the same rhyme, about the mountains south of the capital Ch'ang-an, including Chung-nan [South Mountain] and T'ai-po.*)

Gazing as I climbed a high peak
I saw them huddle closer together,
Angles and corners jutting as the air brightened,
Emerging patterns in a needlework;
Or interfused in a steamy haze 5
Pierced through by sudden glimpses of heights and depths
As it drifted at random, winnowed without a wind,
And dissipated to warm the tender growths.
Sometimes a level plain of cloud settled
With scattered peaks exposed above, 10
Long eyebrows floating in the empty sky,
The lustrous green of paint newly touched up;
And a single strut of broken crag protruded,
The upreared beak of the Roc as it bathes in the sea.

In spring when the Yang waters in secret 15
And from deep within breathes up the glistening shoots,
Though cliff and crag loom tall against the sky
Their outlines soften like a drunken face.
In summer's flames, when the trees are at their prime
Dense and shady, and deeper bury the hills, 20
The magic spirit day by day exhales
A breath which issues in the shaping clouds.
While the autumn frosts delight in punishing
The hills stand starved and stripped, with wasted flanks
And sharp edges which zigzag across the horizon, 25
In inflexible pride scorning the universe.
Though winter's element is inky black
The ice and snow are master jewellers,
And the light of dawn shines over the dangerous peaks
Constant wide and high for a thousand miles. 30
In daylight or darkness never a fixed posture,
From moment to moment always a different scene.

North of the great lake of K'un-ming,
On a brilliant day, I came to view the mountain.

It dropped straight down as far as I could see   35
Trapped wrongside up and steeped in the clear water.
When ripples stirred on the face of the pool
The rowdy monkeys hopped and skipped,
Shrieked with amazement to see their shattered shapes,
Looked up and gaped with relief that they had not fallen in.   40

Fine weather since yesterday.
My old ambition is satisfied at last.
I've clambered all the way to the topmost peak,
Scurrying with the flying-squirrels and the weasels.
The road dips in front, the vista opens   45
Far and wide over crowded bumps and wrinkles,
Lined up in files like processions
Or crouched like grappling fighters,
Or laid low, as though prostrate in submission,
Or starting up like crowing pheasants;   50
Scattered like loose tiles
Or running together like converging spokes,
Off keel like rocking boats
Or in full stride like horses at the gallop;
Back to back as though offended,   55
Face to face as though lending a hand,
Tangled like sprouting bamboos
Or piled like moxa on a wound;
Neatly composed like a picture,
Curly like ancient script,   60
Constellated like stars,
Conglomerated like stationary clouds,
Surging like billows,
Crumbling like hoed soil,
   And some like champions, Fen or Yü,   65
When the stakes are down, eager for the prize ahead,
The foremost and strongest rearing high above,
The losers looking foolish and speechless with rage;
Or like some majestic Emperor
And the vassals gathered in his court,   70
Even the nearest not too familiar,
Even the furthest never insubordinate;
Or like guests seated at a table
With the banquet spread before them,
Or like a cortège on the way to the graveyard   75
Carrying the coffin to the tomb:

    And some in rows like pots
With others sticking up behind like vases:
Some carapaced like basking turtles,
Slumped like sleeping animals,   80
Wriggling like dragons fleeing into hiding,
Spreading wings like pouncing vultures;
Side by side like friends and equals,
Ranked as though in due degree,
Shooting apart like falling spray   85
Or introducing themselves like lodgers in an inn;
Aloof as enemies
Or intimate as man and wife,
Dignified as tall hats
Or flippant as waving sleeves,   90
Commanding like fortresses
Or hemmed in like hunted prey;
Draining away to the East
Or reclining with heads to the North,
Like flames in the kitchen stove,   95
Like the steam of a cooking dinner;
Marchers who will not halt
And the stragglers left behind,
Leaning posts which do not topple,
Unstrung bows which no one draws,   100
Bare like bald pates,
Smoking like pyres;
Unevenly cracked like diviners' tortoiseshells
Or split into layers like hexagrams,
Level across the front like Po ☷   105
Or broken at the back like Kou. ☰

                        Translated by A. C. Graham

THE NORTHERN COLD

Li Ho (791–817)

The sky glows one side black, three sides purple.
The Yellow River's ice closes, fish and dragons die.
Bark three inches thick cracks across the grain,
Carts a hundred piculs heavy mount the river's water.

Flowers of frost on the grass are as big as coins, 5
Brandished swords will not pierce the foggy sky,
Crashing ice flies in the swirling seas,
And cascades hang noiseless in the mountains, rainbows of jade.

Translated by A. C. Graham

AN ARROWHEAD FROM THE ANCIENT BATTLEFIELD OF CH'ANG-P'ING

Li Ho

Lacquer dust and powdered bone and red cinnabar grains:
From the spurt of ancient blood the bronze has flowered.
White feathers and gilt shaft have melted away in the rain,
Leaving only this triple-cornered broken wolf's tooth.

I was searching the plain, riding with two horses, 5
In the stony fields east of the post-station, on a bank where
  bamboos sprouted,
After long winds and brief daylight, beneath the dreary stars,
Damped by a black flag of cloud which hung in the empty night.

To left and right, in the air, in the earth, ghosts shrieked from
  wasted flesh.
The curds drained from my upturned jar, mutton victuals were
  my sacrifice. 10
Insects settled, the wild geese swooned, the buds were blight-
  reddened on the reeds,
The whirlwind was my escort, puffing sinister fires.

In tears, seeker of ancient things, I picked up this broken barb
With snapped point and russet flaws, which once pierced through
  flesh.
In the east quarter on South Street a pedlar on horseback 15
Talked me into bartering the metal for a votive basket.

Translated by A. C. Graham

THE GRAVE OF LITTLE SU

Li Ho

I ride a coach with lacquered sides,
My love rides a dark piebald horse.
Where shall we bind our hearts as one?
On West Mound, beneath the pines and cypresses.
   (Ballad ascribed to the singing girl Little Su, c. A.D. 500)

    Dew on the secret orchid
    Like crying eyes.
    No thing to bind the heart to.
    Misted flowers I cannot bear to cut.
    Grass like a cushion,   5
    The pine like a parasol:
    The wind is a skirt,
    The waters are tinkling pendants.
    A coach with lacquered sides
    Waits for someone in the evening.   10
    Cold blue candle-flames
    Strain to shine bright.
    Beneath West Mound
    The wind puffs the rain.

                    Translated by A. C. Graham

A POET THINKS

Lui Chi (1311–1375)

The rain is due to fall,
The wind blows softly.

The branches of the cinnamon are moving,
The begonias stir on the green mounds.

Bright are the flying leaves,   5
The falling flowers are many.

The wind lifted the dry dust,
And he is lifting the wet dust;
Here and there the wind moves everything.

He passes under light gauze
And touches me.

I am alone with the beating of my heart

There are leagues of sky,
And the water is flowing very fast.

Why do the birds let their feathers
Fall among the clouds?

I would have them carry my letters,
But the sky is long.

The stream flows east
And not one wave comes back with news.

The scented magnolias are shining still,
But always a few are falling.

I close his box on my guitar of jasper
And lay aside my jade flute.

I am alone with the beating of my heart.

Stay with me to-night,
Old songs.

Translated by E. Powys Mathers

THE SNOW

Mao Tse-Tung (b. 1893)

All the scenery in the north
Is enclosed in a thousand li of ice.
And ten thousand li of whirling snow.
Behold both sides of the Great Wall—
There is only a vast confusion left.
On the upper and lower reaches of the Yellow River
You can no longer see the flowing water.
The mountains are dancing silver serpents,
The hills on the plains are shining elephants.
I desire to compare our height with the skies.
In clear weather

The earth is so charming,
Like a red-faced girl clothed in white.
Such is the charm of these rivers and mountains,
Calling innumerable heroes to vie with each other in pursuing her.   15
The emperors Shih Huang and Wu Ti were barely cultured,
The emperors Tai Tsung and Tai Tsu were lacking in feeling,
Genghis Khan knew only how to bend his bow at the eagles.
These all belong to the past—only today are there men of feeling!

Translated by Robert Payne

THE LONG MARCH

Mao Tse-Tung

None in the Red Army feared the distresses of the Long March.
We looked lightly on the ten thousand peaks and ten thousand
    rivers.
The Five Mountains rose and fell like rippling waves,
In the vast darkness we walked through the muddy hills.

Warm were the precipices where Gold Sand River dashed
    into them.   5
Cold were the iron chains of the Tatu Bridge.
Delighting in the thousand snowy folds of the Ming Mountains,
The last pass vanquished, the Three Armies smiled.

Translated by Robert Payne

AFTER SWIMMING
ACROSS THE YANGTZE RIVER

Mao Tse-Tung

Having just drunk the water of Changsha
Now I eat the fish of Wuchang.
Crossing the ten-thousand-li-long Yangtze River
I gaze at the unlimited sky of the southland.
Let the winds and waves batter me,   5

Still it is better than strolling in a quiet garden,
Now that I have found freedom in space.
Did not Confucius say when on a river:
"Such is that which passes and is gone!"
The sails stir   10
But the Snake and Tortoise hills remain still.
Here a grand scheme takes shape.
A bridge flying across
Turning into a broad road Heaven's Moat that used to separate
    the north from the south.
Building a stone wall to the west   15
Will cut off the rain fallen on the Wu Mountain,
To create a towering dam above a mirror-like lake,
The goddess of the Wu Mountain should be unchanged,
But only startled by the changed world.

                                                    Translated by Kai Yu Hsu

SONNET XVI

                                                    Feng Chi (b. 1905)

We stand together on top of a towering mountain
Transforming ourselves into the immense sweep of view,
Into the unlimited plain in front of us,
And into the footpaths crisscrossing the plain.

Which road, which river is unconnected, and   5
Which wind, which cloud is without its response?
The waters and hills we've traversed
Have all been merged in our lives.

Our births, our growth, and our sorrows
Are the lone pine standing on a mountain,   10
Are the dense fog blanketing a city.
We follow the blowing wind and the flowing water
To become the crisscrossing paths on the plain,
To become the lives of the travelers on the paths.

                                                    Translated by Kai Yu Hsu

QUESTIONS

1. What is the character of the African poems here? What qualities make them distinct from western poetry?
2. Are there any characteristic techniques or qualities of western poetry that the African poets adapt to their own purposes? How successful are these adaptations?
3. Examine the African poetry for its use of imagery. Is the distinctive quality it attains a result of the approach it takes to imagery or of the image-making materials the poet has at hand? Is it his environment that makes the difference?
4. How does Chinese poetry differ from all other selections in this book? What is its most notable quality? How is that quality achieved by the poems?
5. Some western readers feel that Chinese poetry is philosophical. Would you agree with this? What might make people feel it is philosophical?
6. Select poems from cultures not represented—for instance, Japanese poems, Latin-American poems, Icelandic poems, or poems of primitive peoples. (You might also select poems that are produced in special cultural circumstances, such as those of a frontier environment.) Comment on what you feel is observable about them. What do they have in common? How do they differ from one another?

Aesthetic Contexts

Visual Arts, Music, and Dance

The Imagists of the early twentieth century responded strongly to artists and their art. Ezra Pound, H. D., William Carlos Williams, Wallace Stevens, and others wrote numerous poems about their aesthetic experiences. The Imagists, however, were not the first poets interested in such subjects. The urge to write about these experiences seems prevalent in all periods and among poets of widely divergent stylistic views.

For the average reader, poems that make a specific reference to an artist or a work of art, no matter what its kind, offer problems of interpretation that do not exist in most poems. When John Berryman refers to Beethoven's music (page 479), he assumes a certain amount of knowledge on the part of the reader. Particularly, he assumes a certain feeling for Beethoven's music and, perhaps, even for Beethoven's life. For some readers, Berryman's poem will have a great richness and meaning that will be missing for a person who has little or no knowledge of Beethoven.

Nonetheless, Berryman's poem may still be of value to one who does not know Beethoven, since it possesses a richness of language and rhythm and meter, and a fullness of metaphor and image that marks all good poetry, no matter what its subject. Berryman's statements about his feelings may be comprehensible and meaningful to such readers, but the poem will become more comprehensible and meaningful to a reader as his knowledge of Beethoven's life and music increases. The experience is like reading a poem whose title is "Syzygy." Even if the poem uses the title meaningfully, we will still understand it better once we look up the word in a dictionary.

Poems whose context is the aesthetic response to works of art offer at least two specific problems for us as readers. The first one is referential: we may simply not know the work of art. We may never have seen the painting, or sculpture, or dance in question. We may never have heard the music the poet refers to. Moreover, we may have had some experience, but not enough to satisfy the demands of the poem. For instance, many of us have heard some of Beethoven's work or know the stories of his stormy romantic years and his ultimate total deafness. But, in order to respond to Berryman as deeply as we might, such fleeting and superficial knowledge may not be enough. We need a deeper, fuller, more comprehensive awareness of the subject. Once this condition is met, the poem becomes accessible and meaningful.

The second problem with reading such poetry has to do with the natural differences in the sensibilities of those who respond to works of art. We cannot necessarily be expected to agree with Sassoon or Pope, and they do not expect agreement. Such agreement is difficult to achieve even among ourselves—and it may well be undesirable anyway. Art may or may not be a matter of taste, but it is a matter of deep feeling. The poets in this section offer a model for feeling in response to works of art that some of us might not be able to match. We may listen to Bach or Charles Mingus and not respond deeply at all. This may be an insurmountable problem for some readers. On the other hand, such readers may well be the first to benefit from reading poems about works of art and music. However, any reader will find his aesthetic sensibilities expanded by examining the responses of the poets whose work follows.

For many poets, a work of art is a special subject that begins a process of contemplation. Marge Piercy and J. D. O'Hara find themselves beginning with a painting, but ending with political and philosophical reflections on the nature of ancillary issues. Mona Van Duyn may be responding to the Cloisters' Pietà, but she soon begins contemplating the relationship of Christ with his mother. In a way, she is offering an extension and an interpretation of the painting.

Like all poems, those with artistic references have problems and limits. But they also have unusual resources and rewards. The impulse to write poetry on the arts—painting, music, sculpture, architecture, dance, and especially poetry itself—has been strong in our history. Examining the poems that follow may help you to understand why.

AT A SOLEMN MUSIC

John Milton (1608–1674)

Blest pair of Sirens, pledges of Heaven's joy,
Sphere-borne, harmonious sisters, Voice and Verse,
Wed your divine sounds and mixed power employ
Dead things with inbreathed sense able to pierce
And to our high-raised phantasy present   5
That undisturbed song of pure concent
Ay sung before the sapphire-colored throne
To him that sits thereon
With saintly shout and solemn jubilee,
Where the bright seraphim in burning row   10
Their loud uplifted angel trumpets blow,
And the cherubic host in thousand quires
Touch their immortal harps of golden wires
With those just spirits that wear victorious palms,
Hymns devout and holy psalms   15
Singing everlastingly;
That we on earth with undiscording voice
May rightly answer that melodious noise
As once we did, till disproportioned sin
Jarred against nature's chime, and with harsh din   20
Broke the fair music that all creatures made
To their great Lord, whose love their motion swayed
In perfect diapason, whilst they stood
In first obedience, and their state of good.
O may we soon again renew that song,   25
And keep in tune with Heaven, till God erelong
To his celestial consort us unite
  To live with him, and sing in endless morn of light.

  2. Sphere-borne: carried on the heavenly spheres; the "Solemn Music" is in heaven. **4. Dead ... pierce:** echoes the creation, in which God breathed into clay and made it living man. **6. concent:** harmony. **10. seraphim:** an order of angels; also cherubim. **23. diapason:** all the harmony in the entire musical scale.

ODE ON ST. CECILIA'S DAY

Alexander Pope (1688–1744)

I

Descend, ye Nine! descend and sing;
The breathing instruments inspire,
Wake into voice each silent string,
And sweep the sounding lyre!
   In a sadly-pleasing strain   5
   Let the warbling lute complain:
     Let the loud trumpet sound,
     Till the roofs all around
     The shrill echoes rebound:
While in more lengthened notes and slow,   10
The deep, majestic, solemn organs blow.
   Hark! the numbers soft and clear,
   Gently steal upon the ear;
   Now louder, and yet louder rise
   And fill with spreading sounds the skies;   15
Exulting in triumph now swell the bold notes,
In broken air, trembling, the wild music floats;
   Till, by degrees, remote and small,
     The strains decay,
     And melt away,   20
   In a dying, dying fall.

II

By music, minds an equal temper know,
   Nor swell too high, nor sink too low.
If in the breast tumultuous joys arise,
Music her soft, assuasive voice applies;   25
   Or when the soul is pressed with cares,
   Exalts her in enlivening airs.
Warriors she fires with animated sounds;
Pours balm into the bleeding lover's wounds:
   Melancholy lifts her head,   30

Ode on St. Cecilia's Day. St. Cecilia is the patron saint of music, and it was customary to write a commendatory poem on her day. See Dryden's "A Song for St. Cecilia's Day, 1687" (page 168).   **1. Nine:** the muses who inspire all the arts.   **12. the numbers:** refers to the rhythm of the music—literally, its meter.

Morpheus rouses from his bed,
Sloth unfolds her arms and wakes,
Listening Envy drops her snakes;
Intestine war no more our Passions wage,
And giddy Factions hear away their rage. 35

III

But when our Country's cause provokes to Arms,
How martial music every bosom warms!
So when the first bold vessel dared the seas,
High on the stern the Thracian raised his strain,
    While Argo saw her kindred trees 40
    Descend from Pelion to the main.
    Transported demi-gods stood round,
    And men grew heroes at the sound,
    Enflamed with glory's charms:
Each chief his sevenfold shield displayed, 45
And half unsheathed the shining blade:
And seas, and rocks, and skies rebound,
To arms, to arms, to arms!

IV

But when through all th' infernal bounds,
Which flaming Phlegethon surrounds, 50
    Love, strong as Death, the Poet led
    To the pale nations of the dead,
What sounds were heard,
What scenes appeared,
    O'er all the dreary coasts! 55
        Dreadful gleams,
        Dismal screams,
        Fires that glow,
        Shrieks of woe,
        Sullen moans, 60
        Hollow groans,
    And cries of tortured ghosts!
    But hark! he strikes the golden lyre;

31. Morpheus: the god of sleep. **34. Intestine war:** civil war or war between close associates. **40. While ... trees:** Peleus, traveling past Chiron and his wife in the Argo, was shown his son, Achilles, destined to be the great hero of the battle of Troy. The image thus links with the first and last lines of the stanza. **50. Phlegethon:** a river of the underworld whose waves are of fire.

And see! the tortured ghosts respire,
　　See, shady forms advance! 65
Thy stone, O Sisyphus, stands still,
　　Ixion rests upon his wheel,
　　And the pale spectres dance!
The Furies sink upon their iron beds,
And snakes uncurled hang list'ning round their heads. 70

V

By the streams that ever flow,
By the fragrant winds that blow
　　O'er th' Elysian flowers;
By those happy souls who dwell
In yellow meads of Asphodel, 75
　　Or Amaranthine bowers;
By the heroes armèd shades,
Glitt'ring through the gloomy glades,
By the youths that died for love,
　　Wand'ring in the myrtle grove, 80
Restore, restore Eurydice to life:
Oh take the husband, or return the wife!
　　He sung, and hell consented
　　　　To hear the Poet's prayer:
　　Stern Proserpine relented, 85
　　And gave him back the fair.
　　　　Thus song could prevail
　　　　O'er death, and o'er hell,
A conquest how hard and how glorious!
　　Though fate had fast bound her 90
　　With Styx nine times round her,
Yet music and love were victorious.

66. Sisyphus: condemned to roll a stone to the top of a mountain for eternity —but every time the stone reached near the top it was cast down to the bottom again. **67. Ixion:** a king condemned to turning on a wheel forever for his insult to Hera, queen of the gods. **69. Furies:** agents of the gods; they tormented the enemies of the gods. **73. Elysian flowers:** the Elysian fields were the classical equivalent of heaven. **77. shades:** ghosts. **81. Eurydice:** the wife of Orpheus; Eurydice had died and Orpheus, the greatest musician of the classical myths, pleaded with Proserpine in song for her return. His song persuaded Proserpine, but he lost Eurydice because he turned to look back on her—something the god had enjoined him against doing—as they made their way up to the world of day (lines 93–94). **84. the Poet:** Orpheus. **91. Styx:** a river in Hades.

VI

But soon, too soon, the lover turns his eyes:
Again she falls, again she dies, she dies!
How wilt thou now the fatal sisters move? 95
No crime was thine, if 'tis no crime to love.
   Now under hanging mountains,
   Beside the fall of fountains,
   Or where Hebrus wanders,
   Rolling in Mæanders 100
     All alone,
     Unheard, unknown,
     He makes his moan;
     And calls her ghost,
     For ever, ever, ever lost! 105
   Now with Furies surrounded,
   Despairing, confounded,
   He trembles, he glows,
   Amidst Rhodope's snows;
See, wild as the winds, o'er the desert he flies; 110
Hark! Hæmus resounds with the Bacchanals' cries—
     Ah see, he dies!
Yet even in death Eurydice he sung,
Eurydice still trembled on his tongue,
   Eurydice the woods, 115
   Eurydice the floods,
Eurydice the rocks, and hollow mountains rung.

VII

   Music the fiercest grief can charm,
   And fate's severest rage disarm:
   Music can soften pain to ease, 120
   And make despair and madness please:
     Our joys below it can improve,
     And antedate the bliss above.
   This the divine Cecilia found,
And to her Maker's praise confined the sound. 125
When the full organ joins the tuneful quire,
   Th' immortal powers incline their ear,
Borne on the swelling notes our souls aspire,
   While solemn airs improve the sacred fire;

99–100. Hebrus and **Mæander:** rivers of classical lore. **111. Bacchanals:** celebrations under the aegis of the god of wine, Bacchus.

> And Angels lean from heaven to hear. 130
> Of Orpheus now no more let Poets tell,
> To bright Cecilia greater power is given;
> His numbers raised a shade from hell,
> Hers lift the soul to heaven.

PICTURE OF A NUDE IN A MACHINE SHOP

William Carlos Williams (1883–1963)

and foundry,
        (that's art)
  a red ostrich plume
in her hair:

Sweat and muddy water,   5
coiled fuse-strips
        surround her
poised sitting—
(between red, parted
        curtains)   10

the right leg
        (stockinged)
up!
    beside the point—
at ease.   15

Light as a glove, light
as her black gloves!
Modeled as a shoe, a woman's
high heeled shoe!

—the other leg stretched   20
out
    bare
        (toward the top—
and upward)
        as   25
the smeared hide under
shirt and pants
stiff with grease and dirt

is bare—
>approaching 30
the centrum

>(disguised)
the metal to be devalued!

>—bare as
a blow-torch flame, 35
>undisguised.

OL' BUNK'S BAND

William Carlos Williams

These are men! the gaunt, unfore-
>sold, the vocal,
blatant, Stand up, stand up! the
>slap of a bass-string.
Pick, ping! The horn, the 5
>hollow horn
long drawn out, a hound deep
>tone—
Choking, choking! while the
>treble reed 10
races—alone, ripples, screams
>slow to fast—
to second to first! These are men!

Drum, drum, drum, drum, drum
>drum, drum! the 15
ancient cry, escaping crapulence
>eats through
transcendent—torn, tears, term
>town, tense,
turns and backs off whole, leaps 20
>up, stomps down,
rips through! These are men
>beneath
whose force the melody limps—
>to 25
proclaim, proclaims—Run and
>lie down,

in slow measures, to rest and
  not never
need no more! These are men!
  Men!

30

SHELDONIAN SOLILOQUY

Siegfried Sassoon (1886–1967)

During Bach's B Minor Mass

My music-loving Self this afternoon
(Clothed in the gilded surname of Sassoon)
Squats in the packed Sheldonian and observes
An intellectual bee-hive perched and seated
In achromatic and expectant curves 5
Of buzzing, sunbeam-flecked, and overheated
Accommodation. Skins perspire ... But hark! ...
Begins the great *B minor Mass* of Bach.

The choir sings *Gloria in excelsis Deo*
With confident and well-conducted brio 10
Outside, a motor-bike makes impious clatter,
Impinging on our Eighteenth-Century trammels.
God's periwigged: He takes a pinch of snuff.
The music's half-rococo. ... Does it matter
While those intense musicians shout the stuff 15
In Catholic Latin to the cultured mammals
Who agitate the pages of their scores? ...

Meanwhile, in Oxford sunshine out of doors,
Birds in collegiate gardens rhapsodize
Antediluvian airs of worm-thanksgiving. 20
To them the austere and buried Bach replies
With song that from ecclesiasmus cries
Eternal *Resurrexit* to the living.

Sheldonian Soliloquy. The Sheldonian is a concert hall in Oxford, England. **5. achromatic:** literally, free of aberrant colors—pure. **10. brio:** vivacity. **13. God's periwigged:** the music is eighteenth-century, when gentlemen wore long white wigs. **20. Antediluvian:** before the flood Noah survived. **22. from ecclesiasmus:** from the church. **23. Resurrexit:** He rises.

Hosanna in excelsis chants the choir
In pious contrapuntal jubilee.   25
Hosanna shrill the birds in sunset fire.
And *Benedictus* sings my heart to Me.

CONCERT-INTERPRETATION

Siegfried Sassoon

Le Sacre du Printemps

The audience pricks an intellectual Ear . . .
Stravinsky . . . Quite the Concert of the Year!
Forgetting now that none-so-distant date
When they (or folk facsimilar in state
Of mind) first heard with hisses—hoots—guffaws—   5
This abstract Symphony (they booed because
Stravinsky jumped their Wagner palisade
With modes that seemed cacophonous and queer),
Forgetting now the hullabaloo they made,
The Audience pricks an intellectual ear.   10

Bassoons begin . . . Sonority envelops
Our auditory innocence; and brings
To Me, I must admit, some drift of things
Omnific, seminal, and adolescent.
Polyphony through dissonance develops   15
A serpent-conscious Eden, crude but pleasant;
While vibro-atmospheric copulations
With mezzo-forte mysteries of noise
Prelude Stravinsky's statement of the joys
That unify the monkeydom of nations.   20

Le Sacre du Printemps. The Rite of Spring—a musical composition by Igor Stravinsky. It has certain pagan overtones and was informed by modern researches in anthropological studies and myth. Easter is a Christian equivalent to this "rite." **14. Omnific, seminal, and adolescent:** refers to the encompassing quality of the music, which seems to take in all experiences (omnific), to suggest the beginnings of things (seminal), and to strike a responsive personal note about the way the poet felt when he was younger and more innocent (adolescent). **15. Polyphony:** melodies played in different keys simultaneously. **18. mezzo-forte:** moderately loud.

This matter is most indelicate indeed!
Yet one perceives no symptom of stampede.
The Stalls remain unruffled: craniums gleam:
Swept by a storm of pizzicato chords,
Elaborate ladies re-assure their lords 25
With lifting brows that signify "Supreme!"
While orchestrated gallantry of goats
Impugns the astigmatic programme-notes.

In the Grand Circle one observes no sign
Of riot: peace prevails along the line. 30
And in the Gallery, cargoed to capacity,
No tremor bodes eruptions and alarms.
They are listening to this not-quite-new audacity
As though it were by someone dead,—like Brahms.

But savagery pervades Me; I am frantic 35
With corybantic rupturing of laws.
Come, dance, and seize this clamorous chance to function
Creatively,—abandoning compunction
In anti-social rhapsodic applause!
Lynch the conductor! Jugulate the drums! 40
Butcher the bass! Ensanguinate the strings!
Throttle the flutes!... Stravinsky's April comes
With pitiless pomp and pain of sacred springs...
Incendiarize the Hall with resinous fires
Of sacrificial fiddles scorched and snapping!... 45

Meanwhile the music blazes and expires;
And the delighted Audience is clapping.

ARTHUR MITCHELL

Marianne Moore (1887–1972)

Slim dragon-fly
  too rapid for the eye
    to cage.

36. **corybantic**: wild, expressive.
   Arthur Mitchell. An American dancer, director of The Harlem Dance Theater.

        contagious gem of virtuosity
        make visible, mentality.   5
        Your jewels of mobility

    reveal
            and veil
                    a peacock-tail.

ON HEARING
A SYMPHONY OF BEETHOVEN

Edna St. Vincent Millay (1892–1950)

Sweet sounds, oh, beautiful music, do not cease!
Reject me not into the world again.
With you alone is excellence and peace,
Mankind made plausible, his purpose plain.
Enchanted in your air benign and shrewd,   5
With limbs a-sprawl and empty faces pale,
The spiteful and the stingy and the rude
Sleep like scullions in the fairy tale.
This moment is the best the world can give:
The tranquil blossom on the tortured stem.   10
Reject me not, sweet sounds; oh, let me live,
Till Doom espy my towers and scatter them,
A city spell-bound under the aging sun.
Music my rampart, and my only one.

ART REVIEW

Kenneth Fearing (1902–1961)

Recently displayed at the Times Square Station, a new Vandyke
    on the face-cream girl.
(Artist unknown. Has promise, but lacks the brilliance shown by
    the great masters of the Elevated age)
The latest wood carving in a Whelan telephone booth, titled
    "O Mortal Fools WA 9–5090," shows two winged hearts
    above an ace of spades.

(His meaning is not entirely clear, but this man will go far)
A charcoal nude in the rear of Flatbush Ahearn's Bar & Grill,
"Forward to the Brotherhood of Man," has been boldly
    conceived in the great tradition.   5
(We need more, much more of this)
Then there is the chalk portrait, on the walls of a waterfront
    warehouse, of a gentleman wearing a derby hat: "Bleecker
    Street Mike is a doublecrossing rat."
(Morbid, but powerful. Don't miss)

Know then by these presents, know all men by these signs and
    omens, by these simple thumbprints on the throat of time,
Know that Pete, the people's artist, is ever watchful,   10
That Tuxedo Jim has passed among us, and was much displeased,
    as always,
That George the Ghost (no man has ever seen him) and Billy the
    Bicep boy will neither bend nor break,
That Mr. Harkness of Sunnyside still hopes for the best, and has
    not lost his human touch,
That Phantom Phil, the master of them all, has come and gone,
    but will return, and all is well.

ART STUDENT

Stephen Spender (b. 1909)

With ginger hair dragged over
                    fiery orange face
Blue shirt, red scarf knotted round his neck,
Blue jeans, soft leather Russian boots
Tied round with bands he ties and unties when   5
His feet are not spread sprawling on two tables—
Yawning, he reads his effort. It's about
A crazy Icarus always falling into
A labyrinth.
            He says   10

8. **Icarus**: in classical mythology, the man who first flew—but he flew too close to the sun, which melted the wax holding his wings together, and he fell. He is cited as an instance of ambition being vastly greater than circumstances should have allowed.

He only has one subject—death—he don't know why—
And saying so leans back scratching his head
Like a Dickensian coachman.
                     Apologizes
For his bad verse—he's no poet—an art student—   15
—Paints—sculpts—has to complete a work at once
Or loses faith in it.
                 Anyway, he thinks
Art's finished.
             There's only one thing left   20
Go to the slaughter house and fetch
A bleeding something-or-other—oxtail, heart,
Bollocks, or best a bullock's pair of lungs,
Then put them in the college exhibition,
On a table or hung up on a wall   25
Or if they won't allow that, just outside
In the courtyard.
             (Someone suggests
He put them in a plastic bag. He sneers at that.)

The point is they'll produce some slight sensation—   30
Shock, indignation, admiration. He bets
Some student will stand looking at them
For hours on end and find them beautiful
Just as he finds any light outside a gallery,
On a junk heap of automobiles, for instance,   35
More beautiful than sunsets framed inside.
That's all we can do now—send people back
To the real thing—the stinking corpse.

BEETHOVEN TRIUMPHANT

John Berryman (1914–1972)

1

Dooms menace from tumults. Who's immune
among our mightier of headed men?
Chary with his loins
womanward, he begot us an enigma.

23. **Bollocks**: testicles.

2

Often pretended he was absentminded
whenas he couldn't hear; and often was.
"... always *he*, he everywhere, as one says of Napoleon"
(Sir John Russell in '21 hearing a Trio)

3

O migratory rooms, the unworthy brothers, the worthless nephew!
One time his landlord tipped a hat to him;
Beethoven moved. Awkward & plangent
charged to the Archduke's foot,—who told his court "Leave him
    alone."

4

My unpretending love's the B flat major
by the old Budapest done. Schnabel did record
the Diabelli varia. I can't get a copy.
Then there's Casals I have, 101, both parts.

5

Moments are, early on in the 4th Piano Concerto
show him at his unrivalled middle best.
It does go up and up, and down lingeringly.
Miser & Timon-giving, by queer turns.

6

They wanted him London, partout. "Too late," "Too late"
he muttered, and mimicked piano-playing.
Prodigious, so he never knew his age
his father'd lied about.

7

Whatever his kindness to Rossini and contempt for Italians,
if down he sat a while in an exquisite chair

6. whenas... hear: Beethoven was totally deaf in his late years. **13. the B flat major:** Quartets number 6 and 13 are both in B-flat major, but Berryman is almost surely referring to number 13, one of the great "late quartets." **15. Diabelli varia:** a piece for piano, "Variations on a theme by Diabelli." **16. 101:** Opus 101 includes the Piano Sonata no. 28 in A major. Berryman may have been thinking of the cello sonatas of Opus 102. **20. Timon-giving:** Shakespeare's *Timon of Athens*, who gave too much. **25. Rossini:** Gioacchino Rossini, Italian opera composer.

it had to be thrown out (five witnesses,
none of whom says quite why).

8

O did he sleep sound? Heavy, heavy that.
Waked at 3:30 not by some sonata 30
but by a botched rehearsal of the Eighth
where all thing has to go right

(Koussevitzky will make it, Master; lie back down)

9

Lies of his fluency from Betty von Arnim
to eager Goethe, who'd not met the man. 35
Fact is, he stumbled at the start
and in the sequence, stumbled in the middle,

10

Often unsure at the end—shown by his wilderness
on-sketchings encrusted like Tolstoy (not Mozart:
who'd, ripping napkins, the whole strict in mind 40
before notes serried; limitationless, unlike you).

11

Inundations out from ground zero.
Back from an over-wealth, the simplification of Necessity.
When brother Johann signed "Real Estate Owner," you: "Brain
 owner."
And what, among fumbling notes, in the nights, did you read? 45

12

Coffee and tallow spot your *Odyssey*
though, and when Schindler was an arse to ask
your drift in Opus 31 and the Appassionata
you uttered at him, cheerful, "Just read *The Tempest.*"

13

Thinking presides, some think now,—only presides— 50
at the debate of the Instincts; but presides,

33. Koussevitzky: Serge Koussevitzky, conductor of the Boston Symphony
Orchestra in the 1940s. **48. Opus 31:** Piano Sonata no. 17 in D minor
(The Tempest). The *Appasionata* is Piano Sonata no. 23 in F minor. The
reference is to Shakespeare's *Tempest.*

over powers, over love, hurt-back.
You grumbled: "Religion and Figured Bass are closed concepts.
Don't argue."

14

To disabuse the "Heiligerdankgesang"? 55
Men up to now sometimes weep openly.
Tortured your surly star to sing impossibly
against the whole (small) thwarting orchestra.
One chord thrusts, as it must

15

find allies, foes, resolve, in subdued crescendo. 60
Unfazed, you built-in the improbable.
You clowned. You made throats swallow
and shivered the backs of necks.
You made quiver with glee, at will; not long.
This world is of male energy male pain. 65

16

Softnesses, also yours, which becomes us.
What stayed your chosen instrument? The 'cello?
At two points. At others, the forte-piano.
At others, the fiddles & viola & 'cello.

17

I'm hard to you, odd nights. I bulge my brain, 70
my shut chest already suffers,—so I play blues
and Haydn whom you—both the which touch but they don't
    ache me.
I'm less inured in your disaster corner,
Master. You interfere.
        O yes we interfere
or we're mere sweetening: what? the alkali lives 75
around and after ours. Sleeking down nerves
Passing time dreaming. And you did do that too.
        There hover Things cannot be banned by you;
damned few.

55. Heiligerdankgesang: song of holy thanks.

If we take our head in our ears and listen
Ears! Ears! the Devil paddled in you   80

18

heard not a hill flute or a shepherd sing!
tensing your vision onto an alarm
of gravid measures, sequent to demure,
all we fall, absently foreknowing . . .
You force a blurt: Who was I?   85
Am I these tutti, am I this rallentando?
This entrance of the oboe?
                          I am all these
the sane man makes reply on the locked ward.

19

Did ever you more than (clearly) cope odd women?
save clumsy uncommitted overtures   90
au moins à Joséphine? save the world-famous unsent
or when retrieved and past-death-treasured letter?

20

Deception spared. No doubt he took one look:
"Not mine; I can't make a kroner there."
Straightforward staves, dark bars,   95
late motions toward the illegible. Musical thighs,

21

spared deep age. Out at prime, in a storm
inaudible thunder he went, upon his height.
The other day I called our chief prose-writer
at home a thousand miles off and began   100
"How are you, Sir?"   out of three decades' amity

22

"I'm OLD," he said. Neither of us laughed.
Spared deep age, Beethoven. I wish you'd caught

---

86. **tutti . . . rallentando:** musical terms meaning "all together" and "slowing down."   91. **au moins à Joséphine:** at least to Josephine. She was the wife of Napoleon, Emperor of France, to whom the *Emperor* Concerto and the Third Symphony were originally dedicated.

young Schubert's last chamberworks and the *Winterreise*
you could have read through, puffing. 105

23

Ah but the indignities you flew free from,
your self-abasements even would increase
together with your temper, evil already,
"some person of bad character, churlish & eccentric"
For refusing to scribble a word of introduction: 110
"He is an unlicked bear"—almost Sam Johnson.

24

An entertainer, a Molière, in the onset
under too nearly Mozart's aegis,
the mysteries of Oedipus old were not beyond you.
Islands of suffering & disenchantment & enchantment. 115

25

But the brother charged the dying brother board & lodging.
Bedbugs biting, stench, unquenchable thirst,
ungovernable swelling. Then the great Malfatti
gave up on, and accorded frozen punch ad lib.

26

Your body-filth flowed on to the middle of the floor 120
"I shall, no doubt, soon be going above"
sweat beading you, gasping of Shakespeare,
knocking over the picture of Haydn's birthplace.

27

They said you died.   "20,000 persons of every class
clashed at the gates of the house of mourning, till they
 locked them. 125
Franz Schubert stalked the five hundred feet to the church.
It's a lie! You're all over my wall!

You march and chant around here! I hear your thighs.

104. Schubert's ... Winterreise: a song cycle of Schubert's on winter themes.
111. Sam Johnson: an eighteenth-century writer noted for his hugeness and bad manners. He compiled the first practicable dictionary of English in 1755.
112. Molière: French comic playwright.

THE PIETÀ, RHENISH, 14TH C., THE CLOISTERS

Mona Van Duyn (b. 1921)

He stares upward at a monstrous face,
as broad as his chest, as long as he is
from the top of his head to his heart. All her
feeling and fleshiness is there.

To be on her lap is to be all shrunken   5
to a little composition of bone
and held away from her upper body,
which, like an upended cot smoothed neatly

and topped with a tight, girlish bolster
of breasts, rises behind him, queer   10
to them both, as if no one had ever rested
upon it, or rumpled it, or pressed it.

And so it stands free of suffering.
But above it, the neck, round and wrinkling
from the downward tilt of the head it's bearing, 15
bears the full weight of that big thing.

It is a face that, if he could see
as we are forced to see, and if he
knew, as we cannot help but know, that
his dead, dangling, featureless, granite   20

feet would again have to touch the ground,
would make him go mad, would make his hand,
whose hard palm is the same size
as one of his mother's tearless eyes,

hit it, since nothing in life can cure   25
pain of this proportion. To see her
is to understand that into the blast
of his agony she turned, full-faced,

The Pietà, Rhenish, 14th c., The Cloisters. "Pietà" is a generic name for representations of Christ lying in his mother's lap after he has been removed, dead, from the cross.

and the face began to melt and ache,
the brows running down from their high arc
to the cheekbone, the features falling toward the chin,
leaving the huge forehead unlined, open,

until, having felt all it could feel,
her face numbed and began to congeal
into this. With horror he'd have to see
the massive girl there, vapidly

gazing, stupid, stupefied.
If he said, "Willingly I dried
out of consciousness and turned to the slight
husk you hold on your knee, but let

an innocent, smaller love of a son
hold me, let not my first stone
be the heart of this great, grotesque mother.
Oh God, look what we've done to each other,"

then from the head her slow wit,
stirring, would speak, "My darling, it was not
I who belittled you, but love
itself, whose nature you came to believe

was pure possibility, though you came through
its bloody straits. And not you,
but love itself, has made me swell
above you, gross and virginal

at once. I touch what's left on my knee
with the tips of my fingers—it is an ugly,
cold corrugation. Here on my lap,
close in my arms, I wanted to keep

both the handsome, male load of your whole
body and the insupportable,
complete weightlessness of your loss.
The holy and incestuous

met and merged in my love, and meet
in every love, and love is great.
But unmanned spirit or unfleshed man
I cannot cradle. Child, no one can."

ARISTOTLE CONTEMPLATING THE BUST OF HOMER: AFTER REMBRANDT

J. D. O'Hara (b. 1931)

His steady hand rests on the vanquished head,
that fading, eyeless, disembodied head,
where once a world of thought was conjured up
for us to set our hearts on and to serve.
Homer has lost, heroes and gods are lost,   5
and Aristotle rules a world of things,
a world of glorious gold and fur and cloth.
His eyes are clear. He sees things as they are
and knows their certain values and their cost.
Nothing was worth it—nothing perhaps but love,   10
whose dancing fountains left no lasting trace
except the dessication of regret
in those bleak eyes that see things as they are.

MAYA

Andrey Voznesensky (b. 1933)

There are ballerinas of silence,
Ballerinas like snowflakes; they melt
But she's like some kind of infernal spark.
When she perishes, half the planet will be incinerated!
Even her silence is frenzied, the roaring silence of expectation,   5
The actively tense silence between lightning and thunderclap . . .
She is tortured by her own gifts—
Inexplicable even to herself, but nothing to joke about . . .

What can be done with this weightless creature in a world of
    ponderousness?
She was born more weightless than anyone.   10
In a world of heavy, blunt objects.
Better able to fly than anyone—
In a world of clumsy immobility . . .
The splendour of genius amidst the ordinary—that's
The key to all her roles.   15

She blazes brilliantly; it is brought on by her boiling blood.
This is no ordinary mythical fairy.
She suffers from a lack of spark, fire and light
In this half-way world ...
She cannot bear half-measures, whispers, and compromises. 20
Her answer to a foreign lady correspondent was cunning.
"What do you hate most of all?"
"Noodles!" ...
Yes of course, noodles are the most repulsive of all things:
A symbol of standardization, of things boiled to mush, of
    commonness; 25
Of subjugation, of anti-spirituality.
Wasn't it about noodles that she wrote in her notes:
"People must stand up for their convictions.
Not by using the police and denunciations,
But only through the strength of their own inner 'I.'" 30
And further: "I don't particularly respect people who live
By the maxim: 'If you don't repent, you won't be saved.'"

Maya Plisetskaya doesn't like noodles!
She's a creator.
"I know Venus is the work of the hands 35
Of a craftsman—and I know a craft!"
We've forgotten the words "gifts," "genius," "illumination."
Without them, art is nothing. As the experiments of Kolmogorov
    proved,
Art cannot be programmed; two human qualities cannot be derivative:
The feeling for religion and the feeling for poetry. 40
Talents cannot be cultivated by agricultural systems invented by
    Lysenko.
They are born. They are part of the national wealth,
Like radium deposits, September in Latvian woods or medicinal
    springs.
Plisetskaya's lines and movements are also miracles like these,
Also part of the national wealth. 45

What a feeling Plisetskaya has for poetry!
I remember her in black, sitting on a sofa:
She looks as if she's put a wall between herself
And the rest of the audience.
She sits in profile, leaning forward. 50
Like the famous statue with a pitcher in the park of Tsarskoye Selo

41. **Lysenko:** head of Russian agricultural biological studies.

Her eyes are switched off.
She listens with her neck.
With her Modigliani neck, with the curve of her spine, with her skin.
Her earrings tremble, like nostrils . . .   55

A woman in grey kept folding and unfolding her arms.
She talked about the role of arms in ballet. I'm
Not going to pass on what she said. Her arms
Flashed and swam under the ceiling—only her arms.
Her legs and torso were no more than little vases   60
For these naked, flashing arms . . .

She is the most modern of our ballerinas.
Poetry, painting, physics have their time in terms
Of style—but not ballet.
She is a ballerina who lives in the rhythms of the Twentieth
    Century.   65

She should dance not among swans, but among cars and jets,
I see her against the background of
The pure lines of Henry Moore and the chapels of Ronchan . . .
Her name is short.
Like those of other girls in tights,   70
And as thunder-like as that of a goddess
Or pagan priestess: Maya.

Translated by George Feifer

MINGUS

Bob Kaufman (b. 1935)

String-chewing bass players,
Plucking rolled balls of sound
From the jazz-scented night.

Feeding hungry beat seekers
Finger-shaped heartbeats,   5
Driving ivory nails
Into their greedy eyes.

54. **Modigliani neck:** Amedeo Modigliani painted women with elongated necks.   68. **Henry Moore:** American sculptor and painter.
Mingus. Charles Mingus is one of the best bass players and band leaders of modern jazz.

Smoke crystals, from the nostrils
Of released jazz demons,
Crash from foggy yesterday
To the light
Of imaginary night.

WALKING PARKER HOME

Bob Kaufman

Sweet beats of jazz impaled on slivers of wind
Kansas Black Morning/First Horn Eyes/
Historical sound pictures on New Bird wings
People shouts/boy alto dreams/Tomorrow's
Gold belled pipe of stops and future Blues Times
Lurking Hawkins/shadows of Lester/realization
Bronze fingers—brain extensions seeking trapped sounds
Ghetto thoughts/bandstand courage/solo flight
Nerve-wracked suspicions of newer songs and doubts
New York altar city/black tears/secret disciples
Hammer horn pounding soul marks on unswinging gates
Culture gods/mob sounds/vision of spikes
Panic excursions to tribal Jazz wombs and transfusions
Heroin nights of birth/and soaring/over boppy new ground.
Smothered rage covering pyramids of notes spontaneously
    exploding
Cool revelations/shrill hopes/beauty speared into greedy ears
Birdland nights on bop mountains, windy saxophone revolutions
Dayrooms of junk/and melting walls and circling vultures/
Money cancer/remembered pain/terror flights/
Death and indestructible existence
In that Jazz corner of life
Wrapped in a mist of sound
His legacy, our Jazz-tinted dawn
Wailing his triumphs of oddly begotten dreams
Inviting the nerveless to feel once more
That fierce dying of humans consumed
In raging fires of Love.

3. Bird: Charley Parker, the great saxophonist of the 1940s. **6. Hawkins, Lester:** Coleman Hawkins and Lester Young were great saxophonists of the 1940s and 1950s. **17. Birdland:** a famous jazz nightclub in New York City.

THE MUSEUM
Sandra Hochman (b. 1936)

In the feathery museum—

Marriage bonds like silky ribbons snap. You're on
Your own. Over the staircase,
Over the widening stairs,

    Climbing and entering. 5
    We walk around—
    I hear my high heels clicking on the floor. We
    Stare at the statues—Imperial Chinese Ladies
    Stuffed in glass cases smile behind white porcelain frowns—
    Walking down hallways—classic vases 10
    Robust under glass—miles away from Greece—
    And bronze statues dancing—here are the Degas nudes—
    You say they look like me—all twirling around
    And we are walking down towards the Rembrandt room.

    We stare at those eyes. At the impossible mouths 15
    Almost about to speak and tell me some secret:
    You say, "They are all close to death"—no, closer to sleep,
    All of the portraits just about to snooze.
    I want to lie down with you,
    Discovering your limbs softly with my hands 20
    As though you were also
    A trip through an unknown museum—
    In a long sleep of teeth and lips
    I would kiss you so many times
    As you come to life in my arms. 25

THE PEACEABLE KINGDOM
Marge Piercy (b. 1936)

A painting by Edward Hicks, 1780–1849, hung in the Brooklyn Museum

Creamcheese babies square and downy as bolsters
in nursery clothing nestle among curly lions and lowing cattle,
a wolf of scythe and ashes, a bear smiling in sleep.
The paw of a leopard with spots and eyes of headlights
rests near calf and vanilla child. 5

In the background under the yellow autumn tree
Indians and settlers sign a fair treaty.
The mist of dream cools the lake.

On the first floor of the museum Indian remains
are artfully displayed. Today is August sixth. 10
man eats man with sauces of newsprint.
The vision of that kingdom of satisfaction
where all bellies are round with sweet grasses
blows on my face pleasantly
though I have eaten five of those animals. 15
We are fat and busy as maggots.

All the rich flat black land,
the wide swirlmarked browngreen rivers,
leafy wheat baking tawny, corn's silky spikes,
sun bright kettles of steel and crackling wires, turn into 20
infinite shining weapons that scorch the earth.
The pride of our hive
packed into hoards of murderous sleek bombs.

We glitter and spark righteousness.
We are blinding as a new car in the sunshine. 25
Gasoline rains from our fluffy clouds.
Everywhere our evil froths polluting the waters—
in what stream on what mountain do you miss
the telltale redbrown sludge and rim of suds?

Peace: the word lies like a smooth turd 30
on the tongues of politicians ordering
the sweet flesh seared on the staring bone.
Guilt is added to the municipal water,
guilt is deposited in the marrow and teeth.
In my name they are stealing from people with nothing 35
their slim bodies. When did I hire these assassins?

My mild friend no longer paints mysteries of doors and mirrors.
On her walls the screams of burning children coagulate.
The mathematician with his webspangled language
of shadow and substance half spun 40
sits in an attic playing the flute all summer
for fear of his own brain, for fear that the baroque
arabesque of his joy will be turned to a weapon.
Five A.M. in Brooklyn: night all over my country.
Watch the smoke of guilt drift out of dreams. 45

When did I hire these killers? one day in anger
in seaslime hatred at the duplicity of flesh?
eating steak in a suave restaurant, did I give the sign?
sweating like a melon in bed, did I murmur consent?
did I contract it in Indiana for a teaching job?   50
was it something I signed for a passport or a loan?
Now in my name blood burns like oil day and night.

This nation is founded on blood like a city on swamps
yet its dream has been beautiful and sometimes just
that now grows brutal and heavy as a burned out star.   55

QUESTIONS

1. On the basis of these poems, do you feel that poets are unusually sensitive to works of art? Do you feel they are especially sensitive to certain arts only? Explain in detail.
2. Do you feel that there is a tendency in these poems (which may be supplemented with choices of your own) to emphasize the life or character of the artist above his work? What evidence is there for answering "yes"? What evidence for answering "no"?
3. Is there a consistent attitude here toward the aesthetic experience? Do you note any inconsistencies? Are there poets whose attitudes seem closely aligned? How many different alliances of thought can you detect?
4. If possible, find one of the works of art (or a reproduction of one) referred to in one of these poems—(*Peaceable Kingdom* and *Aristotle Contemplating the Bust of Homer* appear in numerous art history texts) or a work that correlates with a poem of your choosing. Examine the relationship of the poem to the work of art. What does the poet emphasize? What does he discount? How faithful is he to the work of art? How much does he distort? What is the ultimate result of reading the poem and referring to the work of art?
5. Try the above exercise in a slightly different way. Write a commentary on a poem treating a work of art before you have seen or heard that work. Then, after viewing and

studying the art, write another commentary. How different is your second response? Which, would you say, is more valuable to you?
6. We have purposely omitted poems on poetry and poets because they are so plentiful. If you can, gather from six to twelve poems on the subject of poetry—the Imagists would be good to start with, though all periods abound with such poems. What are the similarities of issues and feelings between these poems and poems about the other arts? What are the differences? Does a greater or a lesser passion command poets when they comment on their own artistic medium?
7. Gather poems on any single artistic medium. Do you detect any unanimity of feeling or attitude on the part of the poets who comment on that medium?
8. Try writing a poem inspired by a work of art. Are there similarities between your work, or that of your peers, and the work of the poets included here? What might that mean?

COPYRIGHTS AND ACKNOWLEDGMENTS
(Continued from page iv)

CORINTH BOOKS, INC. For "In Memory of Radio," "The New Sheriff," and "Vice" from *Preface to a Twenty Volume Suicide Note.* Copyright © 1961 by LeRoi Jones. Reprinted by permission of Corinth Books.

JOHN WILLIAM CORRINGTON. For "A Trip to Omaha (Normandy 6.VI.44)" from *Coastlines* 5:3.

CURTIS BROWN, LTD. For "Foxtrot from a Play" by W. H. Auden from *New Verse*, April–May 1936. Copyright 1936 by W. H. Auden. All rights reserved. Reprinted by permission of Curtis Brown, Ltd.

DAVID DAICHES. For "Not until Doomsday's..."

DOUBLEDAY & COMPANY, INC. For "After Swimming Across the Yangtze River" by Mao Tse-Tung and "Sonnet XVI" by Feng Chi from the book *Twentieth Century Chinese Poetry* by Kai-Yu Hsu, copyright © 1963 by Kai-Yu Hsu. Reprinted by permission of Doubleday & Company, Inc. For "In a Prominent Bar in Secaucus One Day" by X. J. Kennedy from *Nude Descending the Staircase* by X. J. Kennedy; for "Down in Dallas," copyright © 1964 by X. J. Kennedy from the book *Growing Into Love* by X. J. Kennedy. Reprinted by permission of Doubleday & Company, Inc. For "Root Cellar," copyright 1943 by Modern Poetry Association, Inc. from the book *The Collected Poems of Theodore Roethke* by Theodore Roethke. Reprinted by permission of Doubleday & Company, Inc.

EDITIONS SEGHERS. For "The Lines of Our Hands" by Bernard B. Dadié.

NORMA MILLAY ELLIS. For "Love is not all...," "On Hearing a Symphony of Beethoven," and "Conscientious Objector," from *Collected Poems*, Harper & Row. Copyright 1928, 1931, 1934, 1955, 1958, 1962 by Edna St. Vincent Millay and Norma Millay Ellis.

FARRAR, STRAUS & GIROUX, INC. For "Beethoven Triumphant" from *Delusions, etc.* by John Berryman, copyright © 1969, 1971 by John Berryman, copyright © 1972 by the Estate of John Berryman. Reprinted with the permission of Farrar, Straus & Giroux, Inc. For "Invitation to Miss Marianne Moore" by Elizabeth Bishop, from *The Complete Poems* by Elizabeth Bishop, copyright © 1949, 1969 by Elizabeth Bishop. Reprinted with the permission of Farrar, Straus & Giroux, Inc. For "Jonathan's Song" from *Powerful Long Ladder* by Owen Dodson, copyright 1946 by Owen Dodson. Reprinted with the permission of Farrar, Straus & Giroux, Inc. For "For the Union Dead" by Robert Lowell, copyright © 1960 by Robert Lowell. For "Memories of West Street and Lepke" from *Life Studies* by Robert Lowell, copyright © 1958 by Robert Lowell. For Sappho's "Letter to Anaktoria," translated by Robert Lowell in *Imitations* by Robert Lowell, copyright © 1958, 1959, 1960, 1961 by Robert Lowell. Reprinted with the permission of Farrar, Straus & Giroux, Inc. For "Party Piece" by Brian Patten from *Little Johnny's Confession* by Brian Patten, copyright © 1967 by Brian Patten. Reprinted with the permission of Farrar, Straus & Giroux, Inc.

GEORGE FEIFER. For translation of "Maya" by Andrey Voznesensky.

GROVE PRESS, INC. For "The Legend of Shang," "Minister of War" and "Blessings" from *The Book of Songs* by Arthur Waley. Reprinted by permission of Grove Press, Inc. Copyright © 1960, Grove Press, Inc. (All rights reserved.)

HARCOURT BRACE JOVANOVICH, INC. For "anyone lived in a pretty how town" by E. E. Cummings. Copyright, 1940, by E. E. Cummings; renewed, 1968, by Marion Morehouse Cummings. Reprinted from *Complete Poems 1913–1962* by E. E. Cummings by permission of Harcourt Brace Jovanovich, Inc. For "Buffalo Bill's" and "in Just" by E. E. Cummings. Copyright, 1923, 1951, by E. E. Cummings. Reprinted from his volume *Complete Poems 1913–1962* by permission of Harcourt Brace Jovanovich, Inc. For "i sing of Olaf" by E. E. Cummings. Copyright, 1931, 1959, by E. E. Cummings. Reprinted from his volume *Complete Poems 1913–1962* by permission of Harcourt Brace Jovanovich, Inc. For "O sweet spontaneous" by E. E. Cummings. Copyright, 1923, 1951, by E. E. Cummings. Reprinted from his volume *Complete Poems 1913–1962* by permission of Harcourt Brace Jovanovich, Inc. For "sonnet" by E. E. Cummings. Copyright, 1935, by E. E. Cummings; renewed, 1963, by Marion Morehouse Cummings. Reprinted from *Complete Poems 1913–1962* by E. E. Cummings by permission of Harcourt Brace Jovanovich, Inc. For "The Love Song of J. Alfred Prufrock" by T. S. Eliot. From *Collected Poems 1909–1962* by T. S. Eliot, copyright, 1936 by Harcourt Brace Jovanovich, Inc.; copyright © 1963, 1964, by T. S. Eliot. Reprinted by permission of the publishers. For "Art Review" by Kenneth Fearing. Copyright, 1943, by Kenneth Fearing; copyright, 1971, by Bruce Fearing. Reprinted from *Afternoon of a Pawnbroker and Other Poems* by Kenneth Fearing by permission of Harcourt Brace Jovanovich, Inc. For "Mr. Edwards and the Spider" by Robert Lowell. From *Lord Weary's Castle*, copyright, 1946, by Robert Lowell. Reprinted by permission of Harcourt Brace Jovanovich, Inc.

HARPER & ROW, PUBLISHERS, INC. For "The Ballad of Rudolph Reed" from *The World of Gwendolyn Brooks* by Gwendolyn Brooks. Copyright © 1960 by Gwendolyn Brooks Blakely. By permission of Harper & Row, Publishers, Inc. From *On These I Stand* by Countee Cullen: "Scottsboro, Too, Is Worth Its Song." Copyright 1935 by Harper & Row, Publishers, Inc.; renewed 1963 by Ida M. Cullen. "A Brown Girl Dead." Copyright 1925 by Harper & Row, Publishers, Inc.; renewed 1953 by Ida M. Cullen. Reprinted by permission of the publisher. For "The Hawk in the Rain" from *The Hawk in the Rain* by Ted Hughes. Copyright © 1957 by Ted Hughes. Reprinted by permission of the publisher. For "Ariel" by Sylvia Plath. Copyright © 1965 by Ted Hughes. Reprinted by permission of the publisher.

HARVARD UNIVERSITY PRESS. For poems by Emily Dickinson: Numbers 125, 190, 199, 249, 301, 376, 410, 435, 480, 569, 612, 613, 631, 657, 663, 670, 824, 868, 898, 919, 925, 937, 1080, 1123, 1235, 1286, 1408, 1419, 1420, 1545, 1601, 1637, 1726, 1737, 1768. Reprinted by permission of the publisher and the Trustees of Amherst College from Thomas H. Johnson, Editor, *The Poems of Emily Dickinson*, Cambridge, Mass.: The Belknap Press of Harvard University Press, Copyright, 1951, 1955, by The President and Fellows of Harvard College.

HOLT, RINEHART AND WINSTON, INC. For "Design" by Robert Frost from *The Poetry of Robert Frost* edited by Edward Connery Lathem. Copyright © 1964 by Lesley Frost Ballantine. Copyright © 1969 by Holt, Rinehart and Winston, Inc. Reprinted by permission of Holt, Rinehart and Winston, Inc. For "Out, Out—" and "Fire and Ice" by Robert Frost. From *The Poetry of Robert Frost* edited by Edward Connery Lathem. Copyright 1916, 1923, © 1969 by Holt, Rinehart and Winston, Inc. Copyright 1944, 1951 by Robert Frost. Reprinted by permission of Holt, Rinehart and Winston, Inc. For "Epitaph on an Army of Mercenaries" by A. E. Housman. From *The Collected Poems of A. E. Housman*. Copyright 1922 by Holt, Rinehart and Winston, Inc. Copyright 1950 by Barclays Bank, Ltd. Reprinted by permission of Holt, Rinehart and Winston, Inc. For "The True Lover" by A. E. Housman. From "A Shropshire Lad"—Authorised Edition—from *The Collected Poems of A. E. Housman*. Copyright 1939, 1940, © 1965 by Holt,

Rinehart and Winston, Inc. Copyright © 1967, 1968 by Robert E. Symons. Reprinted by permission of Holt, Rinehart and Winston, Inc.

HOUGHTON MIFFLIN COMPANY. For poems by Emily Dickinson: Number 1403, "My Maker—Let Me Be," and Number 1545, "The Bible" from *Life and Letters of Emily Dickinson* edited by Martha D. Bianchi. For Tu Fu, "The Excursion," "The Emperor" and Lui Chi, "A Poet Thinks." For "Venus Transiens" and "The Pond" from *The Complete Poetical Works of Amy Lowell*. Copyright 1955 by Harvey H. Bundy and G. D'Andelot Belin, Jr., Trustees of the Estate of Amy Lowell. Reprinted by permission of Houghton Mifflin Company. For "Ars Poetica" from *The Collected Poems of Archibald MacLeish*. Copyright © 1962 by Archibald MacLeish. Reprinted by permission of Houghton Mifflin Company. For Anne Sexton's "Ringing the Bells" from *To Bedlam and Part Way Back*. Copyright © 1960 by Anne Sexton. Reprinted by permission of Houghton Mifflin Company. For "The Fortress" from *All My Pretty Ones* by Anne Sexton. Copyright © 1962. Reprinted by permission of Houghton Mifflin Company.

INSEL VERLAG. For "Liebes-Lied" by Rainer Maria Rilke. From *Sämtliche Werke*, Band I. Copyright © 1955 by Insel Verlag, Frankfurt am Main. All rights reserved.

CAROLYN KIZER. For "After Tu Fu" from *Poetry*. Copyright 1963 by The Modern Poetry Association.

JOSEPH LANGLAND. For "Hunters in the Snow: Brueghel" © 1963 by Joseph Langland. From *The Wheel of Summer*, Dial Press.

LAURIE LEE. For "First Love."

LITTLE, BROWN AND COMPANY. For Emily Dickinson, Numbers 341, 376, 569, 657, 1080 and " 'Why do I love thee, Sir?' "—Copyright 1929 © 1957 by Mary L. Hampson. Numbers 410, 613, 1095—Copyright 1935 by Martha Dickinson Bianchi, © renewed 1963 by Mary L. Hampson. Numbers 1461, 1333—Copyright 1914, 1942 by Martha Dickinson Bianchi. For "The Turtle" from *Verses From 1929 On* by Ogden Nash. Copyright 1940 by Ogden Nash. By permission of Little, Brown and Company.

MACMILLAN PUBLISHING CO., INC. For "The Walk" and "The Curtains Now Are Drawn" by Thomas Hardy. Reprinted with permission of Macmillan Publishing Co., Inc. from *Collected Poems* by Thomas Hardy. Copyright 1925 by Macmillan Publishing Co., Inc. For "A Glass of Beer" by James Stephens. Reprinted with permission of Macmillan Publishing Co., Inc. from *Collected Poems* by James Stephens. Copyright 1918 by Macmillan Publishing Co., Inc., renewed 1946 by James Stephens. For "An Irish Airman Foresees His Death," "In Memory of Major Robert Gregory," "The People," "A Thought from Propertius," "A Deep-Sworn Vow," "Presences" by William Butler Yeats. Reprinted with permission of Macmillan Publishing Co., Inc. from *Collected Poems* by William Butler Yeats. Copyright 1919 by Macmillan Publishing Co., Inc., renewed 1947 by Bertha Georgie Yeats. For "The Pity of Love," "The Lover Tells of the Rose in His Heart," "He Tells of Perfect Beauty," "He Hears the Cry of the Sedge," "When You Are Old," "Never Give All the Heart" by William Butler Yeats. Reprinted with permission of Macmillan Publishing Co., Inc. from *Collected Poems* by William Butler Yeats. Copyright 1906 by Macmillan Publishing Co., Inc., renewed 1934 by William Butler Yeats. For "Against Unworthy Praise," "Friends," "Words" by William Butler Yeats. Reprinted with permission of Macmillan Publishing Co., Inc. from *Collected Poems* by William Butler Yeats. Copyright 1912 by Macmillan Publishing Co., Inc., renewed 1940 by Bertha Georgie Yeats. For "O Do

Not Love Too Long," "A Prayer for My Daughter" by William Butler Yeats. Reprinted with permission of Macmillan Publishing Co., Inc. from *Collected Poems* by William Butler Yeats. Copyright 1924 by Macmillan Publishing Co., Inc., renewed 1952 by Bertha Georgie Yeats. For "The Folly of Being Comforted" by William Butler Yeats. Reprinted with permission of Macmillan Publishing Co., Inc. from *Collected Poems* by William Butler Yeats. For "Fallen Majesty" by William Butler Yeats. Reprinted with permission of Macmillan Publishing Co., Inc. from *Collected Poems* by William Butler Yeats. Copyright 1916 by Macmillan Publishing Co., Inc., renewed 1944 by Bertha Georgie Yeats. For "Quarrel in Old Age" by William Butler Yeats. Reprinted with permission of Macmillan Publishing Co., Inc. from *Collected Poems* by William Butler Yeats. Copyright 1933 by Macmillan Publishing Co., Inc., renewed 1961 by Bertha Georgie Yeats. For "A Bronze Head" by William Butler Yeats. Reprinted with permission of Macmillan Publishing Co., Inc. from *Collected Poems* by William Butler Yeats. Copyright 1940 by Bertha Georgie Yeats, renewed 1968 by Bertha Georgie Yeats, Michael Butler Yeats and Anne Yeats. For "Leda and the Swan," and "Among School Children" by William Butler Yeats. Copyright 1928 by Macmillan Publishing Co., Inc., renewed 1956 by Bertha Georgie Yeats.

MANYLAND BOOKS, INC. For "The Image of God" by John M. Ruganda, "The Dream of African Unity" by Boevi Zankli, and "Uncle Tom's Black Humour" by Taban Lo Liyong. Reprinted by permission of Manyland Books, Inc., publisher of *African Writing Today*, edited by Charles Angoff and John Povey, in which the poems originally appeared.

THE NEW AMERICAN LIBRARY, INC. For "The Universal Lover" from *Love Poems of Ovid*, selected and in a new English version by Horace Gregory. Copyright © 1962, 1963, 1964 by Horace Gregory. Reprinted by arrangement with the New American Library, Inc., New York, New York.

NEW DIRECTIONS PUBLISHING CORPORATION. For "Mingus" and "Walking Parker Home" by Bob Kaufman from *Solitudes Crowded with Loneliness* by Bob Kaufman. Copyright © 1959, 1965 by Bob Kaufman. Reprinted by permission of New Directions Publishing Corporation. For "October" by Denise Levertov from *O Taste and See* by Denise Levertov. Copyright © 1964 by Denise Levertov Goodman. Reprinted by permission of New Directions Publishing Corporation. For "Dulce et Decorum Est," "Exposure," "Spring Offensive," and "Arms and the Boy" by Wilfred Owen from *Collected Poems* by Wilfred Owen. Copyright Chatto & Windus, Ltd., 1946 © 1963. Reprinted by permission of New Directions Publishing Corporation. For "The Known Soldier" by Kenneth Patchen from *Collected Poems* by Kenneth Patchen. Copyright 1942 by Kenneth Patchen. Reprinted by permission of New Directions Publishing Corporation. For "Canto I" by Ezra Pound from *The Cantos* by Ezra Pound. Copyright 1934 by Ezra Pound. Reprinted by permission of New Directions Publishing Corporation. For "The River-Merchant's Wife: A Letter," "Envoi (1919)," "In a Station of the Metro," "Doria," "Imerro," "Ballad of the Goodly Fere" by Ezra Pound from *Personae* by Ezra Pound. Copyright 1926 by Ezra Pound. Reprinted by permission of New Directions Publishing Corporation. For "Fern Hill," "Poem in October," "A Refusal to Mourn the Death, by Fire, of a Child in London," "Over Sir John's Hill" by Dylan Thomas from *The Poems of Dylan Thomas*. Copyright 1946 by New Directions Publishing Corporation, copyright 1952 by Dylan Thomas. Reprinted by permission of New Directions Publishing Corporation. For "Hold Hard, These Ancient Minutes in the Cuckoo's Month" by Dylan Thomas from *The Poems of Dylan Thomas*. Copyright 1939 by New Directions Publishing Corporation. Reprinted by permission of New Directions Publishing Corporation. For "Picture of a Nude in a Machine Shop" and "Ol' Bunk's Band" by William Carlos Williams from *Collected Later Poems* by William Carlos Williams. Copyright 1948 by William Carlos Williams. Reprinted by permission of New Directions Publishing Corporation. For "Spring Strains," "The Red Wheelbarrow," "Nantucket," "Daisy," "Dawn" by William Carlos Williams from *Collected Earlier Poems* by William Carlos Williams. Copyright 1938 by New Directions Publishing Corporation. Reprinted by permission of New Directions Publishing Corporation. For "The Hunters in the Snow" and "Landscape with the Fall of Icarus" by William Carlos Williams from *Pictures from Brueghel and Other Poems* by William Carlos Williams. Copyright © 1960, 1962 by William Carlos Williams. Reprinted by permission of New Directions Publishing Corporation.

THE NEW YORKER. For "News from the House" by Michael Dennis Browne from *The New Yorker*, January 4, 1969. Reprinted by permission; © 1969 The New Yorker Magazine, Inc. For "Aristotle Contemplating the Bust of Homer" by J. D. O'Hara from *The New Yorker*, December 9, 1972. Reprinted by permission; © 1972 The New Yorker Magazine, Inc. For "To Rosmarie in Bad Kissingen" by Keith Waldrop from *The New Yorker*, October 30, 1971. Reprinted by permission; © 1971 The New Yorker Magazine, Inc.

THE NEW YORK REVIEW OF BOOKS. For "Art Student" by Stephen Spender. Reprinted with permission from *The New York Review of Books*. Copyright © 1971 Nyrev, Inc.

DAVID S. NIVISON. For "New England" by Edwin Arlington Robinson.

W. W. NORTON & COMPANY, INC. For "Two Songs" by Adrienne Rich. Reprinted from *Necessities of Life, Poems, 1962–1965* by Adrienne Rich. By permission of W. W. Norton & Company, Inc. Copyright © 1966 by W. W. Norton & Company, Inc.

HAROLD OBER ASSOCIATES, INC. For "Ballad of the Landlord" by Langston Hughes from *Montage of a Dream Deferred*. Reprinted by permission of Harold Ober Associates, Incorporated. Copyright 1951 by Langston Hughes. For "Let America Be America Again" by Langston Hughes from *A New Song*. Reprinted by permission of Harold Ober Associates, Incorporated. Copyright 1938 by Langston Hughes. Copyright renewed.

OXFORD UNIVERSITY PRESS. For "God's Grandeur," "Spring," and "The Windhover" from *Poems of Gerard Manley Hopkins*.

ROBERT PAYNE. For "The Snow" and "The Long March" by Mao Tse-Tung from *White Pony: An Anthology of Chinese Poetry*.

NORMAN HOLMES PEARSON. For "Heat" and "Oread" from *Selected Poems* by H. D., Grove Press, 1957. Reprinted by permission of the copyright holder, Norman Holmes Pearson.

PENGUIN BOOKS, LTD. For "The Autumn Wastes" and "At the Corner of the World" by Tu Fu. For selections from "The South Mountains" (sic) by Han Yu. For "The Northern Cold," "An Arrowhead from the Ancient Battlefield of Ch'ang-P'ing," and "The Grave of Little Su" by Li Ho. All from *Poems of the Late T'ang* tr. A. C. Graham (Penguin Classics, 1965). Copyright © A. C. Graham, 1965.

A. D. PETERS & CO. For "Epitaph on a Politician" by Hilaire Belloc from *Sonnets and Verse* (Gerald Duckworth & Co.). Reprinted by permission of A. D. Peters and Company.

POETRY. For "After Tu Fu" by Carolyn Kizer. From *Poetry*, October–November, 1963. Copyright 1963 by The Modern Poetry Association. Reprinted by permission of *Poetry* and the author.

PRÉSENCE AFRICAINE. For "Africa" by David Diop. The poem appears in David Diop's *Coups De Pilon*, published by Présence Africaine, Paris (1956). For (*Souffles*) "Breath" by Birago Diop. The poem appears in Birago Diop's *Leurres et Lueurs*, published by Présence Africaine, Paris (1960). For "Nostalgie" ("Nostalgia") by Sembène Ousmane. The poem is taken from Sembène Ousmane's *Voltaigue*, published by Présence Africaine, Paris (1962).

RANDOM HOUSE, INC. ALFRED A. KNOPF, INC. For "In Memory of W. B. Yeats" and "Musée des Beaux Arts" by W. H. Auden. Copyright 1940 and renewed 1968 by W. H. Auden. Reprinted from *Collected Shorter Poems 1927–1957*, by W. H. Auden, by permission of Random House, Inc. For "O What Is That Sound" by W. H. Auden. Copyright 1937 and renewed 1965 by W. H. Auden. Reprinted from *Collected Shorter Poems 1927–1957*, by W. H. Auden, by permission of Random House, Inc. For "Gone Boy" by Langston Hughes. Copyright © 1955 by Langston Hughes. Reprinted from *Selected Poems*, by Langston Hughes, by permission of Alfred A. Knopf, Inc. For "Harlem Sweeties" by Langston Hughes. Copyright 1942 by Alfred A. Knopf, Inc. and renewed 1970 by Arna Bontemps and George Houston Bass. Reprinted from *Don't You Turn Back*, by permission of the publisher. For "A Song of Ch'ang-Kan" by Li Po. From *The Jade Mountain: A Chinese Anthology*, translated by Witter Bynner and Kiang Kang-hu. Copyright 1929 and renewed 1957 by Alfred A. Knopf, Inc. Reprinted by permission of the publisher. For "Point Shirley" by Sylvia Plath. Copyright © 1959 by Sylvia Plath. Reprinted from *The Colossus and Other Poems*, by Sylvia Plath, by permission of Alfred A. Knopf, Inc. For "Bells for John Whiteside's Daughter" by John Crowe Ransom. Copyright 1924 by Alfred A. Knopf, Inc. and renewed 1952 by John Crowe Ransom. Reprinted from *Selected Poems*, Third Edition, Revised and Enlarged, by John Crowe Ransom, by permission of the publisher. For "The Idea of Order at Key West" by Wallace Stevens. Copyright © 1936 by Wallace Stevens and renewed 1964 by Holly Stevens. Reprinted from *The Collected Poems of Wallace Stevens*, by permission of Alfred A. Knopf, Inc. For "Disillusionment of Ten O'Clock" by Wallace Stevens. Copyright 1923 and renewed 1951 by Wallace Stevens. Reprinted from *The Collected Poems of Wallace Stevens* by permission of Alfred A. Knopf, Inc. For "Study of Two Pears" by Wallace Stevens. Copyright 1942 and renewed 1970 by Holly Stevens. Reprinted from *The Collected Poems of Wallace Stevens* by permission of Alfred A. Knopf, Inc.

ISHMAEL REED. For "off d pig" from *Soulscript: Afro-American Poetry*, University of Massachusetts Press. Reprinted by permission of the author.

PAUL R. REYNOLDS, INC. For "Between the World and Me" by Richard Wright. Copyright © 1935 by *Partisan Review*, Inc. Reprinted by permission of Paul R. Reynolds, Inc., 599 Fifth Avenue, New York, N.Y., 10017.

CHARLES SCRIBNER'S SONS. "Speaking of Poetry" is reprinted with the permission of Charles Scribner's Sons from *Now with His Love* by John Peale Bishop. Copyright 1933 Charles Scribner's Sons.

THE SWALLOW PRESS INC. For "Ode to the Confederate Dead" by Allen Tate. Reprinted from *The Swimmers and Other Selected Poems*, © 1970 by permission of the Swallow Press.

THE THIRD PRESS. For "Death" from "Death, Somewhere, and Homeward Bound" by Ezekiel Mphahlele. From *New African Literature and the Arts*. Edited by Joseph Okpaku. Copyright 1970 by Journal of the New African Literature and the Arts. Used with permission of The Third Press–Joseph Okpaku Publishing Co., Inc.

TWAYNE PUBLISHERS, INC. For "The Lynching," "If We Must Die," and "The Negro's Tragedy" from *Selected Poems of Claude McKay,* copyright 1953 by Bookman Associates, Inc., reprinted with the permission of Twayne Publishers, Inc.

UNIVERSAL PUBLISHING AND DISTRIBUTING CORPORATION. For "At That Moment (For Malcolm X)" from *26 Ways of Looking at a Black Man* by Raymond Patterson.

THE VIKING PRESS, INC. For "The Museum" by Sandra Hochman from *Vaudeville Marriage* by Sandra Hochman. Copyright © 1966 by Sandra Hochman. Reprinted by permission of The Viking Press, Inc. For "Spring Morning," "A Youth Mowing" and "Piano" by D. H. Lawrence. From *The Complete Poems of D. H. Lawrence,* edited by Vivian de Sola Pinto and F. Warren Roberts. Copyright © 1964, 1971 by Angelo Ravagli and C. M. Weekley, Executors of the Estate of Frieda Lawrence Ravagli. Reprinted by permission of The Viking Press, Inc. For "Arthur Mitchell" by Marianne Moore. From *The Complete Poems of Marianne Moore.* All rights reserved. Reprinted by permission of The Viking Press, Inc. For "Sheldonian Soliloquy" and "Concert-Interpretation" by Siegfried Sassoon. From *Satirical Poems* by Siegfried Sassoon. Reprinted by permission of The Viking Press, Inc. All rights reserved. For "Counter-Attack" by Siegfried Sassoon. From *Counter-Attack and Other Poems* by Siegfried Sassoon. Reprinted by permission of The Viking Press, Inc. All rights reserved.

WESLEYAN UNIVERSITY PRESS. For "Madonna of the Cello" by Robert Bagg. Copyright © 1961 by Robert Bagg. Reprinted from *Madonna of the Cello,* by Robert Bagg, by permission of Wesleyan University Press. For "The Orb Weaver" by Robert Francis. Copyright © 1946 by Robert Francis. Reprinted from *The Orb Weaver,* by Robert Francis, by permission of Wesleyan University Press. For "Love's Map" by Donald Justice. Copyright © 1959 by Donald Justice. Reprinted from *The Summer Anniversaries,* by Donald Justice, by permission of Wesleyan University Press. "Love's Map" first appeared in *Poetry.* For "Love's Eschatology" by Vassar Miller. Reprinted from *My Bones Being Wiser,* by Vassar Miller, by permission of Wesleyan University Press. For "The Peaceable Kingdom" by Marge Piercy. Copyright © 1968 by Marge Piercy. Reprinted from *Breaking Camp,* by Marge Piercy, by permission of Wesleyan University Press.

JONATHAN WILLIAMS. For "Fastball" from *The Empire Finale at Verona.* Reprinted by permission of the author.

Index

A   Adams, Léonie
      Country Summer   194
Africa   443
After Great Pain, a Formal Feeling Comes   378
After Swimming Across the Yangtze River   461
After-Thought   157
Again—His Voice Is at the Door   382
Against Unworthy Praise   368
Aldington, Richard
      Evening   334
All the Flowers of the Spring   92
Among School Children   192
Ancestral Faces   446
And Did Those Feet in Ancient Time   250
Anonymous
      from *Back of the Bus*   422
      The Bailiff's Daughter of Islington   125
      Bonny Barbara Allan   124
      The Dying Airman   47
      Frankie and Albert   130
      Get Up and Bar the Door   128
      A Happy Time   48
      It Isn't the Cough   42
      The Jam on Gerry's Rock   133
      Jesse James   132
      John Henry   134
      Johnie Armstrong   127
      Mind and Matter   48
      Poor Omie   131
      Relativity   47

Sir Patrick Spens   123
Western Wind   54
Antony and Cleopatra (Act II, sc. ii) (from)   30
anyone lived in a pretty how town   262
Ariel   270
Aristotle Contemplating the Bust of Homer:
    After Rembrandt   487
Arms and the Boy   399
Arrowhead from the Ancient Battlefield
    of Ch'ang-P'ing, An   458
Art Review   477
Art Student   478
Arthur Mitchell   476
Ars Poetica   317
At a Solemn Music   467
At That Moment   117
At the Corner of the World   454
Auden, W. H.
    Foxtrot from a Play   46
    In Memory of W. B. Yeats   115
    Musée des Beaux Arts   328
    O What Is That Sound   142
Autumn Wastes, The   453
Award (from)   414

B

Back of the Bus (from)   422
Bagg, Robert
    Madonna of the Cello   85
Bailiff's Daughter of Islington, The   125
Baite, The   77
Ballad of Rudolph Reed, The   143
Ballad of the Goodly Fere   139
Ballad of the Landlord   141
Baraka, Imamu Amiri (LeRoi Jones)
    In Memory of Radio   271
    The New Sheriff   418
    Vice   416
Bashō
    The Old Pond   425
Because the Bee May Blameless Hum   383
Beethoven Triumphant   479

504   Index

Belloc, Hilaire
    Epitaph on the Politician   41
Bells for John Whiteside's Daughter   114
Berryman, John
    Beethoven Triumphant   479
    Winter Landscape   326
Between the World and Me   411
Bible Is an Antique Volume, The   389
Bishop, Elizabeth
    Invitation to Miss Marianne Moore   264
Bishop, John Peale
    Speaking of Poetry   321
Blake, William
    And Did Those Feet in Ancient Time   250
    The Garden of Love   302
    If You Trap the Moment   42
    London   303
    Mad Song   302
    The Mockers   220
    The Tyger   244
    To Spring   92
Bonny Barbara Allan   124
Breath   441
Brew, Kwesi
    Ancestral Faces   446
Bronze Head, A   373
Brooks, Gwendolyn
    The Ballad of Rudolph Reed   143
Brown Girl Dead, A   410
Browne, Michael Dennis
    News from the House   88
Browning, Robert
    Love Among the Ruins   252
Buffalo Bill's   50
Byron, Lord. *See* Gordon, George, Lord Byron

C   *Canto I* (from)   218
    Carroll, Lewis
        The Crocodile   45
        Jabberwocky   215

Catullus
    Kisses 74
Centuries of Meditations (from) 33
Christian Doctrine, The (from) 32
Chronicles of England, Scotland and Ireland (1577) (from) 27
Clark, John Pepper
    Night Rain 447
Clough, Arthur Hugh
    The Latest Decalogue 39
Coleridge, Samuel Taylor
    Dejection: An Ode 181
    Kubla Khan 306
    Sonnet 307
Collar, The 284
Collins, William
    Ode to Evening 172
Commodity (from) 31
Composed upon Westminster Bridge, September 3, 1802 155
Concert-Interpretation 475
Confucian Ode: Blessings, A 448
Confucian Ode: The Legend of Shang, A 449
Confucian Ode: Minister of War, A 450
Conscientious Objector 398
Corrington, John William
    A Trip to Omaha (Normandy 6.VI.44) 405
Counter-Attack 397
Country Summer 194
Crane, Stephen
    To the Maiden . . . 17
Crashaw, Richard
    On Our Crucified Lord Naked, and Bloody 292
    Sainte Mary Magdalene or The Weeper 286
Crocodile, The 45
Cullen, Countee
    A Brown Girl Dead 410
    Scottsboro, Too, Is Worth Its Song 410
cummings, e. e.
    anyone lived in a pretty how town 262
    Buffalo Bill's 50
    i sing of Olaf glad and big 403
    in Just— 215
    O sweet spontaneous 95
    sonnet 161
Curtains Now Are Drawn: Song, The 63

506 Index

D	Dadié, Bernard B.
	    The Lines of Our Hands 444
	Daiches, David
	    Not Until Doomsday's . . . 227
	Daisy 332
	David's Lament (from *II Samuel*) 395
	Dawn 333
	Dead, The 157
	Death 431
	Dedication, The 295
	Deep-Sworn Vow, A 371
	Dejection: An Ode 181
	Déjeuner Sur L'Herbe 451
	Delight in Disorder 249
	Design 6
	Diary Entry 23
	Dickinson, Emily
	    A Great Hope Fell 386
	    A Little Madness in the Spring 387
	    After Great Pain, a Formal Feeling Comes 378
	    Again—His Voice Is at the Door 382
	    Because the Bee May Blameless Hum 383
	    The Bible Is an Antique Volume 389
	    The Fact That Earth Is Heaven 388
	    The First Day's Night Had Come 378
	    For Each Ecstatic Instant 376
	    He Was Weak 376
	    "Heavenly Father" 389
	    How Happy I Was If I Could Forget 384
	    I Dwell in Possibility 381
	    I Felt a Cleaving in My Mind 385
	    I Reason, Earth Is Short 377
	    I Reckon—When I Count at All 379
	    I Thought That Nature Was Enough 387
	    If All the Griefs I Am to Have 390
	    If I Can Stop One Heart from Breaking 384
	    I'm "Wife" 376
	    Is It Too Late to Touch You, Dear? 390
	    It Dropped So Low 383
	    It Was a Quiet Seeming Day 388
	    It Would Have Starved a Gnat 380
	    Lad of Athens 391
	    Like Rain It Sounded Till It Curved 387
	    Much Madness Is Divinest Sense 379

       My Maker—Let Me Be   388
       Of Course—I Prayed   378
       Of God We Ask One Favor   390
       One Joy of So Much Anguish   389
       One Need Not Be a Chamber   383
       Ourselves Were Wed One Summer—Dear   381
       Rearrange a "Wife's" Affection!   391
       Struck, Was I, Not Yet by Lightning   384
       They Shut Me Up in Prose   380
       To Whom the Mornings Stand for Nights   386
       When They Come Back   385
       "Why Do I Love" You, Sir?   78
       Wild Nights   377
Diop, Birago
       Breath   441
Diop, David
       Africa   443
Disillusionment of Ten O'Clock   329
Dodson, Owen
       Jonathan's Song   413
Donne, John
       Elegie: Going to Bed   280
       The Baite   77
       The Flea   277
       Holy Sonnets 5, 7, 10, 14   151–52
       Song   278
       A Valediction Forbidding Mourning   279
Doria   333
Down in Dallas   145
Dream of African Unity, The   429
Dryden, John
       Mac Flecknoe   38
       A Song for St. Cecilia's Day, 1687   168
Dulce et Decorum Est   402
Durem, Ray
       from Award   414
Dying Airman, The   47

E
       Easter-Wings   283
       Elegie: Going to Bed   280
       Elegy Written in a Country Church Yard   298

Eliot, T. S.
   Hysteria 19
   The Love Song of J. Alfred Prufrock 258
Emerson, Ralph Waldo
   from *Commodity* 31
   The Rhodora 31
Emperor, The 452
Envoi 65
Epitaph on an Army of Mercenaries 396
Epitaph on the Politician 41
Evening 334
Excursion, The 452
Exposure 401

F *Fact That Earth Is Heaven, The* 388
Fallen Majesty 369
Fastball 269
Fearing, Kenneth
   Art Review 477
Feng Chi
   Sonnet XVI 462
Fern Hill 266
Fire and Ice 257
First Day's Night Had Come, The 378
First Love 81
Flea, The 277
Fly That Flew into My Mistress Her Eye, A 282
Folly of Being Comforted, The 367
For Each Ecstatic Instant 376
For the Union Dead 200
Fortress, The 231
Foxtrot from a Play 46
Francis, Robert
   The Orb Weaver 10
Frankie and Albert 130
Friends 369
Frost, Robert
   Design 6
   Fire and Ice 257
   In White 8
   "Out, Out—" 21
Full of Life Now 362

G   Garden of Love, The   302
Garden of Proserpine, The   255
Get Up and Bar the Door   128
Ginsberg, Allen
     A Supermarket in California   268
Glass of Beer, A   45
God's Grandeur   158
Gone Boy   49
Gordon, George, Lord Byron
     Stanzas for Music: There Be None of
       Beauty's Daughters   308
     Stanzas for Music: There's Not a Joy the
       World Can Give Like That It Takes Away   308
Grace Before Beer   49
Grave of Little Su, The   459
Graves, Robert
     The Persian Version   40
Gray, Thomas
     Elegy Written in a Country Church Yard   298
     Ode on a Distant Prospect of Eton College   170
Great Hope Fell, A   386

H   H. D.
     Heat   334
     Oread   316
Han Yu
     from The South Mountains   455
Happy Time, A   48
Hardy, Thomas
     The Curtains Now Are Drawn: Song   63
     The Walk   56
Harlem Sweeties   263
Hawk in the Rain, The   234
He Hears the Cry of the Sedge   366
He Tells of the Perfect Beauty   366
He Was Weak   376
Heat   334
"Heavenly Father"   389
Herbert, George
     The Collar   284
     Easter-Wings   283

Herbert, Lord of Cherbury
   A Fly That Flew into My Mistress Her Eye   282
   To a Lady Who Did Sing Excellently   59
   Sonnet of Black Beauty   282
Herrick, Robert
   Delight in Disorder   249
Heywood, John
   Of Late and Never   48
   Of Loving a Dog   48
Higgins, F. R.
   Grace Before Beer   49
Hobbes, Thomas
   from *Leviathan* (I, iii)   26
Hochman, Sandra
   The Museum   491
Hold Hard, These Ancient Minutes in the Cuckoo's Month   96
Holinshed, Raphael
   from *Chronicles of England, Scotland and Ireland* (1577)   27
Hopkins, Gerard Manley
   God's Grandeur   158
   Spring   93
   The Windhover: To Christ Our Lord   214
Housman, A. E.
   Epitaph on an Army of Mercenaries   396
   The True Lover   138
How Happy I Was If I Could Forget   384
How Soon Hath Time   153
Hughes, Langston
   Ballad of the Landlord   141
   Gone Boy   49
   Harlem Sweeties   263
   Let America Be America Again   408
Hughes, Ted
   The Hawk in the Rain   234
Hunters in the Snow, III The   325
Hunters in the Snow: Brueghel   324
Hysteria   19

I
   I Dwell in Possibility   381
   I Felt a Cleaving in My Mind   385

I Reason, Earth Is Short 377
I Reckon—When I Count at All 379
i sing of Olaf glad and big 403
I Strove with None 51
I Thought That Nature Was Enough 387
Idea of Ancestry, The 415
Idea of Order at Key West, The 63
If All the Griefs I Am to Have 390
If I Can Stop One Heart from Breaking 384
If You Trap the Moment 42
If We Must Die 406
I'm "Wife" 376
Image of God, The 430
Imerro 334
In a Prominent Bar in Secaucus One Day 66
In a Station of the Metro 333
In an Artist's Studio 158
in Just— 215
In Memory of Major Robert Gregory 111
In Memory of Radio 271
In Memory of W. B. Yeats 115
In White 8
Invitation to Miss Marianne Moore 264
Irish Airman Foresees His Death, An 397
Is It Too Late to Touch You, Dear? 390
It Dropped So Low 383
It Is a Beauteous Evening 154
It Isn't the Cough 42
It Was a Quiet Seeming Day 388
It Would Have Starved a Gnat 380

J *Jabberwocky* 215
Jam on Gerry's Rock, The 133
Jesse James 132
John Henry 134
Johnie Armstrong 127
Jonathan's Song 413
Jones, LeRoi. *See* Baraka, Imamu Amiri
Jonson, Ben
    Still to Be Neat, Still to Be Drest 249
    To the Immortal Memory and Friendship of That
        Noble Pair, Sir Lucius Cary and Sir Henry Morrison 164

512   Index

Justice, Donald
    Love's Map 82

K   Kaufman, Bob
        Mingus 489
        Walking Parker Home 490
    Keats, John
        La Belle Dame Sans Merci 312
        Ode on Melancholy 191
        Ode to a Nightingale 188
        On First Looking into Chapman's Homer 146
        On Seeing the Elgin Marbles 313
        To—— 310
        To Autumn 187
    Kennedy, X. J.
        Down in Dallas 145
        In a Prominent Bar in Secaucus One Day 66
    King Lear (Act I, sc. i) (from) 27
    Kisses 74
    Knight, Etheridge
        The Idea of Ancestry 415
    Known Soldier, The 404
    Kubla Khan 306

L   La Belle Dame Sans Merci 312
    Lad of Athens 391
    Lampe, The 294
    Landor, Walter Savage
        I Strove with None 51
    Landscape with the Fall of Icarus, II 327
    Langland, Joseph
        Hunters in the Snow: Brueghel 324
    Latest Decalogue, The 39
    Lawrence, D. H.
        Love on the Farm 79
        Piano 65
        Spring Morning 94
        A Youth Mowing 57
    Leda and the Swan 159

Lee, Don L.
    A Poem Looking for a Reader   420
Lee, Laurie
    First Love   81
Let America Be America Again   408
Letter to Anaktoria   73
Letter to Lady Beaumont, A (from)   25
Levertov, Denise
    October   335
Leviathan (I, iii) (from)   26
Li Ho
    An Arrowhead from the Ancient Battlefield of Ch'ang-P'ing   458
    The Grave of Little Su   459
    The Northern Cold   457
Li Po
    The Nefarious War   396
    A Song of Ch'ang-Kan   224
Like Rain It Sounded Till It Curved   387
Limits of Submission, The   439
Lines of Our Hands, The   444
Litany in Time of Plague, A   248
Little Madness in the Spring, A   387
Lives of Noble Grecians and Romans, The (from)   29
Liyong, Taban Lo
    Uncle Tom's Black Humour   434
London   303
London, 1802   155
Long March, The   461
Love Among the Ruins   252
Love and Life: A Song   26
Love Is Not All: It Is Not Meat Nor Drink   160
Love on the Farm   79
Love Song   79
Love Song of J. Alfred Prufrock, The   258
Love's Eschatology   82
Love's Map   82
Lover Tells of the Rose in His Heart, The   366
Lowell, Amy
    The Pond   315
    Venus Transiens   329
Lowell, Robert
    For the Union Dead   200

Memories of West Street and Lepke 221
Mr. Edwards and the Spider 233
Lui Chi
   A Poet Thinks 459
Lycidas 97
Lyly, John
   To Welcome in the Spring 91
Lynching, The 407

M Mac Flecknoe 38
MacLeish, Archibald
   Ars Poetica 317
Mad Song 302
Madonna of the Cello 85
Mannerly Margery Milk and Ale 247
Mao Tse-Tung
   After Swimming Across the Yangtze River 461
   The Long March 461
   The Snow 460
Marvell, Andrew
   To His Coy Mistress 42
Maya 487
McKay, Claude
   If We Must Die 406
   The Lynching 407
   The Negro's Tragedy 407
Memories of West Street and Lepke 221
Millay, Edna St. Vincent
   Conscientious Objector 398
   Love Is Not All: It Is Not Meat Nor Drink 160
   On Hearing a Symphony of Beethoven 477
Miller, Vassar
   Love's Eschatology 82
Milton, John
   At a Solemn Music 467
   How Soon Hath Time 153
   Lycidas 97
   On Shakespeare 153
   from Paradise Lost (Book VIII) 32
   from Paradise Regained 219
   from The Christian Doctrine 32

　　　　To Leonora Baroni, Singing at Rome　60
　　　　When I Consider How My Light Is Spent　154
　　Mind and Matter　48
　　Mingus　489
　　Mockers, The　220
　　Moore, Marianne
　　　　Arthur Mitchell　476
　　Mphahlele, Ezekiel
　　　　Death　431
　　Mr. Edwards and the Spider　233
　　Mt. Lykaion　160
　　Much Madness Is Divinest Sense　379
　　Musée des Beaux Arts　328
　　Museum, The　491
　　Mutability　156
　　My Maker—Let Me Be　388

N　Nantucket　331
　　Nash, Ogden
　　　　The Turtle　49
　　Nashe, Thomas
　　　　A Litany in Time of Plague　248
　　　　Spring, The Sweet Spring　91
　　Nefarious War, The　396
　　Negro's Tragedy, The　407
　　Never Give All the Heart　367
　　New England　159
　　New Sheriff, The　418
　　News from the House　88
　　Night Rain　447
　　Noiseless Patient Spider, A　10, 232
　　Northern Cold, The　457
　　Nostalgia　427
　　Not Until Doomsday's . . .　227
　　Nuur, Faarah
　　　　The Limits of Submission　439

O　O Do Not Love Too Long　368
　　O sweet spontaneous　95

O What Is That Sound 142
October 335
Ode: Intimations of Immortality from Recollections
   of Early Childhood 174
Ode on a Distant Prospect of Eton College 170
Ode on Melancholy 191
Ode on St. Cecilia's Day 468
Ode to a Nightingale 188
Ode to Duty 179
Ode to Evening 172
Ode to the Confederate Dead 195
Ode to the West Wind 185
Of Course—I Prayed 378
Of God We Ask One Favor 390
Of Late and Never 48
Of Loving a Dog 48
Of the Last Verses in the Book 285
off d pig 419
O'Hara, J. D.
   Aristotle Contemplating the Bust of Homer:
      After Rembrandt 487
Okara, Gabriel
   Piano and Drums 445
Ol' Bunk's Band 473
Old Pond, The 425
On First Looking into Chapman's Homer 146
On Hearing a Symphony of Beethoven 477
On Our Crucified Lord Naked, and Bloody 292
On Seeing the Elgin Marbles 313
On Shakespeare 153
One Joy of So Much Anguish 389
One Need Not Be a Chamber 383
Orb Weaver, The 10
Oread 316
Ourselves Were Wed One Summer—Dear 381
Ousmane, Sembène
   Nostalgia 427
"Out, Out—" 21
Over Sir John's Hill 235
Ovid
   The Universal Lover 75
Owen, Wilfred
   Arms and the Boy 399

       Dulce et Decorum Est   402
       Exposure   401
       Spring Offensive   400
Ozymandias   310

P   *Paradise Lost (Book VIII) (from)*   32
    Paradise Regained (from)   219
    Party Piece   90
    Patchen, Kenneth
       The Known Soldier   404
    Patten, Brian
       Party Piece   90
    Patterson, Raymond R.
       At That Moment   117
    Peaceable Kingdom, The   491
    People, The   370
    Persian Version, The   40
    Piano   65
    Piano and Drums   445
    Picture of a Nude in a Machine Shop   472
    Piercy, Marge
       The Peaceable Kingdom   491
    Pietà, Rhenish, 14th C., The Cloisters, The   485
    Pity of Love, The   365
    Plath, Sylvia
       Ariel   270
       Point Shirley   202
    Plutarch
       from *The Lives of Noble Grecians and Romans*   29
    Poem in October   198
    Poem Looking for a Reader, A   420
    Poet Thinks, A   459
    Point Shirley   202
    Pond, The   315
    Poor Omie   131
    Pope, Alexander
       Ode on St. Cecilia's Day   468
    Pound, Ezra
       Ballad of the Goodly Fere   139
       from *Canto I*   218
       Doria   333

518 Index

Envoi 65
Imerro 334
In a Station of the Metro 333
The River-Merchant's Wife: A Letter 225
Prayer for My Daughter, A 228
Prayer to the Masks 440
Prayer Without Echo 426
Presences 372
Prior, Matthew
    To the Honorable Charles Montague, Esq. 44

Q   Quarrel in Old Age 372

R   Ransom, John Crowe
        Bells for John Whiteside's Daughter 114
    Rearrange a "Wife's" Affection! 391
    Red Wheelbarrow, The 331
    Reed, Ishmael
        off d pig 419
    Refusal to Mourn the Death, by Fire, of a
        Child in London, A 228
    Relativity 47
    Rhodora, The 31
    Rich, Adrienne
        Two Songs 83
    Rilke, Rainer Maria
        Love Song 79
    Ringing the Bells 269
    River-Merchant's Wife: A Letter, The 225
    Robinson, Edwin Arlington
        New England 159
    Roethke, Theodore
        Root Cellar 223
    Root Cellar 223
    Rossetti, Christina
        In an Artist's Studio 158
    Ruganda, John M.
        The Image of God 430

S Sainte Mary Magdalene or The Weeper   286
Sappho
   Letter to Anaktoria   73
Sassoon, Siegfried
   Concert-Interpretation   475
   Counter-Attack   397
   Sheldonian Soliloquy   474
Scottsboro, Too, Is Worth Its Song   410
Senghor, Léopold Sédar
   Prayer to the Masks   440
Sexton, Anne
   The Fortress   231
   Ringing the Bells   269
Shakespeare, William
   from *Antony and Cleopatra* (Act II, sc. ii)   30
   from *King Lear* (Act I, sc. i)   27
   Sonnets 18, 30, 73, 97, 116, 129, 147   147–50
Sheldonian Soliloquy   474
Shelley, Percy Bysshe
   Ode to the West Wind   185
   Ozymandias   310
   Sonnet: England in 1819   309
   To Constantia, Singing   61
Sir Patrick Spens   123
Skelton, John
   Mannerly Margery Milk and Ale   247
Snow, The   460
Solitary Reaper, The   60
Song   278
Song for St. Cecilia's Day, 1687, A   168
Song of Ch'ang-Kan, A   224
Song of Myself (from)   341
Sonnet (Coleridge)   307
sonnet (cummings)   161
Sonnet: England in 1819   309
Sonnet of Black Beauty   282
Sonnet XVI   462
South Mountains, The (from)   455
Speaking of Poetry   321
Spender, Stephen
   Art Student   478
Spring   93
Spring Morning   94

Spring Offensive 400
Spring Strains 93
Spring, the Sweet Spring 91
Stanzas for Music: There Be None of Beauty's Daughters 308
Stanzas for Music: There's Not a Joy the World Can Give Like That It Takes Away 308
Stephens, James
   A Glass of Beer 45
Stevens, Wallace
   Disillusionment of Ten O'Clock 329
   The Idea of Order at Key West 63
   Study of Two Pears 330
Stickney, Trumbull
   Mt. Lykaion 160
Still to Be Neat, Still to Be Drest 249
Struck, Was I, Not Yet by Lightning 384
Study of Two Pears 330
Supermarket in California, A 268
Swinburne, Algernon Charles
   The Garden of Proserpine 255

T   Tate, Allen
   Ode to the Confederate Dead 195
Tennyson, Alfred, Lord
   Ulysses 250
They Shut Me Up in Prose 380
Thomas, Dylan
   Fern Hill 266
   Hold Hard, These Ancient Minutes in the Cuckoo's Month 96
   Over Sir John's Hill 235
   Poem in October 198
   A Refusal to Mourn the Death, by Fire, of a Child in London 228
Thought from Propertius, A 371
To—— 310
To a Lady Who Did Sing Excellently 59
To Autumn 187
To Constantia, Singing 61
To His Coy Mistress 42
To Leonora Baroni, Singing at Rome 60

To My Sister 304
To Rosmarie in Bad Kissingen 84
To Spring 92
To the Honorable Charles Montague, Esq. 44
To the Immortal Memory and Friendship of That Noble Pair,
    Sir Lucius Cary and Sir Henry Morrison 164
To the Maiden . . . 17
To the States 55
To Toussaint L'Ouverture 305
To Welcome in the Spring 91
To Whom the Mornings Stand for Nights 386
Traherne, Thomas
    from *Centuries of Meditations* 33
    Wonder 34
Trip to Omaha (Normandy 6.VI.44), A 405
True Lover, The 138
Tshakatumba
    Prayer Without Echo 426
Tu Fu
    At the Corner of the World 454
    The Autumn Wastes 453
    Déjeuner Sur L'Herbe 451
    The Emperor 452
    The Excursion 452
Turtle, The 49
Two Songs 83
Tyger, The 244

U *Ulysses* 250
   Uncle Tom's Black Humour 434
   Universal Lover, The 75

V *Valediction Forbidding Mourning, A* 279
   Van Duyn, Mona
       The Pietà, Rhenish, 14th C., The Cloisters 485
   Vaughan, Henry
       The Dedication 295
       The Lampe 294
       The World 293

Venus Transiens 329
Very, Jones
   The Dead 157
Vice 416
Voice of the Turtle, The (from *Song of Solomon*) 72
Voznesensky, Andrey
   Maya 487

W   Waldrop, Keith
     To Rosmarie in Bad Kissingen 84
  Walk, The 56
  Walking Parker Home 490
  Waller, Edmund
     Of the Last Verses in the Book 285
  Webster, John
     All the Flowers of the Spring 92
  Western Wind 54
  When I Consider How My Light Is Spent 154
  When Lilacs Last in the Dooryard Bloom'd 103
  When They Come Back 385
  When You Are Old 367
  Whitman, Walt
     Full of Life Now 362
     A Noiseless Patient Spider 10, 232
     from *Song of Myself* 341
     To the States 55
     When Lilacs Last in the Dooryard Bloom'd 103
     A Woman Waits for Me 360
  "Why Do I Love" You, Sir? 78
  Wild Nights 377
  Williams, Jonathan
     Fastball 269
  Williams, William Carlos
     Daisy 332
     Dawn 333
     III The Hunters in the Snow 325
     II Landscape with the Fall of Icarus 327
     Nantucket 331
     Ol' Bunk's Band 473
     Picture of a Nude in a Machine Shop 472
     The Red Wheelbarrow 331

Spring Strains   93
Wilmot, John (Earl of Rochester)
   Love and Life: A Song   26
Windhover: To Christ Our Lord, The   214
Winter Landscape   326
With Ships the Sea   24
Woman Waits for Me, A   360
Wonder   34
Words   24
Wordsworth, William
   After-Thought   157
   Composed upon Westminster Bridge,
     September 3, 1802   155
   It Is a Beauteous Evening   154
   Letter to Lady Beaumont, A (from)   25
   London, 1802   155
   Mutability   156
   Ode: Intimations of Immortality from
     Recollections of Early Childhood   174
   Ode to Duty   179
   The Solitary Reaper   60
   To My Sister   304
   To Toussaint L'Ouverture   305
   With Ships the Sea   24
   The World Is Too Much with Us   156
World, The   293
World Is Too Much with Us, The   156
Wright, Richard
   Between the World and Me   411

Y Yeats, William Butler
   Against Unworthy Praise   368
   Among School Children   192
   A Bronze Head   373
   A Deep-Sworn Vow   371
   Diary Entry   23
   Fallen Majesty   369
   The Folly of Being Comforted   367
   Friends   369
   He Hears the Cry of the Sedge   366
   He Tells of the Perfect Beauty   366

In Memory of Major Robert Gregory 111
An Irish Airman Foresees His Death 397
Leda and the Swan 159
The Lover Tells of the Rose in His Heart 366
Never Give All the Heart 367
O Do Not Love Too Long 368
The People 370
The Pity of Love 365
A Prayer for My Daughter 228
Presences 372
Quarrel in Old Age 372
A Thought from Propertius 371
When You Are Old 367
Words 24
Youth Mowing, A 57

Z   Zankli, Boevi
         The Dream of African Unity 429